The New University of Cologne

Its History from 1919

böhlau

The New University of Cologne

Its History from 1919

Edited by

Habbo Knoch, Ralph Jessen, Hans-Peter Ullmann
on behalf of the Rectorate of the University of Cologne

Böhlau Verlag Wien Köln Weimar

Foreword

In 1919, the city of Cologne took a bold step in deciding to found a university. As World War I was nearing its end, and as revolution and the founding of the Weimar Republic were changing the country, preparations were under way. The National Assembly met in Weimar, peace was negotiated in Versailles, street battles raged in Berlin, the Bavarian Soviet Republic collapsed in Munich, and the city council in Cologne agreed to establish and maintain a university under its stewardship. The Prussian authorities gave the project their approval following intense negotiations.

This was not the first time the citizenry of Cologne had taken this path. One of the oldest universities in Europe had already been established in the city in 1388. After existing without interruption for more than 400 years, it was closed in 1798 while Cologne was under French rule. The advocates of the second founding, however, wanted a "new university" that would be committed to the needs of modern life. It would prepare people academically to master the increasingly complex challenges posed by society and the economy, while also studying their underlying principles.

The university's ties to the city of Cologne were particularly close in the decades immediately following its founding, not only because the city was solely responsible for its financing. The university also emerged directly from the consolidation of existing municipal institutions of higher education: the Commercial College, the Academy for Practical Medicine, and the College of Municipal and Social Administration. In turn, the rapidly expanding university constantly stimulated the city's cultural and economic development.

Today, our university is still—and indeed much more so than in 1919—a campus in the heart of the city. It has become a highly prestigious site of international academic activity and, with its 50,000 students, is among the largest universities in Germany and Europe. However, soon after the end of World War II, the university's expansion made the limits of municipal financing apparent. In the 1950s, the increasing number of students and the growing demands of scientific and medical research led the state of North Rhine-Westphalia to gradually assume responsibility for the university.

The following decades were marked by the struggle to reconcile the successes of educational expansion with the resources available. This struggle led to the significant development of the university at its Lindenthal location in the 1960s and 1970s, but in times of tight budgets the search for solutions often reached its limits. Since the 1980s, it has become increasingly clear just how fundamental the role of the university is in our modern knowledge society. There is hardly an area in which the basic research conducted here does not result in groundbreaking innovations and improvements in the quality of life. And a broad range of research in the social sciences, humanities and cultural studies plays a vital role in enriching our understanding of past and present worlds.

Excellence in research, teaching and administration, rooted in the vision of contributing to the enhancement of freedom and humanity—this has been the mission of our university for many years. The face of the university has changed yet again over the last two decades. We have been able to expand and establish focal points in our research and create state-of-the-art working conditions. The University of Cologne has formed outstanding international connections worldwide, and the city itself is an attractive location for students from near and far. One hundred years after its founding, the University of Cologne is still—and increasingly—a prism of the modern world which it actively helps to shape.

This book recounts the history of the University of Cologne over the past one hundred years. Its descriptive form of presentation was a deliberate choice. Numerous people inside and outside of our university were involved in the process. The staff of the Cologne-based Geschichtsbüro Reder, Roeseling & Prüfer, in particular Dr. Thomas Prüfer as editor and Dr. Thekla Keuck as project manager, deserve our special thanks for their outstanding commitment and great dedication in researching, compiling and producing this volume. Its compelling design is the work of Andrea Högerle of the Cologne agency for visual communication Jefferson & Högerle, commissioned by Geschichtsbüro.

This book was created as part of a project on the history of the new University of Cologne under the direction of Cologne scholars of modern history Professor Habbo Knoch, Professor Ralph Jessen and Professor Hans-Peter Ullmann. They prepared the concept for the volume and were involved throughout its preparation. Furthermore, we would like to highlight the ongoing dedication and constructive support of an advisory committee with Professor Hans-Peter Haferkamp, Professor Axel Karenberg, Professor Elke Kleinau, Professor Uwe Ruschewitz and Professor Michael Wagner as representatives of the individual faculties, headed by Professor Siegfried Hermle.

We would also like to thank the numerous archives, museums and institutions that contributed to the success of this project, in particular the University of Cologne Archives, the Cologne City Museum and the National Socialism Documentation Center of the City of Cologne. Böhlau Verlag's Cologne office, most notably Kirsti Doepner, attended to the project with great care. Special thanks are due to Georg Wamhof, who meticulously coordinated the entire process of the book's creation and whose profound knowledge of the history of the University of Cologne has significantly enriched the project.

All that remains now is for me to wish you an inspiring and enlightening time reading this book. We invite you to rediscover your and our university!

Professor Dr. Dr. h.c. Axel Freimuth
Rector of the University of Cologne

Contents

The Founding Years

Chapter 1

1901–1919

Festmahl im Gürzenich zu Köln
zur Feier der Eröffnung
DER STÄDTISCHEN HANDELS-HOCHSCHULE
am 1. Mai 1901.
GUSTAV VON MEVISSEN
1815 1899

Only a few months after the end of World War I, while Germany's first democracy was taking shape, the city of Cologne stepped boldly into the future and founded a university. At the opening ceremony in Gürzenich Festival Hall on 12 June 1919, Mayor Konrad Adenauer marked the historical significance of the moment, proclaiming, "A solemn hour! What Cologne's intellectual elite has spent a century wishing and striving for has finally come to pass: the alma mater Coloniensis has been revived after lying dormant for one hundred years." Other speakers also invoked the long tradition of the former University of Cologne, established in 1388 and closed in 1798. This new beginning was hailed as a rebirth, and the founding of the university was presented as the fulfillment of a persistent pursuit—but that was just a myth.[1]

The End and a New Beginning

The old university experienced its demise at the end of the eighteenth century. It was antiquated and did not fit into the new education system introduced by revolutionary France, whose troops had occupied Cologne during the War of the First Coalition in 1794. The French closed the time-honored but run-down institution and, in its place, opened a French-style central school. Several attempts by the citizenry of Cologne to restore the university failed. Following the end of the French occupation in 1814, Cologne hoped to re-establish the city's Catholic university. But the new Protestant rulers from Prussia had other plans for their Rhineland province: they envisioned a modern institution in line with the university reforms introduced in Berlin. The conservative, Catholic city of Cologne did not seem to be a suitable location. Instead, the neighboring city of Bonn was chosen and a new university opened there in 1818. Cologne's plans to re-institute its university faded into oblivion.[2]

The emerging interest of the *Wirtschaftsbürgertum* (economic bourgeoisie) rekindled initiatives to re-establish an institution of higher education in the mid-nineteenth century. In 1856, the new president of Cologne's Chamber of Commerce, the entrepreneur Gustav Mevissen, called for the founding of a polytechnic institute. His goal was to turn the rapidly growing commercial hub on the Rhine into the administrative, cultural and academic center of the western provinces. The newly founded polytechnic colleges offered a novel, practice-oriented form of education in the technical and scientific fields not taught at universities. In 1858, the city applied to establish the first Prussian polytechnic to provide training in mining, technology and business. But, as in 1818, Cologne again lost out to another city—Aachen, more industrially advanced, was chosen in 1863.[3]

But Mevissen did not give up. After having called for the creation of a commercial college in Cologne in 1860, he donated 100,000 marks toward its founding in 1879. He noted in a memorandum that business leaders in Germany did not usually attend university but learned their trade through practical experience. The reason, he wrote, was that merchants were wary of the unbridled academic freedom and the theoretical orientation of the universities, where practical aspects were looked down upon. However, Mevissen declared, entrepreneurs also needed a good education. Material wealth should be brought together with education to achieve a balance between materialism and idealism and raise the social status of the merchant class. Mevissen was convinced that a university was not the right place for this kind of education. He therefore called for the founding of independent commercial colleges that would be on an equal footing with universities, where knowledge would be practical, academic disciplines would be taught as applied sciences, and general education would complement specialized professional training.[4]

Mevissen's concept was groundbreaking. To this day, he is viewed as the "father of the commercial college movement" in Germany, a movement in which prominent entrepreneurs, trade associations and teachers from the new commercial schools came together. Their efforts were met with determined opposition from the universities, which did not view the study of commerce as an academic discipline and therefore did not wish to add it to their canon of studies. Most entrepreneurs and merchants also remained skeptical because they saw no sense in academic education and continued to support training through practical experience. The state did not oppose the existence of commercial colleges but did not want to fund them either. As a result, the first German

← The opening ceremony of the Commercial College was held in Gürzenich Festival Hall; a portrait medallion of Mevissen adorned the bottom of the program cover.

commercial colleges stemmed from local initiatives led by members of the business community in cooperation with municipal authorities.[5]

Cologne took the first step. The city accepted Mevissen's endowment within just a few days, and in 1880, the Prussian Ministry of Culture and Education approved the opening of a commercial college. But people in Cologne were not very committed to moving the project forward. Neither the city council nor the *Bürgertum* (bourgeoisie) seemed to have any interest in it. Nothing happened for over a decade. A second initiative led by Mevissen in the early 1890s also failed, and Cologne lost its leading role in the commercial college movement. The first German institution of this kind was founded in Leipzig as part of the university in 1898. In the same year, the polytechnic in Aachen introduced a two-year course in commercial sciences. When Mevissen died in August 1899, the realization of his goal seemed to have vanished into the distant future. But the persistent businessman had made one final effort and bequeathed another 300,000 marks to the endowment, which in the interim had grown to 400,000 marks. The groundwork was laid; the only thing still needed was the political will to put the plan into action.[6]

Germany's First Independent Commercial College

Time was short. In the summer of 1899, Frankfurt am Main decided to establish an academy of commercial and social sciences. Similar plans were being pursued in Berlin, Düsseldorf and Hamburg. German cities embarked upon a race that resulted in the founding of numerous commercial colleges within just a few years. Cologne again risked being left behind.

In late 1899, Wilhelm Becker, the mayor of Cologne, took the initiative and commissioned Eberhard Gothein, a professor of economics in Bonn who had already worked for Mevissen in the early 1890s, to draft a proposal for a municipal commercial college in Cologne. Based on this proposal, the city council on 12 July 1900 approved the founding of the college, increased the assets of the Mevissen foundation to one million marks and provided additional funding. Berlin approved the project in September 1900. A few months later, on 23 April 1901, Germany's first independent commercial college opened on the premises of the Commercial School established in 1899 on Hansaring.[7]

The new college was an institution of the city of Cologne under the supervision of the Prussian Ministry of Culture and Education. The highest governing body was a board of trustees chaired by the mayor of Cologne and made up of city council, state government and chamber of commerce representatives, as well as professors. A director of studies was responsible for the administration of the college. With its four votes, the city had the greatest influence of all entities represented on the board of trustees.[8]

The main fields of study were economics—with a strong historical and geographical focus—and practice-oriented business administration. There were also courses in chemical and mechanical engineering, with a special emphasis on practical aspects of production. Modern languages such as English and French highlighted the international reach of the German economy, which was already heavily export-oriented. In terms of general education and the humanities, students could attend lectures on German and international history, art and art history, philosophy and the history of literature. Legal education focused on branches of law important to business: public law, commercial law and private law. The college also trained teachers for commercial and vocational schools and offered courses in education for them.[9]

Students completed their studies in four semesters and graduated with a degree in "Commerce" or "Commercial Teaching." The college did not restrict admission to secondary school graduates (who had passed the Abitur exam); merchants who had completed an apprenticeship and one year of voluntary military service, along with qualified primary school teachers and foreigners with previous training, were also admitted after taking a college examination. The Commercial College was also open to guest auditors, especially to citizens of the city.[10]

↗ In 1901, the Commercial College moved into the former Commercial School, which had opened in 1899 on Hansaring.

→ Study outings were a special feature of the Commercial College; professors and students on the mail service steamer *Kronprinz* in 1905.

Grosse Prozession
Studenten-Korporationen

Professors and Students

Thanks to the foundation's assets and the city's commitment, Cologne's college had the largest financial resources of any commercial college in Germany. Gustav Mevissen's daughters also supported the college and later the university. They donated funds to improve the situation of the lecturers. Mathilde von Mevissen fought for girls' and women's access to secondary schools and higher education, as well as for women's suffrage. The Commercial College was well staffed. During the college's first year, in addition to its five full-time professors, there were eleven Bonn university professors from the faculties of philosophy and law, as well as twelve part-time practical instructors. Together they taught eighty-six students. By the winter semester of 1902/1903, the college boasted eight full-time professors while the number of students had increased to 205. In addition, there were nearly 1,300 guest auditors.

The Commercial College attracted mostly young men from the Rhineland, especially from Cologne and its surroundings and from the Düsseldorf area. They made up more than forty percent of the students. The second and third largest groups were from southern Germany and the province of Westphalia with more than ten percent respectively. Apparently, proximity to their hometowns played an important role for students choosing their place of study. On average, about fifteen percent of the student body came from abroad, primarily from eastern and south-eastern Europe. This was a lot, but it was significantly less than in Leipzig and Berlin. Half of the German students came from the industrial and commercial classes and were often from industrial areas and larger cities. Many of them were preparing to join the family business. This was reflected in the high proportion of merchants who had completed the middle-level school examination and who made up sixty percent of the student body. Only about thirty percent of all students had the Abitur. Sons of civil servants, who accounted for just seventeen percent of the students at Cologne, tended to study at universities.[11]

Cologne began admitting women in the summer semester of 1907, one year before Prussia opened all institutes of higher education to women, albeit much later than in other western European countries and south-western Germany. The first female student at Cologne was the twenty-one-year-old Luise Chun from Elberfeld. Studying to become a commercial teacher, she chose as the subject of her thesis the organization of credit in small businesses. Up until World War I, women were only a small but steadily growing part of the student body. There were only three at the outset, but by the summer semester of 1914, fifty-seven women were enrolled at the Commercial College, about nine percent of all students. During the war, female students at times accounted for twenty-five percent of all those enrolled. This bolstered their self-confidence, and the first association of female students in Cologne—as at other German institutions of higher education—was founded in 1915.

The share of women from the middle and upper classes was nearly seventy percent, somewhat higher than the figure for their male counterparts. More than forty percent of the women belonged to the economic bourgeoisie. A larger share of women than men—namely, a good twenty-one percent—came from families in the professional classes and high-ranking civil service with academic backgrounds. Four out of five female graduates studied "commercial teaching." The upper-middle classes thus took advantage of the educational opportunities offered to women at the Commercial College. However, they limited themselves to those courses of study that allowed them to pursue the few career opportunities open to women with higher education in Imperial Germany. These included teaching, but not careers in business or social administration. The introduction in 1916 of a program of study at the College of Municipal and Social Administration for women who wished to take up social professions reflected this situation, as its primary purpose was to secure the institution's future. By 1915, more women at the Cologne college had successfully passed their examinations than at all other German commercial colleges put together. Nonetheless, half of all female students at Cologne did not graduate—but neither did nearly two-thirds of the men.[12]

↖ Student associations participate in a procession during the twentieth International Eucharistic Congress in Cologne in August 1909.

← Cologne began admitting women in the summer semester of 1907; female students leaving Gürzenich Festival Hall after the university's opening ceremony in 1919.

Applied and Public Sciences

The Cologne Commercial College focused on further developing its economic disciplines. Much more emphasis was placed on economics here than at universities. Even though the college rather conventionally followed the historical school of economics led by Gustav Schmoller, it did produce something new: economic and social history as an independent field of study. This development is closely associated with Bruno Kuske, who had been teaching at the Commercial College since 1908. The Balance Sheet Archive, which collected documents relating to the economic history of Rhine-Westphalia and had been opened four years earlier, served as a model for other colleges and contributed to the founding of Germany's first regional Rhenish-Westphalian Economics Archive in 1906.

The strong emphasis on practical application in Cologne's approach to teaching economics opened new horizons in this field. Thus, in 1903, the second German professorship for actuarial studies was created at Cologne, one of the centers of Germany's insurance sector. Conversely, systematic principles were applied at the Commercial College to the practice-oriented field of business administration, laying the groundwork for its development into an academic discipline. This process was closely linked to Eugen Schmalenbach, who had been a member of the faculty in Cologne since 1903 and was one of the founders of modern German business administration.[13]

Practical orientation determined not only the content of research and teaching, but also the training offered by the college. From the beginning, lectures, seminars and exercises were supplemented by visits to factories, public agencies and court proceedings. Study trips, which took place from 1905 to 1913, were a special feature of the Cologne college. These trips would sometimes last several weeks and usually involved travel abroad, at times as far as the colony of German East Africa and the USA.

Founded in 1909 with 50,000 marks in funding from the Chamber of Commerce, the Museum of Trade and Industry offered a wealth of resources for the college's educational program. It was the second museum of economics and technology to open its doors in Germany after the Deutsches Museum in Munich. The exhibition was open to the public, and some of the college's lectures took place in the evenings and aimed to attract the citizens of Cologne. The Commercial College was a civic institution in two ways: it was supported by the citizenry and in turn offered them educational opportunities.[14]

Expansion as a Center of Higher Education

The success of the Commercial College encouraged the city to develop Cologne into an important center of higher education. In 1902, the city council decided to construct a new building for the Commercial College in the south of the city. The building, which was located on Claudiusstraße and was inaugurated in October 1907, cost about 2.5 million marks and could accommodate up to 400 students. But actual demand soon outstripped the college's planning. By the winter semester of 1907/1908, 363 students, who were taught by twelve full-time professors, had already enrolled. An extension that increased the Commercial College's capacity to 1,000 students was not completed until 1914. By then, Cologne already had 600 students, which was more than Leipzig, making it the largest commercial college in the German Reich. But the beginning of World War I in August 1914 put an end to this development, and the number of students dropped by half.[15]

A key factor for Cologne's success as a center of learning was its firm practice-oriented approach. When, in 1903, the Prussian Ministry of Culture and Education introduced a year of practical training for graduates of medical school, and Friedrich Althoff, who was responsible for higher education within the ministry, sought cities willing to create educational institutions associated with hospitals that would offer this kind of training, Cologne seized the opportunity. It founded Germany's first academy for practical medicine in 1904. A large, modern hospital was constructed on the grounds of a former psychiatric institution, the Lindenburg; it opened its doors in November 1908. The Cologne Academy for Practical Medicine not only provided young graduates with

↗ The Commercial College on Claudiusstraße opened in October 1907.

→ The new premises at Römerpark also featured a fencing hall.

practical training, it also trained medical specialists and nurses, and offered licensed doctors continuing medical education. Another one of its tasks was the development of practical medicine as an academic field. Later, the academy also began training and providing continuing education for railway doctors, dentists, military doctors, social workers and missionaries. Such diversification was necessary because the academy soon had to deal with decreasing enrollment and was at times even on the verge of closure. This was mainly due to a boycott by practicing doctors who had not been involved in the academy's founding and offered their own courses in continuing medical training. Only the training of specialist physicians proved successful.

Ten full-time professors, almost all of whom had completed their habilitation, taught the most important medical specialties at the academy: internal medicine, surgery, and gynecology and obstetrics. Among them was Ferdinand Siegert, who helped establish the field of child welfare. His research concentrated on diphtheria. The academy was a pioneer in the field of X-ray technology. Gustav Aschaffenburg, who was later to become an internationally renowned scholar, assumed the lectureship in psychiatry at the academy in 1904. He was the founder of criminal psychology in Germany. Overall, the medical academy focused on applied rather than basic research, in keeping with its mission.[16]

Practical work was also central to the College of Municipal and Social Administration founded in 1912. Its goal was to provide training and continuing education for civil servants, offering a practice-oriented alternative or supplement to the usual study of law at a university; this was a prerequisite for a career in the higher ranks of the civil service. The College of Municipal and Social Administration was an offshoot of the Commercial College, which had started offering "academic courses in administration" in 1903, making it one of the pioneers in this field. From 1906 on, the Association for Continuing Education in Law and Political Science also offered six-week courses for civil servants. When Düsseldorf founded an academy for municipal and social administration in 1911, Cologne felt challenged and set up the College of Municipal and Social Administration as an institution of the city. It was headed by Christian Eckert, who at the same time held the position of director of studies at the Commercial College. The college's first full-time lecturer was Fritz Stier-Somlo, a jurist and key figure in promoting public administration as an academic field. The new college advertised its courses in periodicals and by sending out personal letters—an early form of marketing for institutions of higher education. The four-semester program initially included economics and cultural affairs, as well as legal training on the same level. By integrating legal studies into the curriculum, Cologne bolstered an area of study which was underdeveloped at the Commercial College, but which would play an important role in the founding of the university later on.[17]

↖ The new hospital at Lindenburg was opened in 1908; the administration building is on the right.

← Training programs were directed at doctors and nurses, among others; a classroom is pictured here.

The Road to the New University

Nobody in Cologne had seriously pursued re-establishing the old university since having lost out to Bonn in 1818. Although the successful Commercial College deliberately presented itself as distinct from universities, it aimed for academic recognition and equal status. The polytechnics had already partly achieved this: they had been granted the right to award doctorates in 1898, until then a privilege limited to universities. Cologne demanded this right for the first time in 1910, when the city of Frankfurt announced that it wanted to transform its Academy of Social and Commercial Sciences into a university. This was perceived as a threat to the preeminence of Cologne's Commercial College. It was feared that a university with an economic focus would lure away the best students. But the Prussian Ministry of Culture and Education rejected Cologne's application, as well as a second one in 1912.[18]

Christian Eckert, the driving force behind the plans for a university in Cologne, approached Mayor Max Wallraf for the first time in 1913, sending him a memorandum on the "Cologne university question." In it he declared that no other large German city was more entitled to a university than Cologne. The German Reich's fourth-largest city had been home to one of the oldest and most famous German universities for more than 400 years, and at the beginning of the new century it had created a successful, novel kind of institute of higher education through its own efforts. Eckert emphasized how this model differed from existing universities and wanted to make sure that the distinctive features of Cologne's colleges and academies would be preserved in this "novel university." His main concern was the right to award doctorates; the right to be called a "university" was not decisive. Eckert turned it into an issue only for strategic purposes.[19]

The opening of the University of Frankfurt in 1914 and the beginning of World War I seemed to lend more urgency to Eckert's calls for a university in Cologne. In a second memorandum dated 16 March 1915, he explained that the city's desire to establish a university corresponded to both the goals of Germany's higher education policy and the tasks Germans would face after the end of the war. At the time, Eckert assumed as a matter of course that the German Reich would win the war. In the second half of the year, the faculty members of Cologne's institutes of higher learning discussed the university question in three sessions. There were prominent dissenting voices, such as Eugen Schmalenbach, who thought that the character of the Commercial College as a center for applied sciences and practical training would be jeopardized. In the end, they agreed to develop Cologne's colleges by transforming them into a university while preserving their original character; or, if that proved to be impossible, to at least try to achieve the same legal status as universities. This paved the way for negotiations with Berlin.[20]

The Breakthrough

The city endorsed plans for a university, but policymakers had other more pressing problems. The German Reich was in the middle of a war that tied up all the country's resources. Not until Konrad Adenauer became mayor of Cologne in October 1917 did the project receive renewed attention. Christian Eckert reported to Adenauer immediately following his election. Adenauer concluded that the Commercial College would either have to undergo a complete change or it would go under. Adenauer, who was the youngest mayor of a large German city at the time, gave top priority to the founding of a university. It was an essential part of his plan to transform Cologne into a modern metropolis.

Adenauer was aware that the Prussian government continued to oppose the idea of a university in Cologne and therefore wanted to create a fait accomplis. An institute for nutritional physiology and a social science research institute were to be created to complement the practice-oriented areas of higher education that already existed in Cologne. The institute for nutritional physiology was never realized, but Germany's first social sciences institute was established in Cologne with philosopher and sociologist Max Scheler as its founding director. Eckert had drafted the concept for the institute before the end of 1917. As an experienced academic administrator, he formed an effective team with Adenauer, who was an ambitious realpolitiker.[21]

In the spring of 1918, while plans to create the research institutes were underway, Adenauer and Eckert began negotiating with Carl Heinrich Becker, the personnel officer in Berlin responsible for Prussian universities. Becker wanted to turn the Commercial College into the University of Bonn's fifth faculty. Behind this was Becker's goal of consolidating Germany's fragmented academic landscape. Adenauer was not opposed to the idea, but he pressed for a medical faculty for Cologne, a demand that Becker rejected. Negotiations dragged on until the German Revolution of 1918 swept away Imperial Germany and led to the founding of a democratic republic. The Social Democrat Konrad Haenisch became the new Prussian minister of education and endorsed Cologne's plans.

During the early stages of the Weimar Republic, when workers' and soldiers' councils were engaged in a struggle for power with the political parties, the *Freikorps* (paramilitary groups made up of war veterans) were threatening the emerging democracy, and many interpreted the January Uprising as the writing on the wall, Adenauer pressed for a decision be made—and was successful. Approval for a university was granted to Cologne in negotiations in early January 1919. Since 1913, the city had repeatedly adapted its proposals for a university to current educational policy but had maintained the practical orientation that set it apart from the nineteenth-century university model. Following the revolution, the "new university" corresponded to the idea of the need for educational reform of the democratic government in Berlin. Given the imminent occupation of the Rhineland by the Allies, the university was also assigned a cultural-political mission as the keeper of "German culture" in the western part of the country.

The people of Cologne, however, still had to be convinced, as Adenauer and Eckert had not yet made

their efforts public. Although newspapers reacted positively to the news, most of the city's citizens opposed the plans. The hardship faced after the war was too great. Trade and industry voiced their opposition to the founding of a new university. In view of the success of the Commercial College, they considered it superfluous. But Adenauer succeeded in convincing the influential president of the Cologne Chamber of Industry and Commerce, Louis Hagen. Moreover, he obtained a majority in the city council, which unanimously voted to establish the university on 20 March 1919 and approved a good one million marks in funding. On 29 May 1919, Adenauer signed the contract between the city and the Prussian government. The opening ceremony for Cologne's new university took place two weeks later, on 12 June.

The founding of the University of Cologne was the first of a series of measures taken by the Adenauer government to modernize the city; these included the creation of a green belt, the construction of exhibition halls and successfully promoting the city as the site for a new Ford manufacturing plant. Like the University of Cologne, the University of Hamburg was also founded in 1919. Along with Frankfurt, these three city universities were a novelty in the history of German higher education. They all emerged from commercial schools and introduced a new understanding of academic pursuits. For the first time, practice-oriented economic and social sciences, and with them the economic and social dimensions of society, were assigned a significant standing. Of the three universities, Cologne was the most determined in taking this direction.[22]

↑ Mayor Konrad Adenauer and Rector Christian Eckert (2nd and 3rd from left in the foreground) attend the University of Cologne's academic inauguration ceremony on 20 June 1919 in the main building.

The Commercial College on Claudiusstraße

The new university, founded in 1919, took over the premises of the Commercial College as its main building, as well as the facilities of the Academy for Practical Medicine. The Commercial College had been built between 1905 and 1907, based on an award-winning design by Ernst Friedrich Vetterlein, an architect from Darmstadt. Vetterlein's design with its Baroque touches reflected the predominant architectural style of the early 1900s.

The main entrance to the former Commercial College was on the Römerpark side of the building. The building housed "eleven lecture halls; seven departments and their respective archives; two natural science and engineering institutes with their own lecture halls and numerous rooms for practical courses and experimentation, and for storing collections; a library with two reading rooms; two storerooms and auxiliary rooms; an auditorium and antechamber; an examination hall and a consultation room (the former was also used for faculty meetings); four rooms for the director of studies and the secretariat; fourteen rooms for lecturers; a room for the student council; three large halls for the trade museum, including various adjoining rooms; a gymnasium and fencing hall; a refreshment room and smaller adjoining rooms; six apartments and several other rooms available for various purposes."[23]

The university remained on Claudiusstraße until 1934, when the building became the headquarters of the NSDAP Gauleiter Cologne-Aachen, serving that purpose until 1944. A large part of the building was destroyed in an Allied air raid in 1944. Reconstruction work was completed in 1957. Since then, the building has been used by various institutions and public authorities. Today, it is part of the Südstadt Campus of the Technical University of Cologne.[24]

↗ A plot of land located between Agrippinaufer, Oberländer Wall, Claudiusstraße and Maternusstraße in the south of Cologne was available for the construction of the Commercial College. The overall design of the Commercial College was palatial, with Römerpark as its forecourt and entrance.

→ This cross section through the central axis shows the two main floors with classrooms and administration offices. The semi-basement housed six apartments for the stoker, the bedel, and the employees who tended to the library, the museum and the two natural science institutes.

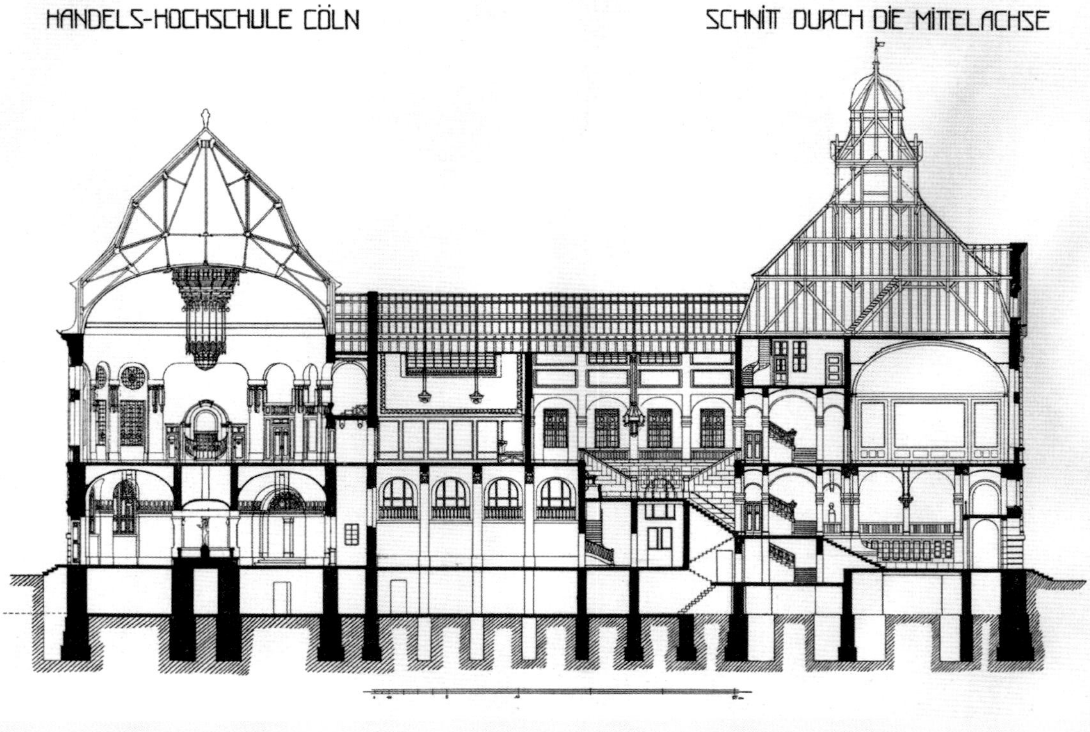
HANDELS-HOCHSCHULE CÖLN
SCHNITT DURCH DIE MITTELACHSE

↑ In designing Cologne's Commercial College, architect Ernst Friedrich Vetterlein from Darmstadt was inspired by the German Baroque style; view of the south-east facade.

A New University

Chapter 2

1919–1933

1919 – 1933

1919

Founding

Mayor of Cologne Konrad Adenauer signs the contract with the Prussian government for the founding of Cologne's new university on 29 May. The opening ceremony takes place on 12 June.

1920

Four Faculties

The two first faculties, the Faculty of Economics and Social Sciences and the Faculty of Medicine, are complemented by the Faculty of Law and the Faculty of Philosophy, which includes mathematics and natural sciences.

1922

Student Self-Help

The financial plight of many students prompts the founding of the Kölner Studentenburse (Cologne Student Services Center). The forerunner of today's Studentenwerk offers needy students financial aid and social services.

1925

Comprehensive Medical Training

The University of Cologne introduces preclinical studies. The expansion of its medical program lays the foundation for the growing success of its medical faculty.

1928

International Orientation

The university opens its Akademische Auslandsstelle (Academic Foreign Office), the precursor of today's International Office, to help foreign students at the University of Cologne.

1929

A New University Building

On 26 October, Mayor Konrad Adenauer lays the cornerstone for the new main building at a ceremony attended by Prussian Prime Minister Otto Braun and Minister of Education Carl Heinrich Becker.

1931

6,000 Students

In the summer semester, enrollment at the University of Cologne during the Weimar era peaks at just over 6,000 students, a number not reached again until twenty years later.

1932

Shift to the Right

In February, the National Socialist German Students' League wins half the seats in the general elections to the Studentenschaft (Student Union). The election is later declared invalid due to low voter turnout.

Kölner Universitäts-Zeitung

Herausgegeben vom **Allgemeinen Studenten-Ausschuß der Universität Köln** mit Unterstützung der **Dozentenschaft** / Verlag der Buchhandlung von **Oskar Müller**, vorm. Hugo Inderau, Köln / Druck von Emil Pilgram, : : : Hoffnungsthal bei Köln. : : : :

Erscheint wöchentlich während der Semesterdauer / Preis jeder Nummer 35 Pfg. / Beiträge werden im Geschäftszimmer des Allgemeinen Studenten-Ausschusses entgegengenommen / Fernsprecher A Nr. 5973 / Anzeigenannahme in der Buchhandlung Oskar Müller.

Nummer 1. Köln, den 20. September 1919. 1. Jahrgang.

Einführung.

Den Freunden und Gönnern, den Herren Dozenten und der Studentenschaft überreicht der Allgemeine Studenten-Ausschuß die erste Nummer der „Kölner Universitäts-Zeitung". Im vergangenen Semester hat es sich herausgestellt, daß ein örtliches Organ an der Universität, ein Nachrichtenblatt für Senat und Ausschuß, eine dringende Notwendigkeit für ein hemmungsloses Arbeiten ist. Was im vergangenen Semester begonnen, gehofft und ersehnt worden war, ist nun zur Tat herangereift.

Wenn alle, Dozenten und Studenten, an dem jungen Unternehmen mitarbeiten und durch zahlreiche Beiträge reiche Unterstützung ihm zuteil werden lassen, wird unsere Zeitung bald zu einer ansehnlichen Zeitschrift heranwachsen. Wir hoffen, daß durch die Zusammenarbeit von Dozenten- und Studentenschaft das schon jetzt bestehende glänzende Einvernehmen noch befestigt und ein noch innigeres Band geschlossen wird.

Aller die an dem Zustandekommen der Zeitung ein Verdienst haben, vor allem aber Sr. Magnifizenz, dem Herrn Rektor, der sich der Sache so warm angenommen hat, sei hier an dieser Stelle gedacht und allen wärmstens gedankt.

Wohlan zur Arbeit!

Der Literarische Ausschuß des A. St.-A.

Zum Geleit,

von

Prof. Dr. iur. et phil. Christian Eckert

Rektor der Universität Köln.

Vor mehr als 400 Jahren, am Dreikönigstage 1389, wurde die erste Kölner Universität unter Beteiligung weiter Kreise des Bürgertums feierlich eröffnet. Schon vor ihrer Errichtung hatte in Köln das wissenschaftliche Studium geblüht. Früher als in anderen deutschen Städten war hier ein wahrhaftes „Studium generale" eingerichtet worden. Wenn man die Unterrichtsziele ins Auge faßt, darf man behaupten, die früheste wahre Hochschule Deutschlands sei in Köln errichtet worden. Ihre geistigen Wurzeln reichten zur künstlerischen und wissenschaftlichen Hochblüte zurück, die für uns in der Frühgotik ihre vollkommenste Ausprägung gefunden hat.

Die Universität Köln ist die erste der deutschen Universitäten gewesen, die nicht gestiftet, sondern geworden war, nicht errichtet durch einen Landesherrn, sondern getragen von dem gemeinsamen Opfersinn der ganzen Bürgerschaft. Lange Zeit hat sie wie wenig andere deutsche Universitäten geblüht, in den Anfängen ihrer Wirksamkeit eigentlich nur in der großen Universität von Paris, als deren Tochter sie vielfach bezeichnet wurde, eine Rivalin besessen. Erst ganz allmählich ist die Universität Köln von der Wirkungsweite einer Weltuniversität mit einer aus allen Landen zuströmenden Studentenschaft zur Universität eines umgrenzten Rheinstaates und schließlich zu einer Stadtuniversität, deren Einfluß nicht sehr über deren Weichbild hinausragte, herabgesunken. Der Niedergang der alma mater coloniensis ging parallel mit dem Zerfall des gesamten deutschen Staates. Hatte sie auch

The new University of Cologne rapidly became one of the German Reich's largest universities. The Faculty of Economics and Social Sciences, which was a special feature of the University of Cologne that had emerged from the Commercial College, played a major role in this development. The university's emphasis on practice-oriented research and teaching and its pronounced interest in the social world were also groundbreaking. Municipal funding set it apart from nearly all other German universities. The city did its best to support the university, but its financial resources were often stretched to the limit. Despite their initially rather positive attitude toward the Weimar Republic, the university and its professors did not fight for democracy and liberal values as the Weimar Republic came to an end.

The Somewhat Different University

The contract between the Prussian government and the city of Cologne had not yet been signed when the university opened its doors. In April 1919, the first students enrolled for the summer semester at the Faculty of Economics and Social Sciences; they were followed by the students who enrolled in mid-May at the Faculty of Medicine, although these two faculties were not formally set up until June 1919. The Faculty of Law opened in January 1920, and the Faculty of Philosophy, which comprised the arts and natural sciences, opened three months later. At first, the university was not much more than a new legal framework for Cologne's three institutions of higher education. This particularly applied to the Faculty of Economics and Social Sciences and the Faculty of Medicine, whose organization, subject matter and professors were adopted from the Commercial College and the Academy for Practical Medicine. There was no theological faculty; Cologne did not want to compete directly with Bonn and saw no need for such a faculty on the part of the church. Furthermore, by positioning itself as a "novel university," it clearly distanced itself from the traditional set of academic disciplines taught at conventional universities. Its focus was on commerce, economics and the social sciences.[1]

The courses offered by the faculties of law and philosophy were initially limited to a few subjects. Only the Faculty of Economics and Social Sciences, one of the first of its kind in Germany, offered a broad range of subjects. Rector Christian Eckert, one of the founders, did not see this as a weakness, but rather a strength that defined the new university: it sought quality rather than quantity. His motto was: "Multum, non multa." This applied both to the university's focus on practice-oriented research and teaching, which had originated in the Commercial College, and to its pronounced interest in subjects from the social world. Although the University of Cologne was at first quite innovative, over the years it sought to include all major academic disciplines. Proclaiming itself "novel" in 1919, the university set out to be different—but only to a certain extent.[2]

A Municipal Undertaking

The city funded the establishment of the university and its operating costs. It provided the university with existing buildings and facilities and committed itself to financing any necessary conversions or expansions. The situation was similar to that in Frankfurt am Main in 1914 and Hamburg in 1919: the urban bourgeoisie initiated the founding of these new universities in Germany—an expression of its economic power, growing self-confidence and pronounced wish to play a formative role.

The University of Cologne was nevertheless not a municipal institution but rather a university founded and financed by the city, which, like all other Prussian universities, was subject to oversight by the Prussian Ministry of Culture and Education in Berlin. This responsibility was entrusted to a state commissioner. During the university's first two years, the commissioner was Philipp Brugger, district president of Cologne, who was succeeded in 1923 by Hans Fuchs, president of the Rhine Province.

Like the Commercial College, the university was governed by a board of trustees, with most of the seats filled by city officials—a special circumstance arising from the city's involvement. The mayor of the city was the chairman of the board; he appointed his

← The first edition of the *Kölner Universitäts-Zeitung* was published on 20 September 1919; on its masthead, the Great Seal with the Three Wise Men appeared for the first time as the symbol of the new university.

deputy, the second managing chairman of the board. The Mevissen family, who had provided the original endowment, was also represented on the board, as was the university with its rector and prorector. Deans took part in board meetings whenever issues relevant to the faculties were being negotiated. The board of trustees' most important responsibilities included drawing up the budget, recruiting administrative staff, evaluating teaching, and forwarding the faculties' recommendations for appointments to the ministry.[3]

The city's strong position inevitably limited the university's administrative autonomy. The determination of Konrad Adenauer, chairman of the board of trustees, and his deputy, Christian Eckert, to take things into their own hands compounded this structural dilemma. Throughout the entire Weimar era, Adenauer and Eckert worked together and were the university's actual center of power, but they also pursued their individual interests. They both repeatedly intervened in affairs that were the domain of the faculties; professors resisted, but not very often and generally not publicly.[4]

Years of Growth

Cologne rapidly began to expand its range of courses. The Faculty of Economics and Social Sciences, the largest faculty by far, at first had four departments, an economics archive and a museum of trade and industry. Only ten years later, the faculty boasted nineteen departments and institutes. The Faculty of Medicine was well positioned from the very beginning with seventeen institutes and clinics, but at first offered only clinical courses—one of the reasons why student enrollment declined year after year. It was not until preclinical courses were introduced in 1925 that this trend was reversed, and by 1932 the number of institutes and clinics had gone up to nineteen.[5]

The faculties of law and philosophy had no forerunners and were established from the ground up. At first, the Faculty of Law had four departments, and by 1930 it had added three more departments and four institutes. Only some of the departments and institutes in the Faculty of Philosophy were housed in the university building on Claudiusstraße, with most of the others spread across the city. The humanities initially consisted of five departments and two institutes, expanding by 1931 to include another department and five more institutes. The natural sciences initially had five institutes, with six more added by 1927.[6]

A unique feature at Cologne were the numerous associated research institutes founded in the 1920s and early 1930s, such as the Financial Research Institute set up in 1927 and the Institute for Trade Research established in 1929. Other important institutions and organizations also emerged in this period. The official, elected student government, the Allgemeiner Studentenausschuß (AStA), was set up in June 1919. Student participation was a major objective of the Weimar Republic's higher education reform. Professors at Cologne, however, opposed any student influence on the curriculum, student participation at meetings of the University Senate, and any organizational connections between the Senate and the AStA. They were willing, at most, to allow students to be heard at disciplinary court sessions. The Senate supported the *Kölner Universitäts-Zeitung*, published by the AStA from September 1919. The student government was renamed Studentenschaft in 1920; it organized many services for students, including department student councils, a housing office and an academic information office. It also ran the Kölner Studentenburse (Cologne Student Services Center) founded in 1922, a forerunner of the modern Studentenwerk. The city and university libraries had already merged in July 1919. The Collegium Musicum was established in 1921 as part of the Institute of Musicology. The Association of Friends and Sponsors of the University of Cologne was formed in late 1924. The Akademische Auslandsstelle (Academic Foreign Office), the forerunner of today's International Office, was in place by the beginning of 1928. And a year later, the university set up a press office.[7]

As the faculties expanded, the number of full professors increased from thirty-eight in the summer of 1920 to sixty-nine in the winter semester of 1932/1933. Cologne's growth rate was thus well above the national average. During the same period, the number of associate professors jumped from one to forty-two.

↗ Student societies also participated in the cornerstone-laying ceremony for the new university building on 26 October 1929.

→ Rector Hans Planitz (3rd from left, foreground), heading the procession from the old university building on Claudiusstraße to the construction site in the Lindenthal district.

The thirty-eight lectureships and untenured positions in 1920 grew to sixty-six by 1932/1933. The first female instructors were appointed in 1922/1923, but there were never more than two in any given semester. During the Weimar Republic, the number of university instructors more than doubled, rising to 177.[8]

The student body grew even more rapidly; 1,299 students enrolled in the first semester. This was about twice as many as had been enrolled in the previous semester at Cologne's colleges. One of the reasons for this sudden increase was the large number of former students returning home from the war. This good start was followed by cycles of growth and contraction. In the winter semester of 1922/1923, Cologne was the second largest university in Prussia after Berlin, and in the following semester the number of students enrolled exceeded 5,000 for the first time. After this initial phase of growth, the number of students dropped to about 4,000 and did not rise again until the summer of 1925. At the peak of this second wave, in the summer semester of 1931, there were 6,019 students enrolled at the University of Cologne. But by the winter semester of 1932/1933, that number had dropped below 5,000 again. These developments reflected the general trend, although growth rates in Cologne were significantly higher than anywhere else in Germany.

When the summer semester of 1920 started, a good two-thirds of the roughly 3,000 students were enrolled at the Faculty of Economics and Social Sciences. The number of students in the faculties of law and philosophy, however, increased from year to year, and by the summer semester of 1930, the Faculty of Philosophy ranked highest for the first time with nearly 2,000 students. This was largely due to the female students, whose number was by far the greatest in the humanities.[9]

New Construction and Crisis

Only a year after the university opened, the unexpectedly large influx of students exceeded the capacity of the university building at Römerpark, which had been designed for 2,500 students. The city constructed new buildings, but only for the Institute of Transportation Economics and the Art History Institute. By the mid-1920s, the university had spread across the city and its main building was hopelessly overcrowded.

Konrad Adenauer and Christian Eckert advocated the construction of a new building. A plan presented in December 1928 estimated that costs would amount to ten million marks. Voting against the Social Democrats, who had called in vain for the further development of compulsory primary education as a supplementary measure, Cologne's city council decided on 29 July 1929 to build a new university building close to the medical facilities in the Lindenthal district. The city made 6.8 million marks available for the project, and citizens of Cologne donated another 4.3 million.

The cornerstone-laying ceremony took place on 26 October 1929, with Otto Braun, Prussia's prime minister, and Carl Heinrich Becker, the minister of education, in attendance. Just a few days later, the New York Stock Exchange crashed and the global economy plunged into the Great Depression. Although Cologne was also affected by this crisis, the mayor continued to support the project, despite all adversity, until the city's level of debt and the rigorous austerity policy of the German government forced him to stop all construction in late 1931. By then, the shell of the building was nearly finished. With the help of private donations, measures were taken to safeguard the building until construction could resume. When construction work was finally completed in 1934, the initiators of this building project, Konrad Adenauer and Christian Eckert, had long since been removed from office.[10]

← At the cornerstone-laying ceremony, Mayor Konrad Adenauer was the first to address the guests; he was followed by Minister of Education Carl Heinrich Becker, Rector Hans Planitz and Allekotte, head of the Korporationsring, Cologne's umbrella organization for dueling student fraternities.

A New University with a Sense of Tradition

From the outset, the new University of Cologne presented itself as innovative. It initially emphasized its Commercial College heritage, which stood for a new approach to applied sciences, designed to deal with the practical needs and problems of the social world. Cologne thus set itself apart from the traditional image of a scholarly university which was detached from the world and dedicated to the pursuit of theoretical insights while paying little attention to new fields of research that addressed everyday realities such as economics, society and technology.[11]

From its very beginnings, the new university coupled its commitment to innovation with a keen awareness that it was continuing the tradition of one of Germany's oldest universities. Even if the claim was not true that Cologne had attempted for over a hundred years to revive its old university, invoking the medieval university's great past and actively cultivating this historical myth resulted in the creation of a culture of remembrance that was even fostered among the professors and continues to shape the university's traditions to this day. In contrast, the memory of the Commercial College soon faded. In 1926, in recognition of its predecessor, the university celebrated the twenty-fifth anniversary of the founding of the Commercial College. But four years later, it discontinued a ceremony first held in 1919 in honor of Mevissen as the founding sponsor of the Commercial College.[12]

Cologne's special mix of innovation and tradition was combined with a humanistic ideal of education that was characteristic of the reform discourse of the time. General education was expected to equip students in specialized areas of study with a broader knowledge of the arts and humanities and to underline the unity of the sciences despite progressive specialization. Eckert invoked the university reforms of the early nineteenth century, clearly placing them in the context of the German Campaign of 1813 against France.[13] In doing so, he emphasized the political significance of the founding of the University of Cologne in the occupied Rhine Province and justified the university's dual cultural-political mission. Through scholarship and education, the University of Cologne was to promote Germany's resurgence and create a "solid bulwark of German culture and scholarship" in the face of other European cultures; at the same time, it would build a bridge of reconciliation and intercultural understanding in Europe. Although this bellicose rhetoric faded with the gradual withdrawal of the occupying troops, the university's image of itself as a "borderland university," whose task it was to safeguard German culture and act as an intermediary in Europe, remained strong.[14]

The idea that scholarship should contribute to the nation's resurgence was a fundamental belief held by German professors. They saw no contradiction in this to their vociferous claim about the political neutrality of scholarship that seeks the truth in a purely objective way. The national interest stood above political parties and therefore above politics. For many professors, the commitment to "*Nation*" and "*Volk*" was not associated with a commitment to democracy. On the contrary, most of them were critical of the Weimar Republic. Cologne, however, had a relatively large number of professors who were democratically minded or at least supportive of the Weimar Republic. In fact, the public perceived Cologne as a "Weimar university," run by the Centre Party, Social Democrats and Liberals.[15]

The parties in the Weimar Coalition had in fact played a role in the founding of the university, not only politically, but also conceptually. To gain the support of Cologne's city council, Konrad Adenauer and Christian Eckert had advocated that the university engage with the decisive social forces of the period. The directors of the Research Institute for Social Sciences—the Catholic philosopher Max

↑ In 1928, Cologne's Municipal Office for Transportation and Commerce published the brochure *Warum studiere ich in Köln* (Why I study in Cologne).

Scheler; the Social Democrat Hugo Lindemann, a politician and expert on social policy; and the sociologist Leopold von Wiese, an economic liberal—would represent a variety of different worldviews. But this hardly played a role for other appointments to the university. Reputation, outstanding achievement and social connections were more important than preserving an ideological balance—much to the displeasure of the Catholic press and politicians who repeatedly called for a stronger Catholic influence at the university.[16]

Founded and funded by the city, the University of Cologne was a civic university that considered itself an integral part of the social world that was the focus of its research. Like the Commercial College, the university opened its doors to the community by organizing many public lectures. It was also involved in setting up and expanding the *Volkshochschule*, a new institution for adult education, and participated in city festivals. Professors were active members of clubs and societies or served as city councilors and consultants. The city, in turn, influenced the university's development through the board of trustees. This restricted academic freedom and repeatedly sparked conflict. The limits of a close association between professors and the citizenry soon became apparent; societal and academic interests could not always be reconciled.[17]

Cologne's urban environment shaped the self-understanding of the university, which from the outset perceived itself as a metropolitan place of study set apart from the provincialism of most German university towns. The new university saw itself as a dynamic force in Cologne's rapid development into a modern metropolis in the 1920s. But although it tried to attract the best students in the German Reich by extolling its vibrant and cosmopolitan urban life, it retained a strongly regional profile during the Weimar era: only one student in ten was not from the Rhine Province or Westphalia.[18]

Gustav Aschaffenburg 1866–1944

Professor in the Faculty of Medicine

Gustav Aschaffenburg, who had gone to school in Cologne, returned to the city from Heidelberg in 1904 to teach at the Academy for Practical Medicine. After becoming the head of the Lindenburg Psychiatric Clinic in 1906, he reformed the clinic, introducing features such as prolonged baths to calm patients. Although this therapy was considered progressive at the time, it had serious side effects.

Aschaffenburg was a pioneer in forensic psychiatry and criminology. He attributed mental illness primarily to physical causes, but also pointed to the influence of social factors. Believing that certain traits leading to illness and crime were hereditary, he was an early supporter of eugenic policies who advocated the sterilization of patients as far back as 1903. Later, however, he also supported the social rehabilitation of criminals.

In 1934, Aschaffenburg referred to the need to "protect the *Volksgemeinschaft* [people's community]" from "vermin" even though by this time he had, as a person of Jewish descent, already become a victim of persecution himself. In 1932, he had withdrawn his candidacy as rector because of antisemitic attacks from the student body. Two years later, the Nazis forced him to resign. An internationally respected scholar, he emigrated to Switzerland in 1938 and from there to the United States, where he taught at Johns Hopkins University in Baltimore.[19]

Ernst Bresslau 1877–1935

Professor in the Faculty of Philosophy

Ernst Bresslau was passionate about zoology. He was the son of a well-known historian, Harry Bresslau, the first German Jew to hold the office of rector at the University of Strasbourg. Ernst Bresslau studied medicine and the natural sciences. A year after completing his habilitation in 1903, he signed up as a ship's doctor and sailed to Brazil. The country never ceased to fascinate him, and he later returned on two research expeditions to explore its nature and wildlife.

Bresslau took up his first professorship in 1909 at Strasbourg. He made significant contributions early on to the study of planarians (flatworms) and proved that mammals had not evolved from marsupials. After heading the zoology department at an institute in Frankfurt am Main, Bresslau went to Cologne in 1924. By then an internationally renowned researcher, he set up the Institute of Zoology, which was first temporarily housed in the Stapelhaus building on the Rhine. Thanks to Bresslau's dynamic leadership, the institute soon expanded after moving to the premises of a former restaurant in the Volksgarten.

In 1933, Bresslau presented his "micro slow-motion" camera for the microscopic analysis of rapid movement. That same year, he was dismissed by the Nazis because of his Jewish background, although he had been baptized as a Protestant as a child. Bresslau emigrated with his family to São Paulo in 1934. There he established a zoological institute at the young University of São Paulo, but died soon after.[20]

Jenny Gusyk
1897–1944

Student in the Faculty of Economics and Social Sciences

On 11 April 1919, Jenny Gusyk became the first female student to enroll in the Faculty of Economics and Social Sciences at the University of Cologne; she was the second student on the matriculation list. Gusyk's Jewish family had fled from pogroms in its Lithuanian hometown of Vilkaujiškis (today Vilkaviškis) to Gräfrath near Solingen in 1911. Her father bought a factory for steel products in Gräfrath. In 1913, the family took on Turkish citizenship. Jenny Gusyk finished secondary school in Solingen, completed her commercial apprenticeship and began studying at the Commercial College in Cologne in 1917. After her mother died in 1918, she raised her two younger siblings.

A socialist and feminist, she was also active in student government. During the winter semester of 1920/1921, she completed her degree thesis on the socialist Jean Jaurès and passed the exam for a graduate degree in business (*Diplom-Kaufmann*) "with distinction." She was the only student to complete a degree in business that year. Her doctoral thesis was reportedly rejected for political reasons.

Gusyk moved to Berlin, where she married left-wing journalist Karl Stucke. He died in 1940 in the Sachsenhausen concentration camp. After being denounced, Jenny Stucke was arrested by the Gestapo in 1943, deported to Auschwitz and murdered there in 1944. Her son Thomas survived with the help of political friends of the family.[21]

Friedrich Moritz
1861–1938

Professor in the Faculty of Medicine

The city of Cologne went to great lengths to appoint Friedrich Moritz as head physician of the Lindenburg Municipal Hospital and a professor at the Academy for Practical Medicine in 1911. A specialist in internal medicine, he had already enjoyed a remarkable career and most recently held the prestigious chair for internal medicine at the University of Strasbourg. The city of Cologne lured him to the Rhine Province with a higher salary. Moritz's reputation and his experience in clinical practice, academic training and medical research played an important role in the young academy.

Moritz was one of the few physicians actively involved in the founding of the new university. As rector and prorector, he advocated preclinical teaching in the natural sciences and anatomy as prerequisites for a comprehensive program of medical studies. His research focused on cardiovascular diagnostics, nutritional science and sports medicine. Moritz was also technically skilled and developed a portable blood pressure monitor and a radiological process for determining the size of a patient's heart. But his approach to patients was never purely technical; he believed that body and soul were one, and that doctors should always combine knowledge with empathy.[22]

The Faculties and Their Key Areas of Study

In the university's early days, its most important division was the Faculty of Economics and Social Sciences. Ten professors transferred directly from the Commercial College, and three new chairs were added by 1927. The departments for economics and business administration, each with four professorships, represented the faculty's core areas of study. The special chairs for actuarial science, social policy studies and economic history had already existed at the Commercial College, and new chairs were created for statistics and finance. In 1921, the faculty founded its first institute, dedicated to transportation economics. By 1929, other increasingly specialized departments and institutes had been created in rapid succession. In 1926, five business administration departments were established, making Cologne one of the leading institutions of higher education in this discipline in Germany. The social sciences, which comprised the Department of Sociology founded in 1920 and the Department for Social Policy and Public Welfare founded in 1923, had almost no connection to the business and economics

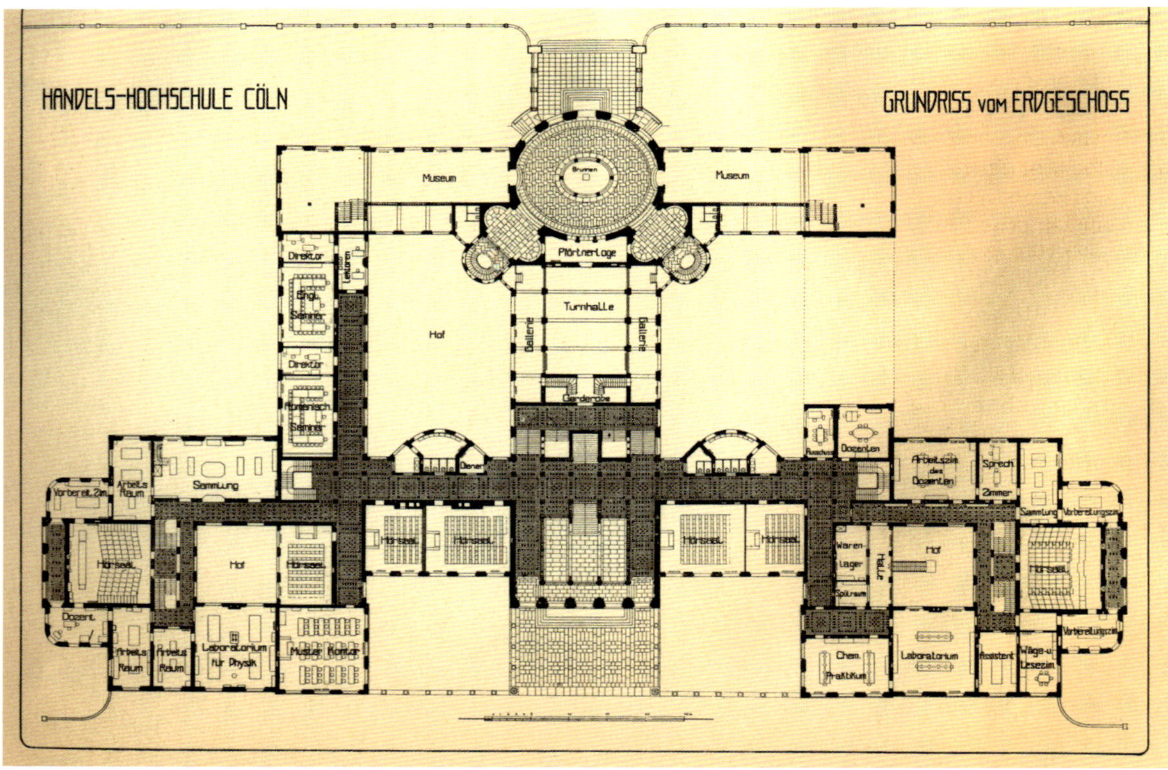

programs. But from 1926, students studying social administration could at least take economics courses with a focus on social sciences.[23]

The Faculty of Medicine emerged from the Academy for Practical Medicine, with thirteen of the academy's professors joining the university. Only the Pharmacological Institute and the Maternity Clinic and Midwifery School were new. In 1924, the latter merged with the Gynecological Clinic at Augusta Hospital to become the Women's Clinic at the Lindenburg. The seventeen institutes and clinics were housed in four hospitals across the city. Lindenburg was the main hospital, the forerunner of today's University Clinic. By 1932, it had expanded to include an anatomical institute, a dental clinic and a surgical clinic. The close cooperation with Cologne's hospitals shaped the university's practice-oriented research and teaching, which was at first limited to clinical subjects. Students could not complete a full medical degree in Cologne until 1925, when preclinical courses and courses in basic sciences and anatomy were introduced.[24]

The Faculty of Law was launched with only two professorships from the Commercial College. Lacking a tradition it could draw on, the faculty soon aimed to include all branches of law typically found at the universities of the period. By 1924, it already had eight full professorships. The appointment of Hans Kelsen in 1930 added a ninth chair for the newly established Institute for International Law. The prime focus of Cologne's law faculty was private law, with four chairs, as well as public law and criminal law, each with two full professorships. Commercial law, a relatively new field, was particularly important at Cologne. In 1927, the Department of Commercial and Industrial Law became an institute. The Institute for Labor and Economic Law later emerged from this. The Institute of Criminology, founded in 1923, was also in step with the times; it combined criminal law and psychology and had its own laboratory. Another noteworthy department, the first of its kind in Germany, was the Department of Politics, which Fritz Stier-Somlo had set up earlier at the Commercial College.[25]

← In 1919, the Commercial College building became the university's main building. Existing disciplines were organized into new faculties but remained in their previous premises.

In the Faculty of Philosophy, the humanities and the natural sciences were not linked by interdisciplinary cooperation. In the university's first year, there were eleven full professors, six of whom had come from the Commercial College and five of whom were newly appointed. By 1932, there were twenty-seven chairs in the faculty, making it the university's fastest-growing division. Philosophy was a main focus in the humanities, with three professorships, one of them Max Scheler's personal chair as of 1922. Initially, the faculty was greatly influenced by independent thinkers such as Hans Driesch, Max Scheler and Nicolai Hartmann; however, during the second half of the 1920s, further appointments resulted in a stronger emphasis on the history of philosophy. The history and German Studies departments each had two full professors. Chairs for English and Romance Studies were added, as were two new institutes, one for studies of journalism and one for musicology. By 1932, five additional institutes and the Department of Education had been added to the humanities portfolio. The training of secondary school teachers quickly became its most important function.[26]

In the natural sciences, the institutes for geography, physics and chemistry evolved from the Commercial College. The Institute for Mathematics was created during the university's first year and a second chair was added to it in 1924. The Botanical Institute was established in the same year and a Zoological Institute set up in 1925. A Department for Experimental Psychology and an Institute for Geology had been already added in 1923. A chair in engineering physics was created in 1926 and was the fourth of its kind in Germany. The intention was to renew and strengthen the practical dimension of natural science education. By the mid-1920s, research-oriented institutes had been set up for theoretical physics and for physical chemistry, the latter a newly emerging discipline. Cologne's natural science professors sought to keep pace with contemporary standards and first talked about forming their own faculty in 1925. But three decades would pass before this idea was realized.[27]

UNIVERSITÄT KÖLN.

Hörerkarte Nr. 1960

Nur gültig für die „Allgemeinen Vorlesungen" im Winter 1919/20.

~~Herrn~~
Frau Teewes
~~Fräulein~~

wird hierdurch die Erlaubnis erteilt, diejenigen umseitig aufgeführten öffentlichen Vorlesungen der Universität Köln, für welche die Gebühren bezahlt sind, zu besuchen. Diese Karte ist nicht übertragbar; sie ist stets mitzubringen und dem Aufsichtsbeamten vorzuzeigen. Mißbräuchliche Benutzung veranlaßt Einziehung der Karte. Rückzahlungen von Gebühren wegen Nichtbesuchs der Vorlesungen finden nicht statt.

Der Rektor
Prof. Dr. Christ. Eckert
Geheimer Regierungsrat.

S. umstehende Anmerkung!

Die Gebühren sind bezahlt für	Die Gebühren sind bezahlt für
Vorlesung 1/35	Vorlesung
mit M. 10,-	mit M.
Köln, den 21.10. 1919	Köln, den 19
Die Universitätsquästur.	Die Universitätsquästur.

KÖLNER VERLAGS-ANSTALT

Guest Auditor Ticket No. 1960

1919

University of Cologne Archives

This guest auditor ticket belonged to a woman. It was issued to Frau Teewes on 21 October 1919 and indicates that it is only valid for "general lectures" in the winter semester of 1919/1920. Opening university lectures to the public had a long tradition. Even when the Commercial College was founded in 1901, the admission requirements stipulated that "guest auditor tickets were to be issued to adults—including ladies" for "evening lectures" which had been announced as "public." Five years after women had first been admitted as guest auditors to universities in Prussia, the Commercial College offered women with the necessary financial means an educational opportunity. The ticket also notes: "A guest auditor ticket entitling the bearer to attend all public lectures costs ten marks per semester, a guest auditor ticket for a weekly one-hour lecture costs three marks per semester or five marks if it is a two-hour lecture."[28]

During the Weimar era, about fifty public lectures were held each semester, giving residents of Cologne access to research-based analyses and new findings from all disciplines. These lectures were very popular. In the winter semester of 1919/1920, the number of auditors who attended general lectures was 3,902—roughly 1,500 more than the 2,432 students enrolled at the university.[29]

Hat Box and Beret

circa 1925
Cologne City Museum

“The beret, which is never taken off during festivities and is an integral part of academic dress, is usually black, but can also be worn in the colors of each faculty, lending the ensemble a more festive appearance. A beret with a flap above the lower ring-shaped headband and a slight bulge is recommended as more becoming to faces that are lean or not so lean. The headband is stiff; the rest is soft.”

This was recommended by Albert Brinckmann, art historian and professor in the Faculty of Philosophy, in his 1924 proposal for the academic dress to be worn by the rector and professors of the University of Cologne. The newly founded university attached great importance to traditional symbols of academic standing. This is apparent in the beret pictured next to a hat box made of cardboard and leather. It belonged to Bruno Kuske, the first German professor of economic history and economic geography and the dean of the Faculty of Economics and Social Sciences in 1923/1924. Brinckmann had proposed a dark green for this faculty, “in harmony with the other colors”—vermilion for the Faculty of Law, crimson for the Faculty of Medicine and dark purple for the Faculty of Philosophy.[30]

Homo Academicus Coloniensis

Initially the new university's faculty was made up mostly of former professors from its three predecessor institutions. Of the thirty-eight who taught during the summer semester of 1920, when all faculties were in operation, thirty had been at the Commercial College, the Academy for Practical Medicine or the College of Municipal and Social Administration. Twenty-two of the thirty were still teaching at Cologne in the early 1930s, providing a stable base during the Weimar era. This group defined and represented the new university, and up until the winter semester of 1932/1933, ten out of fourteen rectors had come from its ranks.[31]

One of them, Christian Eckert, the former director of the Commercial College, was particularly influential. As the founding rector and long-standing executive director of the board of trustees, he functioned as the actual head of the university. Eckert maintained good relations with Mayor Konrad Adenauer, as well as a network of long-time colleagues and professors he had mentored. A restless academic administrator, he did not hesitate to take on the city or interfere in the university's administrative affairs to realize his ideas. As early as 1922, the University Senate complained that Eckert was acting like a majordomo and turning the rector's office into a "quasi-kingdom."[32]

Eckert remained the university's gray eminence until 1933. But as the rectorate, the University Senate and representatives of the various faculties became more confident, they did not shy away from conflicts, even with the powerful board of trustees. One of the reasons for this development was the increasing influence of newly appointed professors, whose relative numbers grew, as did their involvement in academic self-administration. By the winter semester of 1932/1933, thirty-two of the fifty-six deans who had held office since 1919 had come from their ranks.[33]

Most of the new professors were members of the Faculty of Philosophy. They were the pioneers who built their departments and institutes from the ground up—from procuring books for department libraries to furnishing and equipping entire institutes. A sense of new beginnings permeated the humanities and the natural sciences, and this pioneering spirit spread throughout the entire university. Having started with just a rudimentary infrastructure, the Faculty of Law generated a comprehensive program of studies. Professors at Cologne developed the young fields of business administration, sociology and social policy into established academic disciplines. The Faculty of Medicine was the slowest to change; it didn't break new ground until preclinical studies were introduced in 1925.[34]

Physicians had a special status among Cologne's professors because they had the most interaction with the city's residents through their work in hospitals and private practices. In general, the relations between professors and the city differed from one individual to the next. Although Protestant sociologist Leopold von Wiese thought Cologne was provincial and he generally focused on his teaching and research, he became involved in setting up Cologne's *Volkshochschule* and lived in the city for more than fifty years. In contrast, Max Scheler, who was a seasoned cosmopolitan, saw Cologne as the "new Alexandria" and was known about town as an eccentric, chain-smoking figure, but he only spent time there during academic terms and soon set out in search of new horizons.[35]

← Beadles, the rector and professors on their way to the cornerstone-laying ceremony for the new university building in 1929.

Germanist Friedrich von der Leyen from southern Germany was a different story: although everyone had advised him not to move to stuffy Cologne, he found the city culturally stimulating and remained attached to it all his life. Business economist Eugen Schmalenbach from Germany's Sauerland region repeatedly planned to leave Cologne once the Commercial College had been assimilated into the university, but nonetheless cultivated a large circle of friends and students over the years and ran a successful trust company. Law professor Heinrich Lehmann was born in Jena and went to school in Cologne—together with Konrad Adenauer—before starting his career in Jena. Then, after holding a professorship in Strasbourg, he returned in 1919 to his "father city," as he called it, which became his home.[36]

The *Kränzchen* gatherings that existed at nearly all German universities fostered the integration of professors within the university at Cologne. These events allowed "old" and "new" professors from the various faculties to meet, give and listen to lectures, discuss topics pertaining to their different areas of knowledge and undertake excursions together. Special lectures and discussions held by professors of law, history, philosophy, art history and philology generally ended on a sociable note. Invitations to professors' homes, which often included an excellent recital, were an important part of academic life. Formal balls were very popular after the war and contributed to the new university's sense of community.[37]

A housing community for professors was constructed in Marienburg, a wealthy residential district in Cologne, and created a special kind of academic life. From 1921/1922, twelve professors from all faculties lived there with their families. The residential development boasted spacious semi-detached houses with gardens, which could not compete, however, with the mansions of the merchant bourgeoisie in the immediate vicinity. The development was built and managed by a housing cooperative founded by professors and supported by the university. Two-thirds of the new professors who had been appointed before 1921 lived here in their own little world. Children played in the large gardens and families became friends and stayed in touch even after their years at Cologne. Here, the new professors lived the typical life of German scholars in idyllic Marienburg, pursuing their academic work, humanist education, and leisure activities such as music with their families.[38]

Hans Carl Nipperdey 1895–1968

Professor in the Faculty of Law

Hans Carl Nipperdey was one of Germany's most important legal scholars of the twentieth century, having worked actively under three political regimes. After he had completed his habilitation in Jena, his early career came to a standstill in 1920 when he was investigated for high treason in the wake of the Kapp Putsch. By the time he assumed a professorship at the University of Cologne in 1925, he was a supporter of the Weimar Republic. He went on to become Germany's leading specialist on labor law and was an early advocate of the integration of private law into the constitution.

In April 1933, Nipperdey and other colleagues urged the rector Godehard Ebers to resign. This led to the "voluntary *Gleichschaltung*" of the University of Cologne. As dean, Nipperdey interceded on behalf of colleagues who faced repressive measures in 1933/1934. He was a member of the National Socialist Association of Legal Professionals and belonged to the Nationalist Socialist German Lecturers' League. An associate of the Academy for German Law, he headed two of its committees and was involved in writing the National Socialist Civil Law Code. He kept his grandmother's Jewish background secret. After 1945, he joined other professors working to reopen the university. In October 1946, the British military government dismissed him due to his activities during the Nazi era. Nipperdey returned to his chair in May 1947 and served as the first president of Germany's Federal Labor Court from 1954 to 1963.[39]

Ermentrude von Ranke 1892–1931

Privatdozentin in the Faculty of Philosophy

Ermentrude von Ranke belonged to the first generation of women who were admitted to Prussian universities in 1908. A granddaughter of Leopold von Ranke, she received her doctorate in 1915 with a thesis on the Principality of Rudolstadt in the eighteenth century. She was accredited as a teacher and taught at different schools.

In 1918, she began an internship at the Historical Archive of the City of Cologne. Its director, Josef Hansen, was involved in the women's movement and fostered the talented historian. She became the administrator of the history department's library at the University of Cologne in 1921, and in 1922 she completed her habilitation on Cologne's trade relations during the sixteenth and seventeenth centuries. She was the first female historian with a habilitation in Germany and Cologne's first female *Privatdozent* (an academic title for people permitted to teach independently at university level without a salaried professorship). Despite her qualifications, she did not advance any further at the University of Cologne.

In 1926, Ermentrude von Ranke accepted a position as professor of history and civil education at the new Pedagogical Academy in Kiel and taught as a *Privatdozentin* at the University of Kiel. With her husband, philosopher Hermann Bäcker, she switched to the new Dortmund State Pedagogical Academy in 1929, where she taught as a professor of history and didactics. She died aged 39 while giving birth to her second child.[40]

Max Scheler
1874–1928

Professor in the
Faculty of Philosophy

Eugen Schmalenbach
1873–1955

Professor in the Faculty of
Economics and Social Sciences

Max Scheler arrived at Cologne in 1918 as the designated founding director of the Research Institute for Social Sciences. Konrad Adenauer had strongly favored his appointment. A Catholic philosopher and one of the most important figures in his field, Scheler's work on material value-ethics, published in 1913, was a milestone in phenomenological philosophy. Although he had initially supported Germany's war aims, he was later one of only a few German intellectuals to advocate European reconciliation.

His appointment to the University of Cologne, where Scheler also held a personal chair from 1922 on, was his first permanent position. Before that, private affairs had repeatedly hindered the career of this brilliant thinker. In Cologne, Scheler continued to lead an unconventional life; he married his assistant and renounced Catholicism—much to the chagrin of Konrad Adenauer.

Most of Scheler's work stems from the time he spent in Cologne. He was committed to reforming education, laid the groundwork for the sociology of knowledge and conceptualized philosophical anthropology as a new discipline. His enthusiastic and discursive style of philosophizing attracted many students and colleagues, who formed an interdisciplinary discussion circle. Scheler left Cologne in 1928 to take up a professorship in Frankfurt am Main.[41]

Eugen Schmalenbach came from a family of entrepreneurs in Westphalia. Against his father's will, he began studying at the new Leipzig College of Commerce in 1898 after finishing a commercial apprenticeship. He completed his habilitation without a doctorate in 1903 at the Commercial College in Cologne, where he became a professor of business administration in 1906. It was here that he developed important theoretical and practical principles for modern business administration.

Schmalenbach was active as an entrepreneur, auditor and consultant to businesses, public authorities and policy makers. As a liberal democrat who engaged in diverse activities and published numerous articles on the economic issues of the day during the Weimar era, Schmalenbach was influential far beyond his area of expertise. At the University of Cologne, he set up the first department of business administration in Germany and laid the groundwork for the profession of chartered accountant.

After the National Socialists came to power, Schmalenbach, whose wife was Jewish, applied for early retirement in May 1933. During the Nazi era, the couple was subjected to increasing repression and went into hiding in the home of friends in September 1944. After the war ended, Schmalenbach and other professors worked to reopen the University of Cologne, where he taught until 1950.[42]

Male, Catholic, Provincial—Students at Cologne

Many first-generation students at Cologne transferred directly to the university from the colleges that were its forerunners and continued their studies in commerce and economics or medicine at the same place with the same teachers. Many who were studying economics had completed a commercial apprenticeship or had job experience. This raised the average age of Cologne's students; they were among the oldest in the German Reich.

As with the Commercial College, most of the university's students came from the Rhineland and Westphalia. In 1928 they made up 90 percent of those enrolled; a quarter of the student body was from Cologne. Half was from the surrounding areas, with many students commuting daily from their hometowns to the university. There were hardly any foreigners. The students' close ties to the region were also apparent in their religious affiliation, with some fifty-six percent belonging to the Catholic church. About thirty-nine percent were Protestant and between three and four percent were Jewish. These numbers were unusual for Prussia. In 1928, an average of thirty percent of the students at all Prussian universities were Catholic and sixty-five percent Protestant. But in comparison to the percentage of Catholics in the Cologne region, where most of the students came from, the number of Catholic students was still relatively low. Seventy-nine percent of the students had a middle-class background, well above the average at all German universities. Cologne thus contributed to opening the universities to a larger segment of the population, a trend which had already begun before 1918.[43]

Women made up about twelve percent of Cologne's student body, or less than the national average, in the first few years after the university was established. Their share peaked (at nearly twenty-one percent) during the winter semester of 1932/1933. Female students had to overcome many obstacles in daily life at the university, which was tailored to the needs of men. The *Mensa* (cafeteria) close to the university with its inexpensive meals was open only to men. It was also more difficult for women to find accommodations because they were not admitted to student fraternities and therefore could not use this form of housing. The lack of housing for young women meant many had to stay in the homes of their parents, where they often did housework in addition to their studies.[44]

The university was a man's world, defined by male organizations. Nearly sixty percent of the students belonged to one of the many student fraternities that sprang up after the university's founding. These traditional German student societies formed an important part of social life in Cologne, even though their numbers were low compared to the German Reich as a whole. Most of the fraternities in Cologne were Catholic. Predominantly moderate, they were joined together in federations and worked constructively with other student groups. The dueling student fraternities in the Deutscher Waffenring were another matter; they were exclusionary and aggressive. Nearly every fifth male student at Cologne belonged to one of these fraternities, which cultivated nineteenth-century rituals and concepts of honor and were anti-democratic, nationalistic or even racist and antisemitic. Although they always remained a minority, their influence on the student body began to grow around 1930 and contributed to its radicalization.[45]

In addition to social community and contacts, *Studentenverbindungen* offered their members housing and support. Many joined for this reason, because studying was expensive. Numerous fees had to be paid every semester, including lecture hall, library, department and institute fees, charges for health and accident insurance, and dues paid to the Studentenschaft or to the student fund. Even a coat check fee

was charged. During the winter semester of 1920/1921, these all added up to between thirty-five and forty marks. Eight marks per semester hour were also charged for professors' private lectures, which accounted for the major share of courses taught. Fees for lectures that involved experiments, tutorials and seminars were even higher. Foreigners had to pay double the amount "in gold" or a surcharge — certainly not an incentive to study at Cologne.[46]

Fees and charges were a considerable financial burden, in particular for middle-class families—even though half could be waived if a student was "worthy and needy" and had completed the first semester. As much as eighty percent of costs could be waived in exceptional cases. The Student Services Center, founded in 1922, provided all students with support. It offered students opportunities to buy goods at a lower cost, lunch and dinner at reduced prices, and discounts on public transportation, newspapers and theater tickets. As poverty increased during the Weimar Republic's years of economic crisis, many students relied on this financial assistance, and many had to earn money while keeping up with their studies. The "working student" situation was particularly noticeable in Cologne because of the high portion of middle-class students. By the mid-1920s, nearly one in five had to earn their living, in part or in full, while studying. They worked as tour guides and interpreters, gave private lessons to schoolchildren, sold cigarettes or insurance, worked early mornings in bakeries or played music at evening dance events. Others worked in mines, steel plants and foundries. Although the percentage of working students dropped during the years of economic recovery, it went up again sharply during the Great Depression from 1929/1930 onward.[47]

↑ The university was a man's world; students at the Gaststätte ohne Alkohol (GOA), where no alcohol was served, on Claudiustraße.

Chain of Office

1927
The Rector's office

Rectors of the University of Cologne have worn this silver-cast and gold-plated chain of office on celebratory occasions ever since the cornerstone for the new university building was laid in 1929. It features the Great Seal of the old university, the old seals of the faculties of law, medicine and philosophy, the rector's seal of jurisdiction and the seal of the Faculty of Economics and Social Sciences, created in 1925. It also depicts the faculties' symbolic figures: Mercury, Lady Justice, Asclepius and Saint Catharine, as well as the Prussian eagle. An image of Athena, goddess of wisdom, hangs below the Great Seal of the university.[48]

In the first few years after the founding of the university, the chain of the Commercial College was used by the university as the official chain of office for rectors. In 1926, Erwin von Beckerath, a political economics professor, was the first to propose a new chain. He thought that the lettering and the images on the rector's chain were outdated. On 27 April 1927, the University Senate finally decided to commission a new chain. Following a competition, a goldsmith from Cologne, Ernst Riegel, was commissioned to make the chain. The description of the task was: "The chain should [...] be wide and lie on the shoulders, the emblems in pairs on the chest, the seal should lie below the breastbone. [...] No specific style is prescribed; the chain, however, should not have any unnecessary embellishments and should impress through the color of the gold on the rector's Talar [academic gown]."[49]

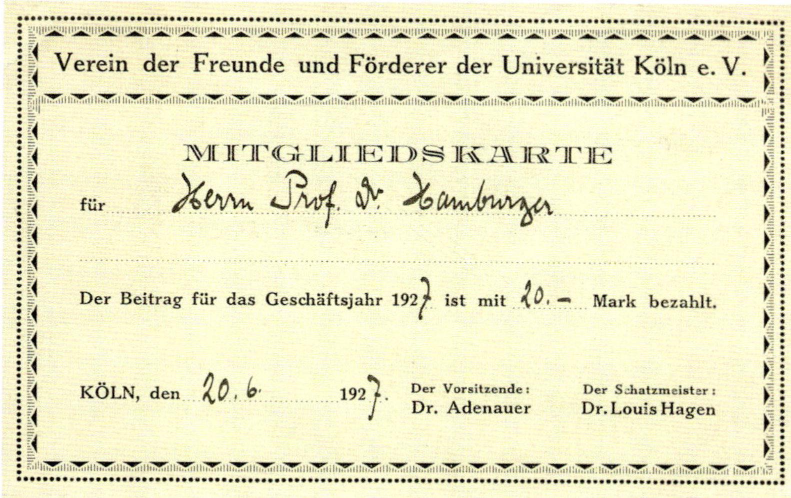
Verein der Freunde und Förderer der Universität Köln e. V.

MITGLIEDSKARTE

für Herrn Prof. Dr. Hamburger

Der Beitrag für das Geschäftsjahr 1927 ist mit 20.– Mark bezahlt.

KÖLN, den 20. 6. 1927.

Der Vorsitzende:
Dr. Adenauer

Der Schatzmeister:
Dr. Louis Hagen

Membership Card for the Association of Friends and Sponsors of the University of Cologne

1927
University of Cologne Archives

Associations of interested citizens who supported "their" university existed in nearly all German university towns. The Association of Friends and Sponsors of the University of Cologne was founded in Cologne on 24 November 1924. It saw itself as a link between the citizenry and the university. Its purpose, as stated in the chronicle published on the occasion of the university's fifth anniversary, was "to support in all ways possible the University of Cologne, which reopened in times of extreme hardship after 120 years, to intensify the ties between research and practice and to promote German intellectual life in the Rhine Province." The members of the association organized guided tours and panel discussions, but above all they sponsored "the establishment of new institutes and facilities, and the maintenance and expansion of existing ones, through fundraising and by granting financial aid."[50]

The first board of the association comprised all the men who played a major role in the founding of the new university: Mayor Konrad Adenauer was the chairman, and the founding rector Christian Eckert was his deputy; the banker Heinrich von Stein acted as secretary; and Louis Hagen, the president of the Chamber of Commerce of Cologne, was the treasurer. Adenauer's and Hagen's names are printed on the membership card which was issued to mathematics professor Hans Hamburger on 20 June 1927.[51]

Eminent Professors

Cologne was already a center of business economics before 1919; one of this discipline's founders was Eugen Schmalenbach. Together with his students Ernst Walb, Erwin Geldmacher and Rudolf Seyffert, Schmalenbach set up the Department for Business Administration in the Faculty of Economics and Social Sciences. This was the first such academic unit in Germany, and it promoted the development of this discipline as a specialized professional field. Schmalenbach transformed accounting into a tool for corporate management, demonstrated the importance of price development for corporate balance sheets, laid the foundations for contribution margin accounting and cost accounting, and introduced an influential accounting system model. The "Cologne school" shaped the development of German business administration into the 1960s.[52]

Heinrich Ewald Hering, the first professor of pathologic physiology in Germany, came from the Academy for Practical Medicine. Early in the 1920s, he discovered the carotid sinus reflex, also known as the Hering reflex, together with his assistant Eberhard Koch. This reflex is a self-regulating mechanism of

the circulatory system, triggered by receptors on the carotid artery when blood pressure is too high. Hering was nominated twice for the Nobel Prize in Medicine. Important preliminary work had been done by Bruno Kisch while he was Hering's assistant. Kisch became a full professor at the University of Cologne in 1925, made significant contributions to cardiovascular research and was a cofounder, in 1927, of the German Society for Cardiovascular Research.[53]

Gustav Aschaffenburg, director of the Lindenburg Psychiatric Clinic, had taught at the Academy for Practical Medicine as well. During his time at Cologne, he published the world's first manual of psychiatry and established forensic psychiatry as an independent field of study. He initiated the founding of Germany's first institute of criminology in 1923 in the Faculty of Law and was its director from 1928 on, together with criminal law expert Gotthold Bohne. The institute brought together legal, psychological and sociological approaches and practical work. One of Aschaffenburg's colleagues at the Psychiatric Clinic was Kurt Schneider. As a young scientist influenced by the phenomenology taught by his doctoral supervisor, Max Scheler, Schneider developed important concepts of clinical psychopathology, published in his classic textbook *Clinical Psychopathology*, and was, with Karl Jaspers, one of the discipline's founders.[54]

Schneider was a member of Max Scheler's interdisciplinary discussion circle. As the founding director of the Research Institute for Social Sciences, Scheler taught philosophy and sociology. A leading figure in the influential phenomenological school of philosophy, Scheler also stimulated developments within the Faculty of Philosophy. One of his fellow debaters was young Helmuth Plessner, who had completed his habilitation in 1920 at Cologne under the supervision of Hans Driesch, a well-known natural philosopher. With Nicolai Hartmann, professor at Cologne from 1925 on, Scheler and Plessner formed the "triumvirate" of philosophy at Cologne in this period. Thanks to their work, Cologne can be called the "birthplace" of philosophical anthropology, with Scheler publishing his book *The Human Place in the Cosmos* in 1927 and Plessner's *Levels of Organic Life and the Human* appearing a year later.[55]

Scheler also did his groundbreaking work in the new field of sociology while he was at Cologne. Plessner was likewise involved in research in this area and contributed to publications of the Research Institute for Social Sciences. Leopold von Wiese, one of the institute's three directors, held one of the first chairs in sociology in Germany. His theoretical and organizational work and publications made Cologne a center of German sociology in the 1920s and contributed significantly to establishing sociology as an academic discipline. Another important area of study carried over from the Commercial College was the interdisciplinary field of colonial science, which, despite Germany's loss of its colonies, was widely represented in research and teaching.[56]

Law professors at Cologne gained a reputation for bringing together legal studies and economics, benefiting from intellectual exchange with university economists and from interaction with the dynamic Rhine-Westphalia region. Cologne appointed Heinrich Lehmann, a recognized specialist in this field, to set up the Department of Commercial and Industrial Law in 1920, one of the first of its kind in Germany. Lehmann's student Hans Carl Nipperdey, who came to Cologne in 1925, produced works on labor law and set standards in this new field, which he was instrumental in shaping until the 1960s.[57]

New horizons opened in the summer of 1930 when Hans Kelsen, a Viennese scholar, accepted a position as a full professor of public law, general jurisprudence and philosophy of law and became the director of the Institute for International Law which had been set up specifically for him. Kelsen published a fundamental work of legal positivism entitled *Pure Theory of Law*, he shaped modern constitutional law and constitutional jurisdiction in Europe and was also the author of important texts on the theory of democracy. With the appointment of Carl Schmitt, whose views on law and the state contradicted Kelsen's, two of the most important legal and constitutional theorists of the twentieth century would have been professors at Cologne during the summer semester of 1933. But in April 1933, Kelsen became the first professor of law at the university to be forced to resign by the Nazis—just a few days before Schmitt began holding his lectures. Schmitt quickly advanced to "crown jurist of the Third Reich" and moved to a new position in Berlin at the end of 1933.[58]

← Professors from the Faculty of Law and the Faculty of Medicine attend the cornerstone-laying ceremony for the new university building in 1929.

Martin Spahn
1875–1945

Professor in the
Faculty of Philosophy

Martin Spahn's beginnings were promising. In 1901, aged only 26, the historian was the first Catholic to hold a chair at the University of Strasbourg. Although liberal-Protestant historians protested his appointment, Kaiser Wilhelm II did not yield to this pressure, in hopes that Spahn would help to strengthen the links between Catholics and the Prussian-Protestant empire. A specialist in early modern history, Spahn became an influential writer on questions relevant to political Catholicism while at Strasbourg.

Through contacts he had as a centrist politician, Martin Spahn was appointed a professor of medieval and early modern history at Cologne in 1920; he also became the director of the new Institute for Journalism and Public Opinion. That same year, he became the founding director of the conservative Politisches Kolleg (Political College) in Berlin, and in 1924 he entered the Reichstag as a member of the German National People's Party (DNVP). The university tried without success to dismiss him, as he was frequently absent and productive only as a writer.

Politically, Spahn shifted more and more to the right. He campaigned for a revision of the Treaty of Versailles, and in 1933 he urged representatives of the DNVP to join the Nazi Party. He remained nominally a member of the "Nazified" Reichstag until 1945. In 1934, he founded the Institute for Spatial Policy, which supported imperialist "*Westforschung*", the study of the regions and countries west of the Rhine.[59]

Fritz Stier-Somlo
1873–1932

Professor in the
Faculty of Law

Fritz Stier-Somlo was an unusual legal scholar. Familiar with all aspects of public law, he was keenly aware of contemporary issues. In order to adapt the training of civil servants to the needs of a modern industrial state, he proposed the founding of Germany's first academy for public administration in Düsseldorf in 1911. As a professor of public law, he also helped to establish Cologne's College for Municipal and Social Administration, which opened the following year.

After the university was founded, he was involved in shaping the new Faculty of Law and set up the Department for Tax Law and the Institute for Foreign and International Law. In 1922, he was a founding member of the Association of German Constitutional Law Teachers and served on its executive board until 1926.

Originally a liberal monarchist, he became a liberal republican in this period. His monograph *Politik* (Politics), published in 1907 and in six subsequent editions until 1925, became a definitive volume in the field. In 1919, he put forward his own draft of a democratic constitution for Germany. Stier-Somlo founded the Department of Politics in the Faculty of Law at Cologne and was its head until his death in 1932.[60]

Franz Thorbecke
1875–1945

Professor in the
Faculty of Philosophy

Leopold von Wiese
1876–1969

Professor in the Faculty of
Economics and Social Sciences

Franz Thorbecke's academic career began just as Germany's colonial policy reached a turning point: after German protectorates were secured militarily, they were to be developed and exploited with the support of academia. Thorbecke, a geography teacher, joined a 1907 expedition led by Cologne geographer Kurt Hassert to Cameroon, which had been a German colony since 1884.

After receiving his doctorate, Thorbecke himself headed an extensive expedition to Cameroon from 1911 to 1913 on behalf of the German Colonial Society. His wife, Marie Pauline, accompanied him as an illustrator and photographer. Thorbecke's most important publication, *Im Hochland von Mittel-Kamerun* (In the highlands of Central Cameroon), was the outcome of this research trip and made him the most authoritative German expert on this part of Africa. The final volume was published by his wife in 1951.

In 1917, Thorbecke became Hassert's successor at Cologne's Commercial College. At the university, he set up the Institute for Geography, which he headed until his retirement in 1942. He continued to focus his research on Africa, believing this to be necessary groundwork for colonialism. In 1933, he joined other professors in pursuing the "*Gleichschaltung*" of the university. He was appointed to the Colonial Geographic Committee of the Reich Research Council and became involved in the National Socialist Working Group for Spatial Research.[61]

Leopold von Wiese was a pioneer in the field of sociology in Germany. Originally a political economist, he came to Cologne in 1915, and in 1919 was one of the founding directors of the first German research institute for social sciences. That same year he assumed one of the first two sociology professorships in Germany and established Cologne's Department of Sociology. From 1921 on, he published the influential *Kölner Vierteljahrshefte für Sozialwissenschaften*, which also served as the bulletin for the German Sociological Association (DGS), of which von Wiese was a founding member and executive secretary. Under von Wiese's influence as a leading representative of his field, the University of Cologne became a center of sociology in the German-speaking world.

Not least to retain his influence, von Wiese actively pursued the "*Gleichschaltung*" of the DGS in 1933, without, however, joining the Nazi Party. He aimed to integrate his Beziehungslehre (relationship doctrine), as a conceptualization of relations between people, into the Nazis' racist schemes for reorganizing society, but his ideas were not taken up. In 1934, he went to the USA for a year of research.

Involved in the reopening of the University of Cologne from 1945 on, von Wiese became the first president of the DGS when it was re-established in 1946. In this position, he advocated allowing National Socialist sociologists to again join the DGS and opposed critical engagement with the Nazi era.[62]

The Beginning of the End

For a long time, antidemocratic forces were hardly visible in the public sphere at the University of Cologne. The professors emphasized their political neutrality as academics, and at first, the majority of representatives voted into the student parliament were political moderates. But an antisemitic movement of right-wing fraternities arose early on that was not subjected to sanctions by the university leadership, and by the mid-1920s, the influence of right-wing groups was increasing. This development became apparent in November 1927 when the Prussian Ministry of Culture and Education called on students to vote on a regulation that was directed against ethnic-nationalist and antisemitic activities by the Deutsche Studentenschaft. With a voter turnout of just over fifty-six percent, only one in five students at Cologne was in favor of this regulation and of measures to protect fellow students from discrimination.[63]

The minister of education responded by dissolving the official student unions in Prussia. The University of Cologne suspended student representation elections for several years. This policy deprived right-wing radical groups of an important forum, which meant that the local chapter of the National Socialist German Students' League (NSDStB) at Cologne, founded in 1927, remained insignificant at first. But by the end of 1929, the league had intensified its activities, claiming in a leaflet that there was a Jewish-capitalist conspiracy at the university and attacking the deans Fritz Stier-Somlo and Gustav Aschaffenburg as "Jews." On 18 January 1930, as the university celebrated the founding of the Weimar Republic, Nazi students showed up wearing brown shirts and carrying banners with swastikas. The university administration played down the significance of these incidents. It was only after violent confrontations early in February during an NSDStB event at the university that the rector banned the Nazi group for a year—not because of its political agenda, however, but because it had violated the university's rules of conduct. As the year came to an end and the NSDStB was awaiting reinstatement in February 1931, it demonstrated the strength it had gained in the interim. Some 600 demonstrators marched to a rally in front of the university, and there were clashes with the police. Rector Josef Kroll speculated that a "large share of the student body had National Socialist tendencies," but saw no reason for concern, since he believed the majority of students rejected the NSDStB's course of action. Professors, he maintained, only had to make it clear to everyone that the university needed to remain "free of political activities and disturbances under all circumstances."[64]

In November 1931, Kroll and his successor as rector, Bruno Kuske, recommended reinstating the NSDStB so that it could be monitored and sanctioned more closely. Kuske pointed out to the Senate that there might be a regime change after the upcoming elections in Prussia, and that Berlin would then order the group's reinstatement anyway. With the intention of preserving the autonomy of the university under all circumstances, the university leadership preempted a possible Nazi government policy before the National Socialists even came to power. This set a fatal precedent for 1933 when the university implemented Nazi policy before any pressure was brought to bear on it ("voluntary *Gleichschaltung*").[65]

When student body representation was reintroduced and elections were held early in 1932, the NSDStB won eight seats out of sixteen. The remaining seats were filled by the right-wing National Block. However, voter turnout was only twenty-two percent; liberal, moderate and socialist groups boycotted the election, which had been exploited by right-wing parties for propaganda purposes. Kuske did not accept the election outcome because of its low turnout, but the NSDStB made much of its success, portraying itself as the only legitimate representative of the student body. Kuske's strategy of integration and

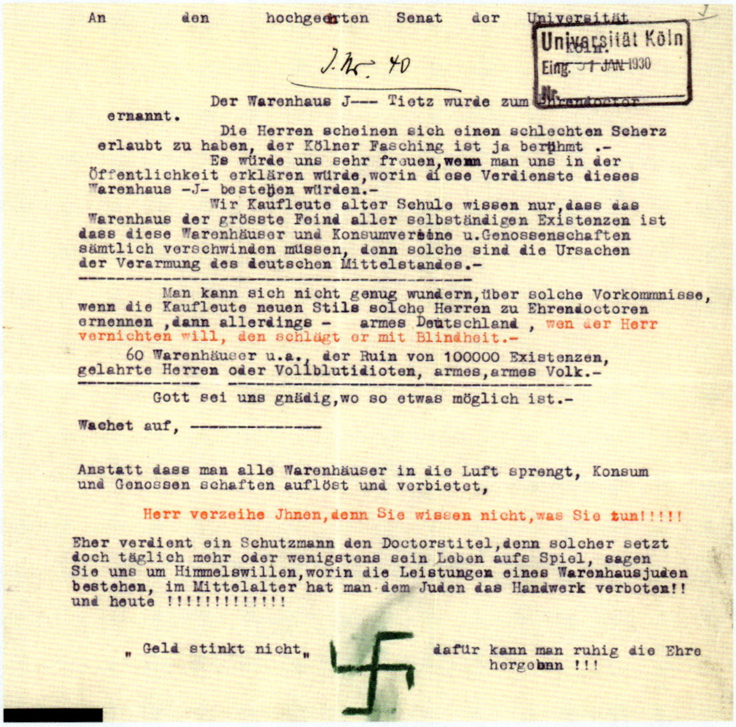

An den hochgeehrten Senat der Universität Köln.

Universität Köln
Eing. 31 JAN 1930
Nr.

J. Nr. 40

Der Warenhaus J--- Tietz wurde zum Ehrendoctor ernannt.

Die Herren scheinen sich einen schlechten Scherz erlaubt zu haben, der Kölner Fasching ist ja berühmt .-

Es würde uns sehr freuen, wenn man uns in der Öffentlichkeit erklären würde, worin diese Verdienste dieses Warenhaus -J- bestehen würden.-

Wir Kaufleute alter Schule wissen nur, dass das Warenhaus der grösste Feind aller selbständigen Existenzen ist dass diese Warenhäuser und Konsumvereine u.Genossenschaften sämtlich verschwinden müssen, denn solche sind die Ursachen der Verarmung des deutschen Mittelstandes.-

Man kann sich nicht genug wundern, über solche Vorkommnisse, wenn die Kaufleute neuen Stils solche Herren zu Ehrendoctoren ernennen, dann allerdings - armes Deutschland, wen der Herr vernichten will, den schlägt er mit Blindheit.-

60 Warenhäuser u.a., der Ruin von 100000 Existenzen, gelahrte Herren oder Vollblutidioten, armes, armes Volk.-

Gott sei uns gnädig, wo so etwas möglich ist.-

Wachet auf, ------------

Anstatt dass man alle Warenhäuser in die Luft sprengt, Konsum und Genossen schaften auflöst und verbietet,

Herr verzeihe Jhnen, denn Sie wissen nicht, was Sie tun!!!!!

Eher verdient ein Schutzmann den Doctorstitel, denn solcher setzt doch täglich mehr oder wenigstens sein Leben aufs Spiel, sagen Sie uns um Himmelswillen, worin die Leistungen eines Warenhausjuden bestehen, im Mittelalter hat man dem Juden das Handwerk verboten!! und heute !!!!!!!!!!!!!

„ Geld stinkt nicht„ dafür kann man ruhig die Ehre hergeben !!!

control had failed. All he could do was invoke the credo of professors in the university's newspaper on 19 February 1932: "Attempts by political forces within the student body to influence and regulate the university administration are contrary to German tradition and culture."[66]

The professors' efforts to maintain their purported political neutrality seemed futile in the face of the general politicization and the NSDStB's radical seditionist activities. It became apparent that a heavy price would have to be paid when even a committed Social Democrat like Kuske, who declared his "resolute resistance" against attempts by enemies of the republic to "conquer" universities, nonetheless regarded the university administration as merely an "executive organ" of the state and left the defense of democracy to the government. In the end, the professors' primary concern was to keep academic life free of the influence of political parties.[67]

Behind this was the contention that the German university was rooted in an intellectual tradition and community that had evolved naturally with its own values. But no one was willing or able to defend this idea when antisemitic threats against psychiatrist Gustav Aschaffenburg prompted him to withdraw his candidacy as rector in the summer of 1932. Cologne's professors and the university's board of trustees had strongly and publicly objected to the criticism expressed in Catholic newspapers and its antisemitic undertones when Hans Kelsen was appointed professor in 1930. Now, no one urged the internationally respected Aschaffenburg to remain a candidate, and no one supported him publicly. At a crucial moment, the University of Cologne did not defend the academic values it supposedly upheld—long before the dictatorship finally destroyed them.[68]

↑ Antisemitic attacks also increased in Cologne; inflammatory text from 1930 targeting the decision to award an honorary doctorate to Alfred Tietz, a graduate of the Commercial College, patron of the university and owner of Germany's largest department store group, based in Cologne.

Match Case Belonging to a Member of the Corps Suevia

circa 1930
University of Cologne Archives

Religio, scientia, amicitia—these are the principles of the Corps Suevia Cologne, which was founded in 1904 and to this day remains part of the association of Catholic German student fraternities. Piety, knowledge and friendship "refer to the values of the Christian worldview and idea of humanity, of academic effort and intellectual honesty, and the responsibility of members toward the friends of the league and the association," Joachim Cardinal Meisner explained on the one-hundredth anniversary of the Suevia.

Several Catholic student fraternities were founded in Cologne after the Commercial College opened. These student societies adopted the ritualized lifestyle of the traditional university corporations (elite German student fraternities) and played a major role in student social life. One regular Corps Suevia event was the founding anniversary celebrated every year by its members, young and old. The high point of the corporation's twenty-fifth anniversary in 1929 was the presentation of its new coat of arms, which from then on graced even common items such as the match case pictured above: "The jumping lion symbolizes the name of the Corps Suevia, which has its own coat of arms; the cross and the coat of arms of the city of Cologne symbolize the home of all Suevians, and the small ship on the crest symbolizes Suevia's fortunate journey through its decades of development and growth."[69]

Wassily Kandinsky, *Scene XVI— The Great Gate of Kiev*

1931
Theater Studies Collection

What do Cologne and Paris have in common? Kandinsky. The original series of stage designs created in 1928 by the Russian artist Wassily Kandinsky for his theater production of Modest Mussorgsky's *Pictures at an Exhibition* are preserved today only in the Theater Studies Collection of the University of Cologne and the Centre Pompidou in Paris.

Kandinsky was so fascinated by Mussorgsky's music that, during his time as a Bauhaus master in Dessau, he began to express his impressions of the sounds in artwork for a theater project. While the orchestra played, the various paintings with geometric elements were supposed to be pushed around or lowered onto the stage, creating images that followed the music.

Kandinsky's production premiered in Dessau in 1928 but was subsequently forgotten. It was not until the 1983 Berliner Festspiele that the Russian painter's only stage production was reconstructed by students at Berlin University of the Arts, based on original stage directions and the stage designs from Cologne University's Theater Studies Collection.

The stage designs became part of the Theater Studies Collection in 1931. On 26 October of that year, Kandinsky wrote to the founder and director of Cologne's Theater Institute, Carl Niessen, that he intended to "reproduce them in a more palatable form," as the original designs were "somewhat dirty" from having been used for the theater production.[70]

Exclusion and Adaptation

Chapter 3

1933–1945

1933 – 1945

1933

"Voluntary *Gleichschaltung*"

On 11 April, following the forced resignation of Rector Godehard Ebers, the University Senate elects Nazi sympathizer Ernst Leupold as the new rector with seventy-five out of seventy-nine votes. All deans with one exception are members of the NSDAP, making Cologne the first university to conform to and implement National Socialist policies.

1933

Expulsion

On 13 April, jurist Hans Kelsen is one of the first professors in Germany to be suspended because of his Jewish background; he is later forced to retire. Over the following years, the university dismisses a fifth of its faculty members for racist or political reasons.

1935

Inauguration of the New University Building

The university officially inaugurates its new main building on 5 April. The modern structure was nearly completed during the Weimar Republic, but construction was suspended for a long time due to financing difficulties during the Great Depression.

1938

550th Anniversary Celebration

Cologne celebrates the founding of the old university in 1388 with National Socialist pomp. In the wake of the pogroms of 9 November, the rector declares that the university no longer has any "Jewish students."

1939

Murdered by the SS

Benedikt Schmittmann, a Cologne professor of social sciences and politician focusing on social policy, who had been suspended and taken into "protective custody" in April 1933, is arrested a few hours after Germany attacks Poland on 1 September and later brought to the Sachsenhausen concentration camp, where he is brutally murdered by the SS on 13 September. Philologist Goswin Frenken dies in 1944 at the Flossenbürg concentration camp.

1939

Rhineland Center for Racial Policy

During the "Third Reich," Cologne becomes a focal point for racial policies in the Rhineland. One of the institutions involved is the university's Institute for Hereditary Biology and Racial Hygiene, established in 1939.

1942

Destruction

University buildings are badly damaged by an air raid over Cologne on the night of 31 May. By the end of the war, extensive parts of the University of Cologne and its clinics have been destroyed or can no longer be used.

1944

Suspension of Teaching

The university stops all teaching activities on 10 October. Parts of the university are moved to Marburg and other locations. The last Nazi rector leaves Cologne in November.

In April 1933, Cologne became the first university to voluntarily implement the policy of "*Gleichschaltung*." Shortly thereafter, the university began expelling faculty members and met with little resistance from those who remained. In the end, one-fifth of all faculty members were dismissed for racist or political reasons. Those who remained hastened to conform. All of the Jewish students were driven from the university within just a few years. The number of students overall dropped steadily, and fewer and fewer women began their studies. The faculty shrank in size and the number of professorships did not rise until after World War II began and new institutes were opened. Conscription led to a decline in male students and rapid increase in female students. Some of the university buildings were destroyed by extensive air raids. In October 1944, the university was moved to Marburg.

Nazifying a Weimar Republic University

It came as a surprise when, on 11 April 1933, the University of Cologne became the first German university to proactively meet the demands of Nazi "*Gleichschaltung*" and fill all administrative positions with professors who conformed to Nazi policies. The newly appointed Reich Minister of Education Bernhard Rust reacted with "satisfaction" and praised the university's actions as exemplary. He was quoted in the local newspaper *Stadt-Anzeiger für Köln und Umgebung* the next day: "Cologne's Gleichschaltung developed and was executed from within the university"—despite the fact that "this university until now has been the farthest removed from the current political course." For the National Socialists, Cologne's self-enforced conformity was a triumph; for other universities, it was a portent. On 21 April 1933, they faced the same fate by decree.[1]

↖ Rector Hans von Haberer (seated) and Reich Minister of Education Bernhard Rust (3rd from left) at the opening ceremony for the new university building on 5 April 1935.

← Professors of the University of Cologne marching on 1 May 1936 at the "Day of National Work" parade, giving a "German salute" to the *Gauleiter* as they pass; Rector Hans von Haberer is in the middle of the photo.

After 30 January 1933, University Rector Godehard Ebers tried to prevent the Nazification of the university, initially with the backing of the professors. But from the very beginning, the new regime also had its supporters. By the end of March, possibly even earlier, they had begun collaborating with the Nazi mayor, Günter Riesen, and the National Socialist state commissioner Peter Winkelnkemper. In early April, the university leadership faced mounting external and even greater internal pressure. Ebers no longer had enough support within the university. On 11 April, the Nazi Party "liaison officer" at the university, pathologist Ernst Leupold, told the assembled professors that they could not prevent the university's "*Gleichschaltung*." Ninety-five percent of the professors present elected Leupold as the university's first Nazi rector. The new deans had all been actively involved in the "voluntary *Gleichschaltung*" of the university, and all but one were members of the Nazi Party or became members later.[2]

Cologne was now on its way to becoming a "*Führeruniversität*," following the "*Führerprinzip*," a principle of organization requiring a hierarchy of leaders. In October 1933, Rust completely abolished academic self-administration. From then on, the university rector was installed by the Reich Ministry of Education as a "*Führer*." The University Senate was reduced to an advisory role. The student body and the faculty members were organized as independent units subordinate to the rector, with their heads appointed by the ministry. Four further university rectors were appointed after Leupold, all members of the Nazi Party.[3]

Disbanding an Academic Class

The National Socialist "cleansing" of the universities began on 7 April 1933 with the "Law for the Restoration of the Professional Civil Service," a cynical title for a law intended to force all "non-Aryans" and "unreliable" political elements out of public service. One of the first affected in Cologne was the law professor Hans Kelsen. An internationally renowned expert in constitutional and international law and an ardent democrat from a Jewish family with left-leaning political tendencies, he embodied everything the Nazis opposed.[4]

The Faculty of Law expressed solidarity with Kelsen. On 18 April 1933, all full professors with the exception of Carl Schmitt signed a multiple-page letter addressed to the Prussian Ministry of Culture and Education in which they referred to their active role in the university's "voluntary *Gleichschaltung*" and requested that their esteemed colleague be retained in his academic post. "Taking leave" of him, the letter argued, would be a "severe loss for the University of Cologne" and "damaging to the reputation of the German academic community." The new dean, Hans Carl Nipperdey, personally took the letter to Berlin—and achieved nothing at all. Hans Kelsen was forced to retire on 1 January 1934.[5]

The case was unique: no other expression of solidarity with persecuted colleagues followed. Academics limited themselves to occasional acts of support and attempts to find new positions for their colleagues abroad. The academic community, which had repeatedly defended its interests against interference during the Weimar Republic, disintegrated under pressure from without and exclusionary forces within. Of those University of Cologne professors forced to leave, seventy percent were affected by the "non-Aryan" provisions of the law of 7 April 1933, and thirty percent were persecuted for their political attitudes, including seven Catholic professors. For the Reich overall, this ratio was eighty to twenty. The few women who taught at German universities were particularly hard hit and accounted for forty-four of those affected by the purge. One of two women teaching at the University of Cologne in 1933 was forced to leave her position. Altogether, one-fifth of the faculty was fired, forced into retirement or driven from the university for racist or political reasons. Although this reflected the average number at German universities as a whole, Cologne was in the top third, as most universities lost considerably less personnel.[6]

Losses

In many cases, the University of Cologne failed to seek or find suitable replacements for the professors who had been forced to leave. The Department for Social Policy practically ceased to exist after Hugo Lindemann, Theodor Brauer and Benedikt Schmittmann were dismissed. The Institute for Labor Policy, founded in 1938, was of no relevance. The chair formerly held by the renowned financial expert Fritz Karl Mann remained empty for a long time. There were no replacements for Eugen Schmalenbach and Hans Kelsen. The internationally recognized psychiatrist Gustav Aschaffenburg was succeeded by Max de Crinis, a National Socialist with inferior academic credentials who later was among those responsible for planning and carrying out the "Aktion T4" program in Berlin, which involved the murder of mentally ill and disabled persons. The Faculty of Philosophy lost a number of academics now considered to be among the most outstanding representatives of their disciplines: Romance language scholar Leo Spitzer, philosopher and sociologist Helmuth Plessner, ethnologist and sociologist Julius Lips, sociologist and social education expert Paul Honigsheim and historian Hans Rosenberg.[7]

From 1933 to the summer of 1939, the overall number of full professors at the University of Cologne sank from seventy-one to sixty-two, while the number of associate professors increased from forty-two to fifty-one. Positions for lecturers and untenured professors fell sharply from seventy to forty-nine. These declines were a direct result of the National Socialists' restrictive university policies. For ideological reasons, they excluded "non-Aryan" students and instructors, devalued academic education and limited women's access to university studies. The number of students declined considerably throughout Germany, including in Cologne, where enrollment went from 4,445 in 1933 to 2,588 in the summer of 1939.[8]

New Partnerships

The National Socialists had strong reservations about universities and lacked a comprehensive concept for research and teaching, beyond instrumentalizing them for their ideological goals. However, they also needed academic experts and well-educated graduates that only universities could provide. In Cologne, the Nazi municipal government began investing in the university again in 1934, despite ideological reservations. The new university building, which had long been the subject of fierce dispute, was completed, and subsidies increased from

↗ The windows of the new university building facing the northern courtyard were designed by Wilhelm Gessler in 1937 and displayed the names of Cologne students who had died in World War I.

→ The Cologne student leader Georg Neeb marching ahead of students on 1 May 1938.

year to year. The overall university budget grew from 2.7 million marks in 1934 to nearly 4 million marks in 1939. A large portion of the additional capital went to maintaining the new main building. Its completion in late 1934 signaled a shift in municipal and university policy: the National Socialists had gone from criticizing the university to cautiously supporting it.[9]

Quite a few professors supported the attempt to establish *völkisch* or ethnic-nationalist scholarship at the university. But the research policies introduced in 1934 by some Nazi administrative entities in an attempt to exploit the country's research capacity for political ends were of greater consequence. The Four Year Plan of 1936 marked the increasing incorporation of academic research into the National Socialist regime's preparations for war. This also benefited the University of Cologne. The regime's need for scholarly expertise was mostly filled by disciplines and professors in place before 1933 rather than by the newly founded and truly Nazi institutes such as the ineffectual Institute for German Socialism, the obscure Rhine Provincial Institute for Research on Kinship and the Racial Corpus, or the Institute for Hereditary Biology and Racial Hygiene established in 1939.[10]

At War

Like most German universities, the University of Cologne closed its doors during the first months of the war in September 1939. The mobilization of entire cohorts of male students and young lecturers emptied lecture halls and seminar rooms. When teaching resumed in January 1940, student attendance dropped by about one-third. Only four out of five vacant associate professorships were filled. The university compensated by radically expanding the number of untenured professorships and other instructors from forty-nine in the summer of 1939 to ninety-one in the summer of 1940, a makeshift solution that endured. In this situation, women were also given opportunities. In 1941, physician Asta von Mallinckrodt-Haupt, who had been a *Privatdozentin* at Cologne since 1939, became the first woman in Germany to be appointed professor of dermatology and the University of Cologne's first female untenured professor. The number of full professors rose by a third to eighty-one by 1944, although some were conscripted in the course of the war. Enrollment of male students dropped to 1,000 by 1944, while the number of female students increased year after year. In the end, there were nearly as many women as men studying at Cologne, marking a complete reversal of Nazi educational policy.[11]

The university tried to maintain a normal teaching schedule, but this became increasingly difficult, especially from 1942 on, when Cologne was hit by devastating air raids. Students served in air defense units and cleared rubble. In the summer of 1942, buildings that housed the natural sciences, in particular, were heavily damaged and partially destroyed. In February 1943, large parts of the Lindenburg Clinic were hit, and a few months later, the natural science institutes were damaged a second time. In the summer of 1943, the city began to relocate parts of its administration to the main university building. Regular teaching had become nearly impossible.[12]

Institutes deemed essential for the war effort, such as the institutes for physiological chemistry, applied physics and theoretical physics, were transferred to secure locations from 1943. When the Allies reached Aachen from the west, the university was moved to Marburg on 12 October 1944. The clinics were to continue their courses but gave up after an air raid in late October 1944. Damage to the main university building was so extensive it could no longer be used. Most of the teaching staff left Cologne. The lecturers and students who remained in the city were conscripted into the *Volkssturm* (people's army). Unable to deal with the situation, Rector Friedrich Bering appointed the classicist Josef Kroll as acting rector. On 6 March 1945, American troops occupied the city. The university faced an uncertain future.[13]

↖ Transfer of the university rectorate from Hans von Haberer to Otto Kuhn at the university auditorium on 18 November 1938.

← Members of the municipal Social Office for Air Raid Victims distribute food rations in front of the main university building.

Anticipatory Obedience

The University of Cologne's new rector Ernst Leupold announced to his colleagues at the Rectors' Conference in Wiesbaden on 12 April 1933 that the former heads of the university had "resigned their posts on their own initiative" in "agreement" with Bernhard Rust, the acting Prussian Minister of Culture and Education. The university rector and Senate completely supported "the policies of the government on national renewal," Leupold added. He presented this drastic and surprising change—from an institution that had upheld the values of the republic to one that toed the National Socialist line—along with a message: "The Reich Commissioner welcomes the move and recommends that all other universities implement Gleichschaltung as well." Cologne was the first German university to officially commit itself to serving the Nazi regime. At first, the other university rectors did not heed Leupold's call. Rust therefore passed a decree ordering the "Gleichschaltung of universities" on 21 April 1933.[14]

After Adolf Hitler was appointed chancellor on 30 January 1933, Cologne, like all German universities, faced pressure from increased agitation by National Socialist students. The NSDAP's victories in both the Reichstag and Prussian Landtag elections on 5 March and in the municipal elections on 12 March emboldened representatives of the new regime to intervene directly in the universities. In Cologne, where Konrad Adenauer was forced out of power on 13 March, the National Socialist Günter Riesen was appointed acting mayor—a move that fundamentally changed the situation for the university due to the city's strong position on the university's board of trustees. In a letter to Riesen dated 20 March, the rector and Senate declared their "firm intention" to work together on "the renewal of Germany" and to serve as an "intellectual border guard in the stead of Strasbourg University to the west, which has been snatched from Germandom." The university thus drew a parallel to its Weimar-era self-image as a "bulwark" and a "bridge," but adopted a nationalistic, one-sided interpretation and adapted it carefully to the revolutionary rhetoric of the new political leaders.[15]

The rector at the time, Godehard Ebers, a conservative Catholic and political centrist, had tried to stop the appropriation of the university by the National Socialists—with little success. He was forced to tolerate a National Socialist German Students' League (NSDStB) rally on the square in front of the university and the hoisting of the Nazi flag on the main university building. The university's existence was indeed at stake. For years it had been under constant attack by the National Socialists, especially by the Nazi newspaper *Westdeutscher Beobachter*. According to rumors, Hermann Göring, Prussian Minister of the Interior, was threatening to close the university, and Riesen, the acting mayor of Cologne, viewed it as a costly expense for the heavily indebted city. He therefore insisted on the appointment of a state commissioner to restructure the university's financial resources and personnel. The position went to the editor-in-chief of the *Westdeutscher Beobachter*, Peter Winkelnkemper, who assumed office on 25 March 1933.[16]

Within the university, a group had formed that was pushing for rapid "voluntary *Gleichschaltung*." The driving force was Ernst Leupold, the dean of the Faculty of Medicine, who had joined the NSDAP in 1923, but left it again in 1926, fearing a negative effect on his career. He was supported by a considerable majority of colleagues in his faculty. Leupold was appointed the Nazi Party "liaison officer" at the university in late March. On 5 April, he consulted with Winkelnkemper, who met with representatives of all faculties at the Cologne City Hall the next evening. Present at the meeting with Leupold were the business economist Erwin Geldmacher, the legal scholar Hans Carl Nipperdey, the philosopher Heinz Heimsoeth and the geographer Franz Thorbecke. Heimsoeth

↑ The acting mayor, Günter Riesen (center), and other National Socialists on the balcony of Cologne City Hall on 13 March 1933.

and Geldmacher had joined the NSDAP in March. Leupold had not invited the acting rector of the university or the deans of the other faculties because of their democratic political views. The conspiratorial group discussed personnel and organizational issues related to the "*Gleichschaltung*" of the university. Ten days later, Leupold reported that all present that evening considered Ebers unable to lead the university in the new political situation, so Nipperdey had suggested they should call on the rector to resign.[17]

At first, Heinrich Lehmann, Cologne's most senior professor of law after Ebers, tried unsuccessfully to convince him to resign. Mayor Riesen then summoned Rector Ebers to the city hall on 8 April. "History," he explained to Ebers, required a "right-leaning rector." Ebers wavered but did not want to set a precedent with his resignation. At midday he met with Leupold, Geldmacher, Nipperdey and the law professor Hans Planitz. The four men finally convinced him to resign. Late in the evening Ebers sent a telegraph to Berlin announcing that the rector, Senate and deans of the University of Cologne would resign on 11 April "in the interest of the university."[18]

Leupold, backed by Rust, was the only candidate to run for election. He explained to the assembled professors that they had no alternative. A clear majority of seventy-five out of seventy-nine voted for Leupold. As was standard procedure, Ebers assumed the post of prorector; Nipperdey, Geldmacher and Heimsoeth became the deans of their faculties. Nearly all leadership positions in the university thus went to men who had served in World War I. The new dean of the Faculty of Medicine, the dermatologist Friedrich Bering, joined the NSDAP on 1 May, and Leupold renewed his membership in 1937. Now the leadership of the University of Cologne was largely in the hands of the National Socialists.[19]

Kurt Alder
1902–1958

Professor in the
Faculty of Philosophy

In 1950, the Nobel Prize for Chemistry went to Kurt Alder, full professor at the University of Cologne, for research work he had done nearly 25 years earlier. While doing postdoctoral work at the University of Kiel with his supervisor Otto Diels, Alder discovered a new general principle of chemical reactivity, later named the Diels-Alder reaction. Diene synthesis is one of the most important reactions for forming carbon ring compounds and is frequently used to this day in the industrial synthesis of pharmaceuticals and pesticides, for example.

After receiving his doctorate in 1926, Alder earned his habilitation in 1930 at Kiel, where he was given an associate professorship in 1934. Two years later, he was appointed department head of the main scientific laboratory of IG Farben's Bayer plant in Leverkusen, where he continued to work on the development of Buna, a synthetic rubber. This substitute material was essential to the war effort and was produced in several plants. A large production facility was built next to the Auschwitz III-Monowitz concentration camp, but it never went into operation. Alder began lecturing at the University of Cologne in 1937 and was appointed professor of experimental chemistry and chemical technology in 1940. His research focused on developing diene synthesis. After the war, he rebuilt the Institute of Chemistry and was involved in establishing the Faculty of Mathematics and Natural Sciences in 1955 as an entity separate from the Faculty of Philosophy.[20]

Marta Baerlecken
1909–2007

Lecturer in the
Faculty of Philosophy

Marta Baerlecken was the grande dame of Dutch studies in Germany but never held a professorship. Linked by family ties to the Netherlands, Baerlecken received her doctorate in 1936 in Cologne with a thesis on Walther von der Vogelweide. She then worked at the German-Dutch Institute, founded in 1931, but only as a graduate assistant. During World War II, Baerlecken kept the institute running.

Besides her work at the university, she translated authors such as the Flemish poet Gerard Walschap into German. She was promised a position as an assistant professor in 1942 but did not receive it because she refused to hang a photo of the Dutch Nazi leader Anton Mussert in the German-Dutch Institute. Her political views prevented her from completing her habilitation.

After the war, Marta Baerlecken worked in the Dutch studies division of the German Department as an untenured lecturer. She also served as a recognized expert in key professional commissions, setting up Dutch studies programs throughout Germany. Baerlecken was head of the Working Group for Dutch-German Cultural Exchange. Involved in reconciliation with the Netherlands and Belgium early on, in 1954 she was the first German to be awarded the Erasmus Medal by the city of Rotterdam for her services.[21]

Stefan Cohn-Vossen 1902–1936

Privatdozent in the Faculty of Philosophy

Hermann Corsten 1889–1968

Director of the University and City Library of Cologne

Stefan Cohn-Vossen made a name for himself early in his career. With David Hilbert, one of Germany's most renowned mathematicians, he published the textbook *Anschauliche Geometrie* in 1932 (*Geometry and the Imagination*, 1952), which was considered one of the best introductory works on the subject. It was translated into several languages and appeared in many German editions. The young mathematician was about to embark on a promising career.

Cohn-Vossen studied mathematics in Göttingen and his hometown of Breslau. After receiving his doctorate in 1924, he earned a habilitation in Göttingen in 1929, supervised by Richard Courant, one of Hilbert's former students. A year later he received a lectureship for geometry and geometric analysis at the University of Cologne, where he worked intensively on differential geometry. His inaugural lecture in February 1932 was on the topic of convex planes.

The National Socialists and their racist policies put an end to Cohn-Vossen's career in Germany. He was suspended at the beginning of May 1933 and lost his authorization to teach in September. Cohn-Vossen emigrated to Switzerland with his wife, where he taught in Locarno and Zurich. In 1934, he became a professor at the University of Leningrad. After moving with the institute to Moscow in 1936, he died there in June of pneumonia.[22]

Hermann Corsten's influence on the University and City Library of Cologne was second to none, despite the fact that his academic career first pointed in another direction. He was seriously injured in World War I and completed his degree in the natural sciences rather late. After obtaining his doctorate from the Faculty of Economics and Social Sciences in Cologne in 1927, he began a traineeship for library management in Bonn, which he completed at the State Library in Berlin. In early January 1931, he was appointed a civil servant, and on 1 May 1933, he joined the NSDAP.

Corsten was head of the Cologne University and City Library from October 1933 to 1954. Within the first year, he gathered the scattered library collections in the university's new main building and set up a universal card catalog. During the war, Corsten was interim director of the National Library in occupied Luxembourg. In at least one case, the holdings he acquired from a private library can be considered property looted by the Nazi regime. In other cases, he played an instrumental role in securing and restituting endangered libraries. Corsten protected the Cologne collections by moving them out of the city. After the war ended, he managed the library's reconstruction, was involved in setting up a national book lending system and established a training program for librarians in Cologne.[23]

The Book Burning

As elsewhere in Germany, a book burning was planned in Cologne for 10 May 1933, organized by the Deutsche Studentenschaft. At the last minute, the rector canceled participation by the faculty members because of bad weather, apparently without consulting the organizers. Rumors about disagreements between the university management and the Studentenschaft were countered by a joint statement released by both parties the following day, explaining that the "*Führer*" of the Studentenschaft had postponed the event so as not to expose attendees to "pouring rain." But in neighboring Bonn and far-away Berlin, book burnings took place in the rain, accompanied by long speeches by professors and numerous guests.[24]

It all began with the "Twelve Theses of the Deutsche Studentenschaft" published on 13 April 1933 entitled "Against the un-German spirit!", a call to "cleanse" literature and the universities as prescribed by *völkisch* and racist principles. "Our most dangerous enemy is the Jew and those who are his slaves," the fourth thesis states. The aim of the students was to "overcome Jewish intellectualism and the resulting

liberal decay in German intellectual and cultural life." The authors demanded that "subversive writing" be eradicated and "undesirable university instructors" be reported. Since the response from the universities was muted, the Deutsche Studentenschaft decided to separate the denunciation campaign from the planned book burnings.[25]

But even at this point, not all universities were willing to be pressured into serving the interests of the Deutsche Studentenschaft. At a meeting in Zurich on 30 April 1933, representatives of German universities deliberated on steps to take against the student campaign. They agreed that the university rectors should approach the government "individually" to intervene against the "comportment of the Deutsche Studentenschaft," especially with regard to the "Twelve Theses." It did not correspond with the "spirit of the university," reported the prorector of the University of Cologne, Godehard Ebers, to Rector Ernst Leupold. The professors were particularly opposed to the construction of "pillories" to which the banned books were to be nailed. The ministry reacted immediately and prohibited this spectacle.[26]

The professors who gathered in Zurich did not speak out against the action as such; they were more concerned about the "comportment" of the radical students and certain elements of the campaign. And neither did the Senate of the University of Cologne have any fundamental reservations. But the professors only wanted to participate if the university library was spared. Nazi state commissioner Peter Winkelnkemper agreed with this condition, upon which the Senate ruled that the members of Cologne's faculty and the rector should take part in the book burning but were not to wear gowns or the rector's chain of office. Apparently, there was no desire to lend the propaganda event the aura of the highest university ceremonies. Legal scholar Heinrich Lehmann also requested that the "Twelve Theses" be toned down. Ernst Leupold spoke with the head of the propaganda section of the National Socialist German Students' League (NSDStB), who then agreed that "the theses will not be mentioned in the speeches."[27]

← The book burning in Cologne took place on Claudiusstraße in front of the main university building on 17 May 1933.

The changes requested by the Senate did not pertain to the core of the book burning, namely publicly stigmatizing and marginalizing authors deemed "un-German" by Nazi ideology, particularly "Jewish" authors. The Senate wanted to protect the university's libraries, not these books or their authors. Rector Leupold downplayed the book burning as a "symbolic" action, referred in Nazi-inflected jargon to the "burning of degenerate Jewish books," and thus legitimized the antisemitic agitation. By appearing without the usual ceremonial accoutrements—gowns and the rector's chain of office—the professors were mainly targeting the Studentenschaft's claim to leadership, which they considered presumptuous.[28]

The cancellation of the book burning was thus a declaration of professorial power vis-à-vis students who had questioned their authority rather than a covert expression of critique of National Socialist university policies. On the evening of 17 May 1933, student paramilitary units and student corporations marched in front of the university building, just minutes before the student "leaders" welcomed their guests in the Senate Hall. The university group leader of the NSDStB, Manfred Garben, criticized the fact that only few professors had fought alongside the Deutsche Studentenschaft for a *völkisch* renewal of the universities before 1933. He expressly praised Cologne's pioneering role in implementing "*Gleichschaltung*." According to a report in the *Kölner Tageblatt*, Rector Leupold declared that the professors wished to "extend their hands to their students and guide them, not only in grappling with intellectual questions, but also in their aspirations for the fatherland and the Volk." Political neutrality was a thing of the past.[29]

After the reception, the student "leaders" went with the university rector and members of the Senate to the university square, where a pyre had been erected in front of the memorial to the fallen soldiers of World War I. Students burned 344 books and over a thousand magazines, including works by Alfred Kerr and Emil Ludwig, Heinrich Mann and Erich Maria Remarque. There were no "fiery tirades;" the "Twelve Theses" were not read aloud. Instead, Peter Winkelnkemper commemorated the dead of the "national revolution" and World War I. According to the *Westdeutscher Beobachter*, Rector Leupold praised the "collapse of the foreign spirit" and the "men" who "in just a few weeks had carved a new Germany out of chaos." The student organizations marched past their "leaders" with torches and fanfare to Horst-Wessel-Platz, now Rathenauplatz.[30]

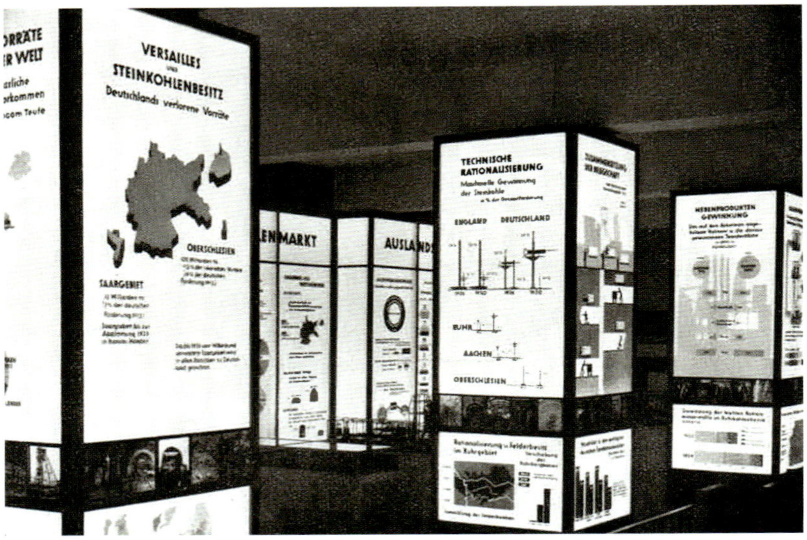

Exhibition of Western German Economy

1933

University of Cologne Archives

Light, color and movement: the curators of the Museum of Trade and Industry hoped that this new exhibition concept would revive the museum's popularity with the public. Re-opened as the Exhibition of Western German Economy on 9 February 1933, the old university museum was the first institution to move into the university's new main building. A brief glimpse of the mining section in the first room shows that the exhibition—directed not only at students but at the interested public as well—was meant to convey a "contemporary" view of Rhine-Westphalian economic life. According to the museum guide, "The mining section is a windowless room lit by glass walls and columns with indirect lighting." It went on to say, "Statistics are displayed on these large, illuminated glass surfaces, not as lifeless strings of numbers, but in color images that visualize interrelationships, using easy-to-understand symbols and imagery. The use of light to display statistics also offers the museum the advantage of being able to update information quickly and at a relatively low cost, putting the technology in place to achieve the dynamic effect desired." The highlight of the exhibition was the mining tunnel, which gave an impression of what underground operations in the coal mining industry were like. The Barbarastollen, as the mine tunnel is called, is roughly forty meters long; it still exists and is open to visitors.[31]

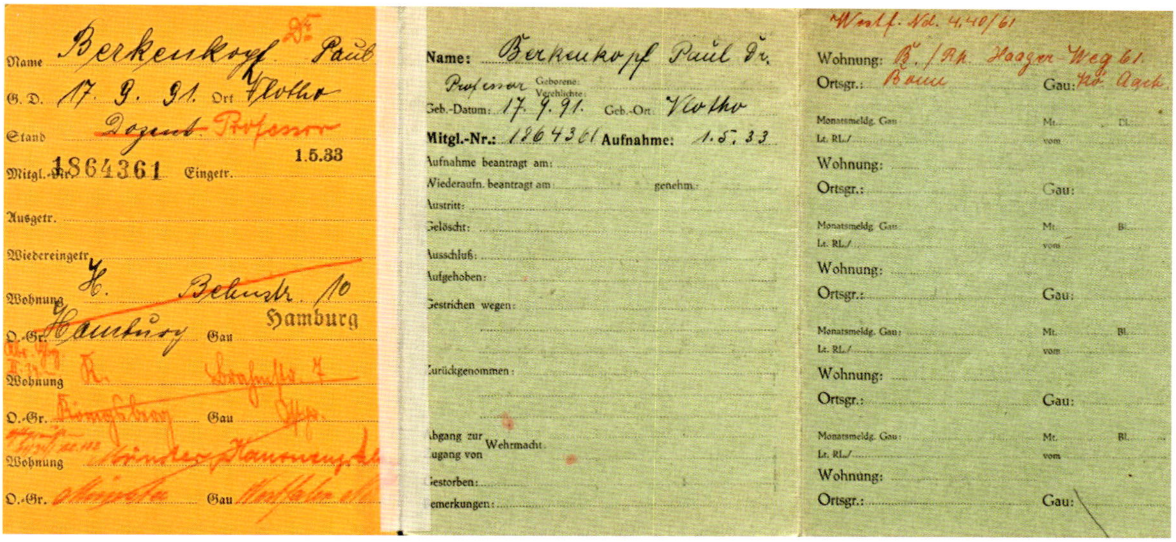

Paul Berkenkopf's Membership Card from the NSDAP Master File

1933
Federal Archives

According to paragraph 3 of the articles of the National Socialist German Worker's Party of 22 May 1926, "any upstanding member of the German Volk who has reached the age of 18 and is of pure Aryan stock" could join the NSDAP. The admission process was initiated by submitting an application for membership which had to be signed in person. After the NSDAP won the manipulated elections of 5 March 1933, millions of Germans—"*Märzgefallene*" (March casualties) as people mockingly referred to them at the time—applied for membership to the ruling party. Among them was Paul Berkenkopf, "member no. 1864361" who was admitted to the NSDAP on 1 May 1933. He was a full professor of political economics at the University of Cologne from 1939 to 1962 and head of the Institute of Transportation Economics.[32]

Membership numbers were assigned only once. Numbers that became available due to suspension or withdrawal of membership or death were not reassigned. This meant that the master card file, which from 1937 on was kept in fire-proof safes in what was known as the card file hall in the NSDAP's administration building at Königsplatz in Munich, allowed quick access to the personal data of all active, inactive and terminated NSDAP members. Seven million of the original fourteen million cards in the master membership file were transferred to the Berlin Document Center in 1945.

The Expulsion of Cologne Academics

Hardest hit by the Nazi purges at the University of Cologne was the Faculty of Law, which lost a quarter of its professors and instructors, including three of the eight full professors. Hans Kelsen was one of the first to lose the right to teach in 1933. Franz Samuel Haymann, a specialist for civil and Roman law, and Godehard Ebers, whose focus was public, constitutional and church law, were relieved of their duties in September 1935, ostensibly on account of the "termination of the chair." The real reasons were different: Haymann was Jewish and a member of the left-liberal German Democratic Party, Ebers was a Catholic and sympathized with the Center Party. Haymann emigrated to the United Kingdom in 1938 but was unable to gain a foothold there. Ebers went to the University of Innsbruck in 1936, was jailed repeatedly after Germany's annexation of Austria in 1938, but was able to return to his position in Innsbruck after 1945.[33]

At the Faculty of Economics and Social Sciences, the largest at the university, one out of five instructors fell victim to the Nazi purges. Four out of twelve full professors were forced to leave, including, in fall 1933, the conservative Catholic political economist Christian Eckert—once the most powerful man at the university—and the liberal head of the Cologne school of business administration, Eugen Schmalenbach. Both remained in Germany. Fritz Lehmann, assistant at the Cologne International Press Research Institute, emigrated to the United States in 1934 and committed suicide there in 1940. The two social policy experts Hugo Lindemann and Theodor Brauer lost their positions as directors when the Research Institute for Social Sciences was closed in 1934. Brauer, a Catholic, was able to stay at the university as an honorary professor for a time, while the Social Democrat Lindemann was deemed "politically unreliable" and lost his teaching authorization in September 1933. Benedikt Schmittmann, full professor of social policy and a friend of Konrad Adenauer's, was suspended in April 1933 and taken into "protective custody" for several weeks. When war broke out, he was again arrested and taken to the Sachsenhausen concentration camp, where he was murdered by the SS on 13 September 1939.[34]

The Faculty of Medicine lost around nineteen percent of its staff, including five of fourteen full professors. The psychiatrist Gustav Aschaffenburg was expelled because of his Jewish heritage, and the physiologist Bruno Kisch because of his Jewish faith. Walter Brandt and Otto Veit, professors of anatomy, were suspended in 1936 and 1937 respectively, because of "Jewish family ties," which could mean that a spouse or an ancestor had been classed as "Jewish" according to Nazi racial laws. The national-conservative Veit remained in Germany and was able to continue working intermittently with the help of colleagues. Brandt, formerly a Social Democrat and an NSDAP member in 1933/1934, found little support. He emigrated to the United Kingdom in 1937. Hans Eppinger, professor of internal medicine, was a special case. His close ties to Konrad Adenauer piqued Nazi officials in Cologne, who pressured him to move to Vienna in May 1933. After Austria's "annexation," he joined the NSDAP and conducted lethal experiments on prisoners in the Dachau concentration camp. He committed suicide in 1946.[35]

In the Faculty of Philosophy, a good twenty-three percent of the faculty members were expelled, including the only woman on the faculty, *Privatdozentin* Edda Tille-Hankamer. Only five of twenty-seven full professors lost their positions. Although the two mathematicians Hans Hamburger and Ernst Fischer and the zoologist Ernst Bresslau were affected, overall the natural sciences lost fewer faculty members than the humanities. Leo Spitzer, a full professor for Romance languages, and a Nazi opponent, lost his authorization to teach at the university in September 1933 for racist reasons and accepted a chair at the

University of Istanbul. The national-conservative professor of German language and literature Friedrich von der Leyen was forced from his post in 1937 because his wife's grandfather was considered Jewish, despite having been baptized in 1810.

A large number of high-ranking associate professors had their teaching privileges revoked early on. The ethnologist and sociologist Julius Lips, a Social Democrat, was dismissed as the director of the Rautenstrauch-Joest Museum in March 1933 and suspended by the university the following month. He emigrated to the United States in the same year. Paul Honigsheim, a sociologist, lost his authorization to teach in March 1934 for political reasons, having already been removed from his position as head of the Cologne *Volkshochschule* in September 1933. A Social Democrat and Nazi opponent, he fled to the USA. The philosopher and sociologist Helmuth Plessner was suspended in July 1933 and emigrated to the Netherlands after losing his teaching authorization in 1934. After the Wehrmacht occupied the country in 1940, Plessner went into hiding. *Privatdozent* Hans Rosenberg, in January 1933 the last scholar with Jewish ancestry to receive his habilitation in Cologne, emigrated to the USA in 1934.[36]

Goswin Frenken, associate professor at the Department of German Studies, was a member of the Nazi Party from 1933 to 1935 but repeatedly came into conflict with authorities because of negative comments about Adolf Hitler and the NSDAP. In April 1935, he was detained by the Gestapo for several days. The university reacted by suspending his teaching authorization and then revoking it altogether in August 1936. He was sentenced to three months in prison in 1937 for speaking out against Hitler, at which point the university revoked his doctoral title. After repeatedly criticizing Hitler in public, Frenken was imprisoned in July 1944. He died on 23 January 1945 in the Flossenbürg concentration camp.[37]

↓ Max Günther, an assistant doctor at the Lindenburg Psychiatric and Neurological Clinic, was dismissed in 1933 because he was Jewish. He and his family emigrated to the Soviet Union in 1935/1936.

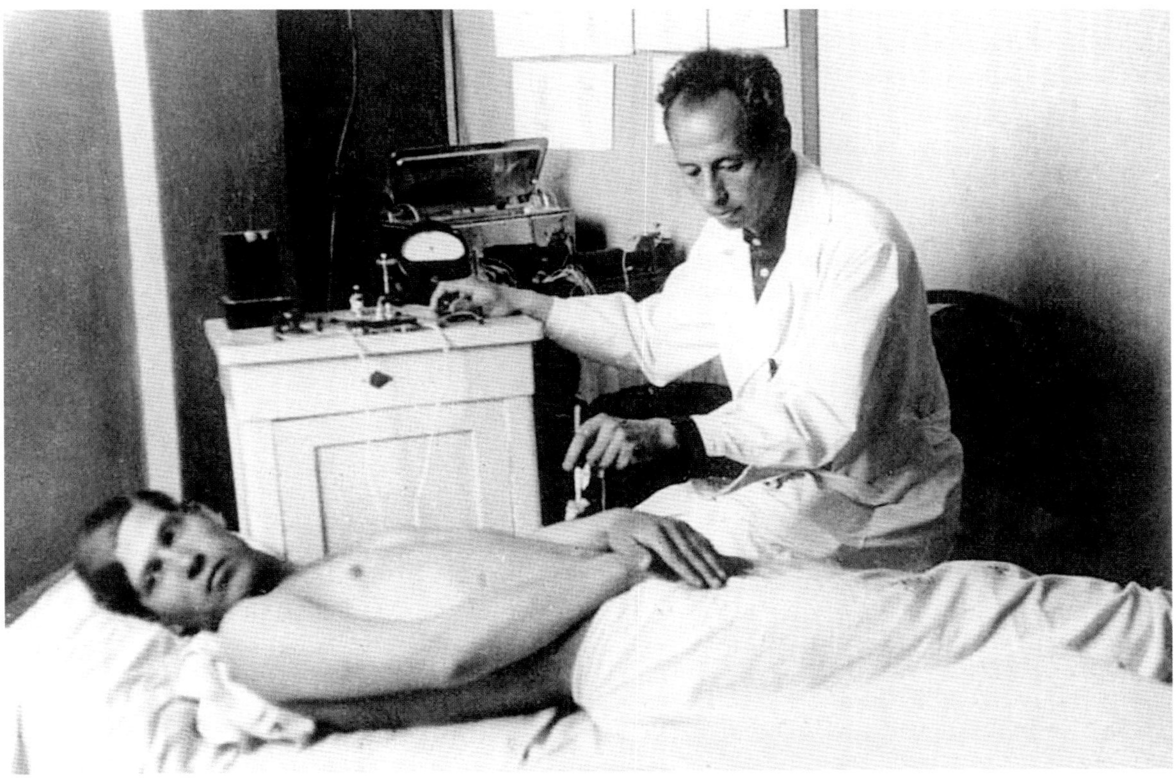

Expelled Faculty Members

Faculty of Economics and Social Sciences

Theodor Brauer (1880–1942)
Honorary professor of social policy

Paul Eckardt (1884–1979)
Lecturer in economics education

Christian Eckert (1874–1952)
Professor of political economics

Hermann Halberstädter (1896–1966)
Lecturer in business administration

Reinhold Heinen (1894–1969)
Lecturer in municipal policy

Clodwig Kapferer (1901–1997)
Lecturer in international market research (related to export)

Karl Kumpmann (1883–1963)
Honorary professor of economics

Fritz Lehmann (1901–1940)
Lecturer in capital markets research

Hugo Lindemann (1867–1949)
Honorary professor of municipal and social policy

Fritz Karl Mann (1883–1979)
Professor of financial economics

Anton Felix Napp-Zinn (1899–1965)
Associate professor of political economics

Eugen Schmalenbach (1873–1955)
Professor of business administration

Benedikt Schmittmann (1872–1939)
Professor of social policy

Faculty of Law

Godehard Ebers (1880–1958)
Professor of constitutional, administrative, international and church law

Hans Goldschmidt (1881–1940)
Associate professor of administrative law, history of German law and German private law

Franz Haymann (1874–1947)
Professor of Roman law, civil law and philosophy of law

Hans Kelsen (1881–1973)
Professor of international law, general jurisprudence and philosophy of law

Ludwig Waldecker (1881–1946)
Professor of public law

Alfred Wieruszowski (1857–1945)
Honorary professor of civil and commercial law

Faculty of Medicine

Gustav Aschaffenburg (1866–1944)
Professor of psychiatry

Walter Brandt (1889–1971)
Professor of anatomy

Max Günther (1901–?)
Privatdozent in psychiatry and neurology

Victor Hoffmann (1893–1969)
Privatdozent in surgery

Walther Jahrreiss (1896–1985)
Privatdozent in psychiatry

Bruno Kisch (1890–1966)
Professor of physiology

Eduard Krapf (1901–1963)
Privatdozent in psychiatry

Daniel Laszlo (1902–1958)
Privatdozent in internal medicine

Rudolf Leuchtenberger (1895–1990)
Privatdozent in internal medicine

Emil Meirowsky (1876–1960)
Associate professor of dermatology

Helmut Seckel (1900–1960)
Privatdozent in pediatrics

Otto Veit (1884–1972)
Professor of anatomy

Faculty of Philosophy

Ernst Barthel (1890–1953)
Privatdozent in philosophy

Isaak Benrubi (1876–1943)
Lecturer in philosophy

Walter Braunfels (1882–1954)
Lecturer in improvisation studies and organology

Ernst Bresslau (1877–1935)
Professor of zoology

Stefan Cohn-Vossen (1902–1936)
Privatdozent in mathematics and lecturer in geometry and geometric analysis

Ernst Fischer (1875–1954)
Professor of mathematics

Goswin Frenken (1887–1945)
Associate professor of Medieval Latin philology and comparative history of medieval literature

Hans Hamburger (1889–1956)
Professor of mathematics

Johannes Hasebroek (1893–1957)
Professor of ancient history

Johannes Hessen (1889–1971)
Associate professor of philosophy

Paul Honigsheim (1885–1963)
Associate professor of philosophy, sociology and social education

Herbert Kühn (1895–1980)
Associate professor of prehistoric art and prehistory

Hans Lassen (1897–1974)
Privatdozent in engineering physics

Friedrich von der Leyen (1873–1966)
Professor of German philology

Julius Lips (1895–1950)
Associate professor of ethnology and sociology

Ernst Alfred Philippson (1900–1993)
Privatdozent in English philology

Helmuth Plessner (1892–1985)
Associate professor of philosophy

Hans Rosenberg (1904–1988)
Privatdozent in modern history

Isidor Scheftelowitz (1876–1934)
Honorary professor of Indo-Iranian philology

Hans Sperber (1885–1960)
Associate professor of German and Nordic philology

Leo Spitzer (1887–1960)
Professor of Roman philology

Edda Tille-Hankamer (1895–1982)
Privatdozentin in German philology

The list comprises fifty-three names of the University of Cologne academics who, between 1933 and 1945, lost their positions or their authorization to teach, or were forced into early retirement for racist, political or religious reasons. In general, formal criteria were decisive for inclusion in this list, even though in some cases the suspension of rights affected individuals with a pronounced affinity to National Socialist ideology and its worldview. Twelve persons have not been included in the list because they lost their rights only temporarily or their cases do not clearly meet the criteria for inclusion, or because they participated in Nazi crimes. In four other cases, the evidence currently available is not conclusive enough to allow an assessment.[38]

Franz Haymann
1874–1947

Professor in the Faculty of Law

Law, philosophy and history: the work of jurist Franz Haymann reflects a lively interdisciplinary exploration of these three disciplines. Born in Frankfurt am Main as the son of a merchant, Haymann studied law and philosophy in Lausanne, Strasbourg and Berlin. After completing his dissertation on Rousseau in 1898, he went first to Frankfurt and then to Rostock, where he assumed his first post as a full professor. The University of Cologne offered the multifaceted jurist a chair for Roman law, German civil law and philosophy of law in 1923. Just one year later, his colleagues appointed him dean of the Faculty of Law.

In his legal works, Haymann combined philological-historical interpretations with reflections on legal dogma. Although he was from a Jewish family, Haymann had been baptized and raised as a Christian. At times he was politically active in the left-liberal German Democratic Party. The National Socialists forced him into early retirement in 1935 for racist reasons. He emigrated to England following the November Pogroms in 1938. After the war ended, his friend Hans Carl Nipperdey, dean of the Faculty of Law, and university rector Josef Kroll tried unsuccessfully to convince Haymann to return to Cologne. He died in Oxford in 1947.[39]

Hermann Jahrreiß
1894–1992

Professor in the Faculty of Law

Hermann Jahrreiß, honorary citizen of the University of Cologne, was a full professor for public law, international law, and philosophy of law and the state from 1937 to 1962, with short interruptions. He was rector and president of the German Rectors' Conference from 1956 to 1958.

In Cologne during the war, Jahrreiß drew on the work of Carl Schmitt to develop a *Großraumtheorie* (theory of greater space), rejecting the discipline of classical international law as an instrument of Anglo-Saxon power politics and conceiving of a Europe dominated by Germany and Italy as a "community of defense and economics." He was involved in the University Working Group for Spatial Research and led the Group for International Law, part of a huge research undertaking, the *Kriegseinsatz der Deutschen Geisteswissenschaften* (the war effort of the German humanities).

After the end of the war, the university refused to allow Jahrreiß to return because of his anti-British publications. He only resumed teaching in late 1947. Until then, Jahrreiß worked as a defense attorney and expert at the Nuremberg War Crimes Trials, again contending that the international law system was biased against Germany. The argument he presented in Nuremberg—that German jurists had complied with Nazi laws because they adhered to the legal positivism of the Weimar period and were thus not responsible for their actions—shaped the self-perception of the legal profession in Germany into the 1980s.[40]

Bruno Kisch
1890–1966

Professor in the
Faculty of Medicine

In the midst of World War I, Bruno Kisch sent his habilitation submission via military post to Cologne. He had finished writing his thesis supervised by the physiologist Heinrich Ewald Hering while serving on the Russian front. In December 1918, he returned to work as an assistant professor with Hering and became a full professor of physiology in 1925. He made significant contributions to research on the heart and circulatory system.

Kish was faced with antisemitic hostility as soon as he returned from military duty. After the National Socialists took power in 1933, he was hard hit by exclusionary and racist policies: he had no remaining students and was forced to relinquish his membership in the men's society Schlaraffia and resign from the board of the Cologne Association for Natural and Local History. The German Society for Circulatory Research terminated his membership, although he was one of its founders.

After the National Socialists revoked his teaching authorization in 1934, Kisch founded the first cardiology practice in Cologne. As the situation deteriorated, he avoided imminent imprisonment by fleeing with his family in 1938 to the USA, where he settled permanently and continued his research. With the aid of the recently developed electron microscope, he discovered, among other things, the mitochondria in heart muscle fibers and their function.[41]

Bruno Kuske
1876–1964

Professor in the Faculty of
Economics and Social Sciences

In Cologne, Bruno Kuske found his life's work. The economist, who arrived in the city in 1903 with a Mevissen scholarship to work at the Historical Archive of the City of Cologne, studied the history and geography of the Rhineland and Westphalia like few before him. After completing his habilitation in 1908, Kuske taught at the Cologne Commercial College, where he became Germany's first professor for economic history in 1917. His chair was transferred to the new university in 1919 and extended in 1924 to include economic geography.

Kuske had close ties to politics and business, was active in applied sciences and worked with popular media early on. He joined the Social Democratic Party in 1919. Although he left the party in 1933, he was suspended for four months in 1933/1934 for political reasons. In 1944, as part of "Aktion Gewitter," he was imprisoned in the Deutz satellite concentration camp for a few weeks. During the "Third Reich," Kuske supported Nazi policies on western Europe with his work on spatial research. In World War II he propagated an "economic union of the Westland," comprising the Rhineland, Westphalia, the Netherlands and Belgium, with Cologne as the capital.

After 1945, Kuske continued his "*Westforschung*" (western studies), but now in the context of European integration. Well-connected and visible in the media, Kuske presented concepts for the formation of North Rhine-Westphalia.[42]

“Doctorate Revoked!”

The Nazi policies of exclusion took hold in every area of the university. Even graduates no longer at the university were persecuted relentlessly by the Nazi regime. By 1942, the University of Cologne had revoked at least sixty-five academic titles; most were doctorates, but some were *Diplom* degrees (equivalent to a master’s in certain fields) or both. To the extent that comparative figures exist, this appears to be slightly lower than the average number of degrees revoked at all German universities within the Reich’s borders of 1937. It should be kept in mind, however, that Cologne only began issuing doctoral titles in 1919. The revocation of doctoral titles, a rare phenomenon before 1933, became a common occurrence in the Nazi period. Two decrees enacted in the first half of 1933 stipulated that doctoral titles could be revoked if the person in question lost their German citizenship or was prosecuted for “dishonorable conduct.” In 1935, this was extended to all other academic degrees. At first, the University of Cologne did not apply this discretionary provision, but in 1936, the Faculty of Medicine revoked the first two doctoral titles. The number of such cases then rose sharply in Cologne when the Reich Ministry of Education declared that a person stripped of German citizenship for political reasons would also lose their doctoral degree. In 1939, a new law on academic titles provided a final national regulation. An academic title could be revoked from persons deemed “unworthy,” a flexible term that also applied to those who had lost their civil rights or been convicted of serious crimes. From 1943 on, expatriation led automatically to the revocation of a doctoral title, without the involvement of the university.[43]

About half of all doctoral revocations in Cologne were due to the loss of German citizenship; in the entire Reich, this figure was around three-quarters. The other half came in the wake of criminal convictions. The large number of revocations due to criminal convictions in Cologne indicates an active approach by the university. Among the most prominent Cologne graduates to have their doctoral titles revoked because of expatriation was Paul Ludwig Landsberg. He completed his doctorate in 1923 under Max Scheler, was a *Privatdozent* in Bonn and was considered one of the most talented philosophers in Germany. In the spring of 1933, Landsberg emigrated to France; in the same year he lost his teaching authorization because of his Jewish ancestry. In 1939, Cologne revoked his doctoral title. Landsberg was arrested in 1943 as a member of the Résistance and sent to the Sachsenhausen concentration camp, where he died, completely debilitated, in 1944.[44]

Many of the criminal proceedings that led to doctoral revocations were politically motivated; this was clearly the case when it came to accusations of high treason and “treachery,” the justification for three revocations in Cologne. Jakob Schiefer, who came from a family of farmers, qualified to study in Cologne after attending evening school and earned a degree in economics. A labor union member, Schiefer received his doctorate in May 1933 and emigrated shortly thereafter to the Netherlands. Unable to earn a living there, he returned to Germany in 1934 and was active in the Social Democratic resistance movement. In 1935, he was arrested and convicted of “preparing to commit high treason.” In 1937, the University of Cologne revoked first his *Diplom* and then his doctoral title.[45]

Cases involving abortion—which resulted in six revocations of doctoral degrees—also followed National Socialist policies. Homosexuality could also be grounds for revoking all academic titles; five such cases are known for the University of Cologne. Alwin Kresse, a general practitioner born in Cologne in 1895, who received his doctorate in 1921 from the Faculty of Medicine, was convicted for homosexual activities in December 1938. Although he was given a mild sentence, the university deemed Kresse a

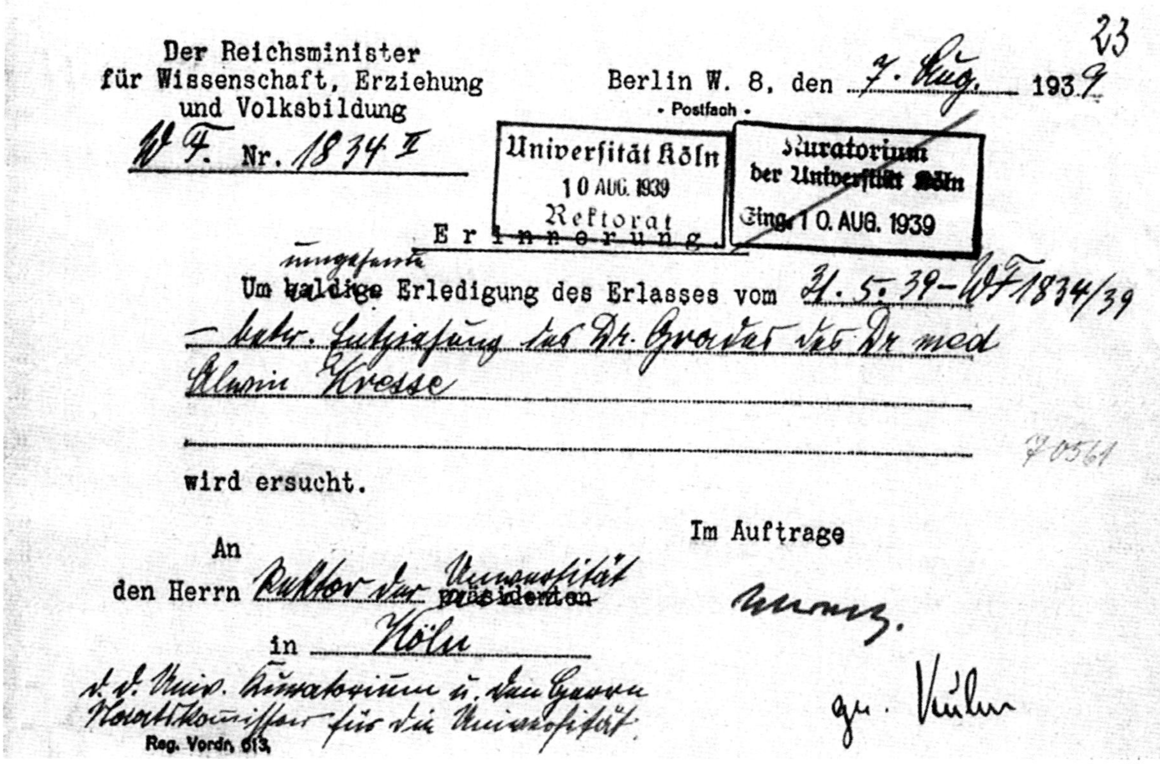

Der Reichsminister
für Wissenschaft, Erziehung
und Volksbildung
WF Nr. 1834 II

Berlin W. 8, den 7. Aug. 1939
• Postfach •

Universität Köln
10 AUG 1939
Rektorat

Kuratorium
der Universität Köln
Eing. 10. AUG. 1939

~~Erinnerung~~

Um umgehende ~~baldige~~ Erledigung des Erlasses vom 31.5.39 – WF 1834/39
– betr. Entziehung des Dr.-Grades des Dr med
Alwin Kresse

wird ersucht.

An
den Herrn Rektor der Universität ~~Präsidenten~~
in Köln
d. d. Univ. Kuratorium u. den Herrn Staatskommissar für die Universität.

Im Auftrage

gez. Kühn

Reg. Vordr. 613

↑ The Reich Ministry of Education demanded in 1939 that the university revoke physician Alwin Kresse's doctoral title.

"criminal homosexual" and revoked his doctoral title. Kresse's efforts to appeal the charges were still ongoing in 1939 when, based on forced confessions, he was sentenced to two and a half years in prison and a five-year loss of civil rights for carrying out "professional abortions." Kresse lost his doctoral title and his license to practice medicine. After he was released from prison, he administered medical treatment to forced laborers at the Ford plant in Cologne and also conducted abortions in this capacity—this time acting in compliance with Nazi policies.[46]

Foreign currency offenses were common in the context of Jewish emigration due to restrictions that were tantamount to expropriation. The University of Cologne revoked five academic titles because of such convictions. The high number of such cases was presumably due to the relatively large size of the Faculty of Economics and Social Sciences. Michael Arenz received a degree in economics there in 1923 and his doctorate in 1926. He joined the NSDAP in 1933 and worked as a business executive in Cologne, where in 1938 he became involved in procuring Dutch currency for a Jewish person who had emigrated. After the transaction was discovered, he was convicted in 1939 and served a nine-month sentence. Both of his academic titles were revoked in 1941.[47]

After 1945, twenty graduates made efforts to have their doctoral titles reinstated, most of them successfully. But the Faculty of Economics and Social Sciences was the only faculty that, in 1953/1954, proactively restored all academic titles revoked during the Nazi period as a result of expatriation. It was not until 2005 that the university repealed as unethical the revocation of academic titles during the "Third Reich," citing sixty-five identified cases and all as yet unidentified cases.[48]

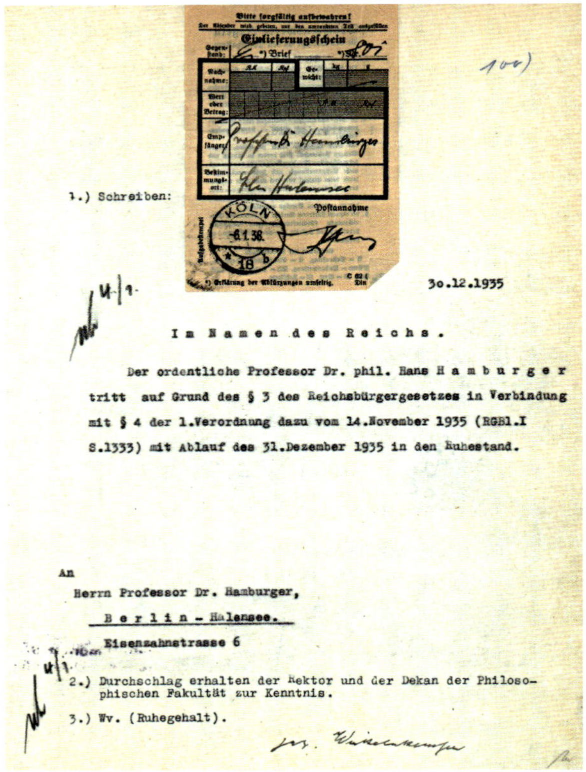

Bitte sorgfältig aufbewahren!

Einlieferungsschein

1.) Schreiben:

30.12.1935

I m N a m e n d e s R e i c h s .

Der ordentliche Professor Dr. phil. Hans H a m b u r g e r tritt auf Grund des § 3 des Reichsbürgergesetzes in Verbindung mit § 4 der 1.Verordnung dazu vom 14.November 1935 (RGBl.I S.1333) mit Ablauf des 31.Dezember 1935 in den Ruhestand.

An

Herrn Professor Dr. Hamburger,

B e r l i n - Halensee.

Eisenzahnstrasse 6

2.) Durchschlag erhalten der Rektor und der Dekan der Philosophischen Fakultät zur Kenntnis.

3.) Wv. (Ruhegehalt).

Notice of Dismissal Issued to Hans Hamburger

1935

University of Cologne Archives

Professor of mathematics Hans Hamburger was among the victims of the National Socialist purges at the University of Cologne. He had been baptized Protestant as a child in 1896. In the summer semester of 1924, Hamburger was appointed professor of mathematics and director of the Institute of Mathematics in Cologne. Although he had been a soldier in World War I, that offered him protection for only two years once antisemitic persecution began in 1933. In compliance with the "Reich Citizenship Law" of September 1935 and its regulatory statutes, the University of Cologne's board of trustees suspended him with immediate effect on 14 November 1935. According to the new law, Germans of Jewish descent were not "Reich citizens" and were barred from holding "public office." The actual notice of dismissal was sent shortly thereafter. The notice, dated 30 December 1935, read: "In the name of the Reich. Full professor Dr. phil. Hans Hamburger will retire in compliance with Article 3 of the Reich Citizenship Law in conjunction with Article 4 of the First Regulation to that law of 14 November 1935 (RGBl. I, p. 1333), effective 31 December 1935."[49]

Hamburger received a pension at first, but when he emigrated to England, benefits were suspended as of 1 February 1940. He was re-appointed to his former chair in 1953 as part of Germany's reparations program.[50]

Leitz Forensic Comparison Microscope

1936
Institute of Criminology

Researchers at the Institute of Criminology, founded in 1923, studied criminalistics, criminal law history and criminal biology in addition to the traditional field of criminal justice. A profile of the institute, published in 1938 noted that to carry out "microscopic and other optical analyses, as well as the chemical and physical analysis of trace evidence, especially for the examination of fingerprints, bullets and documents," the institute was equipped with the "most modern apparatuses currently in use for forensics in these areas." One of these was the large forensic comparison microscope produced by the Ernst Leitz company in Wetzlar; a desktop model is pictured above.[51]

With this microscope, images of two objects could be examined and compared side-by-side. For example, traces of the unique scratches produced on a bullet by the barrel of a gun could be compared to those left on the casing. The optical paths of the two images were combined by means of an optical bridge, so they could be viewed with a single eyepiece. The large forensic comparison microscope was launched in 1936 and soon became an essential forensic tool because of its "excellent properties," which included various illumination features. The Federal Criminal Police Office continued to swear by this device well into the late 1950s.[52]

Studying during the Nazi Era

The National Socialists aimed for lower student enrollment; they did not value academic education and considered universities unsuited to the task of cultivating a new political elite. As early as April 1933, the Nazis had radically limited access to academic higher education by enacting a law countering "overcrowding in schools and universities." Women were particularly affected since, according to Nazi ideology, their role was that of mothers and housewives. The number of female students at the University of Cologne sank from about 1,000 in the 1932/1933 winter semester to 381 in the summer of 1939. But, above all, the law targeted "non-Aryans," whose numbers were not to exceed 1.5 percent. In Cologne, the number of Jewish students dropped from 188 in the 1932/1933 winter semester to seventy-three in the summer of 1933. By the 1934/1935 winter semester there were only twenty Jewish students left, and these included all students who had any Jewish heritage as defined by Nazi racial ideology. From then on, Jewish students stopped enrolling, so that by November 1938 there no longer any "Jews" studying at the university.[53]

In May 1933, well over a month before the corresponding decree was passed by the Reich Ministry of Education, the Cologne branch of the NSDStB demanded that "communist" students be expelled from the university. At first, the university did not comply with these demands, but in October 1933 the three student representatives in the university disciplinary committee forced the university to act. The group denounced "left-wing" and "anti-national" fellow students and formally launched several politically motivated disciplinary proceedings. A climate of fear spread throughout the university. A student law passed by the Nazi government in April 1933 abolished student self-government by elected representatives, banned political or denominational organizations (with the exception of the NSDStB), limited the influence of the student fraternities, and declared that the heads of the Studentenschaft were now their "*Führer*." Jewish and left-leaning organizations were disbanded; other political organizations were suppressed in the course of 1933. The vast majority of students welcomed the new regime or adapted to the new situation. The right-leaning fraternities supported those in power but were subjected to "*Gleichschaltung*" during the 1930s. The Catholic organizations, which had many members in Cologne, kept their distance but did not protest against the activities of the Nazis. Many students joined Nazi organizations.[54]

Student life was now subject to a multitude of new rules and duties. A so-called "duty book" introduced by the Cologne section of the NSDStB in the winter semester of 1933/1934 as a pilot project for all German universities revealed the extent of regimentation. Students were required to list all memberships in Nazi organizations, their participation in "compulsory working groups and compulsory lectures of the student representatives," as well as their activities in "fellowship houses, student corporations, camp service, labor service, and voluntary semester-break labor service." Other activities included political education courses and long hours of paramilitary athletic training conducted by the SA. The effects were apparent at every university: many courses could not be held, student performance declined, and students often fell asleep during lectures after long nighttime SA drills. As early as 1934, the Reich Ministry of Education was already pressing for a reduction of compulsory student activities. Attempts to indoctrinate students through student organizations, working groups and training camps also proved to be counterproductive. The student leader of the Cologne-Aachen Gau, Manfred Garben, noted "general fatigue" in June 1935, because "various entities take up so much of the individual student's time with lectures and other activities." Many students avoided more intense commitments. In the summer of 1939, half of all Cologne students excused themselves from harvest duty, and one in five did not even react to letters from the Studentenschaft.[55]

After the war began, more duties were added. Pressure to help with the harvest or to work in industry or other areas during semester breaks increased considerably. While student participation in these activities fluctuated, studying became less and less the focus of attention for other reasons. Teaching activities were curtailed due to more frequent Allied air raids from 1942 on, and students assumed more and more tasks within the university institutes, in municipal services and in air defense or civil protection. By this time, conscription had caused enrollment to drop by half, to a mere 1,000 students, as compared to the figures for the 1939 summer semester. Many of those who were able to study because of a military exemption were forced to return to the front during semester breaks. The empty seats were filled by female students, whose numbers had increased fourfold after the admissions quotas for women were rescinded during the war, reaching a total of nearly 1,000 in 1944.

Most women were initially involved in the Working Group of National Socialist Women Students (ANSt), which was subordinate to the NSDStB. The local Cologne group reported membership rates of about ninety percent in 1940, up from fourteen percent only three years before. In the course of the war, however, the figure again dropped. A few chosen female students were active in the "Facheinsatz Ost" (Field Operation East). Their task was to prepare the homes of local residents who had been murdered or expelled for "settlers" and then supervise the new arrivals. In the autumn of 1944, when the university was moved to Marburg, all students who had studied for fewer than six semesters at the Faculty of Medicine and fewer than three semesters at all other faculties were sent to compulsory labor service; most of them were women.[56]

← The matriculation celebration in the university auditorium on 19 January 1943 was staged as a National Socialist spectacle.

Fritz Karl Mann
1883–1979

Professor in the Faculty of
Economics and Social Sciences

Fritz Karl Mann assumed the first German chair for financial economics in Cologne in 1926. He had received his doctorate of law in Göttingen in 1906; afterward, he studied languages at the University of London and history, philosophy and national economics in Paris and Berlin. During his archival research, he discovered writings by John Law, Montesquieu and Marshal Vauban. He earned his doctorate of philosophy in 1913 with a thesis on economics in absolutism under the supervision of Gustav Schmoller in Berlin and completed his habilitation in 1914 at the University of Kiel, where he was appointed to his first professorship in 1920.

In Cologne, Mann systematized the lectures in public finance and developed the fundamental elements of his concept of financial sociology, which later led to his groundbreaking work on "intermediary economic forces." In 1927, he founded the Institute for International Public Finance. While in Cologne, Mann also wrote *Steuerpolitische Ideale*, a sweeping survey of 300 years of tax policy concepts. The National Socialists revoked his teaching authorization in 1935 because of his Jewish background. He emigrated to the United States in 1936 and was a professor at the American University in Washington, D.C., until he retired in 1954. From 1953 on, Fritz Karl Mann was also a guest professor in the summer semesters at the University of Cologne.[57]

Hans Christian Naujoks
1892–1959

Professor in the
Faculty of Medicine

The Reich Ministry of Education appointed Hans Christian Naujoks in mid-1934 as a full professor for gynecology and obstetrics—without consulting the city or the University of Cologne. In Marburg, where he was a specialist for obstetrics, abortions and sterilizations, Naujoks had ingratiated himself with the Nazi regime by joining the NSDAP and many other Nazi organizations. He was also instrumental in ensuring that the "Law for the Prevention of Offspring with Hereditary Diseases" enacted in July 1933 would include provisions for abortions for "eugenic" reasons. Naujoks enhanced the reputation of the University of Cologne's Women's Clinic by improving the medical services offered.

While a professor in Cologne, Naujoks carried out or was responsible for more than 1,000 forced sterilizations of women at the clinic. At least one patient died as a result. The clinic called on the police and the judicial system to ensure that women who did not appear voluntarily to be sterilized were brought there under duress. Naujoks was one of a handful of doctors who had permission during the Nazi period to conduct radium sterilizations on older women for "eugenic" reasons. After 1945, Naujoks' career continued as a professor at the universities in Marburg and Frankfurt am Main. In 1957, he was awarded the Order of Merit of the Federal Republic of Germany.[58]

Lotte Schlesinger 1901–1962

Doctoral student in the Faculty of Philosophy

A Jewish woman in Nazi Germany submits her doctoral thesis on Jewish culture during the Weimar Republic to a prominent National Socialist—an astonishing story. But Lotte Schlesinger from Breslau did indeed read modern history, German studies and education at the University of Cologne from 1929 to 1933, and in January 1937 the historian Martin Spahn accepted her dissertation *Die wichtigsten jüdischen Zeitungen in Deutschland in der Zeit vom November 1918 bis Januar 1933* (The most important Jewish newspapers in Germany from November 1918 to January 1933). A month later, Schlesinger passed her doctoral viva.

To be awarded her degree, Schlesinger needed only to deliver the required copy of her doctoral thesis. In April 1937, however, a new decree went into effect prohibiting those considered to be Jews from obtaining a doctorate. Pending titles could be awarded within a three-month period. But Otto Kuhn, the new Nazi dean of the Faculty of Philosophy, refused Schlesinger's request for an extension in mid-May and had the Gestapo confiscate all of her documents. Schlesinger emigrated to England that same month.

After the war, Schlesinger requested in June 1946 that her doctorate be issued to her. Two months later, the Faculty of Philosophy replied that it was "pleased" to confirm that she could use the doctoral title. The actual doctoral certificate arrived two years later; there was never an official apology.[59]

Walter Stokar von Neuforn 1901–1959

Professor in the Faculty of Philosophy

Walter Stokar von Neuforn was one of the most committed Nazis at the university. He asserted publicly that he had been a member of the NSDAP from 1921 to 1924 and had taken part in the Beer Hall Putsch in November 1923. This is not documented, but there is proof that he joined the Nazi Party in 1936.

Stokar von Neuforn was granted a cumulative habilitation—at the time a very rare exception—thanks to special efforts by the Faculty of Philosophy. In 1939, Stokar von Neuforn, who was also a member of the SA, was appointed untenured professor and director of the Institute for Prehistory and Early History. He had a doctorate in archaeology and a degree in pharmacy and was an expert in applying methods from the natural sciences to examine organic prehistorical artifacts. He set up a modern archeology department with its own laboratory. In 1942, the university appointed him full professor of prehistoric archeology.

During World War II, Stokar von Neuforn was active in the Forschungsgemeinschaft Deutsches Ahnenerbe, an SS research project founded to give Nazi racist ideology scholarly backing. He joined the Waffen-SS in 1943. As the official university advisor to the Reich Commissioner for the occupied Netherlands, Stokar von Neuforn was one of the key figures in the Germanic Research Institute from 1943 on and was active in Nazifying Dutch universities. After the war, the University of Cologne prevented him from returning, and he went back to working as a pharmacist.[60]

Serving the Nazi Regime

The astonishing rapidity with which the universities adapted to the new rulers in 1933 was soon matched by an accelerated phase of (self-)mobilization. As the regime's need for academic expertise grew, so did the intensity of academics' commitment to support it. "*Westforschung*" at the University of Cologne was a case in point. Bruno Kuske, who had engaged in research in economic history and geography and been active in applied research and political consulting since the 1920s, initiated a faculty committee for spatial research in late 1934, anticipating the requirements of those in power. After the Reich Working Group for Spatial Research was founded in December 1935, Kuske—a former Social Democrat—assumed leadership of the Cologne University group. The decentralized, large-scale research project was intended to "maintain and secure the völkisch existence" of the Germans. The key concepts were "blood and soil" and "people and space." From the perspective of the National Socialists, the aim was to integrate academia into their political ideology. For academics, this was an opportunity to secure recognition, additional resources and rapid career advances.[61]

The concepts and methods of spatial research, as well as the interdisciplinary research conducted together with other universities, were highly compatible with the *völkisch*-racist approach of Nazi spatial policy. Kuske was tireless in wooing new colleagues. In 1938, the working group numbered approximately forty professors from all faculties; the majority were from the Faculty of Economics and Social Sciences and the Faculty of Philosophy, and roughly a quarter were active members. After the war began, the working group assumed tasks "essential to the war effort." The Cologne professors contributed expertise legitimizing the Nazi regime's expansion to the west, justifying the annexation of the Netherlands and Belgium, Luxembourg and parts of northern France.[62] Prominent National Socialists were also active in this field. The Institute for Spatial Policy, founded in 1934 by Martin Spahn, and the German-Dutch Institute led by historian Franz Petri both played an important role in the field of "*Westforschung*." Petri later became a full professor and advocated the "re-Germanization" of the west. As a military administration officer, he was involved in the occupation of Belgium and northern France. The archaeologist Walter Stokar von Neuforn contributed to the founding of the Germanic Research Institute in the occupied Netherlands.[63]

In the medical field, "racial hygiene" and "eugenics" offered numerous opportunities for academics to serve National Socialism. After 1933, Cologne became a center of Nazi racist policies in the Rhineland. In 1940, the Faculty of Medicine founded an Institute for Hereditary Biology and Racial Hygiene and appointed Ferdinand Claußen, a student of Germany's leading "racial hygienist" Otmar von Verschuer, as its director. Claußen believed the "life form" of the "Jewish people" was that of a "rootless parasite," which he argued should be fought like an "infectious disease."[64] Gynecologist Hans Christian Naujoks, who went to Cologne in 1934, was also a proponent of "racial hygiene." The National Socialist and member of the SA was one of the propagandists and executors of forced sterilization for "eugenic" reasons. Doctors performed at least 1,600 such procedures at the Women's Clinic headed by Naujoks, as well as at the Weyertal Protestant Hospital and the Surgical University Clinic. Doctors in Cologne were also involved in the "euthanasia" murders during the war, because their medical reports decided whether people with mental or physical disabilities were sent to institutions to be killed. One of the masterminds and organizers of this program was Max de Crinis, who headed the University Psychiatric Clinic from 1934 to 1938.[65]

The Academy for German Law, founded in May 1933, prepared a National Socialist law reform. The Cologne jurist Heinrich Lehmann was an active member of this academy, and in the fall of 1933, he published a

new edition of his textbook *Allgemeiner Teil des Bürgerlichen Gesetzbuches* (General part of the Civil Law Code) in order to contribute to what he considered a "revolutionary" political shift. Together with his colleague Hans Carl Nipperdey, he was involved in drafting the Volksgesetzbuch which was intended to replace the Civil Law Code. Cologne economists also worked for the academy. Erwin von Beckerath led the Central Committee for Political Economy within the economics group. Günter Schmölders, who became a professor in Cologne in 1940 and had joined the NSDAP in 1933, was head of the Committee for Pricing Policies. After the economics group was disbanded in 1943, both worked on plans for a new ordoliberal post-war economic order.[66]

During the war, several institutes in Cologne were considered "essential to the war effort," including the Institute for Applied Physics, whose director, Johannes Malsch, was a member of the Nazi Party and was associated with the "German physics" movement. Malsch was an expert in high-frequency technology and conducted research on behalf of the German Luftwaffe. Since the beginning of the war, the Institute of Physics had worked for the Army Ordnance Agency on problems of how to generate energy by nuclear fission. The director of the institute, Fritz Kirchner, joined the NSDAP in 1940. The humanities also became involved in the "war effort" from 1940 on as part of "Aktion Ritterbusch." This "joint effort" was a huge project that mobilized scholars from a range of disciplines, including Cologne professors such as philosopher Heinz Heimsoeth, who had been a member of the NSDAP since 1933. The international law expert Hermann Jahrreiß headed the Group for International Law and helped develop an expansionary theory of greater space. Like some of his colleagues, he was involved in the University Working Group for Spatial Research, where the threads of the network of Cologne professors working for the Nazi regime came together.[67]

↑ Map room of the Faculty of Economics and Social Sciences in 1935; Cologne's spatial research served Nazi *Lebensraum* ideology.

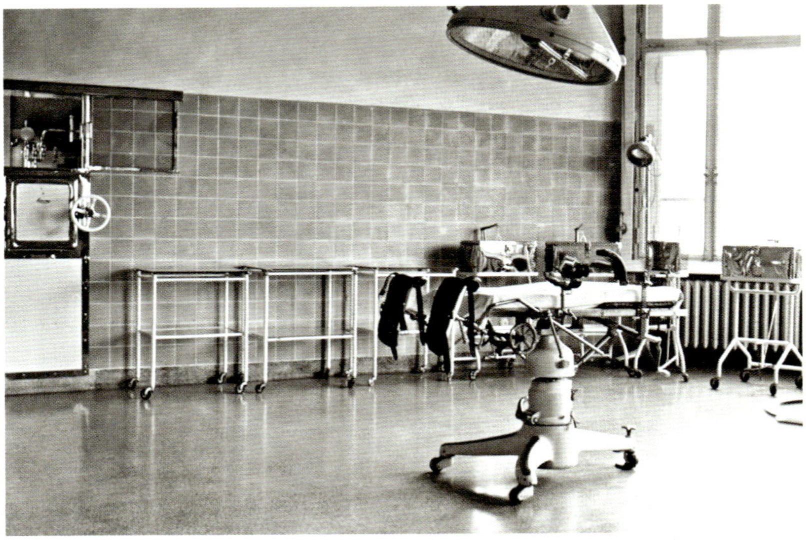

Operating Table at the University Women's Clinic

1938

University Archive Frankfurt am Main

On 14 July 1933, the National Socialists enacted their first racial law, the "Law for the Prevention of Offspring with Hereditary Diseases." It went into effect on 1 January 1934 and formed the basis for the forced sterilization of some 400,000 people. Cologne was the center of Nazi racial policy in the Rhineland. The Nazi party, the city and the courts were not alone in implementing these policies in Cologne. Many university institutes and clinics, including the Institute for Hereditary Biology and Racial Hygiene, the Lindenburg Psychiatric and Neurological Clinic, the Center for Historical Research on the Racial Corpus, the Surgical University Clinic and the University Women's Clinic, also participated. The latter two were authorized to carry out forced sterilizations and abortions for "eugenic" reasons, as was the Weyertal Protestant Hospital.[68]

Of the roughly 4,070 people from the Cologne city district who underwent forced sterilization, about one-third were subjected to the procedure at the University Women's Clinic. One of them was the twenty-one-year old Berta R., whose case was brought before the Hereditary Health Court of Cologne. Following an "intelligence test," the court determined that she suffered from "congenital feeble-mindedness." Neither a school report submitted later nor her husband's protests succeeded in changing the verdict. In April 1937, Berta R. was taken by the police to the Cologne University Women's Clinic and forcibly sterilized.[69]

Ex Libris from the Richter Library

1942

Cologne University and City Library

"I am, as you know, one of those without rights," wrote Elise Richter on 24 August 1941 from Vienna to Hermann Corsten, the director of the University and City Library of Cologne. Elise Richter, a distinguished Romance language scholar and linguist, and her sister Helene Richter, an Anglicist and theater studies scholar, owned an impressive library that comprised some 8,000 books. Following the "annexation" of Austria by the "Third Reich" in March 1938, the two women were forced to sell their library because of the Nazis' racist policies of exclusion. After months of "sales negotiations," a sum of 4,000 marks for 2,700 volumes was agreed upon. But even this "ridiculously low price," as Corsten himself described the amount to his superiors, was never received by the sisters. Elise and Helene Richter were deported on the same day that the boxes full of books were picked up to be sent to Cologne. Both died in Theresienstadt.[70]

From 2005 to 2009, the University and City Library of Cologne reconstructed the Richter Library and attempted to identify the books that had originally belonged to the Richter sisters. This ex libris, designed by Austrian commercial artist Alfred Cossmann, was part of the evidence that allowed researchers to clearly determine the provenance of the books.[71]

The New University Building

On 29 July 1929, Cologne city council approved the construction of the new university building on the Inner Greenbelt between Bachemer Straße and Zülpicher Straße. Ground was broken on 26 October 1929, and the shell of the building was completed a year and a half later in the spring of 1931. Work was halted at the end of the year for lack of funds due to the Great Depression. Construction resumed when the Nazis approved a Reich loan on 23 June 1933. On 2 November 1934, university operations in the new building began. The official opening ceremony was held on 5 April 1935.

The plans for the new university building were drawn up by the director of Cologne's Office of City Planning, Adolf Abel. He designed a functional structure with geometric lines in the New Objectivity style. The building complex comprised three structural groupings: an administrative wing, twenty-two lecture halls and about forty seminar rooms. An elongated front building housed the rooms for the academic self-government bodies, including the Senate's meeting room, the rector's and deans' offices, the building management office and the secretariat, as well as the university library and some departments. The auditorium was an extension that jutted back from the center of the building and could be divided with a movable partition wall into two separate spaces. Carl Niessen, a professor of theater studies in Cologne, had ensured that it was equipped with a fully furnished stage. Parallel to the auditorium were two octagonal lecture hall wings with courtyards in between. At the rear of the building, there were six connected pavilions that housed the departments.

The move from Cologne's Südstadt to Lindenthal brought the university closer to the Faculty of Medicine's facilities at the Augusta Hospital and the Lindenburg Clinic. A university quarter began to take shape and more and more buildings were added over the decades as the university expanded.[72]

↗ During the Nazi period, an eagle and swastika hung over the main entrance of the university.

→ A refreshment room with a view of the Greenbelt was located on the ground floor at the rear of the main building.

↑ View of the rear of the new university building with the six connected pavilions that housed the departments. The newly constructed main building had a facade of tufa stone from Ettringen in the Eifel region; the window surrounds were made of basalt volcanic rock.

A Professorial University

Chapter 4

1945–1960

1945–1960

1945

Reopening

On 10 December, seven months after the end of World War II, the University of Cologne celebrates its reopening in the main building, which had undergone makeshift reconstruction work.

1947

Central University Library Catalog of North Rhine-Westphalia

A central library catalog is created at the University and City Library of Cologne. It is used to manage the newly established book lending system between the academic libraries of North Rhine-Westphalia (NRW).

1950

First Nobel Prize

Chemist Kurt Alder is the first University of Cologne professor to receive a Nobel Prize. He and his mentor Otto Diels are awarded the prize for their discovery of the Diels–Alder reaction, one of the most important reactions for forming carbon ring compounds.

1953

France in Cologne

The Institut Français, built by the university with the help of a grant from France, opens on Am Sachsenring. The designer of the modern building is the well-known Cologne architect Wilhelm Riphahn.

State University

1954

The University of Cologne is retroactively incorporated into the state of North Rhine-Westphalia's budget as of 1 April 1953, ending the university's status as a city institution. Cologne becomes a state university.

1955

A Fifth Faculty

On 1 April, the Faculty of Philosophy is divided into the Faculty of Philosophy and the Faculty of Mathematics and Natural Sciences. Cologne is one of the last German universities to abandon the traditional understanding of the humanities and natural sciences as a single branch of learning.

Master Plan

1959

The city approves the "general plan" for new construction submitted by Chancellor Wolfgang Wagner. The rapid increase in student enrollment made this large-scale expansion project necessary.

1960

WiSo High-Rise

The new building of the Faculty of Economics and Social Sciences (WiSo for short) is officially inaugurated. The ensemble designed by Wilhelm Riphahn comprises two-story buildings for auditoriums and seminar rooms and a high-rise for offices and libraries.

Despite the immense destruction wrought by the war, Cologne managed to reopen its university surprisingly quickly in late 1945. The reopening was marked by a desire to restore the classical professorial university and Christian neo-humanism. But the attempt to reconstitute the University of Cologne as an elitist ivory tower soon failed; the twin pressures of rapid student body growth and the differentiation of research and teaching forced the university to go with the times. As it expanded, the university also became too costly for the city of Cologne, so control and funding responsibility passed to the state government of North Rhine-Westphalia in 1954. A year later, an independent Faculty of Mathematics and Natural Sciences was established. With the Riphahn building, completed in 1960, the Faculty of Economics and Social Sciences acquired its own complex.

Rising from the Ruins

By the end of the war, thirty-seven of Cologne University's ninety buildings had been entirely destroyed. A further thirty-three were heavily damaged, while twenty had suffered slight damage. The medical and scientific facilities were hardest hit. By contrast, the main university building suffered relatively little damage, with an estimated twenty-eight percent destruction rate. Many of the science laboratories and much of their equipment were no longer usable. Most of the libraries had moved their collections to safe sites, and they now needed to be retrieved. In the first few weeks after the end of the war, the most urgent concern was to inspect and secure the university's facilities.[1]

In early May 1945, the US military government, hoping to quickly reopen the university, appointed classical philologist Josef Kroll as managing rector, who had been recommended by the reinstated mayor, Konrad Adenauer. Kroll began by convening a small committee of professors. All members of the founding committee had at least not been members of the Nazi Party and were thus not considered politically compromised. The committee included the legal scholars Hans Carl Nipperdey and Ernst von Hippel, the sociologist Leopold von Wiese, the business economists Eugen Schmalenbach and Rudolf Seyffert, and Otto Veit, a specialist in anatomy who had been forced into retirement by the Nazis. Over the following weeks this circle expanded to include nine more professors.[2]

A quarter of Kroll's group consisted of professors who had already taught at the Commercial College or the Medical Academy. The decisive cohort, however, were those professors who had been appointed to their chairs before 1925. These accounted for more than half of the new provisional university leadership. With the exception of three professors who had only come to Cologne during the war, all members of this group had known each other for more than twenty years and were among the leading figures at the university during the Weimar era. With a single exception, all of them had previously served as deans, and Kroll had been rector twice before. The founding committee filled the faculty committees during the reopening phase and also constituted the first elected university leadership. It was therefore instrumental in shaping the development of the University of Cologne during the early post-war years.[3]

Reconstruction as Restoration

On 21 June 1945, the British replaced the Americans as the occupying power in Cologne, leaving the existing structures for university self-government in place. These included the provisional university leadership. In late October, the British sanctioned the reopening of Cologne University. The first courses began a month later, and an official opening ceremony was held on 10 December 1945. In his speech at this event, the newly elected rector Josef Kroll invoked the nineteenth-century ideal of a neo-humanist university based on the intellectual tradition of the *Abendland* (Occident) as the model for the new university which had now adopted the name of Universität zu Köln.[4]

Like most university rectors of the post-war era, Kroll drew on the myth of the Humboldtian university in order to restore the University of Cologne as an institution in the hands of the full professors. By 1949, the number of full professorships at the university had returned to the level of the last semester of the Weimar period. However, the number of associate

← The University and City Library, which was housed in the main building, required extensive repairs after 1945.

professorships in 1949 was twenty-five percent lower than in the winter semester of 1932/1933, while the number of lectureships and untenured professorships had fallen by half. The shortage of positions other than full professorships hampered the entry of women into academic roles, and the University of Cologne began the 1945/1946 winter semester with just a single female instructor. By 1947, there were four women on the academic staff, one of whom was an associate professor. The following year, the university employed seven women: five instructors, an associate professor and a lecturer. Together they accounted for five percent of the entire teaching faculty. Barely twenty percent of the students were women in 1949, a lower proportion than at the end of the Weimar Republic.[5]

When the patriarchal professorial university was restored, so too was the paternalistic approach to students. The professors tended to look upon the student body with a mixture of optimism and apprehension, believing that the future elite of the nation had been "seduced" and "misguided" by National Socialism and was therefore potentially dangerous. This was one of the reasons why the University Senate resisted the election of a student council (AStA) until pressure from the British forced them to concede. The British also pushed for the publication of the *Kölner Universitäts-Zeitung* from May 1946 in order to promote democratic practices among the student body. Kroll viewed this newspaper as an instrument to promote his vision of *civitas academica*, an academic culture that he presented as "democratic" but that in fact maintained hierarchical and corporative structures. He shut the newspaper down in 1948 after the students began to assert greater editorial freedom.[6]

Most of the professors supported Kroll's conservative stance. A small group led by law professors Hans Carl Nipperdey and Gotthold Bohne pushed for a more liberal course, especially in relation to the students. Their attempts to replace Kroll with one of their own finally bore fruit in 1949 with the election of Bohne as rector. By then, Kroll's increasingly authoritarian regime had also brought him into conflict with the liberal-minded British university officer Harry Beckhoff, who later described him and the majority of the Cologne professors as obstinate reactionaries. Cologne's Social Democratic Party (SPD) also accused Kroll, who relied on the support of the Christian Democratic Party's (CDU) majority in the city council, of protecting ex-Nazis while doing nothing to support the return of former faculty members who had fled the Nazi regime. Only in March 1946 were these professors invited to return to their posts. The letters of invitation sent by the deans varied in tone from solicitous to business-like, depending on the faculty, though in most cases they tended to advise against returning, pointing out the difficult living conditions in post-war Cologne. The overall response was surprisingly friendly, but of those who had fled the country, only the mathematician Hans Hamburger actually reassumed his chair. Most of the expelled academics who accepted the offer to return had remained in Germany after 1933. By 1950, thirteen academics who had been persecuted had again become faculty members. There was no active and open debate about the legacy of the Nazi era in the two decades following the reopening of the University of Cologne. The few critical remarks tended to come from émigrés such as Richard Alewyn or René König, but these were swallowed up by the general collective silence.[7]

The Beginning of Expansion

The elitist ethos of the University of Cologne was quickly undermined by increasing student numbers. In the winter semester of 1951/1952, the student body had reached nearly 6,400, exceeding its previous peak of 6,000 in 1931. By the summer of 1957, the university counted more than 10,000 students for the first time, and by 1960 the figure had risen to just under 14,000. The largest faculty was the Faculty of Economics and Social Sciences with around 5,500 students, followed by the Faculty of Philosophy with just under 3,200. The Faculty of Law came in third with approximately 1,900 students. Medicine had 1,650 students, while Mathematics and Natural Sciences, which had become an independent faculty in 1955, had nearly 1,600 students. The proportion of female students fell slightly after 1949 to 19.5 percent by 1960. Most of the women, about 1,100, were in the Faculty of Philosophy, where they made up about a

↗ The professorial university of the 1950s was a male domain; ceremony commemorating the university's founding, 1954.

→ Suit and tie were obligatory for students, even at the Campi Bar in 1955; only one-fifth of the students were women.

third of all students. The lowest number of female students was in the Faculty of Law, with just under 190, accounting for a share of less than ten percent. In the Faculty of Economics and Social Sciences and the Faculty of Mathematics and Natural Sciences, fourteen percent of the students were female. Among the medical students, their share was twenty-five percent. It was not until the 1960s that there was a fundamental change in the numbers of female students.[8]

The number of full professors grew rapidly, from thirty-nine in the winter of 1945/1946 to 127 in the summer of 1960. During the same period, the number of associate professorships rose from seven to sixteen. In contrast, the number of lectureships and untenured professorships grew steadily from six to 154. The number of instructors rose from twelve to ninety-three. In addition to the full professors, the non-professorial academic staff saw the greatest expansion in the first phase of growth. In 1958, they founded the Association of Non-Habilitated Assistant Professors, the first such organization established to represent the interests of this group of university employees. Thanks to the overall increase in teaching staff, the ratio of instructors to students declined only slightly in this period, from 1:26 in 1949 to 1:32 in 1960. However, the situation varied from faculty to faculty. In 1960, there was one member of teaching staff for every ninety students in the Faculty of Economics and Social Sciences, whereas in medicine the ratio was one to sixteen.

For women, the University of Cologne remained a dismal place to build a career during the 1950s. Not a single female professor held a chair in Cologne and there was never more than one female associate professor. By 1960, seven women held lectureships or untenured professorships in the Faculty of Philosophy, the Faculty of Mathematics and Natural Sciences and the Faculty of Medicine. The Faculty of Economics and Social Sciences employed just two women as instructors. In the Faculty of Law, only men held teaching positions. In 1960, a total of 22 female academics worked in teaching and/or research at the University of Cologne. This was a share of five percent.[9]

Major Changes

Rapid growth led to a major expansion of university facilities. By the middle of the 1950s several specialist clinics independent of the old Lindenburg Clinic complex had been established. These included the first neurosurgical clinic in Germany. The construction of the clinics represented a major achievement for the city of Cologne. The state government did inject some money, but between 1948 and 1953 much less funding flowed into the city's university than to the other universities maintained by the state. While Cologne received about twenty-one million marks, more than sixty million went to the neighboring University of Bonn. After several years of negotiation, the state assumed full financial responsibility for the University of Cologne in 1954. A year later, the mathematical and natural science disciplines were separated from the Faculty of Philosophy. With the founding of a fifth faculty in 1955, Cologne became one of the last universities in the German-speaking countries to abandon the traditional model of humanities merged with natural sciences.[10]

This process of differentiation and rising student numbers forced a physical expansion of the university, which was finally possible thanks to an increase in state funds. The Faculty of Economics and Social Sciences, whose student body quadrupled to 4,800 between 1949 and 1954, was the first to receive its own building. This was designed by Cologne architect Wilhelm Riphahn. The building complex, completed in two phases between 1954 and 1960, was connected to the old university building at its northern end. It was clearly divided into two functional areas: an eight-story central block, which housed the offices and libraries, and a lower section containing lecture halls and seminar rooms, which was connected by a corridor to the WiSo high-rise and the main university building. Following the completion of the first phase of construction in 1958, it had already become clear that the new space would not suffice. The university responded to the challenge in 1959 with a new "master plan" that provided for the creation of a unified university quarter modeled on an American campus. The modernity of this design would fundamentally alter the face of the University of Cologne for the following two decades.[11]

← A sculpture entitled *Hercules the Archer Killing the Stymphalian Birds* by Émile-Antoine Bourdelle was erected in front of the new Economics and Social Sciences complex designed by Cologne architect Wilhelm Riphahn.

Reopening with Difficulties

On 6 March 1945, US troops occupied the districts of Cologne on the west bank of the Rhine. Just a few days later, American officers surveyed the state of the university. The Americans found that three-quarters of the facilities had been destroyed or badly damaged. In April 1945, the provisional city administration appointed by the US military government entrusted the legal scholar Hans Carl Nipperdey with securing the university buildings. In early May, the economist Rudolf Seyffert, bacteriologist Reiner Müller, historian Peter Rassow and Nipperdey were appointed provisional deans of their faculties under the leadership of the provisional rector Josef Kroll. Nipperdey, who served as prorector at Kroll's request, dealt with all financial and legal issues. At this time, Nipperdey and Kroll, who would later become staunch rivals, were still cooperating.[12]

Numerous students participated in the reconstruction and restoration of the buildings in exchange for food and meager wages, but also in the hope of securing a place at the university. When the British took over the military government from the Americans on 21 June, they too supported a rapid resumption of teaching, since the universities were central to the British plan for national re-education, and specifically for the formation of the future German elite. The British suggested that the university adopt a new constitution as a basis for rapid reconstruction. Nipperdey, as the prorector responsible for introducing the new statutes, convened a drafting committee, which on 26 July reinstated the constitution of 1919 in slightly amended form. Another important step was the appointment of a personnel commission under Kroll's leadership in early August, which developed guidelines for the dismissal of those compromised as supporters of the Nazi regime. In late August, Nipperdey asked the faculties to form tripartite commissions to review their academic staff. This was intended to ensure that classes could quickly resume once staff had been vetted. The British had not yet specified how the denazification process should be conducted.[13]

In the third week of August, Major James Mark was commissioned by the Foreign Office to assess the situation at the University of Cologne. He asked the rectorate to conduct a comprehensive review and presented a catalogue of questions to be answered. At that time, the British military government still assumed that only the universities in Göttingen and Hamburg would be ready to open for the winter semester. The main building at Cologne was still unfit for use, even though the city theaters and orchestra had been performing in the auditorium since mid-August. At several administrative conferences in August, Adenauer addressed the fact that construction was not proceeding as quickly as expected. His greatest concern was that other universities in the British occupation zone would soon open, rendering Cologne superfluous and therefore threatening its existence.[14]

In addition to restoring the main building and other facilities, the university staff also worked on the required survey, the results of which fed into a *Memorandum for the Reopening of Cologne University*. This document formed the basis for the "request for permission to reopen the university," which had to be submitted to the military government by the end of September. The six universities located in the British zone were managed by the University Section of the Education Branch, which appointed a civil servant as an education control officer at each university. In Cologne this was Dr. Harry Beckhoff, who had studied in Heidelberg and visited Cologne before going into exile. Beckhoff advocated for the speedy reopening of the university, arguing that this would boost the morale of the population.[15]

The university did its bit and presented the enrollment regulations to the British on 15 October. Capacity was limited, as the military government had approved only 1,500 student places due to the poor housing situation in the heavily bomb-damaged city. On 24 October, Cologne finally had cause to celebrate as the British military government approved the reopening of the city's university. On 5 November, the University Senate met and elected Kroll as its regular rector. The faculties also confirmed the provisional deans. The pharmacologist Joseph Schüller had taken over as head of the Faculty of Medicine in the meantime, presumably due to Müller's prior involvement with the Hereditary Health Court in Cologne, which had implemented the Nazis' forced sterilization policy.[16]

From mid-November, the restoration of the main building also proceeded apace. Finally, sufficient glass and cement were available to properly weatherproof the building. Heating, however, remained a problem. The old system did not work, and there were not enough stoves and fuel. The result was a further delay, so that when the University of Cologne was finally reopened on 10 December 1945, it was the last university in the British zone to do so. Rector Josef Kroll professed in his speech at the opening ceremony just before the first students returned: "In our minds, we want to inscribe before the gates of this university that has been brought back to life the following word, to which we commit ourselves as this new period of academic study begins: Humanitati."[17]

↓ 10 December 1945. The ceremonial reopening of the university was attended by (from left to right) the governor of the state of North Rhine-Westphalia Brigadier John Barraclough, Rector Josef Kroll, Auxiliary Bishop Wilhelm Stockums, Mayor Hermann Pünder and Prorector Otto Veit.

Richard Alewyn 1902–1979

Professor in the Faculty of Philosophy

Germanist Richard Alewyn attracted attention early on with his work on German Baroque literature. In 1932, he succeeded Friedrich Gundolf as a professor in Heidelberg. He was headed for a brilliant career when the Nazis expelled him in August 1933 because of his Jewish grandmother. Alewyn and his family emigrated to the USA via France, Austria and Switzerland. He taught at Queens College in New York from 1939, becoming an American citizen in 1944.

Alewyn was one of the few émigrés to return to Germany. Arriving in 1948, he became a professor of German philology in Cologne in 1949. He not only revived the German Department but was also active in the public sphere through lectures, articles and radio programs. Alewyn laid the foundations for a modern social and cultural history of German literature, reinterpreted Hugo von Hofmannsthal's writings and initiated German research on the literature of sensibility. In 1955, a year after becoming a citizen of the Federal Republic of Germany, Alewyn left Cologne for the Free University of Berlin. He then moved to the University of Bonn in 1959, where he remained until retiring in 1967.[18]

Gerhart Baum born 1932

Student in the Faculty of Law

As a politician, lawyer and politically active citizen, Gerhart Baum has had a formative influence on the law and the understanding of legal concepts in Germany. Born in Dresden, he moved to Cologne in the early 1950s. He completed his Abitur in 1954 and studied law at Cologne University until 1957. He joined the Liberal Students' Association during his first semester. Baum's political commitment became his vocation and a defining part of his career.

After passing his second state examination in law in 1961, Baum held a management position at the Confederation of German Employers' Associations in Cologne. In 1966, he joined the executive committee of the Free Democratic Party (FDP) as chairman of the Young Democrats organization. He belonged to the left wing of the party. From 1969 to 1973, Baum was chairman of the FDP parliamentary group in Cologne's city council. In 1972, he became parliamentary state secretary of the Federal Ministry of the Interior and was elected to the Bundestag, remaining a member of parliament until 1994.

At the height of his political career, he headed the Federal Ministry of the Interior, but stepped down when the social-liberal coalition collapsed in 1982. Baum led the German delegation to the UN Commission on Human Rights from 1992 to 1998. As a lawyer, he has also successfully pursued cases before Germany's highest constitutional court in the interest of protecting civil rights.[19]

Gotthold Bohne
1890–1957

Professor in the Faculty of Law

Cornelia Harte
1914–1998

Professor in the Faculty of Mathematics and Natural Sciences

Criminal law expert Gotthold Bohne was a man of many interests. He first studied theology and philosophy, then medicine and law. After fighting in World War I, he received his doctorate in law from the University of Leipzig in 1920 and completed his habilitation on the history of criminal justice at the same institution a year later. Bohne taught criminal law and civil and criminal procedural law at Cologne from 1923 to 1957. He was one of the first two directors of the Institute of Criminology, founded in 1923, which he headed until his retirement in 1957. He also served as dean of the faculty, first in 1926/1927 and again in 1934/1935.

Bohne took an interdisciplinary approach in his work on criminal law and criminology, combining legal, sociological, psychological, medical and scientific aspects. He studied psychoanalysis (still a young field at the time), explored the influence of society on individual behavior and developed methods from the natural sciences for the preservation of evidence. Despite his work on "hereditary hygiene" and the fact that he had defended forced sterilization to "preserve the racial and eugenic purity of the German people" in an article published in 1935, he was not considered after 1945 to have been an active supporter of the Nazi regime. Bohne was on the two commissions for constitutional and personnel matters established in the summer of 1945. He was rector of the university from 1949 to 1951 and was instrumental in reopening the university.[20]

Cornelia Harte was the first female full professor at the University of Cologne. A biologist, Harte had studied botany, zoology and chemistry during a period in which the Nazis had restricted and impeded women's opportunities to study. She received her doctorate at Freiburg in 1941, earned her habilitation at the same university in 1948 and was offered an associate professorship in developmental physiology at Cologne in 1951. She was thus one of a small group of women who pursued careers at German universities at the time. In 1961, Harte was made a full professor. A specialist in the cytogenetics of higher plants, she conducted research and taught at the University of Cologne until she retired in 1982.

Cornelia Harte was one of the founders of the Society for Developmental Biology in 1975, and she endowed the Cornelia Harte Award for outstanding research in developmental biology. In addition to her scientific research, she was committed to promoting female scientists. She was deputy chair of the German Association of Women Academics and one of the founding members of the working group of female university lecturers. She provided the University of Cologne with considerable financial support to promote women in the sciences. In 2001, Cologne's equal opportunities officer named the university's mentoring program for female students and doctoral and post-doctoral candidates after Cornelia Harte.[21]

In the Spirit of the *Abendland*

The reopening of the university raised the question of the self-conception of an institution that had spent almost half of its existence serving a dictatorship. The Constitutional Commission convened by the provisional prorector Hans Carl Nipperdey on 26 July 1945 provided an initial response to this question. It adopted the 1919 statutes but amended the first paragraph, according to which the purpose of the university was now to "teach and propagate scholarship." In doing so, it was to be "guided by the true and highest ideals of humanity, directed solely toward the goals of knowledge and education." In contrast to the 1919 version, practice-oriented professional training was treated as a mere adjunct to the actual purpose of building character through scholarship. What was missing from the text was the commitment to democracy called for and promoted by the occupying powers. Instead, the statutes proclaimed the normative foundational principles of the university to be not the values of democracy, but rather purportedly "timeless values" and "universal human ideals." This was to be an institution that stood above party-political opinion. This Humboldtian "idea of a university" was typical of post-war German academia. The majority of the Cologne professors rejected calls by the British to adapt the statutes to the new era.[22]

Only a minority of academics pushed for a liberal-democratic orientation. Their spokesman was the jurist Hans Carl Nipperdey, who interpreted the humanism of the university statutes in terms of a modern rule of law and universal human rights, and advocated for greater student participation. The group of professors around Nipperdey, one of the few social-democratic professors in Cologne, favored a stronger practical orientation, greater engagement with social issues, and opening up the university to broader sections of the population. Most of the professors, however, supported Kroll's attempt to return to the *status quo ante*. His desire to restore the university to a nineteenth-century ethos was not only about dissociation from the "Ungeist," the cultural nihilism, but above all from the university policy of the Weimar era, which had been criticized even prior to 1933. Kroll first publicly expounded his Catholic-conservative idea of a university in the tradition of the *Abendland* in his address at the reopening ceremony on 10 December 1945. This became part of the official image of what was henceforth known as Universität zu Köln—the University of Cologne. It was Kroll, the classical philologist, who pushed through this formulation (the "*zu*" is not modern German usage), insisting it was the only correct translation of the Latin *Universitas Coloniensis*. He also maintained that the university was founded in 1388.[23]

Kroll saw the university as a bulwark of Greco-Christian culture, which he believed was in crisis even before the Nazis came to power. He lamented the "masses" that accompanied the increasing democratization of higher education, and advocated a return to its elitist roots. Kroll saw the primary purpose of the university not in training people for professions, but rather in building character. He rejected both the increasing specialization of academic research and a regimented approach to teaching. These trends endangered the integrity, spirit and standards of higher education. He contrasted the intellectually creative "academic" with the mere "hordes," and wanted to see his old university reborn to represent a timeless, universalist and non-partisan humanism. There was no need to draw lessons from Nazism since, in his eyes, the university had been a victim of an "Ungeist" and the "Antichrist" (Hitler). As Kroll saw it, individuals had behaved wrongly, but the institution had remained intact at its core. Kroll was convinced that the university did not need to profess its commitment to democracy, since the *civitas academica* was "democratic" by nature, as a free and equal community of teachers and students—though founded on a hierarchical order. Cultural understanding between nations as a characteristic of the

university was taken to be self-evident, based as it was on the principle of humanism.[24]

Kroll's idea of an *abendländische* university, founded on the pathos of a concept of scholarship and education inflated to become a quasi-religious idea, matched the general restorationist sentiment of the post-war era. One of the few liberal counter-proposals came from the Cologne Germanist Richard Alewyn in his essay on the spirit of the university, which appeared in 1951 in the first guide to the University of Cologne. Alewyn roundly rejected the amalgam of a notion of an *Abendland* culture and the Humboldtian myth. He declared both the medieval university and its nineteenth-century successor dead: "The dome of faith has been broken and the figure of the humanist being has been toppled." Specialization, he claimed, was merely a consequence of progress in scholarship. While Alewyn also referred to a unifying "spirit" that permeated all aspects of the university, this was not a religious or idealistic construct for him, but rather a practical process of (self-)criticism and discussion. It was from this spirit that knowledge was created, then refined through academic exchange. Alewyn saw the university as a communicative space where social issues could be debated, not as a cloistered ivory tower. But Alewyn's views were not representative. More typical was the vision presented by the theologian and philosopher Josef Koch in the 1953 university guide. He invoked the danger of the "massification" of the university, through which it risked "degenerating into a factory." He stressed that the university was "one of the greatest creations of the spirit of the Abendland" and was now called upon to preserve that spirit amidst the "cultural crisis of the present day." Mere professional training did not do justice to this ideal. For Koch, the "honorific title of civis academicus" was reserved for the "cultivated person," not for the "philistine." This high-flown rhetoric was in keeping with the elitist spirit.[25]

↑ Gerhard Marcks' sculpture of Albertus Magnus was erected in front of the university in 1956. The medieval polymath Magnus was regarded by many as the progenitor of the *Abendland* university tradition.

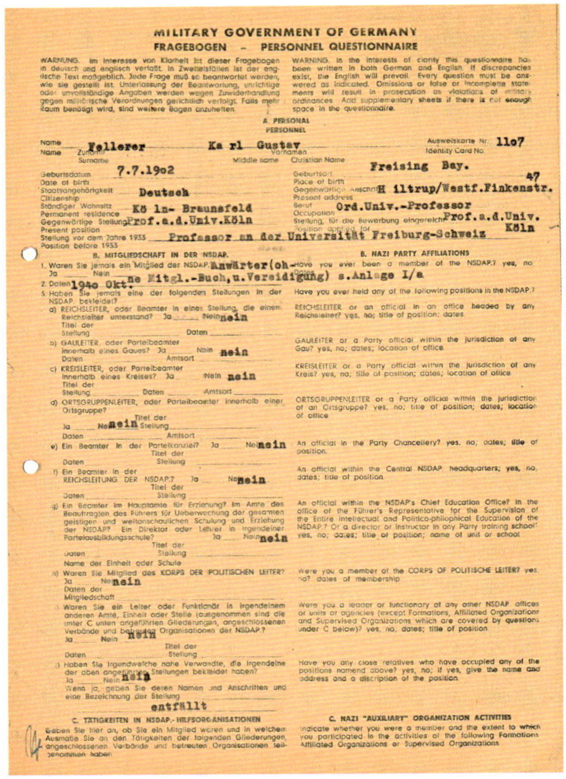

MILITARY GOVERNMENT OF GERMANY
FRAGEBOGEN – PERSONNEL QUESTIONNAIRE

WARNUNG. Im Interesse von Klarheit ist dieser Fragebogen in deutsch und englisch verfaßt. In Zweifelsfällen ist der englische Text maßgeblich. Jede Frage muß so beantwortet werden, wie sie gestellt ist. Unterlassung der Beantwortung, unrichtige oder unvollständige Angaben werden wegen Zuwiderhandlung gegen militärische Verordnungen gerichtlich verfolgt. Falls mehr Raum benötigt wird, sind weitere Bogen anzuheften.

WARNING. In the interests of clarity this questionnaire has been written in both German and English. If discrepancies exist, the English will prevail. Every question must be answered as indicated. Omissions or false or incomplete statements will result in prosecution as violations of military ordinances. Add supplementary sheets if there is not enough space in the questionnaire.

A. PERSONAL / PERSONNEL

Name / Name: Zuname / Surname: Fellerer — Vornamen / Middle name, Christian Name: Karl Gustav — Ausweiskarte Nr. / Identity Card No.: 1107
Geburtsdatum / Date of birth: 7.7.1902 — Geburtsort / Place of birth: Freising Bay.
Staatsangehörigkeit / Citizenship: Deutsch — Gegenwärtige Anschrift / Present address: Hiltrup/Westf. Finkenstr. 47
Ständiger Wohnsitz / Permanent residence: Köln-Braunsfeld — Beruf / Occupation: Ord. Univ.-Professor
Gegenwärtige Stellung / Present position: Prof. a. d. Univ. Köln — Stellung, für die Bewerbung eingereicht / Position applied for: Prof. a. d. Univ. Köln
Stellung vor dem Jahre 1933 / Position before 1933: Professor an der Universität Freiburg-Schweiz

B. MITGLIEDSCHAFT IN DER NSDAP. / B. NAZI PARTY AFFILIATIONS

1. Waren Sie jemals ein Mitglied der NSDAP.? Ja — Nein — / Have you ever been a member of the NSDAP.? yes, no: Anwärter (ohne Mitgl.-Buch, u. Vereidigung) s. Anlage I/a
2. Daten / Dates: 1940 Okt.
3. Haben Sie jemals eine der folgenden Stellungen in der NSDAP. bekleidet? / Have you ever held any of the following positions in the NSDAP.?
   a) REICHSLEITER, oder Beamter in einer Stellung, die einem Reichsleiter unterstand? Ja — Nein: nein. Titel der Stellung — Daten — / REICHSLEITER or an official in an office headed by any Reichsleiter? yes, no; title of position; dates
   b) GAULEITER, oder Parteibeamter innerhalb eines Gaues? Ja — Nein: nein. Daten — Amtsort — / GAULEITER or a Party official within the jurisdiction of any Gau? yes, no; dates; location of office
   c) KREISLEITER, oder Parteibeamter innerhalb eines Kreises? Ja — Nein: nein. Titel der Stellung — Daten — Amtsort — / KREISLEITER or a Party official within the jurisdiction of any Kreis? yes, no; title of position; dates; location of office
   d) ORTSGRUPPENLEITER, oder Parteibeamter innerhalb einer Ortsgruppe? Ja — Nein: nein. Titel der Stellung — Daten — Amtsort — / ORTSGRUPPENLEITER or a Party official within the jurisdiction of an Ortsgruppe? yes, no; title of position; dates; location of office
   e) Ein Beamter in der Parteikanzlei? Ja — Nein: nein. Daten — Titel der Stellung — / An official in the Party Chancellery? yes, no; dates; title of position.
   f) Ein Beamter in der REICHSLEITUNG DER NSDAP.? Ja — Nein: nein. Daten — Titel der Stellung — / An official within the Central NSDAP headquarters; yes, no, dates; title of position.
   g) Ein Beamter im Hauptamte für Erziehung? Im Amte des Beauftragten des Führers für Ueberwachung der gesamten geistigen und weltanschaulichen Schulung und Erziehung der NSDAP? Ein Direktor oder Lehrer in irgendeiner Parteiausbildungsschule? Ja — Nein: nein. Daten — Titel der Stellung — Name der Einheit oder Schule / An official within the NSDAP's Chief Education Office? In the office of the Führer's Representative for the Supervision of the Entire Intellectual and Politico-philophical Education of the NSDAP.? Or a director or instructor in any Party training school? yes, no; dates; title of position; name of unit or school
   h) Waren Sie Mitglied des KORPS DER POLITISCHEN LEITER? Ja — Nein: nein. Daten der Mitgliedschaft — / Were you a member of the CORPS OF POLITISCHE LEITER? yes, no? dates of membership
   i) Waren Sie ein Leiter oder Funktionär in irgendeinem anderen Amte, Einheit oder Stelle (ausgenommen sind die unter C unten angeführten Gliederungen, angeschlossenen Verbände und betreuten Organisationen der NSDAP.? Ja — Nein: nein. Daten — Titel der Stellung — / Were you a leader or functionary of any other NSDAP offices or units or agencies (except Formations, Affiliated Organizations and Supervised Organizations which are covered by questions under C below)? yes, no; dates; title of position
   j) Haben Sie irgendwelche nahe Verwandte, die irgendeine der oben angeführten Stellungen bekleidet haben? Ja — Nein: nein. Wenn ja, geben Sie deren Namen und Anschriften und eine Bezeichnung der Stellung: entfällt / Have you any close relatives who have occupied any of the positions named above? yes, no; if yes, give the name and address and a discription of the position

C. TÄTIGKEITEN IN NSDAP.-HILFSORGANISATIONEN / C. NAZI "AUXILIARY" ORGANIZATION ACTIVITIES

Geben Sie hier an, ob Sie ein Mitglied waren und in welchem Ausmaße Sie an den Tätigkeiten der folgenden Gliederungen, angeschlossenen Verbände und betreuten Organisationen teilgenommen haben / Indicate whether you were a member and the extent to which you participated in the activities of the following Formations Affiliated Organizations or Supervised Organizations

Karl Gustav Fellerer's Denazification File

1946

North Rhine-Westphalia State Archive, Rhineland Department

Allied Control Council Ordinance No. 24 of 12 January 1946 provided for the systematic assessment and classification of all civil servants into five categories. The ordinance permitted universities to allow persons whose role as supporters of the Nazi regime was deemed less significant, to retain their positions so that teaching and administrative activities could continue.

Karl Gustav Fellerer, born in 1902, was a professor of musicology at the University of Cologne from 1939 to 1970. After moving from Fribourg in Switzerland to Cologne, he joined the Nazi Party on 1 October 1940. In the questionnaire of 5 May 1946 provided by the Military Government for Germany, he wrote, "After I was called from Fribourg, Switzerland, to take up my appointment in Cologne in 1939, the executive chairman of the university's board of trustees and the Nazi Party liaison officer repeatedly urged me to join the party." On 8 August 1947, the denazification committee in Cologne assigned Fellerer to Category V, thus exonerating him. This decision did not reflect the fact that Karl Gustav Fellerer had used his scholarly expertise to serve the Nazi regime. Fellerer participated in planning the music department for the Nazi's Hohe Schule der Partei (Advanced School of the Nazi Party) and was active in the Sonderstab Musik (Special Task Force for Music) of the Einsatzstab Reichsleiter Rosenberg (Reichsleiter Rosenberg Taskforce).[26]

Nobel Diploma for Kurt Alder

1950
University of Cologne Archives

KURT ALDER—this name is inscribed in gold on the diploma for the 1950 Nobel Prize in Chemistry, which is kept in the University of Cologne Archives. Alder, a chemist who had lectured at Cologne University since 1937, and his mentor Otto Diels received the highest scientific award for their work on the Diels–Alder reaction. Alder was the fortieth German and the first faculty member from the University of Cologne to win the Nobel Prize. He was able to continue his research for only a few years after his discoveries in the field of carbon ring compounds had been honored, before dying of a chronic heart ailment on 20 June 1958. Shortly before his death, Alder wrote to the Standing Working Committee for Nobel Prize Winner Meetings, which he had always attended: "The constant and ever-increasing strain experienced by active German university professors with a never-ending number of new responsibilities has, in my case, after years of strain, resulted in severe over exhaustion. I am therefore under strict medical orders to take a complete rest for the time being." Today, Kurt Adler's presence is still felt at his former place of work. The largest auditorium of the Physical Chemistry Institute is named after him, and his widow established the Kurt Alder Prize with an endowment in 1991. It has been awarded every year since then to students for outstanding work in the field of organic chemistry.[27]

Failed Denazification

The denazification of the universities, which had been one of the main concerns of the victorious Allies, was initially undertaken in Cologne by the professors themselves in the summer of 1945. They took advantage of the fact that the military government had not yet offered any concrete guidelines. The British wanted first and foremost to ensure that "Nazis" were removed or kept away from the universities. However, lacking the necessary resources and insight to conduct their own review, they left this work to those professors they considered politically uncompromised and who had been entrusted with the reconstruction of the universities.[28]

In early August, a staff commission in Cologne set out guidelines for the political evaluation of academic personnel and instructed the faculties to form review committees. Former senior Nazi Party officials, professors who had joined the party after their appointment, and those who had been appointed under pressure from the party despite lacking full academic qualifications, were to be "removed from their positions." In principle, only those who "had not in any way fallen for National Socialist ideology" were to remain in office. But there were significant exceptions: a full professor who had become a party member for fear of dismissal was spared, and one who

could prove an "oppositional attitude" despite having been a party member would only be temporarily suspended. The latter rule also applied to associate and untenured professors for whom party membership had been a prerequisite for promotion.[29]

These elastic guidelines and their charitable interpretation reveal how empty any talk of genuine "self-cleansing" was. Singling out a few leading Nazis for punishment provided an easy and convenient shield for the many supposed "fellow travelers." From the outset, the group around Kroll wanted to avoid making party membership a core criterion for dismissal. They estimated that about half of the professors in Cologne had been members of the Nazi Party. A strict rule to that effect would have made the resumption of classes considerably more difficult, or even impossible in Kroll's eyes. Thus, for practical reasons alone, a benevolent evaluation of the academic staff appeared necessary. This pragmatic reticence was buttressed by a strong esprit de corps and by collegial networks. Professors wanted to get rid of some of their fellows and keep others. In some cases, colleagues attested to a humanistic outlook; in others, people were advised to quietly retire or keep a low profile.[30]

In September 1945, the provisional university administration submitted its list to the British military government. It showed that, of the 283 teaching staff employed by the university in 1944, 130 had been Nazi Party members, eighty-seven of whom were now deemed untenable. Surprisingly, only two of the five Nazi rectors were included among that latter group. Of the sixty-seven full professors, forty-three were classified as acceptable. The full professors were less discerning in evaluating those who had not completed their habilitation: sixty-two of ninety-two were to be dismissed without further examination. The British followed the proposals with a few exceptions; most notably, they classified all Nazi rectors as politically compromised. In the first post-war semester, sixty-four former members of the teaching staff were permitted to resume their work: thirty-nine full professors, seven associate professors, six lecturers and untenured professors, and twelve instructors, including one woman. The patriarchal professorial university thus restored itself.[31]

← Seat of the British military government on Hohenzollernring; this is where the provisional university leadership submitted its denazification list in September 1945.

A second phase of denazification began with the British military government's Order No. 3 of 17 January 1946. It contained implementation provisions and a specification of five categories: I. Major Offenders, II. Offenders, III. Lesser Offenders, IV. Followers, and V. Persons Exonerated. In August 1946, the Subcommittee for the Political Review of University Professors and Other Instructors took up work in Cologne; a second subcommittee dealt with the denazification of students, a matter of particular concern to the British. The committee for university instructors, chaired by Josef Kroll, consisted of three additional professors and one representative of each of the political parties. All full professors and lecturers were required to fill out a 132-point questionnaire drafted by the British military authorities specifying, for example, whether they had been a member of the Nazi Party or other Nazi organizations. The subcommittee forwarded its assessment to the main denazification committee for the city of Cologne. The military government conducted the final classification—and revised some decisions of the university committees. Only fifty-six people were fully exonerated. However, people were allowed to appeal their classification, and in doing so they could rely on the support of the university leadership, which deliberately played for time and delayed passing information on to the military authorities. As a rule, the longer the denazification process dragged on, the greater were the chances of success in appeal. The exonerating denazification certificate became a kind of currency, known throughout Germany colloquially as a *Persilschein* after the popular brand of laundry detergent.[32]

On 1 October 1947, Decree No. 110 heralded the final phase of denazification in the British zone. From then on, responsibility largely passed to German hands. The military government merely reserved the right to assign people to categories I and II. Gradually, most of the professors who had been dismissed, including several who were heavily implicated, either returned to the University of Cologne or retired with a full pension and benefits. By the end of the 1940s, all of the professors who had taught during the last semester of the war had been reinstated, with the exception of the most notorious Nazi officials.[33]

Alfred Herrhausen 1930–1989

Student in the Faculty of Economics and Social Sciences

Alfred Herrhausen was viewed by many as a visionary, but he also had many opponents. He became one of Deutsche Bank's two chairmen in 1985 and led the bank's transformation into an international financial services provider, long before "globalization" and "investment banking" had become buzz words. An advocate of increased transparency and ethical responsibility in the banking industry, he presented himself as a modern business executive. In the late 1980s, his calls for debt relief for "Third World countries" sparked fierce debate.

From 1942 to 1945, Herrhausen attended the Reichsschule Feldafing, a Nazi Party school, and after completing his Abitur he studied business administration in Cologne from 1949 to 1952. The highly talented young man began his career in 1952 as a management assistant at Ruhrgas AG. At the same time, he wrote his dissertation on the principle of marginal utility under the supervision of Theodor Wessels. In 1955, the year he completed his doctorate, Herrhausen joined Vereinigte Elektrizitätswerke Westfalen; in 1970, he became a member of the executive board of Deutsche Bank.

The career of this influential banker and political consultant was cut short. After being appointed the first sole chairman of Deutsche Bank since Josef Abs in May 1988, Herrhausen was murdered in 1989, with the Red Army Faction claiming responsibility for his death.[34]

Josef Koch 1885–1967

Professor in the Faculty of Philosophy

Even as a student, Josef Koch was already drawing connections between theology, philosophy and philology. After being ordained in 1908, he worked in the seminary of the Archdiocese of Cologne, obtained his doctorate in philosophy in Bonn in 1915, and asked to be released from the priesthood in 1921 to pursue an academic career. He went via Rome to Breslau (Wrocław), where he received a doctorate and completed his habilitation on Durandus of Saint Pourçain at the Faculty of Theology in 1925. Koch was appointed associate professor in Breslau in 1933 and then professor of fundamental theology. He conducted research on the mystic Meister Eckhart and published a standard edition of Eckhart's Latin writings.

After fleeing from Breslau in 1945, Koch returned to the Rhineland and lectured as a visiting professor at the University of Bonn until becoming a professor of philosophy at the University of Göttingen in 1947. In 1948, he was appointed professor of medieval philosophy at the University of Cologne, a position he held until he retired in 1954.

While in Cologne, Koch devoted himself to the work of theologian and philosopher Nikolaus von Kues and edited parts of the historical-critical edition of his collected works. In 1950, Koch founded the interdisciplinary medievalist conference in Cologne, and he was the first director of the Thomas Institute, which became a research center for medieval philosophy.[35]

René König
1906–1992

Professor in the Faculty of Economics and Social Sciences

René König, a polyglot who grew up in Paris and Magdeburg, obtained his doctorate in Berlin in 1930 with a thesis on French naturalistic aesthetics. He was denied his habilitation after his book, *Vom Wesen der deutschen Bildung* (On the nature of German education), published in 1935, was banned. As an opponent of the Nazis, he emigrated to Switzerland in 1937 and earned his habilitation in Zurich in 1938. He was one of the founders of the International Sociological Association established in 1949. His programmatic publication *Soziologie heute* (Sociology today) appeared in the same year.

König was appointed in 1949 to Cologne's first independent chair for sociology. His Cologne school established empirical social research in the Federal Republic of Germany and made Cologne a center of West German sociology. König promoted quantitative social research until his retirement in 1974, but in his own work he took a more ethnological approach. From 1955 to 1985, he was the editor of the *Kölner Zeitschrift für Soziologie und Sozialpsychologie*, making a major contribution to the specialization and professionalization of this field of study. The versatile sociologist saw himself as a "citizen of the world" and always regarded his discipline as an assessment of contemporary society. Early on, he engaged in a critical examination of sociology during the Nazi era. His encyclopedic volume entitled *Soziologie* (Sociology), first published in 1958, made the field of sociology accessible to a wide audience.[36]

Alfred Müller-Armack
1901–1978

Professor in the Faculty of Economics and Social Sciences

Alfred Müller-Armack earned his doctorate under the supervision of Leopold von Wiese in Cologne in 1923 and then completed his habilitation thesis on the business cycle and economic policy in 1926, also in Cologne. With his pamphlet *Staatsidee und Wirtschaftsordnung im neuen Reich* (The concept of the state and the economic order in the new Reich) published in 1933, the economist and cultural sociologist espoused Nazi ideology. He joined the Nazi Party that same year. Müller-Armack became an untenured professor at Cologne in 1934 and then moved to Münster in 1938, where he was granted a chair in 1940. He was head of the Research Center for Spatial and Housing Economics there, which developed plans for the colonization of the "Eastern Territories." In 1941, he founded the Research Center for General and Textile Market Economy.

After the war, Müller-Armack, in collaboration with Walter Eucken and his Freiburg school, formulated the concept of *Soziale Marktwirtschaft* (social market economy), according to which state-regulated competition would create "prosperity for all." In 1950, he joined the University of Cologne, where he set up the Institute for Economic Policy. Ludwig Erhard made him provisional head of the central policy unit at the Federal Ministry for Economic Affairs in 1952. Müller-Armack left his chair at Cologne when he became state secretary for European affairs in the ministry in 1958. After resigning in 1963, he returned to Cologne where he remained until retiring in 1969.[37]

Student Life in Hardship

When it reopened in late 1945, the University of Cologne faced a backlog of at least seven cohorts desiring entrance to the university. By October, around 4,000 applications had been received. Given the precarious supply of basic necessities and lack of livable accommodation in the heavily damaged city, the British military government approved just 1,500 study places for the first post-war semester, 150 of which were reserved for displaced persons (DP) who had remained in Cologne. Since the occupying forces had instructed the university to give preference to those who had actively opposed or avoided involvement with the Nazi regime, applicants were subjected to political scrutiny. At first, this was relatively mild and conducted by the university itself, but from the summer semester of 1946 applicants were subject to the British denazification process. The university's own denazification subcommittee processed the admission applications. The last word, however, came from the military government, which in some cases rejected students who had been admitted in the first post-war semester. This situation continued until the Youth Amnesty of October 1946, when the British military authorities automatically exonerated everyone born after 1 January 1919. In order to have greater control over admissions, the university developed its own selection criteria in 1946. By means of a complex system of categories and points, applicants were assigned to one of forty-three groups based on their qualifications and level of education. In some of the early post-war semesters, the university rejected up to eighty percent of applicants. The high rejection rate disadvantaged women in particular, since men were given priority as future family breadwinners. In stark contrast to the final university semester of the war, when women comprised half of the 2,000 students enrolled, female students formed a minority of eighteen to twenty-two percent in the immediate post-war years.[38]

In Cologne, as at other German universities, the average age of the first post-war students was nearly twenty-four, as the war had forced many young people out of education. In the lecture halls, students in their late twenties who had completed their Abitur in the 1930s before serving for years in the Wehrmacht sat alongside eighteen-year-olds who had received only a rudimentary upper-secondary education and left without a full graduation certificate in 1944. Almost all students had one thing in common: they had been exposed to twelve years of Nazi indoctrination and had been deeply affected by the violence of war. In a survey conducted in the winter semester of 1946/1947, ninety-eight percent of Cologne students stated that they had served as soldiers or anti-aircraft assistants, nurses or armaments workers. DP students had a special status. Their number reached its peak in the summer semester of 1947 with 113 men, mainly from Poland and the Baltic. Most of them lived in a camp in the former Benedictine Brauweiler Abbey on the western edge of the city.[39]

During the first post-war semesters, day-to-day student life was marked by frequent shortages of food and necessities. The food situation remained calamitous, reaching its lowest point in 1947 when the student population survived on an average daily ration of 737 calories. Although the churches offered free meals to students and the university received food donations from abroad, around ninety-five percent of Cologne students were underweight in 1947. Students collapsing from hunger in lecture halls was an everyday occurrence. Many students worked during the semester to make ends meet. The housing situation was also precarious. In the winter semester of 1946/1947, fewer than half of the students had a room of their own; many shared with four or more people. They often lived in unheated cellars, sheds or bunkers and, in the cold months, wrapped themselves in blankets in their beds while studying. Many travelled long distances, even on foot, to get to their classes.

In the winter semester of 1946/1947, over a quarter of the students spent up to two hours a day travelling to classes. Even in the lecture halls and libraries of the university, the students were afflicted by cold.[40]

Notwithstanding the difficult conditions, many students actively supported a new democratic system, though rarely as members of political parties. In the winter semester of 1946/1947, about eighty-five percent of Cologne students eschewed joining a political society, deterred by their experience of Nazism. But these young men and women were not apolitical or disinterested, as some contemporaries believed. The Student Council (AStA), which was first elected in July 1946, was active in areas such as culture, social affairs and sport. Cologne students also sought out new forms of student association as an alternative to the deeply discredited student fraternities. In 1946, for example, they founded the Catholic and Protestant student congregations, the English Society and the Orion group, which organized well-attended discussion evenings on political topics. This creation of new social and political groupings was typical of the first post-war generation.[41]

Moreover, following the deep national isolation of the Nazi era, students in the immediate post-war period showed great interest in the world beyond Germany's borders. The British university officer Harry Beckhoff promoted international exchange in multiple ways. He organized foreign trips for students and invited British guest speakers to Cologne. He was also instrumental in initiating the first international summer school to be held on German soil since the war, at Schloss Wahn in Cologne in July 1947. Nearly 150 students from Great Britain, Switzerland and Cologne took part. New associations such as the Cologne section of the International Student League (ISSF) and the German-Scandinavian Students' Association also embraced international exchange and cultural diplomacy.[42]

↑ The enthusiasm of post-war students for education was tempered by material hardship; female students wearing heavy coats while reading in 1946/1947.

University Guide

1951

Cologne University and City Library

The cover of the Cologne University guide published for the first time in 1951 is reminiscent of posters in the New Objectivity style. The introduction by the two editors of the booklet sounds just as modern: "Fellow students, the Student Council has published this university guide to provide you, and especially the freshmen among you, with a practical guide designed to make it easier to find your way around the university, and to offer you information on the facilities and institutes outside your own faculty." The 170-page brochure provided information on the city, the faculties, the board of trustees, the Association of Friends and Sponsors, the University and City Library, the Student Services Center, the Heinzelmännchen Studentenschnelldienst (a student job placement service), student sports activities and the numerous student associations. In addition to practical tips, the guide featured ads for local businesses accompanied by the editors' request to give preference "to these businesses when shopping." There was also an essay on the modern concept of a university by German literature professor Richard Alewyn, who had returned to Cologne after emigrating, and an expert opinion by the Academic Commission on University Reform appointed in 1948 by the military governor of the British occupation zone—two texts that gave incoming students the feeling that they once again held their academic future in their own hands.[43]

Husserliana

1954
Husserl Archives Cologne

The first volume of the Husserliana series that the Husserl Archives in Cologne helped publish in 1954 was entitled *The Crisis of European Sciences and Transcendental Phenomenology*. The archive in Cologne was founded on 27 August 1951 following the signing of a basic agreement between the Faculty of Philosophy and the Husserl Archives of the University of Leuven in Belgium, making Cologne a branch of the Leuven archives. After the death of the philosopher Edmund Husserl in 1938, his widow Malvine Husserl and Herman Leo van Breda, a young Franciscan priest, rescued Husserl's literary estate from the Nazis, taking it to Belgium, which at the time had not yet been occupied by the Germans. The first Husserl archive was created there in 1939. After World War II, some of Husserl's former long-time research associates opened two further Husserl archives in Freiburg im Breisgau and Cologne. Together with the Leuven and Freiburg archives, the archives in Cologne were intended to secure academic access to the estate of the founder of phenomenology, transcribe some 40,000 pages of his manuscripts written in Gabelsberg shorthand and prepare editions of his work for publication. International contacts were also an important aspect of the work in Cologne, with many distinguished philosophers invited to lecture in Cologne, among them Hannah Arendt, Aron Gurwitsch and Gabriel Marcel. Today, the Husserliana series comprises nearly 40 volumes, about half of which were compiled in Cologne.[44]

Academic Profile of the University

During the 1950s, the university's academic profile was shaped by academic appointments and the establishment of new institutes. One of the latter was the Institute for Social and Administrative Sciences, founded in 1947. This carried on the work of the Research Institute for Social Sciences, which had been shut down by the Nazis in 1934. This publicly financed associated institute was affiliated to two of the university's faculties and pioneered interdisciplinary collaboration between the social sciences, economics and law. It also developed new areas of focus; in addition to sociology and social policy, departments were established dealing with social law, municipal and administrative law, and housing law and economics.[45] The department heads were among the most distinguished academics at the University of Cologne. Only one of them, Hans Carl Nipperdey, had already taught in Cologne in the 1920s. He was one of the leading German experts on labor law, and in 1954 became the first president of the Federal Labor Court. The sociologist René König, who came to Cologne from exile in Switzerland in 1949, was a pioneer of empirical social research and founded one of the most influential schools of social science in Germany. The jurist Hans Peters, appointed in 1949, had been a member of the Kreisau Circle of anti-Nazi dissidents and co-founded the Hamburg section of the CDU after the war. At the University of Cologne, he developed a modern, practice-oriented study of public administration, combining legal with sociological, economic and psychological approaches. Gerhard Weisser also took a decidedly practical approach to the study of social policy and co-operatives, a field in which he held a professorial chair from 1950. He was a highly influential member of the SPD and was one of the authors of its 1959 Godesberg Program.[46]

However, anti-Nazis and former dissidents were a minority among the professorial faculty. Ultimately, the character of the University in Cologne was largely shaped by researchers who had begun their careers during the "Third Reich." Many simply continued their work, while others adapted or changed their approaches to fit the new political order. The younger generation of professors included the economist Alfred Müller-Armack, one of the founders of *Soziale Marktwirtschaft* (social market economy) who was appointed in 1950, and Erich Gutenberg, who moved to Cologne in 1951 and laid the theoretical foundations for the academic study of business administration in Germany. The Faculty of Economics and Social Science distinguished itself by establishing one of the first German chairs of political science in 1951, a post that was held from 1959 on by the political scientist Ferdinand A. Hermens. The former émigré founded the Cologne school of political science, which places institutions at the center of its empirical analysis.[47]

Theodor Schieder, who was appointed to the Faculty of Philosophy in 1948, helped establish history as the flagship discipline of the faculty. The historian, whose pre-1945 work had lent support to Nazi expansionism in eastern Europe, opened the discipline to social-historical research approaches and promoted a European perspective on German history. He also considerably enlarged the Department of History to include study centers for American, Ibero-American and Eastern European history. In the field of philosophy, the Thomas Institute was founded in 1950 with a focus on medieval research; the Husserl Archives, established a year later, turned Cologne into a center of phenomenological research. Fritz Schalk, who had taught Romance philology in Cologne since 1936, built his department into one of the most important of its kind in West Germany. And in German studies, Richard Alewyn, who returned to Germany in 1949, introduced socio-historical methods.[48]

But it was in the natural sciences that the post-war University of Cologne achieved its first great successes. In 1950, Kurt Alder, who had been a professor in Cologne since 1940, was awarded the Nobel

Prize for Chemistry. The botanist Joseph Straub, who had worked at the Kaiser Wilhelm Institute of Biology until 1944 and was appointed to the University of Cologne in 1949, opened his department to modern genetic research and raised funding to found the first German Institute of Genetics in 1959. Very few of the Cologne physicians who were politically compromised by their involvement with the Nazi regime distinguished themselves in the first post-war years. An exception was Hugo-Wilhelm Knipping, who became one of the first to apply the isotope method in clinical research. In 1948, Wilhelm Tönnis, who had worked at the Kaiser Wilhelm Institute for Brain Research until 1945, took up the first German chair in neurosurgery. This was followed a year later by the foundation of Germany's first neurosurgical clinic. Together with Klaus-Joachim Zülch, with whom he had already worked at the Kaiser Wilhelm Institute, Tönnis brought two departments of the Max Planck Institute for Brain Research to Cologne.[49]

The emigrants who returned to Germany were instrumental in ensuring that the university caught up to the level of international research, as was the financial economist Fritz K. Mann, who remained in the USA after having been fired and forced to emigrate in 1936 but regularly returned to lecture at the University of Cologne. Similarly, the émigré Max Delbrück, who won the 1969 Nobel Prize for Medicine, was founding director of the Institute of Genetics at the University of Cologne. Scientists such as Tönnis and Alder ultimately continued their research in the same context. Schieder brought his Königsberg research on eastern Europe to bear in a major project on the history of the post-war displacement of ethnic Germans, though now devoid of the previous *völkisch* ideology. Müller-Armack adapted his ideas of a market economy within a totalitarian dictatorship to a democratic ordoliberal concept. The transformation of the university's academic profile therefore included a large element of continuity.

↓ Rector Josef Kroll talking to Carl Diem, former Nazi sports official and director of the newly founded Physical Education College in Cologne, 29 November 1947.

Hans Peters
1896–1966

Professor in the Faculty of Law

Hans Peters was a "political professor" who combined scholarly and practical activities throughout his life. An expert in administrative and municipal law, he joined the Center Party in 1923 and worked for the municipal department of the Prussian Ministry of the Interior and for the provincial government in Breslau. From 1928 to 1933, he held a post at the Prussian Ministry of Culture and Education. At the same time, Peters completed his habilitation in Breslau in 1925 with a thesis on the limits of municipal self-government in Prussia. From 1928 on, he lectured as an associate professor at the University of Berlin and was dean of the Berlin Academy for Administration Studies. An opponent of the Nazis, Peters was a member of the Kreisau Circle, for whom he produced expert opinions on cultural, church and administrative matters.

After the war, Peters was one of the founding members of the CDU in Hamburg and a member of the city council of Berlin, where he helped draft the constitution of the state of Berlin. In 1949, he went to Cologne as a professor of constitutional and administrative law. His *Lehrbuch der Verwaltung*, a classic textbook for interdisciplinary administration studies, was published the same year. As president of the Görres Society, Peters modernized that traditional Catholic academic organization. The prominent lawyer spent many years on the city council of Cologne, drafted the 1963 constitution of the University of Cologne and served as university rector in 1964/1965.[50]

Martin Schwarzbach
1907–2003

Professor in the Faculty of Mathematics and Natural Sciences

Geologist Martin Schwarzbach's career began in Breslau, where he obtained his doctorate in 1933 with a study of the Cambrian Period in Upper Lusatia. His habilitation, completed in 1937, dealt with Silesia's carbon deposits. Schwarzbach was a *Privatdozent* and professor in Breslau until 1945. After a brief stint in Göttingen, he went to Cologne in 1947, where he assumed the chair for geology and rebuilt the Geological Institute, which had been destroyed in the war.

Schwarzbach was viewed as one of the last remaining polymaths in the geosciences due to the wide scope of his research in a variety of subdisciplines. He turned his attention to the study of past climates from 1940 on and is considered the "father" of paleoclimatology. In 1950, he published the textbook *Klima der Vorzeit* (*Climates of the Past*), which quickly became an internationally acclaimed standard work.

His experience of earthquakes in the Lower Rhine region sparked his interest in research in this area. He initiated the founding of the University of Cologne Bensberg Earthquake Station following a particularly strong earthquake in 1951, and he lived and worked in Bensberg for over thirty years. Schwarzbach was particularly interested in the history of the geo- and natural sciences. After retiring in 1975, he oversaw the Archive of Geology in Freiburg until 1988.[51]

Wilhelm Tönnis
1898–1978

Professor in the Medical Faculty

Wilhelm Tönnis was a pioneer of neurosurgery in Germany. He completed his habilitation in Würzburg in 1929 and headed Germany's first independent neurosurgical department from 1934 on. In 1936, he founded the *Zentralblatt für Neurochirurgie*, the world's first academic journal for neurosurgery. Three years earlier, in 1933, he had become a member of the paramilitary German Air Sports Association, and he joined the Nazi Party in 1937. That same year, he was granted the first German associate professorship of neurosurgery in Berlin and took charge of a new department at the Kaiser Wilhelm Institute for Brain Research in Berlin. It has not yet been established whether he was involved in research that accompanied the Nazis' "euthanasia" program. During World War II, Tönnis was a "brigadier surgeon" responsible for treating brain and nerve injuries, first in the Luftwaffe and later in the entire Wehrmacht.

Tönnis assumed the first German chair of neurosurgery in Cologne in 1948. He integrated his department, now part of the Max Planck Institute for Brain Research, into the university's new Neurosurgical Clinic and was its head from 1949 until his retirement in 1968. Tönnis was also director of the Max Planck Institute for Brain Research from 1957 to 1968. In Cologne, Tönnis continued to focus on the early detection of brain tumors and vascular malformations of the brain, and he served as rector in 1960/1961.[52]

Otto Veit
1884–1972

Professor in the Medical Faculty

Anatomist Otto Veit became interested in medicine through zoology. His work on the anatomy and developmental history of the vertebrate head made him one of Germany's most distinguished experts in the field of comparative anatomy. Veit received his doctorate in Freiburg and earned his habilitation in 1911 at the Institute of Anatomy in Marburg, where he became an untenured professor in 1916. He fought as a volunteer in World War I. In 1925, the University of Cologne appointed him founding director of the Institute of Anatomy, which was an integral part of the preclinical studies program that had been introduced that same year.

Despite a lack of funding and space, Veit established the study and research of anatomy in Cologne and secured its academic reputation. He was a German nationalist but lost his *Prüfungserlaubnis* (authorization to teach) in 1934 because his great-grandparents had been Jewish. His colleagues in Cologne and even high-ranking National Socialists did what they could to enable him to remain at the university. Veit, an active member of the Confessing Church, was nevertheless forced into retirement in 1937. He stayed in Cologne and became prorector of the university when it reopened in 1945. Veit rebuilt the Institute of Anatomy, which had been destroyed in the war, restored its collections and continued to be actively involved in the institute long after his late retirement in 1957.[53]

From a Municipal to a State University

The speedy reopening of the university was supported not only by the political leadership of the city, but also by a broad civic consensus, which included the political parties, business leaders and the church. However, as early as 1945 the question of who should bear the financial burden was contentious. The CDU, which was the largest party in the city council, wanted to finance the university solely from municipal funds, while the SPD favored the participation of the Province of North Rhine, the predecessor to the state of North Rhine-Westphalia that was created in the summer of 1946. The Social Democrats hoped that this might dilute the dominance of the Catholic-conservative "Cologne clique." Robert Görlinger, chairman of the SPD in Cologne city council before 1933 and again after 1945, repeatedly raised this issue. A politician who had influential ties to state and federal politics, Görlinger strove to open the university to all strata of society, to imbue it with a democratic spirit and give it a strong practical orientation. He was convinced early on that the reconstruction of the university would have to be followed by its expansion, the cost of which exceeded the city's financial means.[54]

But the SPD was unable to advance its agenda due to the combined resistance of the CDU and the university leadership. When the currency reform of 1948 exacerbated the city's financial difficulties, the SPD proposed that the state government at least partially cover the costs of running the university. The CDU majority rejected this proposal. Rector Kroll argued that Cologne should not cede control of an institution that was "as old as the cathedral and the city's next most prized possession." The situation changed fundamentally when, following a stalemate in the city assembly in November 1948, the SPD began to annually alternate control of the mayoralty with the CDU. Robert Görlinger subsequently became mayor and succeeded in getting the CDU-led state government on board. He was supported by the Minister of Education Christine Teusch, who was from Cologne and had been a member of the university's board of trustees after the war. In the spring of 1949, North Rhine-Westphalia took on half of the city's share of the running costs and supported the redevelopment of the university and the construction of new buildings. The status of the university as a municipal institution remained unchanged.[55]

While the CDU saw the agreement as a way of safeguarding the city's continued control of the university, the SPD considered it the first step toward its transfer to the state. The lack of detailed regulation led to repeated discussions about which of the two sponsors should bear which costs. In order to resolve the impasse, the board of trustees chaired by Cologne Mayor Ernst Schwering, who had been appointed by the CDU, ruled on 7 August 1950 that the city should enter into negotiations with the state government to replace the old state treaty of 1919 with a new agreement that regulated the financial participation of the state. While the CDU still had great reservations about "selling our university to the state," the resistance in the Cologne professorship was gradually eclipsed by a fear that the university might fall behind Bonn or Münster. The universities there, as state institutions, had received significantly more development assistance and grants, even though they had fewer students.[56]

← Minister of Education Christine Teusch with cabinet colleagues in 1950. The CDU politician from Cologne was a member of the board of trustees and favored the takeover of the university by the state.

Following intensive negotiations, in which Robert Görlinger was again involved as mayor for a year, the state government, city and university concluded the Agreement Between the State and the City on the University of Cologne in May 1952. It provided for the incorporation of the university into the state budget of North Rhine-Westphalia on 1 April 1953. However, the negotiations on the exact form of that incorporation dragged on until March 1954. Max Adenauer, municipal director and son of the former mayor, expressed the ambivalent mood of the CDU at the adoption of the agreement on 4 March: "What use was it to consider the feelings and sentiment of the people of Cologne when we were simply no longer able to ensure the necessary conditions for the proper running of the university?" The transfer took place on 1 April 1954 and applied retroactively from 1 April 1953.[57]

The city now paid fifty percent of the required subsidy to the state and transferred all the university's property to state ownership. Although the board of trustees remained in place, its powers were greatly reduced. The Ministry of Education nominated a representative, while the number of municipal members was reduced. From now on, the city retained a right to participate in decisions related to the university, but it relinquished co-determination. For the first time, an administrative committee was set up and a chancellor was appointed by the Ministry of Education to run the university. The autonomy of the university was safeguarded by Article 16 of the State Constitution of 1950. The Cologne professors regarded this transition to a state university as a gain. In the first few years, the state's higher education policy was limited to construction funding. It pushed ahead with the expansion of the university from the mid-1950s onward. The situation was not as beneficial to the city; although Cologne had lost control of its university, the rapidly increasing financial requirements meant that it was hardly relieved of any financial burden. In a supplementary agreement dated 24 October 1960, the state agreed to take over the city's entire share of the running costs within five years. In return, the city undertook to provide the state with free development land for new university buildings and to continue to cover twenty percent of the subsidy requirements for the university medical clinics. This final financial commitment was rescinded in October 1963. Only then were new university statutes passed to replace the statutes of 1919.[58]

Bronze Statue of Albertus Magnus by Gerhard Marcks

1955
Ludwig Museum

In 1954, the city of Cologne commissioned Gerhard Marcks to create an Albertus Magnus monument to be placed in front of the university. The sculptor had moved to Cologne in 1950 at the invitation of lawyer and collector Josef Haubrich. The city council provided him with a studio house designed by the architect Wilhelm Riphahn in the Müngersdorf district. It was here that the models of the seated Albertus Magnus were created in 1955. One of these models, the bronze figurine from the Ludwig Museum pictured above, is only 23.5 centimeters tall. Marcks showed the great thinker and theologian of the Middle Ages looking into the distance and toward the sky. Wearing only a cloak and sandals, Marcks depicted him as a humble scholar without worldly wants, who conveyed a new way of thinking to his students based on the interpretation of traditional works, represented by the open book in his lap. With this sculpture, Marcks gave shape to the timeless image of a scholar whose real appearance remains unknown.

The 2.60-meter bronze statue was erected in 1956. Over the years, it has occupied several different places on Albertus Magnus Platz in front of the university. Today, it is back where it originally stood, directly in front of the entrance to the main building. Additional casts were made of the sculpture in 1965 for the University of Bologna, in 1970 for the University of Texas in Houston, and in 1996 for the University of Jena.[59]

Punch Cards

circa 1960

Central Archive for Empirical Social Research

These punch cards are from the Central Archive for Empirical Social Research in Cologne (ZA), founded in 1960. The archive was merged with two other institutes—the Mannheim Center for Surveys, Methods, and Analyses, and the Social Sciences Information Center in Bonn—to become the Leibniz Institute for the Social Sciences (GESIS) in 1986. From the very beginning, the staff at the Central Archive for Empirical Social Research used modern technology, thus acquiring a reputation for being technically up to date. They used punch cards, an early electronic data processing technology, to streamline workflows. The punched cards in the 80-column format were processed by external mainframe computers. The holes in the data carrier, which was made of stiff paper, were similar to braille. A 1960 reference book states: "The punch card system can be used for nearly all areas of business accounting, including statistics, payroll and commission accounting, invoicing, accounts receivable and payable, and other bookkeeping tasks [...], as well as by public authorities for administrative purposes." The ZA had established procedures: the programmers punched the cards, which contained a considerable amount of information for statistical analysis, in a separate room equipped with keypunch machines. Then the punch cards were stored in the archive, where they remain to this day.[60]

ROSA
UXEM

The Great Transformation

Chapter 5

1960 – 1975

1960–1975

1961

Genetics Research Begins

The Institute of Genetics starts work in a new six-story building. Max Delbrück, the founding director of this first research institute at a German university dedicated exclusively to molecular biology, is later awarded the Nobel Prize.

1962

Internationalization

The University of Cologne signs its first international partnership agreement with the University of Clermont-Ferrand in France, providing for regular student exchanges and scholarships.

1965

Europe's Largest Faculty

The Faculty of Economics and Social Sciences, the University of Cologne's flagship, is the largest of its kind in Europe, boasting 8,500 students.

1966

The KVB Battle

Some 8,000 pupils from Cologne schools protest together with university students against substantial fare increases imposed by KVB, the city's transport company. Violent clashes with the police make national headlines.

1968

Student Protests

After the assassination attempt on Rudi Dutschke, student protests at Cologne become more radical, culminating in the occupation of the rectorate in November 1968.

1968

A Campus University

The central lecture hall building and the University and City Library of Cologne are officially opened. Together with the main building, inaugurated in 1935, and the Philosophikum, completed in 1974, they constitute the new Universitätsforum (University Forum) at the center of the first urban campus university in Germany.

1970

First Collaborative Research Centers

The first two Collaborative Research Centers, the *Sonderforschungsbereiche* (SFBs), begin their work: one in the Faculty of Medicine and one in the Faculty of Mathematics and Natural Sciences.

1974

The Boom Ends

The last large buildings to be constructed are the Philosophikum, the institutes for physics and chemistry, the *Mensa* (student cafeteria) and the hospital ward building. The financial crisis halts further expansion. The central hospital, only partly finished, is not completed until 1990.

RAUCHEN VERBOTEN

Increases in student enrollment, as well as in the number of professors and other teaching staff, new courses of study, new research institutes and numerous new buildings, characterized the development of the University of Cologne after 1960. Although the university was already planning to expand by the end of the 1950s, it initially did not keep pace with rapidly growing demand. By the mid-1960s, overcrowding and partially outdated university facilities and structures made comprehensive reforms unavoidable; students demanded improved conditions and a more democratic university system. The majority of Cologne professors were skeptical or even hostile toward the student movement and most of its demands for political reform. As student protests tailed off in the early 1970s, the university's criticism of North Rhine-Westphalia's higher education policies resulted in serious conflict. The University of Cologne attempted to preserve traditions through cautious reforms, but it nevertheless changed fundamentally in this period.

From an Elite University to a "Mass" University

The steadily growing number of students changed West Germany's university landscape. Driven by the first cohorts of baby boomers, a growing middle class seeking advancement, and accelerated government modernization policies, the university completed its transition from an elite educational institution to an institution of professional training for larger segments of the population. The University of Cologne, one of the largest in West Germany, grew by two-thirds within fifteen years: from nearly 14,000 students in 1960 to some 23,000 in 1975.

A key factor in this growth was the Faculty of Philosophy. Its student numbers doubled during this phase, reaching about 6,700. By late 1970, it had become the largest faculty, superseding the Faculty of Economics and Social Sciences. This increase was due in particular to the growing number of women, which surpassed the number of male students in the Faculty of Philosophy for the first time in the winter semester of 1974/1975. Meanwhile, the share of women in the Faculty of Economics and Social Sciences remained at less than one-fifth. Student numbers at that faculty had risen from about 5,500 in 1960 to 8,500 in the winter semester of 1965/1966, making it the largest of its kind in Europe. However, by 1970 this number had fallen to 5,000 students because North Rhine-Westphalia had opened new universities. The numbers rose only slightly to 6,000 over the following five years. The largest increase in growth rate was in the Faculty of Mathematics and Natural Sciences, where the number of students rose from nearly 1,600 to just over 4,000, a quarter of whom were women. The Faculty of Medicine grew by fifty percent to nearly 2,400 students; here too, a quarter of the students were women. The rise in the number of law students was also substantial, from about 1,900 to 3,650, a fifth of them women—a dramatic increase compared with the first post-war semester, when women made up less than three percent of law students.[1]

← By the end of the 1960s, students created an "alternative public sphere" with new actions such as teach-ins. Among other things, they called for better study conditions both inside and outside the lecture halls.

Vigorous Expansion

As the student body grew between 1960 and 1975, so did the teaching staff, rising from 435 to 964. In the mid-1960s, the creation of teaching positions surpassed the increase in students for several years, meaning that the student-to-instructor ratio continued to improve until the early 1970s. Initially this was because new positions opened up for non-professorial academic staff, who took on more and more teaching and organizational responsibilities, but later on it was primarily due to additional professorships. After Germany's "economic miracle" ended, job expansion slowed. From 1974/1975, the ratio of university instructors to students declined again.[2]

It is notable that the number of regular professors rose significantly; the number of chairs alone increased from 127 to 288. In the summer of 1966, biologist Cornelia Harte was the first woman to be appointed to a chair. Ten years later there were fourteen women holding chairs, six of them in the Faculty of Philosophy alone. This figure later stagnated at thirteen. The number of associate professors increased sharply—from sixteen to 145. This growth occurred mostly in the faculties of medicine, philosophy, and mathematics and natural sciences. The share of women who were associate professors was significantly lower than among the full professorships: from 1964 on, the number of female associate professors did not exceed three or four. Although the overall increase in associate professors meant the end of Cologne as a professorial university, it continued to be dominated by men.[3]

During its period of expansion from 1960 to 1975, the university developed its academic institutions and degree programs, which led to increased specialization but also to a focus on specific areas. Professorships, seminars, institutes and clinics increased by about fifty percent in the Faculty of Economics and Social Sciences, the Faculty of Philosophy and the Faculty of Medicine. During the same period, the Faculty of Law doubled the number of its departments. The Faculty of Mathematics and Natural Sciences expanded mostly due to specialization and had two of Cologne's three Collaborative Research Centers (SFBs), thanks to an increase in external research funding from 1.4 million German marks in 1960 to nearly twelve million in 1975.[4]

A Modern Campus University

This rapid growth meant that the University of Cologne was bursting at the seams. As early as 1959, Chancellor Wolfgang Wagner had proposed a "master plan" for the major extension and modernization of the university's buildings—a year before the Wissenschaftsrat (German Council of Science and Humanities) recommended the massive expansion of West Germany's universities. Using British and American urban universities as a model, the University of Cologne was to become the first campus university located in a major German city. Separate, functional sites were to be created for each faculty on this new campus to facilitate a modern form of interdisciplinary, transparent and urban academic life and work. To realize this ambitious project, which would nearly double the university's existing building space, the administration had acquired a total area of about thirty-seven acres by 1969, costing almost twenty-two million German marks.[5]

The area in front of the main building was redesigned to make room for the Universitätsforum, as the center of the new campus was called. The university commissioned a prestigious architect, Rolf Gutbrod, for this project. The street directly in front of the main building was diverted underground as an underpass, creating a continuous space above it. By 1968, the university had built a functional and architecturally sophisticated university and city library there, as well as a central lecture hall building in the Brutalist style popular at the time. The building complex was embedded in an artistically designed garden landscape with small ponds. The Philosophikum, designed by Cologne architect Georg Lohmann to house the Faculty of Philosophy's departments, was completed in 1974.[6]

The most spacious campus area, separated from the Universitätsforum only by Zülpicher Straße, was allotted to the Faculty of Mathematics and Natural Sciences. In the early 1960s, the university had already put up new buildings for the mathematics, geosciences and biology departments and institutes. Between 1964 and 1975, modern institutes for physics and chemistry were built on a site approximately twenty-two acres in size. Opposite that site, adjoining the green area behind the main building, the new central *Mensa* opened its doors in 1974 and began serving nearly 13,000 meals per day.[7]

The largest project was the construction of a central hospital on the grounds of the old Lindenburg Clinic. After the university had built a new Institute of Pharmacology, Institute of Anatomy and Women's Clinic between 1960 and 1966, work began late in 1969 on the service center of the central hospital and the approximately eighty-meter-tall hospital ward building with 1,150 beds. These buildings set architectural and technical standards. But after 1974, the general financial crisis delayed completion of the rest of the complex by more than ten years.[8]

→ Rapid growth forced the university to expand. The new central student cafeteria on Zülpicher Straße opened in 1974

VolksBlatt

Cologne's Path

The heated debate on education and higher education reform that started in the mid-1960s resonated among students at Cologne. They opposed admission restrictions and prescribed periods of study, and they demanded better conditions for students, binding curricula and degree requirements, and participation in university decision-making. From the spring of 1967 to the summer of 1969, students articulated their demands with activities ranging from sit-ins to the occupation of the rectorate. However, these protests never reached the scale and force of those in Berlin or Frankfurt. This might be attributed to the fact that Cologne's student movement was closely connected to the city's progressive cultural, political and religious circles. Students in the Republican Club, a left-wing association, talked with journalists, trade unionists and professors from the liberal left. Students met with progressive Christians once a month at the Politisches Nachtgebet, a political evening prayer group that gathered in the Antoniter Church, and a lively music and art scene opened new horizons. The *Kinderläden* (self-run day care groups for children), shared housing and women's groups founded by students all had a far-reaching effect on the city's society.[9]

The political balance of power within the student body also shaped Cologne's development. Left-wing university groups held a majority in the Student Council (AStA) only once, from February until November 1968. Even though left-wing groups such as the Socialist German Student Union (SDS) dominated the scene with sensational actions, conservative groups defined student politics. One of these was the Aktion 1967 group, a special feature of the University of Cologne founded in early 1967 with roots in the Catholic student corporations. It soon

↑ When the Emergency Acts were passed on 30 May 1968, student protesters renamed the University of Cologne "Rosa Luxemburg University." Conservative students countered with spontaneous humor.

changed its name to the Cologne Student Union (KSU) and assumed the chair of the AStA in November 1968. Conservative students also wanted to reform their alma mater, but in cooperation with its professors. When this approach failed, the KSU also worked together with left-wing university groups, joining protests against the 1972 Anti-Radical Decree, for example.[10]

On the Defensive

In the course of the 1960s, Cologne's professors increasingly felt forced to adopt a passive role. With its 1959 "master plan" and new constitution of 1963, the university had taken control of its future, but the rise of student protests and changes in higher education policy put the professors on the defensive. Most professors opposed the students' demands. They criticized the politicization of the university and perceived many protest actions as a personal threat. The university's leadership hoped to maintain the upper hand with a tough stance on some issues combined with offers to engage in a dialog with students, but it could not prevent fundamental changes in academic culture around 1970. Academic gowns and Latin names seemed outdated, and the authority of professors waned. Supported by a handful of progressive professors, students had asserted their right to have a say and to ensure greater transparency. While Cologne's professors continued to fight the idea of a *Gruppenuniversität*, in which all groups participate in self-government, everyday university life had long embraced change and left the old professorial university behind.[11]

In addition to opposing equal student representation in the university's decision-making bodies, the University of Cologne resisted most other reform initiatives and presented itself as the guardian of academic interests in negotiations with policymakers, whose proposals it characterized as lacking the necessary expert knowledge. Accordingly, the university took a conservative stance. When confronted with the idea of establishing more independent assistant professorships, Cologne's professors emphasized the "formative effect of close cooperation between those who teach and their assistants in developing the personality required of a researcher." They were against the introduction of a presidential system based on the American model because they said the university should not be headed by managers or politicians with no relevant expertise, and they resisted the introduction of specialized departments because they saw this as a threat to the individual initiative of researchers. Work on a new university constitution compliant with North Rhine-Westphalia's Higher Education Act of April 1970 dragged on and was finally abandoned in 1973.[12]

At the beginning of the 1970s, the University of Cologne also strongly resisted the establishment of a *Gesamthochschule* (comprehensive university) in Cologne as envisaged by the state government. This would have incorporated the university, the departments of the Rhineland College of Teacher Education located in Cologne, the German Sports College, the State College of Music and the University of Applied Sciences of Cologne. The University Senate and deans feared a loss in quality and prestige and emphasized the differences between these institutions of higher education. The spirit of 1919, when the city's various colleges had been merged to create a novel university, introducing an independent and modern form of applied research and teaching, was no longer in evidence.[13]

Managing Growth

Early in the 1960s, the student body continued to grow rapidly, posing problems for the University of Cologne, as neither the available space nor the size of the teaching staff kept pace with these increases. Educational policymakers recognized that this trend was likely to continue and sought solutions. The Wissenschaftsrat (German Council of Science and Humanities), founded by West Germany's federal and state governments in 1957, presented its first recommendations for the expansion of higher education in October 1960. In the case of Cologne, experts suggested numerous construction measures, fifty-two additional professorships and the creation of new areas of study. They expected the number of students to increase to 9,600. But this estimate was long outdated by the time their recommendations were published. Nearly 14,000 students had enrolled at Cologne for the winter semester of 1960/1961.[14]

At the time, the university had 445 faculty members, with an average of about thirty-one students per teacher. In January 1962, the University Senate discussed various ways of dealing with this situation, which was seen as an unacceptable workload. The ideas proposed differed widely. The only consensus was that the academic staff needed to be increased substantially, the administration should be expanded and more part-time help hired for the university library. The Senate could not agree on the question of employing more non-professorial academic instructors because the extent to which each faculty relied on them varied considerably. The Faculty of Philosophy and the Faculty of Economics and Social Sciences, the two biggest, required high numbers of non-professorial academic staff to conduct their courses with large numbers of students. Under no circumstances did the Senate want to improve conditions in major departments to the detriment of the smaller ones.[15]

Despite these differing viewpoints, the university substantially increased its number of instructors over the next few years, especially that of those who were not full professors. But these measures were unable to reverse the trend, and during the winter semester of 1965/1966, the 554 instructors each had an average of nearly thirty-five students. The situation was similar in terms of space, with the number of students who statistically had to share one lecture hall seat rising by ten percent to three. Distribution of the workload for those who taught courses varied enormously, however: those in the Faculty of Economics and Social Sciences had an average of 101 students, whereas an instructor in the Faculty of Medicine had just under thirteen.[16]

Students as well as teaching and other staff continued to complain about overcrowded lecture halls and libraries, the lack of work spaces and inadequate book stocks. The expansion of the university's buildings had been on the agenda since 1959, but planning and construction took time. Several projects were postponed or interrupted during the first half of the 1960s because of the state's financial constraints. When the budget was announced for 1964, the chancellor reported that all applications for increases in construction funding and academic staff had been dropped. In January 1964, deans complained that overcrowding was having adverse effects on teaching, and that it was impossible for students to pursue "a proper course of study" in particularly popular areas such as business administration or German language and literature. The University of Cologne had already implemented some of the "emergency measures against overcrowding" proposed by the West German Rectors' Conference—such as longer opening hours for libraries, tutorials during the semester break, and counseling services for first-semester students—without lasting effects, and other measures had failed due to the lack of personnel and material resources.[17]

As new universities opened in North Rhine-Westphalia, the situation at the University of Cologne improved to a certain degree in the second half of

the 1960s, but the problem of the rapidly growing student body remained unresolved. The first issue of *Hausmitteilungen*, published on 15 May 1968, reported that the Ministry of Education expected the number of students in Cologne to increase to 50,000 in the long term—an unusually realistic estimate. To cope with this predicted growth, study programs needed to be streamlined, shortages of personnel and space eliminated, faculties further expanded and "other forms of education and training" developed outside the university. The University of Cologne created more jobs and significantly improved the instructor-to-student ratio, so that by the early 1970s, it was about one to twenty-four, but this figure then stagnated. One of the key reasons for this positive development was a substantial increase in non-professorial academic staff in the Faculty of Philosophy and the Faculty of Economics and Social Sciences. The number of regular professorships also increased significantly in all faculties. New buildings were opened almost every year, providing more modern and improved conditions for studying and working. Nevertheless, university committees increasingly restricted admissions to the Faculty of Medicine, as well as to studies in the natural sciences, economics and humanities. Beginning in the 1970s, a numerus clausus was introduced and became a regular means of limiting the number of students admitted. After years of expansion, the university had developed into a modern mass university, but it continued to struggle with unresolved issues associated with this transformation.[18]

↑ Packed courses were the norm in many departments by the end of the 1960s; a lecture on economics for law students in lecture hall B.

Marianne Baudler
1921–2003

Professor in the Faculty of
Mathematics and Natural Sciences

Marianne Baudler studied chemistry in Göttingen and Dresden during World War II and graduated with honors in 1943. Three years later, she obtained her doctorate in Göttingen with a thesis on polysulfanes. Baudler followed her doctoral advisor Franz Fehér to Göttingen in 1947; two years later, they both transferred to the Inorganic Chemistry Institute of the University of Cologne, where she worked as an assistant professor.

She was offered a position as *Diätendozentin* (a *Privatdozentin* employed as a probationary civil servant) a year after having completed her habilitation on pyrophosphoric acids in 1959. In 1963, the university appointed her associate professor of inorganic chemistry. Baudler became director of the Institute of Inorganic Chemistry in 1968 and was given a personal chair. A year later, she was appointed full professor, a position she held until retiring in 1986.

The German National Academy of Sciences Leopoldina accepted Marianne Baudler as a member in 1982. As an expert in the chemistry of nonmetals, she was a corresponding member of the Göttingen Academy of Sciences and Humanities from 1991 onward. She was honored in Würzburg with the Alfred Stock Memorial Prize in 1986 and was a member of the Society of German Chemists for more than 50 years.[19]

Max Delbrück
1906–1981

Professor in the Faculty of
Mathematics and Natural Sciences

The German-American biophysicist Max Delbrück was one of the founders of modern molecular genetics. He went to the University of Cologne as a visiting professor in 1956 and was the founding director of the university's Institute of Genetics, established in 1961. It was Germany's first university research institute dedicated exclusively to molecular biology and a model for other such institutes in Heidelberg, Freiburg and Constance. Delbrück worked as a professor in Cologne from 1961 to 1963 and maintained close ties to the institute throughout the rest of his life.

Delbrück, who came from a family of scholars, received his doctorate in 1929 as a student of physicist Max Born in Göttingen with a study on quantum mechanics. He then left Germany to work abroad. Upon his return in 1932, he went to work at the Kaiser Wilhelm Institute for Chemistry in Berlin, where he was an assistant to Otto Hahn and Lise Meitner and published a groundbreaking study on gene mutation together with other scientists in 1935. Delbrück emigrated to the USA in 1937 and worked first at the California Institute of Technology in Pasadena before moving to Vanderbilt University in Nashville, Tennessee, in 1939. In collaboration with Salvador E. Luria and Alfred D. Hershey, he investigated the replication mechanism and the genetic structure of viruses. In 1969, the three researchers received the Nobel Prize in Medicine for their work.[20]

Rudolf Gross 1917–2008

Professor in the Faculty of Medicine

Rudolf Gross was one of Germany's leading researchers in the field of internal medicine. Originally from Stuttgart, he received his doctorate at Strasbourg in 1944 and then worked as a military doctor and at prisoner of war hospitals for a year. In 1946, he took a position at the University Hospital Tübingen where his mentor Hans Erhard Bock awakened his interest in hematology and oncology. In 1949, they both left Tübingen for the University Hospital of Marburg. Additional training with the distinguished oncologist Hans Lettré in Heidelberg in 1951/1952 influenced his further work. After earning his habilitation in Marburg in 1954, Gross was appointed senior clinical physician there in 1957 and untenured professor in 1960. In 1964, Gross accepted a professorship for internal medicine and was named head of the Medical Clinic I in Cologne. In 1968/1969 he was dean of the Faculty of Medicine.

As a researcher and lecturer, Gross shaped the development of internal medicine at Cologne until retiring in 1982. He co-authored *Die Innere Medizin*, still regarded as a standard textbook on internal medicine to this day. In 1978, he served as president of the German Society for Internal Medicine and, from 1980 to 1988, as head of the academic editorial board of the medical journal *Deutsches Ärzteblatt*. Gross was also interested in philosophical problems related to medicine beyond the strict limits of his discipline. He was honored in 1988 with the Paracelsus Prize of the German Medical Association.[21]

Erich Gutenberg 1897–1984

Professor in the Faculty of Economics and Social Sciences

After 1945, Erich Gutenberg made a decisive contribution to establishing the academic foundations of the field of business administration in Germany. He came from a family of entrepreneurs and enlisted in the German army to fight in World War I. He was awarded a doctorate in economics at the University of Halle in 1921 and graduated with a degree in business administration in Frankfurt am Main in 1926. He obtained his habilitation in Münster in 1928 with a study of corporations as the focus of theories in business administration.

Gutenberg worked for several years in the business sector, including as a certified auditor on the executive board of Deutsche Wirtschaftsprüfungs-AG. In 1938, he was appointed associate professor of business administration at the Bergakademie Clausthal. Gutenberg joined the Nazi Party in 1937, was a member of various Nazi organizations and became a member of the SA in early 1939. He served as an officer in World War II from 1939 to 1943.

His first appointment as full professor was at the University of Jena in 1940, from where he moved to the university in Frankfurt am Main in 1948. But he carried out his most significant work in Cologne. As Eugen Schmalenbach's successor, he established a second Cologne school of business administration between 1951 and 1966. Students jokingly called the volumes of his standard work on the fundamentals of business administration "the Gutenberg bible."[22]

Specialization and Focus

The expansion of Cologne's faculties accelerated in the 1960s, driven by a governmental policy of modernization, the desire to catch up with international developments in the sciences and humanities, and the growing number of students. Many new departments were set up, and in the process, increasing specialization was combined with a focus on specific areas of study and interdisciplinary cooperation. After an intensive initial phase in the first half of the 1960s, university expansion continued vigorously until 1970 and then lost momentum, except in the Faculty of Medicine.[23]

The Faculty of Mathematics and Natural Sciences, the youngest faculty, sought to group its disciplines into departments for mathematics, physics, chemistry, biology, geosciences and human sciences. Here, too, expansion was the result of specialization and the creation of focus areas. The only new institutes added were for nuclear physics in 1961 and crystallography in 1966. In 1961, the Chemistry Institute was divided into the Organic Chemistry Institute and the Inorganic Chemistry Institute. Botany and zoology each had three chairs and geology had two. Mathematics grouped its specialized disciplines into one institute in 1965. The Institute of Genetics established six departments by 1972, and it set up one of Cologne's first Collaborative Research Centers (SFBs), specializing in microbiology, in 1970. The Department of Physics substantially increased its professorships with a focus on nuclear and solid-state physics, establishing an SFB for the physics of metals in 1974.[24]

The Faculty of Mathematics and Natural Sciences created a department of human sciences bringing together a rather amorphous group of disciplines that encompassed both natural sciences and cultural studies. These included geography, prehistory, early history, ethnology and psychology. In 1963, the study of psychology was split into a natural science branch and a more comprehensive branch that was integrated into the Faculty of Philosophy. It moved with the Institute of Social Psychology—founded by sociology professors in 1962—into a shared building complex in 1964.[25]

The Faculty of Philosophy also experienced a period of rapid expansion until 1966, founding nine of the twelve new institutes it set up between 1960 and 1975. The East Asian Department and Germany's first phonetics institute opened up new areas of research. The Martin Buber Institute for Jewish Studies, established in 1966, was the second of its kind in West Germany. In 1965, the Department of History became an influential center for research into the history of the nation-state in Europe. In view of the heterogeneity of its disciplines, the faculty sought to bring order to the diversity of its many departments and special areas of study by drawing on the liberal arts tradition and forming units based on the concepts of philosophy, language, history and art. Its disciplines, as stated in 1969, provided useful insights and methods "to be shared across all faculties" in order to "understand the world." As disciplines that "served" other faculties and their areas of study, they maintained a reciprocal exchange with these other faculties.[26]

Twenty-four new institutes were set up in the Faculty of Economics and Social Sciences, more than half of them by 1965. The research institutes of sociology, social policy, political science and European affairs emerged in 1960 from predecessor organizations. The Central Archive for Empirical Social Research established in 1960 was the first of its kind in Europe. The Institute for Comparative Social Research set up in 1965 was an important addition to the study of sociology in Cologne. The vocational, economic and social education programs were grouped into a single institute, and an institute for economic and social history was created. The first chair for computer science was established in 1971. The accelerated specialization was particularly pronounced in business administration, which established ten new special chairs by the mid-1970s. Two new institutes in the fields of insurance and transportation studies strengthened cooperation with other faculties.[27]

The Faculty of Law expanded especially in the areas of civil law, public law and international law, which had a strong tradition in Cologne. More than half of these fifteen new institutes were established by 1966. A striking number of special institutes were founded, some dedicated to traditional areas of study, such as insurance and procedural law, and others in the newer fields of legal studies focusing on energy, East Germany and broadcasting; the latter worked in close cooperation with the public radio and television broadcasting network WDR (Westdeutscher Rundfunk) based in Cologne. The study of international law was further expanded in 1960 with the establishment of the Institute of European Community Law, which moved into the new House for International Law in 1970, along with two other institutes with an international focus.[28]

In the Faculty of Medicine, new institutes and special disciplines were continually created as a result of ongoing progress in medical research and the development of West Germany's health care system. These included institutes for nuclear medicine, anesthesiology and virology, which were complemented by a new chair for cardiology in 1971. From 1970, an SFB for cardiovascular research consolidated Cologne's traditional strength in this area of medicine. Such areas of focus, combined with interdisciplinary cooperation, played an increasingly important role in basic research. The Center for Experimental Medicine emerged in 1972 from Germany's first department for experimental surgery. The Institute of Medical History, founded in 1965, was also innovative. In 1974, two new clinics opened for urology and radiation therapy.[29]

↓ The Faculty of Philosophy's seminar building was officially opened in 1974.

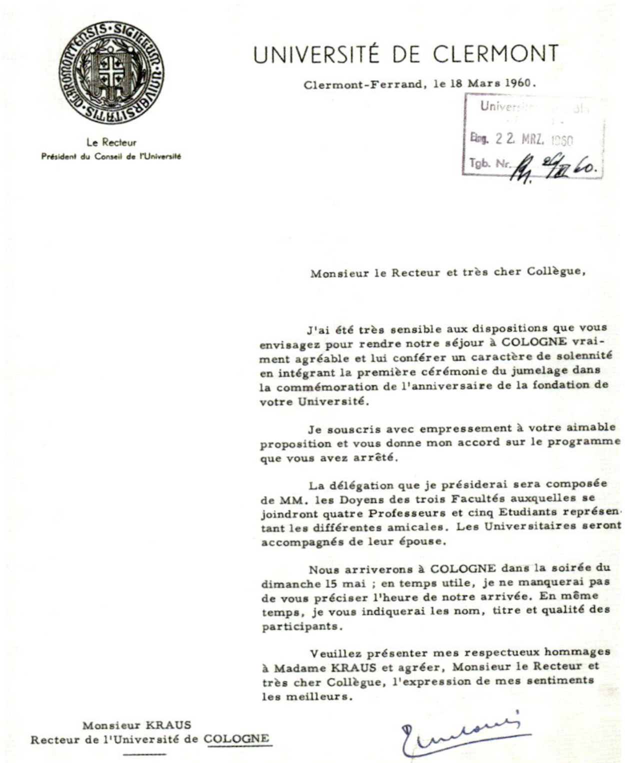

Le Recteur
Président du Conseil de l'Université

UNIVERSITÉ DE CLERMONT

Clermont-Ferrand, le 18 Mars 1960.

Eing. 22. MRZ. 1960
Tgb. Nr.

Monsieur le Recteur et très cher Collègue,

J'ai été très sensible aux dispositions que vous envisagez pour rendre notre séjour à COLOGNE vraiment agréable et lui conférer un caractère de solennité en intégrant la première cérémonie du jumelage dans la commémoration de l'anniversaire de la fondation de votre Université.

Je souscris avec empressement à votre aimable proposition et vous donne mon accord sur le programme que vous avez arrêté.

La délégation que je présiderai sera composée de MM. les Doyens des trois Facultés auxquelles se joindront quatre Professeurs et cinq Etudiants représentant les différentes amicales. Les Universitaires seront accompagnés de leur épouse.

Nous arriverons à COLOGNE dans la soirée du dimanche 15 mai ; en temps utile, je ne manquerai pas de vous préciser l'heure de notre arrivée. En même temps, je vous indiquerai les nom, titre et qualité des participants.

Veuillez présenter mes respectueux hommages à Madame KRAUS et agréer, Monsieur le Recteur et très cher Collègue, l'expression de mes sentiments les meilleurs.

Monsieur KRAUS
Recteur de l'Université de COLOGNE

Partnership Program between Cologne and Clermont-Ferrand

1960
University of Cologne Archives

Germany and France became close partners after 1945. The reconciliation between the two countries also created opportunities to strengthen academic cooperation. In 1960, the universities of Cologne and Clermont-Ferrand established a partnership program, resulting in the increased exchange of academic faculty and students—nearly three years before Chancellor Konrad Adenauer and President Charles de Gaulle signed the Franco-German Elysée Treaty on 22 January 1963. It was the University of Cologne's first formal partnership program with another European institution of higher learning. A delegation from Clermont-Ferrand visited Cologne from 15 to 19 May 1960 and attended the university's anniversary celebration on 18 May. Two months before, Rector Pierre Louis had written to his counterpart in Cologne, Theodor Kraus, and informed him that he would be coming to Cologne along with three deans, four professors and five students, and that the professors would be accompanied by their wives. Two years after this visit, on 24 July 1962, the universities of Cologne and Clermont-Ferrand signed a partnership agreement focusing on the exchange of students and academic staff.[30]

Megaphone

1967
University of Cologne Archives

Loud and clear—making themselves heard was what the student protests in Cologne from 1967 to 1969 were all about. The megaphone pictured above was used at rallies and teach-ins. Today it is housed in the University of Cologne Archives and is a popular showpiece in exhibitions on Cologne's student movement. A megaphone was also essential for students protesting on 28 May 1968. This is the day they decided, during a discussion of the Emergency Acts organized by the AStA in lecture hall A, to march to the city center, where the printing and paper industry union was already holding a demonstration. An article in the local press the next day was headlined "Attack on the Emergency Acts: 1,500 students charge toward Alter Markt square." At the fore was Lothar Gothe of the German Socialist Student Union (SDS) of Cologne, holding a megaphone in his hand and chanting slogans; beside him was Bernd Peterson, head of the AStA. The *Kölner Stadt-Anzeiger* reported that the students were "greeted enthusiastically by the union members."[31]

The Beginnings of Internationalization

In late 1959, the University of Cologne participated in the founding of the European Rectors' Conference (CRE), sending a clear signal of interest in a stronger international orientation. The CRE was created in the context of the first steps toward European integration. The University of Cologne was one of the driving forces behind this first organization of European universities. As president of the West German Rectors' Conference, Cologne representative Hermann Jahreiß headed the German delegation. One of the first vice-presidents of the CRE, he was jokingly referred to as the "Foreign Minister of German Universities" because of his influence.[32]

It was Jahreiß and his successor in the rector's office, Theodor Kraus, who initiated the first partnership with a foreign university. Kraus, an economic geographer, had complained to the University Senate that although partnerships with German universities existed, there were none with French universities; he was then given the mandate to change this. On 24 July 1962, the University of Cologne signed an agreement with the University of Clermont-Ferrand providing for regular student exchanges with reciprocal scholarship awards. During the 1960s, Cologne offered ten one-semester scholarships for each winter semester, and Clermont-Ferrand offered seven scholarships for each academic year. Initially, the participants were mostly students from Cologne pursuing Romance language and literature studies and students from Clermont-Ferrand pursuing German studies, but law students also began participating in the mid-1970s. There was also academic cooperation in the form of guest lectures and university weeks which were attended by delegations on a reciprocal basis.[33]

The student exchange program fostered the University of Cologne's international ties. The university had agreed to a first regular exchange scholarship with the University of Copenhagen back in 1948. By the end of the 1960s, twelve more agreements had been concluded with universities abroad. They led to a rapid increase in the number of foreign students at Cologne, whereas the number of Cologne students studying abroad was at first significantly lower. Some 1,200 students from ninety-three countries around the world were studying at Cologne in 1969. Foreign students were looked after by the Akademisches Auslandsamt (Academic Foreign Office) founded in 1951, formerly the Akademische Ausstauschstelle.[34]

Exchanges were generally initiated by individual professors, departments or faculties. The exchange program with Pennsylvania State University that began late in 1961 was the first between a West German and an American university. It was initiated by Professor Dagobert de Levie, founder and director of the Study Abroad Program, who had studied at Cologne and fled antisemitic persecution in Germany in 1938. In the spring of 1962, twenty-five American students came to Cologne for the first time to spend a semester at the Faculty of Economics and Social Sciences. But the decisive factor was reciprocity: in 1964, the first group of Cologne students went to Pennsylvania. By the summer semester of 1971, about a hundred German and some two hundred American students had participated in the program. In December 1970, the University of Cologne made Dagobert de Levie a lifetime honorary senator for his achievements.[35]

An important step toward internationalization was the founding in 1960 of the Staatliches Studienkolleg, a state preparatory college for foreign students. Housed in a new building in Cologne-Lindenthal, the college was conceived specifically for students from developing countries. In two semesters that preceded university study programs, more than forty teachers taught some eighty students German, academic methods and basic knowledge in relevant subject areas. Students from Africa, who were not numerous in West Germany in the 1960s, were

looked after by the university in collaboration with the White Fathers, a Catholic society now called Missionaries of Africa. In 1962/1963, the missionaries built a residence for about eighty students in Cologne-Bickendorf, in which half the students were African and half were German—a modern approach to integration and a model that would set a precedent.[36]

The cooperation between the University of Cologne and Kabul University was a pioneering project of a special kind. Contacts based on guest lectures led to the signing of a partnership agreement between both universities on 3 March 1962. The agreement was designed to support Kabul University in establishing an economics faculty to provide specialist training in economics and administration in Afghanistan. A contract between West Germany and Afghanistan created the legal basis for this new form of educational development aid. The Faculty of Economics and Social Sciences carried out the project and set up a working group especially for this purpose. Despite many financial, organizational and linguistic obstacles, the cooperation was successful. On average, five university instructors from Cologne and one assistant worked in Kabul each semester. Afghan scholarship holders studied in Cologne. The agreement was revised in August 1966 and the instructors from Cologne were joined by colleagues from Bonn and Bochum. There were now eight university instructors and two assistants in Kabul. The University of Cologne ended its partnership on 21 January 1981 following the invasion of Afghanistan by Soviet troops in late 1979.[37]

↑ The partnership agreement with Kabul University was extended on 27 October 1976: (from left) Prof. Dr. Clemens Menze, rector of the University of Cologne; Ambassador of Afghanistan G. Farugh; Prof. Dr. Rolf Leis, rector of the University of Bonn.

Ulla Hahn
born 1945

Student in the
Faculty of Philosophy

In her novel *Im Spiel der Zeit*, published in 2014, the celebrated poet and author Ulla Hahn writes about her alter ego Hilla Palm's days as a student in Cologne, a defining period in the author's own life. Hahn grew up in a working-class family in Monheim am Rhein, obtained her Abitur through adult education courses and enrolled at the University of Cologne in 1965. She studied German language and literature, sociology, and history. While in Cologne, she became involved in the student movement and was confronted with her literature professor's Nazi past.

Hahn immersed herself in reading and became deeply involved in political activities; for a time, she was a member of the German Communist Party. She worked as a journalist and published her first poems. In 1973, she continued her studies in Hamburg, obtaining her doctorate in 1978 with a thesis on West German democratic and socialist literature in the 1960s. She worked as an editor of the cultural program at Radio Bremen from 1979 to 1989 and as a lecturer at the universities of Hamburg, Bremen and Oldenburg.

Hahn's breakthrough as a poet came in 1981 with the publication of her first collection of poems, *Herz über Kopf*. Hahn has been a freelance writer since 1989 and published her first novel, *Ein Mann im Haus*, in 1991. Ten years later, she wrote *Das verborgene Wort*, the first of a series of successful autobiographical novels. Ulla Hahn has received numerous awards for her literary work.[38]

Georg Heberer
1920–1999

Professor in the
Faculty of Medicine

Georg Heberer was an exceptionally talented surgeon. Rudolf Zenker, with whom he worked as a resident in Mannheim after obtaining his doctorate in Tübingen in 1945, helped him find his calling. In 1951, Heberer followed his mentor to the University Hospital of Marburg, where he completed his habilitation in 1953 and was awarded his first associate professorship. In 1958, Heberer and Zenker performed the first open-heart surgery in Germany.

Heberer was granted a full professorship at the University of Cologne in 1959. Initially head of the University Surgical Clinic in Cologne-Merheim, he was appointed director of the Surgical Clinic Cologne-Lindenthal in 1963. He assumed the position of dean of the Faculty of Medicine in 1967/1968.

In Cologne, Heberer promoted experimental surgical techniques and advocated the establishment of anesthesia and urology as independent disciplines. Under his leadership, the Surgical Clinic in Cologne became a leader in the surgical replacement of blood vessels and the clipping of aneurysms. He also developed innovative procedures in gastrointestinal and endocrine surgery. Heberer accepted a position at the Ludwig Maximilian University in Munich in 1973, where he helped turn the Großhadern Clinic into one of the world's leading organ transplantation clinics.[39]

Ferdinand Hermens 1906–1998

Professor in the Faculty of Economics and Social Sciences

Securing parliamentary democracy was the life work of political scientist Ferdinand Hermens. The avowed Catholic studied economics in Bonn, earning his doctorate in 1930 with a thesis on democracy and capitalism under the supervision of Joseph A. Schumpeter. His post-doctoral dissertation at the Technical University of Berlin was rejected in 1934. The Centrist democrat emigrated to the USA via the United Kingdom in 1935. Hermens initially worked at the Catholic University of America in Washington, D.C., transferring in 1938 to the University of Notre Dame in Indiana, where he was appointed a full professor of political science in 1945. His most important work, *Democracy or Anarchy? A Study of Proportional Representation*, was published in 1941.

From 1948 on, Hermens assumed visiting professorships in Germany, and in 1959 he succeeded Heinrich Brüning as chair for political science at the University of Cologne. In 1960, he became the director of the newly founded Research Institute for Political Science and European Affairs. At Cologne, Hermens established empirical political science research in Germany, but he remained an outsider. He was a vocal but unsuccessful advocate of a majority voting system. After resigning in late 1971, he returned to the USA in 1972, continuing his work as a lecturer and researcher to an advanced age.[40]

Hilde Kaufmann 1920–1981

Professor in the Faculty of Law

In 1970, Hilde Kaufmann was the first woman to be appointed a professor in the Faculty of Law at the University of Cologne. Holding a postdoctoral degree in criminal law, she made criminology the focus of her research and founded the Criminological Research Center within the Institute of Criminology in 1971. The close connection between her field of study and criminal law, in particular criminal proceedings and the penal system, enabled Kaufmann to introduce new perspectives in criminology.

Kaufmann studied law in Münster and in Bonn, where she was awarded a doctorate in 1950. Following her second state examination in law in 1952, she worked at the Bonn district attorney's office, and from 1953 to 1956 for the Parole and Clemency Board for War Criminals. She then took a position at Bonn University as an assistant professor, completing her habilitation in 1961 with a study entitled *Die Abgrenzung des materiellen vom formellen Strafrecht* (The distinction between substantive and formal criminal law). She was appointed untenured professor at Bonn in 1965 and full professor at the University of Kiel in 1966.

At Cologne, Kaufmann was head of both the research center and the renowned Institute of Criminology. She died at a relatively young age and was only able to complete two of the three volumes of her textbook of criminology which deals with the causes of crime and forms of punishment: *Kriminologie I* (1971) and *Kriminologie III* (1977).[41]

“No Advanced Seminar without an Intermediary Exam”

The transition from an elitist institution to a university for a larger section of society was particularly noticeable at the University of Cologne, even though the changes varied from discipline to discipline. The expansion of the institutes and departments lagged behind the rapid pace of development, despite many newly created jobs and building projects. Students complained about overcrowded courses and inadequate facilities. They took longer to finish their studies, and the number of university dropouts increased. In 1964, calls for radical reform became louder, intensified by the heated debate surrounding the “educational state of emergency.” The University of Cologne, however, took a long time to act. In July 1965, the Senate adopted a proposal by the West German Rectors’ Conference and decided to limit the length of study to eight plus two semesters as of the summer semester of 1966. The student representatives agreed to this measure but also urged that binding curricula should finally be introduced for all courses of study, a step they had long demanded. This, however, was a long way off for the University of Cologne.[42]

The debate on university education was given a boost by the recommendations for academic reform drafted by the German Council of Science and Humanities in the summer of 1966. Although the committee was fundamentally in favor of preserving the Humboldtian notion of the "unity of research and teaching," it proposed restricting the length of studies to a standard four and a half years and the introduction of a three-part structure. The core of this concept was a career-oriented educational program from which students could graduate with a master's degree, a *Diplom* or a state examination. Students in the first semesters were to be provided with student counseling, benefit from small seminar groups and attend compulsory courses until they passed their mandatory intermediate examinations. For students who were particularly gifted, the experts proposed a research-oriented, two-year graduate study program that could be completed with a doctoral degree. In view of the need for lifelong learning in a modern knowledge society, they additionally recommended that universities offer continuing education and degree programs for people who already held jobs and were seeking further academic training.[43]

The recommendations of the German Council of Science and Humanities met with some severe criticism, particularly because the council proposed a uniform solution for all faculties and watered down the concept of the unity of research and teaching in favor of professional training. In Cologne there was no immediate official reaction. The opening of the Ruhr University in Bochum in 1965 had helped ease the situation at Cologne's Faculty of Economics and Social Sciences, reducing its most pressing problem. However, the recession of 1966/1967 put a damper on long-term plans to expand capacities. As a result of austerity measures, there were insufficient funds, especially for non-professorial academic staff, "to enable the university to take significant steps toward the urgently needed reform of the academic system, such as streamlining and structuring study programs to facilitate intensive work in smaller groups," as stated in the rector's 1967 annual report. The reform dragged along, as did the drafting of curricula. The strongest opposition to the introduction of compulsory intermediate examinations came from the student body.[44]

Considering the diversity of the faculties, it was difficult to implement a uniform reform, but some disciplines made progress. The English Department, one of the largest at the university with some 1,300 students, developed its own concept and had already implemented parts of it in early 1968. The key element of the reform drew on the council's main recommendations: "No advanced seminar without an intermediate exam; no intermediate exam without a proseminar; no proseminar without a successfully completed introductory course." With the exception of lectures, there were to be no more than twenty to thirty-five students in the classes. This necessitated a complex organizational process involving central planning with the help of a letter board, the creation of a student file using punch cards and a standardized course registration system, enabling administrators to place all students in more than ninety courses and seminars in only a few hours. This entailed considerable bureaucratic effort which was to be handled by a "modernized central administration" in the future.[45]

Nevertheless, all of these initiatives implemented by the University of Cologne were provisional. The success of the reform depended on the State Higher Education Act. Work on the draft had begun in fall 1968, and it was hotly debated in the Cologne University Senate. Rector Heinz Hübner, chair of the influential Commission for the Development of Higher Education in North Rhine-Westphalia, was the advocate of Cologne's viewpoint in the commission and opposed the feared "centralization of academic activities." The Higher Education Act, which went into effect in April 1970, adopted some of the proposals made by the German Council of Science and Humanities in 1966 and established a legal framework. Over the following years, the faculties of the University of Cologne would apply this framework in drafting new rules and regulations for admissions, study requirements, and examinations. Despite the differences between the various disciplines, the duration of most degree programs was limited, and they were divided into basic and advanced courses with intermediate examinations.[46]

← The University of Cologne became a modern mass university in the 1960s; crowded hall in the university's main building during enrollment.

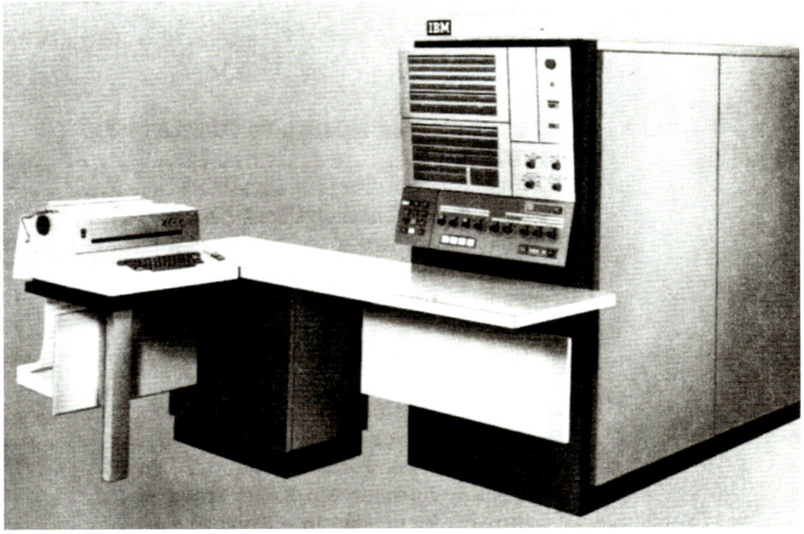

IBM 360/30

1969
Regional Computing Center

To satisfy the university's need for increased computing and data processing power, the Computing Center of the University of Cologne (RZK), founded in 1964, rented the IBM 360/30 electronic data processing system in 1966. The IBM 360 was the first universal mainframe computer and is regarded today as the American company's most important invention. The number 360 refers to the 360 degrees of a circle and the universal applicability of the system. The smallest model in the series, the 360/30, was 43 times faster than its predecessor and had 66 times more memory. The rented computer system was installed in a seminar room in the basement of the Institute of Mathematics. Despite a significant increase in capacity compared to Cologne's first and long outdated ER 56 computer, the limits of the IBM computer were also soon reached. In a memo of 3 November, the RZK informed university staff that "the old IBM 360/30 mainframe computer will be removed after Christmas 1969. All software must be migrated to the new computer system by that time." The memo gave rise to concern among users. Worried that moving the programs to the new system would slow down workflows, they protested against the dismantling of the IBM system—to no avail: The rental agreement between IBM Germany and the University of Cologne ended on 31 December 1969.[47]

Skeleton Collection

1972
Anatomical Collection of the Center of Anatomy

The anatomical collection is one of the treasures of the University of Cologne. When the Institute of Anatomy moved into the last available rooms in the new building on Joseph Stelzmann Straße in the late 1960s, it was considered one of the most modern facilities of its kind.

On the occasion of the 67th meeting of the German Anatomical Society in Cologne in 1972, the holdings of the macroscopic educational collection were reclassified and labeled, and drawings of each were prepared. Anyone who sets foot in the building today will—like the guests attending the event nearly 50 years ago—see lots of bones. Mammals arranged by size provide an insight into evolutionary changes. The visitor's gaze wanders over the enormous neck vertebrae of an elephant to the expansive lumbar vertebrae of a Greenland whale. In the locked showcases in the corridors leading to the lecture halls, one can see human organs floating in alcohol, including an adult human's stomach. There are also specimens that were produced using a special technique called corrosion casting. The cavities of a corrosion-cast kidney, for example, were injected with colored plastic, which then hardened, allowing the soft tissue to be removed. The large hall full of mostly anatomic pathology specimens, both wet and dry, is also very impressive. These specimens are still used by students today as points of reference for comparative anatomy.[48]

The Discourse on Research and Teaching

When the University of Cologne opened in 1919, the aim was to introduce new approaches to teaching and research. After 1945, the emphasis shifted to the allegedly classical values of a *universitas litterarum* based on humanist and Christian ideals. But regardless of their differing positions, the professors all believed in the ideals of unity and freedom of research and teaching as the university's core principles. As early as the 1920s, but especially after 1945, academics discussed whether the increasing number of students and the "massification" of higher education posed a threat to this concept. Fundamental changes taking place during the 1960s again raised this question, this time with far greater urgency.[49]

At the height of these turbulent developments, two of Cologne's most influential professors discussed the prospects for teaching and research in the University of Cologne's 1968/1969 yearbook: Theodor Schieder, a historian and well-connected academic administrator who served as rector of the university from 1962 to 1964 and vice-president of the West German Rectors' Conference in 1965/1966, and Heinz Hübner, a legal scholar and experienced educational policymaker who was vice-president of the German Association of University Professors and Lecturers from 1961 to 1969 and rector of the university from 1968 to 1970. At the association's fourteenth annual conference in 1964, both had jointly opposed the radical demands for reform put forward by Hans Dichgans, a CDU Bundestag member who wanted to abandon the concept of "Humboldtian academic freedom." Dichgans also called for a presidential constitution based on the American model and fundamental changes in habilitation and appointment procedures. Schieder and Hübner were open to reform, but in response to students and policymakers, they insisted that the university's well-established organizational structure be maintained, while conceding that changes would have to be made to meet modern-day needs; these changes, however, would require professional competence and a sense of proportion. They categorically rejected equal participation in decision-making processes at all levels, and believed in preserving the traditional model of a professorial university in which the "community of instructors and students" was based on a master-pupil relationship.[50]

Theodor Schieder wrote in 1968 that the "unity of teaching and research as a structural principle of the university" was in grave danger. He felt that university research was under pressure due to an "excessive strain on educational capacities," especially in the so-called "mass" subjects, but also because of the new trend toward "big science" which was incompatible with the university's structural framework. Among other things, Schieder proposed that lecturers should alternate between research and teaching semesters so as to be relieved of teaching duties while they were engaged in research, and that in the "large-scale" disciplines, "departments with regular teaching" should be separated from associated "research institutes." The University of Cologne had already benefited from this dual arrangement, and Schieder had himself set up a successful research unit in 1965 in the Department of History. To secure the "future of university research," Schieder considered creating "professorships for advanced students" and "research professorships" based on the American model, even if this was not consistent with German university tradition. He found the proposal of the German Council of Science and Humanities to "establish focal points" to be sensible. He thus consciously abandoned the "old principle of university equality, that is, the equal representation of all subjects at all universities" in favor of "collaborative systems." As a member of the main committee and senate of the German Research Foundation, Schieder was personally involved in setting up Collaborative Research Centers. He believed that the faculties should be responsible for the advancement of interdisciplinarity and cited cooperation between the social and historical sciences as an example.[51]

In his 1969 article, Heinz Hübner, then presiding rector, dealt with specific financial and organizational issues in more detail than Schieder had, and he did not hold back with his criticism of the demands of the student movement. He shared his predecessor's conviction that the unity and freedom of research formed the essence of the university. Hübner wrote that even though teaching was currently paramount, it was conceivable only on the basis of the primacy of research. The "continued existence of our society" depended on this combination. Schieder had used similar arguments. Hübner called for a high degree of autonomy for colleges and universities, as well as "freedom of research." This was the only way new ideas could be developed in scholarship. He was concerned about early career scholars being "burdened with didactic assignments," deprived of research opportunities, and exposed to an uncertain professional future. To preserve the unity of research and teaching, given society's demand for educational programs that were of practical benefit and the increasing tendency toward specialization, Hübner proposed that students should study in phases, starting with preliminary courses followed by a structured phase of basic education; only once they had completed these would students learn to conduct actual research. He wanted to adapt Humboldt's combination of "specialist education" and "cultivation of the personality" to conditions at a modern mass university. However, Hübner himself questioned whether this could work. Theodor Schieder, on the other hand, expressed such concerns only privately. In July 1968, he wrote to his friend and colleague Werner Conze: "To a certain extent, the severance of research and teaching is unavoidable."[52]

↓ Close cooperation between instructors and students was also typical of research and teaching in the natural sciences; working in the lab at the University of Cologne around 1970.

Alex Meyer
1879–1978

Honorary professor
in the Faculty of Law

The legal scholar Alex Meyer had a passion for aviation. While still a young court assessor, he published a paper in 1908 entitled *Die Erschließung des Luftraums in ihren rechtlichen Folgen* (The legal consequences of "opening up" air space)—a new field of law at the time. A year later he obtained his balloon pilot license, and he was one of the founders of the German Pilots' Association in 1910.

Meyer was awarded his doctorate in Leipzig and pursued a career in the Weimar Republic as a civil servant of the *Reich*. In 1933, he worked in the provincial government in Düsseldorf, where he was forced into retirement in 1936 due to his Jewish background. In 1938, he was unable to accept a teaching position in aviation law at New York University as he was denied a visa, so he emigrated in 1939 to Zurich instead. His book *Freiheit der Luft als Rechtsproblem* (The freedom of air space as a legal problem), published in 1944, confirmed his reputation as a leading expert in international aviation law.

In 1950, Meyer accepted a teaching position at the University of Cologne. One year later he founded a research unit for air law that became, in 1960, the Institute of Air and Space Law, which still exists today. He began publishing the internationally acclaimed journal *Zeitschrift für Luftrecht und Weltraumrechtsfragen* in 1952. Meyer was appointed honorary professor a year later. He was head of the institute and the journal until the age of 95.[53]

Fritz Schalk
1902–1980

Professor in the
Faculty of Philosophy

Fritz Schalk was one of Germany's most important scholars of Romance languages and literature. He was born in Vienna, where he obtained his doctorate in 1927 for his work on Blaise Pascal. Schalk earned his habilitation in Hamburg in 1932 with a thesis on the French Enlightenment. He assumed his first professorship in Rostock in 1933 but came under attack for his liberal views and was relocated to Cologne in 1936. At Cologne, he was given a chair in 1941. As the dean of the Faculty of Philosophy in 1948/1949, he played a significant role in the reconstruction of the university. He reopened the university's Petrarca Institute in 1949 and, despite retiring in 1970, continued to be its head until he died.

During Schalk's time as professor, the Romance Department developed into the largest such department in West Germany. The student exchange program with Romance countries was promoted by Schalk who, as head of the Academic Foreign Office, was internationally well connected. He combined the study of language, literature and cultural history in his work on Western European Enlightenment. His book on the audience in Italian humanism, published in 1955, gave new impetus to the study of the early modern period. As the publisher of the internationally recognized academic journal *Romanische Forschungen*, and an administrator and successful lecturer, Schalk had a lasting influence on the study of Romance languages and literature in West Germany.[54]

Theodor Schieder
1908–1984

Professor in the
Faculty of Philosophy

Theodor Schieder had a formative influence on historical research in the young Federal Republic of Germany. His professional career during the Nazi period has been a matter of much debate since the 1990s. From 1935 on, Schieder played a leading role in "*Ostforschung*" (eastern studies) at the University of Königsberg. These studies were intended to provide the Nazi regime with arguments for the revision of the Treaty of Versailles. In 1937, Schieder joined the Nazi Party and became involved in propaganda and training. In his memorandum of October 1939 on the "Germanization" of Polish territories, he called for the "de-Judaization of the rest of Poland" and warned against a "new Polish leadership." After having completed his habilitation under the supervision of Kurt von Raumer, Schieder assumed von Raumer's chair at the University of Königsberg in 1942.

Schieder was appointed to a professorship at the University of Cologne in 1948. Although his work as the editor of *Documents on the Expulsion of the Germans from Eastern-Central Europe* (1953–1961) initially followed in the tradition of "*Ostforschung*," in a later statement he insisted that the expulsion was to be viewed as "a reaction to National Socialist policies." Schieder paved the way for social history in West Germany, and many of his students later became distinguished historians. He established important academic institutions, held influential positions in academia and—as dean and then rector from 1962 to 1964—contributed to shaping his University.[55]

Dorothee Sölle
1929–2003

Privatdozentin in the
Faculty of Philosophy

Dorothee Sölle, daughter of legal scholar Hans Carl Nipperdey, was one of the most controversial representatives of theological Protestantism. She studied philosophy, classical philology, Protestant theology and German literature, earning her doctorate in Göttingen in 1954 with a thesis on German literature. After working as a teacher and radio journalist in Cologne, she assumed a position as an assistant professor at the University of Aachen in 1962 and moved to the University of Cologne's German Department in 1964. The mother of four completed her habilitation on the relationship between theology and poetry there in 1971 and became a *Privatdozentin*.

Dorothee Sölle was most influential as an author and public intellectual. In 1968, she published *Atheistisch an Gott glauben* (An atheist approach to believing in God) and drafted a proposal for a new Christian ethic, in which Christ, who shares our life and is active among us, replaces God as the central figure. During the nationwide meeting of German Catholics that same year, she established the Politisches Nachtgebet, political evening prayers that were held until 1972 in Cologne's Antoniter Church. As a politically active theologian, she opposed the Vietnam War, supported Latin American liberation movements and was involved in the German peace movement. This stood in the way of her appointment to a professorship in Germany. Instead, she was a professor of systematic theology at the Union Theological Seminary in New York from 1975 to 1987.[56]

The Politics of Protest

Rudolfplatz was in a deadlock. Young people had blocked rail tracks, and streetcars were being attacked by angry demonstrators. On 21 October 1966, some eight thousand pupils and students protested against a sharp increase in fares imposed by the KVB, the city's transport company. Ruthless police action led to violent clashes that lasted until the early hours of the morning. This "KVB battle" made headlines throughout Germany.[57]

Broader political issues did not play a part in this protest yet. The politicization of Cologne students first became apparent following Benno Ohnesorg's violent death in Berlin on 2 June 1967. Five days later, six thousand students gathered for a silent march in Cologne. Hundreds attended a commemorative ceremony where Rector Werner Scheid was one of the speakers. During the following weeks, hundreds of students joined events to protest the banning of the Communist Party of Germany (KPD) and the Emergency Acts, which were seen as attacks on democracy. Protests against the German government's grand coalition policies, which until then had been led primarily by the Extra-parliamentary Opposition (APO), were linked to student demands for fundamental change in the university.[58]

Students created an "alternative public sphere" using new forms of action, such as go-ins, sit-ins and teach-ins, and their own communication media, including magazines, leaflets, posters and happenings. Their sometimes spectacular protests expressed a new understanding of democracy, attracted a great deal of media attention, and forced professors to engage in public debate about (university) policy issues. Cologne students staged their first sit-in on 19 June 1967 to block the entrance to the Faculty of Economics and Social Sciences and protest against looming admission restrictions. Other actions targeted new study regulations, new rules on the duration of studies, and the poor study conditions.[59]

Students from groups across the entire political spectrum called for the democratization of the university, focusing at first on the question of which issues they could have a say on. The university's constitution merely referred vaguely to "student affairs." At their first general meeting late in 1967, students called on the Senate to define their rights of participation more clearly. To underline the urgency of their demands, up to 3,000 people staged a sit-in on 1 February 1968 in what became the largest of the actions of the Cologne student movement. Two days later, the Senate put together a "negative catalog," stating that student representatives were not to be involved in issues considered to be the internal affairs of the faculty, nor in nominations and appointments. As of July 1968, two representatives of the non-professorial academic staff without a habilitation degree and two student representatives were allowed to participate in Senate meetings.[60]

But the students were not satisfied with these concessions. The assassination attempt on Rudi Dutschke on 11 April 1968 radicalized the protest movement even further. Around 1,500 students blocked traffic at Rudolfplatz on 13 April, and 800 students ran through the streets chanting. That evening, about 400 people in the city center tried to prevent the *Bild* newspaper from being distributed because they blamed it for the attack on Dutschke. On 17 April, more than 1,400 students joined a sit-in at the university auditorium. When the grand coalition passed the Emergency Acts on 30 May, students set up a barricade in front of the main entrance of the university they had renamed "Rosa Luxemburg University."[61]

The rift between the two sides deepened. While the rector and deans were still talking with students about university reforms during the 1968 summer semester, the situation escalated to the point that, by mid-October of the same year, the rectorate changed hands for the first time under police protection with only a few people in attendance, rather than in the usual official public ceremony. On 23 November 1968, students occupied the rectorate over the weekend and demanded access to all university committees. A teach-in with 1,600 participants underlined this demand. Students forced their way into a meeting of the Faculty of Philosophy on 4 December, after their request that the meeting be open to the public had been rejected; the rector called in the police to end the protest. And shortly before Christmas, a university building was locked to protect a Senate session convened there to discuss the incident.[62]

A ten-year-old exhibition on German jurists during the Nazi era came to Cologne early in 1969, after it had already caused a furor at other universities; curators supplemented it with information on the Nazi past of legal scholars at Cologne. On the day it opened, about 1,200 students participated in a teach-in titled "Smash the Political Justice System." Rector Heinz Hübner called in the police to break up the event. Students then occupied the Institute of Criminology, whose director, Richard Lange, was one of the professors revealed to have had an active Nazi past. Although the confrontation with the university's Nazi legacy became part of the conflict about (university) policy, it was not a central issue.[63]

The new law on higher education planned by the state of North Rhine-Westphalia had dominated debate within the university since the 1969 summer semester. It was widely rejected by students because it failed to fulfill their demands for student participation. Strikes, some of which lasted for weeks, boycotts of lectures, and protests followed. Left-wing activists impeded the election of the rector, occupied the AStA office, damaged parts of the rectorate, and disrupted an event presided over by the rector. After that, the protest movement lost its momentum.[64]

← Students barricaded the university's main entrance in the early hours of 30 May 1968.

The Schlesinger Collection

1972

Martin Buber Institute for Jewish Studies

The founding director of the Martin Buber Institute for Jewish Studies at the University of Cologne, Professor Johann Maier, stated in his speech at the institute's inauguration in 1966 that "only an institute of Jewish studies equipped with sufficient source material and specialist literature can […] fulfill its task of conveying a historically sound understanding of Judaism based on its own knowledge of sources." Obviously, "the destructive actions of the past" would not make it easy "to procure the material that was once so abundant in this country." The foundation for today's specialist Jewish library comprising some 38,000 volumes was laid with the support of the German Research Foundation in 1972, when the institute acquired the private library of Kalman Schlesinger, a bookseller and Judaica specialist originally from Cologne who had emigrated to Jerusalem. This brought to Cologne around 100 prints produced before the nineteenth century, North African manuscripts from the sixteenth to the eighteenth centuries and correspondence between Jewish scholars of the nineteenth and twentieth centuries. These include original letters written by literature Nobel Prize winner Shmuel Josef Agnon, by Rabbi Joseph Eschelbacher and by Orientalist Moritz Steinschneider.[65]

studiobühneköln

1974
studiobühneköln

In 1974, the University of Cologne decided to make its theater and film workshop (studiobühne) one of its central institutions. Since then, it has maintained and promoted the studiobühne as an independent open cultural center. A hard-to-miss sign on Universitätsstraße directs theatergoers to Germany's oldest existing university theater. It was founded in 1920 by the Cologne theater studies scholar Carl Niessen. In the 1950s, his successor Hermann Wetzke made contemporary works by authors such as Albert Camus and Alfred Jarry a focal point of the repertoire. In the 1960s, studiobühneköln became the city's most important political theater. It was a place where many generations of students explored theoretical and practical opportunities for engaging with the arts at the university. The experimental theater was an important part of the city's cultural scene for students, as well as audiences interested in Cologne's budding independent theater landscape. "Many well-known actors performed on this stage: Lambert Hamel, Eberhard Feik, Jürgen Flimm and Annette Frier. Karin Beier also appeared here," Dietmar Kobboldt, director of studiobühneköln, noted in 2014. "We are a kind of incubator, a launching pad for young theater talents."[66]

Development in Times of Educational Expansion

During the German economic boom of the 1950s and 60s, growth was the defining feature of the period at the University of Cologne, as well as many other West German institutions of higher education. The university's "master plan" of 1959 foresaw doubling the available space and enlarging the university grounds by one third. Thanks to Konrad Adenauer, who had set aside land for the future expansion of the university when he was mayor, the first building projects were completed rapidly. In 1966, the street in front of the main building, Universitätsstraße, became an underpass, and in 1968 the University and City Library and the lecture hall building, the first two large-scale buildings, were completed. Both buildings formed part of the central Universitätsforum to be located opposite the main building, turning the university into a modern campus university.

In addition to the Universitätsforum, the "master plan" of 1959 comprised two other important projects: moving the institutes for geosciences, physics and chemistry to a location between Luxemburger Straße and Zülpicher Straße, and the construction of several new buildings for the Faculty of Medicine and the University Hospital in Lindenthal. Completed in 1969, the building that was to house the physics institutes was a reinforced concrete skeleton structure with a curtain wall facade made of pre-fabricated metal elements. The same building materials and the same basic design were used for the construction of the chemistry institutes, completed in 1975. Both buildings were connected by a shared forum. They reflected the contemporary architectural style in the Bauhaus tradition, featuring a functional design language. The building housing the physics institutes was awarded the architecture prize of the city of Cologne in 1971.[67]

↗ The lecture hall building was part of the new Universitätsforum. Six lecture halls of different sizes providing room for 2,100 students were grouped around a spacious foyer with entrances on all sides. The floor was designed to match the pavement of Albertus Magnus Platz outside.

→ The lecture hall building planned by Rolf Gutbrod was also designed to link Albertus Magnus Platz to the library. The reinforced concrete expressed the energy and dynamics of an "open" architectural design. Other materials such as the brick used on the exterior walls of the lecture hall building allowed the building to blend into its architectural environment.

↑ Modern buildings, such as the physics and chemistry institutes, seen here from Zülpicher Straße, were also constructed for the Faculty of Mathematics and Natural Sciences; the Unicenter, opened in 1973 and one of Europe's largest residential buildings, towers in the background.

Dealing with Deficits

Chapter 6

1975–1990

1975 – 1990

1975

More Women

The winter semester sees more women than men enroll at the Faculty of Philosophy. The trend continues and by 1980, women make up more than 60 percent of the faculty's students.

1977

Cologne's Tumor Center

The Cologne Tumor Center is opened. Twenty-six departments and institutes of the Faculty of Medicine are involved in the project funded by German Cancer Aid. Internationally acclaimed researchers come to Cologne as guest scholars, consolidating Cologne's position as a research hub.

1980

Two New Faculties

In accordance with a new law, two departments of the Rhineland College of Teacher Education, a training college for teachers with a branch in Cologne, are incorporated into the University of Cologne as the Faculty of Educational Sciences and the Faculty of Curative Education; the university now has seven faculties.

1980

Largest University in NRW

With nearly 40,000 students, Cologne becomes the state's largest university for the first time. By 1990, the number of students increases to nearly 54,000.

1984

First Research Training Group

Germany's first *Graduiertenkolleg* (Research Training Group) is established in Cologne. Funded by the Fritz Thyssen Foundation, the group is part of the Faculty of Medicine and a model for many further such groups.

1985

Moving Forward

Following years of pressure from the university and the city, the state of North Rhine-Westphalia finally allocates 200 million German marks to complete construction of the University Hospital building, interrupted in 1974.

1988

The University's 600th Anniversary

The university celebrates its founding six hundred years earlier, presenting itself as one of Europe's oldest universities with strong ties to the city of Cologne and its citizens.

1989

A Center of Genetics Research

A research center for gene technology is established in Cologne. It is one of four such centers in Germany. In the same year, two *Sonderforschungsbereiche* (Collaborative Research Centers) for molecular biology are initiated.

UNI-Frühlings Fest

PHIL-FAK
10.000-129.999
und
A
WISO
10.000
-104.999
JURA
WISO-FAK
105.000-155.999

A lack of financial resources dictated the University of Cologne's development from the mid-1970s on. Increases in faculty size and new university buildings could not keep pace with the steadily rising enrollment. Overcrowding and the insufficient facilities shaped students' everyday lives. The university's criticism of North Rhine-Westphalia's higher education policies was a source of conflict that did not subside until the state's new Higher Education Act came into force in 1980. In the following years, the university implemented this law, incorporating the Cologne-based departments of the Rhineland College of Teacher Education and devising a new basic structure. Despite the constant lack of funds and increased strain on teaching staff, Cologne managed to continue developing its research and teaching capabilities in the 1980s and further enhance its academic reputation. The university started the new decade with self-confidence and optimism.

Austerity Measures

North Rhine-Westphalia, which had previously invested quite heavily in developing its higher education facilities, cut back on funding in the mid-1970s. The University of Cologne was forced to reduce staff and spending in all areas and could not realize construction projects as planned. In late 1975, Rector Wolf Isselhard spoke of "negative growth"—a new experience after twenty-five years of expansion. Universities were no longer a high priority on the political agenda and thus were not spared when the government was forced to implement budget cuts. This was most conspicuous in the lack of new construction. After building projects that had started in the 1960s were completed, construction work ended abruptly in 1975. Only some sections of the central hospital complex had been finished; the building pit for the diagnostic and treatment wings lay abandoned for years, testifying to the halt of Cologne's once-ambitious plans.[1]

↖ The new *Mensa* was a central meeting place at the Cologne University campus; view from its main entrance across Zülpicher Straße toward the physics building.

← Each semester, students stood in long lines to enroll at the registrar's office in the basement of the main building.

The university's total expenditure for conversions and extensions of existing buildings and the construction of new ones fell from about twelve million German marks in 1975 to a low of 664,000 German marks in 1983; the number of students nearly doubled during the same period. The Tumor Center, which opened in 1977 and had been financed by external sources, and the construction of a new heating plant and the annex of the Institute of Genetics in 1980, were the last major investments made for years. Due to the drastic funding cuts, even the wing of the main building that housed the lecture halls and had been gutted by fire in 1981 could not be reconstructed right away. The university undertook only basic building maintenance and measures needed to comply with safety standards and prevent hazards.[2]

In Conflict

Austerity measures intensified the conflict between the university and the North Rhine-Westphalian state government. When the University of Cologne's rector and deans publicly protested against the state's higher education policies in the summer of 1975, the state ministry was not amused. In his annual report in late 1975, Rector Wolf Isselhard declared that the university could no longer handle the high number of student applications and that a further increase in student admissions would jeopardize "the other tasks required of a research university." Isselhard pointed out that the University of Cologne was willing to undergo reform, but he rejected the state government's plans as inappropriate and demanded that the university have a greater say in decisions.[3]

The first federal Higher Education Act was adopted by the German government in 1976, and the ensuing revision of state legislation further fueled tensions between the university and policymakers. The debate once again centered on university autonomy, the professors' rights, and self-administration. The University of Cologne perceived the quantity and scope of new legal regulations as an unacceptable political intervention that would result in paralyzing bureaucratization and the downgrading of university courses to a rigidly structured, school-like form of education. Most professors rejected the participation of students and non-academic staff in decision-making processes, even though the German Constitutional Court ruling of 1973 ensured that professors would continue to hold a majority on university committees. The university leadership also complained that financial resources were inadequate in view of increasing student enrollment, and that the resulting work overload was restricting research. "Mandatory measures" in the form of a centralized student placement system and the "strict" numerus clausus for subjects such as medicine had not solved these problems, they argued. Furthermore, the university maintained that young academics were in a precarious situation which would have a long-term impact on the quality of research and teaching.[4]

Despite poor study conditions, there was surprisingly little student protest. The Association of German Student Unions called for a two-week boycott of classes in November 1977, mainly to protest the proposed introduction of a standard duration of studies, but students at Cologne hardly responded. By contrast, the long-standing conflict between the university and the state government escalated in a dispute over the merging of teacher-training colleges and universities. The University of Cologne believed this would weaken its academic proficiency and compromise teacher education. At a state public hearing in November 1978, Cologne University representatives walked out in protest together with representatives of other institutions of higher education. The University of Cologne questioned both the rationale and the legality of the Merger Act. Following a judicial review of the administrative decision, instigated by the political opposition, the state government amended the law, granting institutions of higher education greater latitude.[5]

Reorientation under Difficult Conditions

Although implementation of the state's new Higher Education Act and the Merger Act did not end the dispute over higher education policy, which had lasted for more than ten years, the conflict did recede into the background. The University of Cologne was forced to begin complying with the new legislation. In addition to taking care of its everyday business, it had to incorporate the new faculties of educational sciences and curative education, transform various professorships into career civil servant positions and introduce a new salary scheme. The introduction of the new basic structure proceeded more slowly than at other universities and tied up resources for nearly a decade.[6]

These ongoing pressures and financial constraints were the hallmark of the 1980s. In the winter semester of 1980/1981, there were nearly 40,000 students enrolled at Cologne, making it the largest university in North Rhine-Westphalia; by 1990, there were about 54,000. The ratio of instructors to students steadily deteriorated. Nevertheless, the state government's 1983 *Konzentrationserlass*, a decree that provided for the reorganization of degree programs, forced the University of Cologne to transfer a total of ninety-three positions to the state's central job pool by 1989.[7]

Lectures and seminars in many subjects were overcrowded. Students organized themselves to cope with their studies. A student-run service that transcribed economics lectures became a flourishing business; its services were indispensable for most students. Private refresher courses became a must for law students. There was not enough space available for lab work in the natural sciences, and students sometimes fell behind by a semester. During exams, the university library was filled with business and law students, which made normal use of the library impossible.

In addition to the lack of space and teachers, there was a shortage of teaching materials, since the university's budget for such resources had dropped in the mid-1980s to its 1978 level. However, funding for construction increased again from 1984, so the wing of the main building that housed the lecture halls could finally be restored. But the university's investments did not come close to the level of the early 1970s. In the summer of 1981, the rectorate, together with the board of trustees, founded the Building Pit Association to hasten completion of the central hospital. The joint action by the university and the city was successful and by the end of the year, the state government had decided to invest two hundred million German marks in the hospital. Construction resumed in 1985 and the building was completed in 1990.[8]

Despite the challenging situation, the university continued to develop its research and teaching. Between 1983 and 1987 alone, the number of research projects increased from some 1,350 to nearly 2,000. A large share of inner-university investments continued to flow into the university's clinics. Expansion in other faculties was mostly limited to isolated measures. For example, the Forschungsstelle Afrika (African Research Unit) was set up in 1984 at the Institute of Prehistoric Archeology, and a year later, the university established a professorship for applied mathe-

matics. In 1986, it responded to the opening of communist China by setting up an interdisciplinary research unit that focused on modern China in the Institute of East Asian Studies, underlining the political and economic relevance of the university's academic work. Between 1980 and 1990, the number of study programs offered rose from just under ninety to about 120.[9]

New Research Funding

Compared to the university's own total expenditure, which rose very slowly, external research funding played an increasingly important role. At the beginning of the 1980s, the University of Cologne was already one of the West German universities receiving the most external funding. By 1983, research grants from external sources exceeded the university's own stagnating budget for research. This reflected a far-reaching shift in research funding away from long-term public funds to temporary grants based on project-related applications.[10]

This additional money flowed into top-level research. In the 1980s, the German Research Foundation (DFG) financed six *Sonderforschungsbereiche* or SFBs (Collaborative Research Centers). Germany's first Research Training Group, sponsored by the Fritz Thyssen Foundation, began its work at Cologne in 1984. In addition to state and federal grants, European Community funding became increasingly important by the end of the 1980s. Heisenberg and Humboldt scholarships supported young scholars from Germany and abroad. Close cooperation with Cologne's Max Planck institutes and major research facilities such as the Jülich Nuclear Physics Institute and the German Aerospace Center consolidated the position of Cologne as a research hub. Private companies, including Bayer and BASF, invested in projects and endowed chairs.[11]

↑ The new *Mensa* was well frequented within a few years of its opening.

In 1985, the university set up a research transfer office to focus on further developing its good, long-standing relationship with the business sector, which actively sponsored many affiliated institutes. The office maintained close contact with companies and promoted cooperation to make the university's research results available to industry and commerce and, in turn, to provide researchers with insight into the companies' work. Together with other institutes of higher education, the University of Cologne presented the results of its basic research at the Hannover Trade Fair for the first time in 1986.[12]

On the Upswing

In 1988, exactly six hundred years after the founding of the old university, the University of Cologne largely finished drafting its new constitution and could present itself confidently as a special kind of "reform-oriented university," one which continued to adapt its successful and established traditions—such as research, international reach and practical relevance—to modern needs. Collaborative Research Centers, a research center and a new degree program nurtured promising disciplines such as genetics and computer science. In 1989, the new Institute of the Legal Profession promoted the practical dimension of legal research and teaching. The university also advanced the internationalization of its degree programs. In December 1988, the Faculty of Economics and Social Sciences founded the Community of European Management Schools (CEMS) together with other European institutions of higher education to establish common standards for business and economics education in Europe. The University Senate voted in 1989 to establish a binational master's program in law, which required students to study for two years in Cologne and two years in Paris.[13]

Despite the prevailing mood of optimism, the university continued to struggle with the consequences of overcrowding and underfunding. But the state's austerity measures were now facing widespread resistance. Some 10,000 students joined in strikes, demonstrations and a week of actions to protest the elimination of university positions, and restructuring measures, foreseen in the 1988 "structural plan." The protests had the Senate's full support. At the request of the university, even the city of Cologne and the board of trustees spoke out against the proposed measures. Although the jobs were eliminated nonetheless, the federal and state governments responded to public pressure and decided in the spring of 1989 to launch a *Hochschulsonderprogramm*, an initiative intended to ease the situation in the disciplines most affected. This special budget provided Cologne with thirty-one positions for its new study program in business information technology. Between 1983 and 1990, the university had gained a total of eighty new positions and lost ninety-three, mostly in the humanities. During the same period, the number of students rose by nearly fifteen percent, but by the late 1980s, the student population seemed to have peaked. The University of Cologne entered the new decade with confidence.[14]

↗ The large reading room in the new University and City Library quickly became one of the few quiet places on campus for studying.

→ Research funding from external sources became increasingly important during the 1980s, especially for the natural sciences; a bird's-eye view of the physics and chemistry buildings.

Pushed to the Limit

Overcrowding was the university's biggest problem during this period. In the mid-1970s, it was clear that the expansion of the university could not keep pace with the steadily growing number of students. Politicians had expected enrollment to decline after the last of the baby boomers entered universities in the second half of the 1980s, but this did not happen. Each year, more and more pupils finished school with the Abitur, encouraged by an educational policy that regarded higher qualification as a key factor in a knowledge society. Between 1975 and 1990, the number of students at the University of Cologne rose from 25,000 to about 54,000. When the Rhineland College of Teacher Education became part of the university in 1980, this alone resulted in an increase of more than 4,000 students, so that Cologne replaced Münster as North Rhine-Westphalia's largest university. That year, West Germany's student population exceeded one million for the first time. By the end of the decade, this figure had gone up to 1.5 million.[15]

The attempt to control student numbers by regulating capacity and restricting admissions did not ease the problem. Political pressure and the *Öffnungsbeschluss*, a decision made by the German states in 1977 to maintain access to university education, forced universities to exclude many degree programs from the university placement system run by the German Central Office for University Admissions. In Cologne, this affected a wide range of subjects including English, chemistry, history, mathematics, physics, Romance languages and literature, and economics. The University Senate was forced to accept the decision, even though it was convinced that the liberalization of admission procedures was likely to have unforeseen consequences for the university. Although the University of Cologne no longer clung to the ideal of an elite university, it still hoped to limit the number of students and to be able to select the more qualified of the many applicants. As enrollment numbers continued to rise despite a lack of capacity, the university introduced its own admissions restrictions for up to thirty-five subjects per semester in the 1980s.[16]

North Rhine-Westphalia's financial problems meant that the University of Cologne was not allowed to create enough new positions. The ratio of instructors to students continued to deteriorate. In 1975, there had been one full professor for every fifty-three students; by 1989, that figure had dropped to one to ninety-six, statistically speaking, while the national average was one to sixty-five. Cologne complained that while it was responsible for the largest share of the state's university education, it lacked adequate staffing. The situation was particularly drastic in economics, where the professor-to-student ratio was one to 160 in 1988. Almost twice as many students as foreseen had enrolled in the very popular business administration program. The teaching faculty could "no longer cope with the onslaught" and was on the verge of "collapse," the university's *Journal* reported.[17]

In addition to inadequate staffing levels, there was a lack of space. A large portion of the severely reduced funds for renovating and extending university buildings was invested in medical facilities. When the state reduced funding yet again in 1982, Chancellor Johannes Neyses spoke of an emergency and declared that only the "most urgent and unavoidable measures to maintain buildings" could be financed. By the end of 1988, the University of Cologne was "bursting at its seams," as the *Journal* stated in its headline. "Chaotic conditions" prevailed in the lecture halls and rooms for advanced seminars. The university leadership demanded better and sustained funding for universities rather than special short-term funding measures. To draw attention to the deplorable conditions, the chancellor together with Rector Peter Hanau publicly presented a folding chair and a legal textbook to an incoming law student, the 53,000th student to enroll for the winter semester of 1988/1989.[18]

Overcrowding made studying a daily struggle, especially in subjects with high enrollment levels. Affordable living space was in short supply and the search for accommodation was a time-consuming endeavor for the many students who were not from Cologne. Rooms in student dormitories had already become scarce in the late 1970s. Many rooms in older residences were smaller than the required minimum of twelve square meters, and their sanitary facilities were inadequate. Ten years later, the situation had become even worse. In the course of 1989, the waiting list for the existing 3,500 dormitory rooms grew from 1,000 to 2,100 students. However, demand was in fact much greater due to the lack of available rental apartments in Cologne and increasing rents. The end of subsidized housing construction in the mid-1980s meant that students from low-income families had to compete for a handful of affordable apartments. The situation was so precarious that the AStA arranged "short-term solutions," among them a tent city on the university meadows and trailers on the Unicenter parking lot. Only then did politicians address the "new housing shortage." Together with the university, the Student Services Center and the city, they looked for possibilities for expansion and new construction. But that took time. Accommodation, like overcrowding, remained a constant problem.[19]

↓ The public was aware of university overcrowding; a film crew documented a day at the registrar's office.

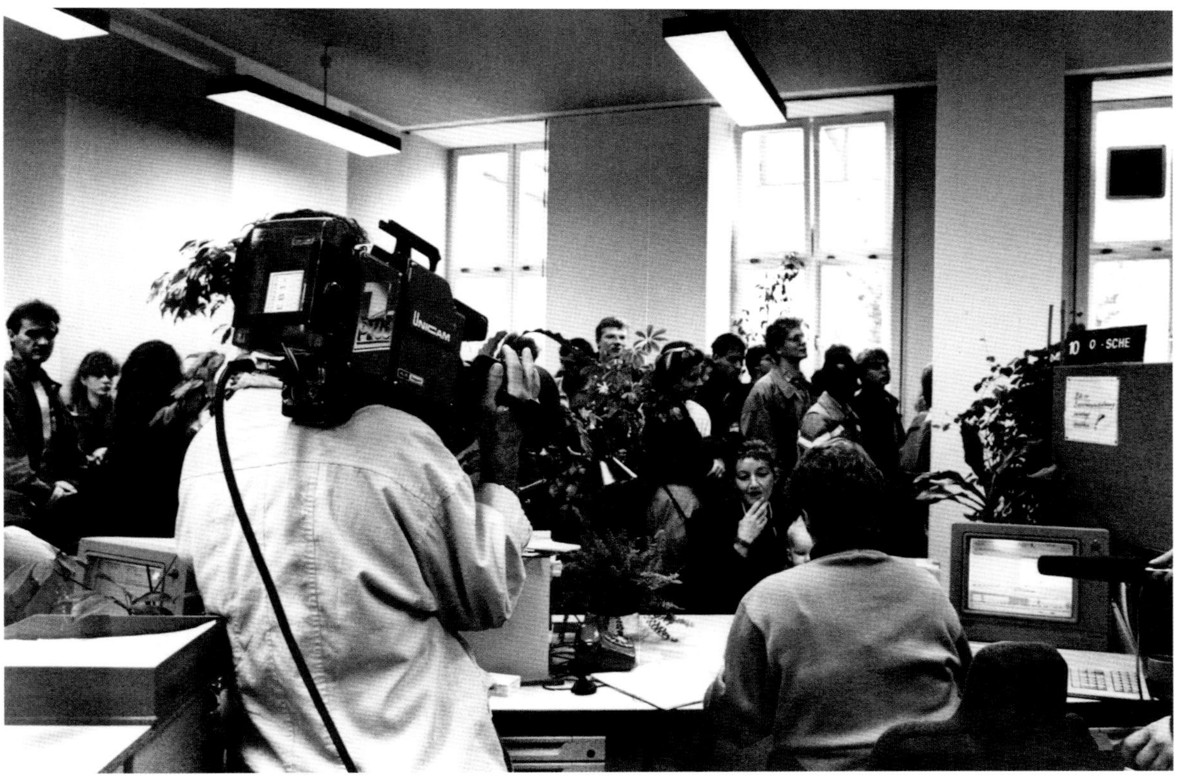

Christa Berg
born 1940

Professor in the
Faculty of Educational Sciences

After passing her state teaching examination in 1963, Christa Berg began doctoral studies at the University of Cologne in education, history and philosophy. She completed her doctorate in 1970 with her thesis titled *Die Okkupation der Schule. Eine Studie zur Aufhellung gegenwärtiger Schulprobleme an der Volksschule Preußens (1872–1900)* (The occupation of the school: A study illuminating contemporary school problems in Prussia's elementary school system). In 1974, she was appointed professor of education at the Rhineland College of Teacher Education in Cologne. After the college was incorporated into the University of Cologne in 1980, she taught at the Faculty of Educational Sciences until her retirement in 2000.

The social history of education was the focus of Berg's work. In addition to studying the history of schools and teachers, Berg carried out research in the history of socialization and the history of family, childhood and youth. She also worked in the fields of general education and the development of educational theory. Berg was on the editorial board of the *Jahrbuch für Historische Bildungsforschung*. As coeditor of the influential *Handbuch der deutschen Bildungsgeschichte* (Handbook on the history of education in Germany), she edited the fourth volume which dealt with the period of the German Empire. From 1986 to 1990, she was a member of the board of the German Educational Research Association, and she was named an honorary member in 2000. Berg received the Ernst Christian Trapp Prize in 2008.[20]

Erwin Grochla
1921–1986

Professor in the Faculty of
Economics and Social Sciences

Erwin Grochla is considered one of the most influential economists of the former West Germany. After completing an apprenticeship, he was drafted into the military in 1941. Following World War II, he was an architectural draftsman at Dürener Metallwerke AG and an administrator for the municipality of Greater Berlin. He completed his Abitur in 1947 and studied business administration in East and West Berlin. Grochla received a degree in business management at the Free University of Berlin in 1950, where he was awarded his doctorate in 1953 with a thesis on *Interne und externe Betriebsplanung* (Internal and external business planning) and his habilitation in 1957 with a study on various types of business cooperation titled *Betriebsverband und Verbandsbetrieb*.

Grochla lectured at the University of Mainz in the summer of 1958 and in the same year assumed Germany's first chair in general business administration and organizational theory at the Mannheim College of Economics. The University of Cologne appointed him to a professorship in 1960. In Cologne, Grochla founded the Institute of Business Administration for Organization and Automation in 1964 with the support of the business community, and he headed it until his death. His focus on business organization and information studies made him a sought-after expert worldwide in the early phase of digitization, and he remained loyal to Cologne despite offers from other universities.[21]

Ulla Johansen
born 1927

Professor in the Faculty of Philosophy

Anna Gisela Johnen
1925–2014

Professor in the Faculty of Mathematics and Natural Sciences

Ulla Johansen, born in Estonia, began studying history and then ethnology at the University of Hamburg in 1947. She received her doctorate there in 1953 for her thesis *Die Ornamentik der Jakuten* (The ornaments of the Yakuts). After taking a position at the Museum of Ethnology in Hamburg, Johansen conducted her first field research in 1956 in Turkey, where she lived with a family of nomads for several months.

Johansen worked for various museums in Scandinavia and at the Academy of Sciences of the Soviet Union. She was head of the South and East Asia Department of the Museum of Ethnology in Hamburg from 1962 to 1965. In 1966, she assumed a position as a research associate at the South Asia Institute of the University of Heidelberg, where she completed her habilitation two years later with a thesis on shamanism. In 1970, Johansen accepted a guest professorship in Istanbul. In 1973, she was appointed to the chair of ethnology at the University of Cologne, which she held until she retired in 1990. Johansen raised substantial external funding and expanded the Cologne Institute of Ethnology. The geographical focus of her work was on the Near East, central Asia, Siberia and north-eastern Europe. Her main areas of research were ethnohistory, material culture, social structures and religions. Her studies on Turkey were seminal. In 1999, Johansen was awarded the Werner Heisenberg Medal.[22]

Anna Gisela Johnen was born and raised in Cologne and began studying botany at the University of Cologne in 1944. She was forced to interrupt her studies after her first semester when the university closed due to the war. Following the reopening of the university, she enrolled in zoology in the winter semester of 1945/1946 and participated in the reconstruction of the university.

In 1953, Johnen received her doctorate in Cologne for her thesis on developmental biology. A year later, she joined an international research team in the field of developmental physiology at the Hubrecht Institute in Utrecht. She was a fellow of the German Research Foundation from 1954 to 1957 and a research assistant at the Institute of Zoology at the University of Cologne from 1958 to 1960, where she obtained her habilitation in developmental biology in 1964.

Johnen became a full-time lecturer at the University of Cologne in 1967 and was appointed university professor of zoology in 1970. The focus of her research was the developmental physiology of vertebrates and ornithology. She maintained close ties to her native city and bequeathed her estate to the Cologne Gymnasial- und Stiftungsfonds (a foundation dedicated to promoting education) and her books to the University and City Library.[23]

On the Way to a New Constitution

Even after a decade of intense debate and higher education reform, the University of Cologne's constitution of 1963 still remained in effect in 1975, with only a few minor changes. The university had begun drafting a new constitution, but it suspended that work because the German government was in the process of drawing up its first federal Higher Education Framework Act (HRG). When the act came into effect in January 1976, it required universities to reorganize the courses offered, shorten the standard duration of studies, improve administrative efficiency, introduce a new personnel structure and group-based participation, and expand external research funding. Its detailed provisions strengthened state regulation of universities.[24]

North Rhine-Westphalia revised its higher education legislation on the basis of the HRG. This meant that the state's plans for a *Gesamthochschule* (comprehensive university) in Cologne had to be abandoned. Instead, the departments of the Rhineland College of Teacher Education located in the city were to be incorporated into the university. However, as in other locations, both institutions rejected

these plans. Other parts of the amended legislation also met with harsh criticism. When the draft bill for the law governing institutes of higher education in North Rhine-Westphalia was presented, the University Senate drew up a ninety-one-page position paper in February 1978 that was not supported by the non-professorial academic staff and student representatives. In particular, the Senate rejected the introduction of the so-called *Gruppenuniversität*, in which all groups have the right to participate in self-government, a concept meant to strengthen the influence of non-professorial academic staff, students and non-academic employees. The Senate feared that politically charged conflicts and a "bloated self-government" caused by the new organizational structure would lead to higher costs and place restrictions on research and teaching. The Senate also believed the new regulations would limit the university's autonomy and adversely affect its productivity.[25]

The protests had no effect. The 1979 Higher Education Act and the 1980 Merger Act foresaw the incorporation of teacher education colleges, required the drafting of new study regulations and called for a redistribution of voting rights in decision-making university committees. Universities were to transpose these legal requirements into new basic regulations by 1982 at the latest. But the University of Cologne took its time compared to other institutions of higher education in North Rhine-Westphalia. The responsible commission did not submit a first partial draft to the Senate until February 1984. Cologne did not even have a new constitution in place in 1986 when existing university constitutions were scheduled to expire. The state government extended the deadlines several times, and many consultations and alternative drafts followed. After the first complete version was finally submitted early in 1989, approval procedures were slow due to changes requested by the state, but the new constitution finally went into effect in late 1990.[26]

The university had already begun implementing uncontested parts of the new constitution in 1989. This included the reorganization of (self-)government at all levels. The university was now headed by a rectorate in which the rector, chancellor and three prorectors worked together. State and university administration were to form an effective unit. The prorectors were elected in December 1989. They held office for two years and were responsible for planning and finances, teaching, study programs and academic reform, research and early-career researchers. The rector headed the university for a four-year term. The rectorate was elected by the newly created Council, a body comprising professors, academic staff, students and non-academic staff that replaced the former University Senate and put into practice the principle of the *Gruppenuniversität*. In contrast to its predecessor, the Council no longer included all regular and emeritus professors, but only twenty-two professorial representatives and seven representatives from each of the other three groups. The Council approved the rector's report and monitored changes to the general rules of the university. A scaled-down Senate was chaired by the rector and composed of seven professorial representatives and two representatives from each of the other three groups. The governing bodies of the faculties were organized in a similar way.[27]

The long time it took to finalize the constitution reflected the University of Cologne's sustained resistance to university reform. The university felt forced to implement legal requirements while its real problems, overcrowding and underfunding, worsened from year to year. But by the end of the difficult process, the university's initial concerns had evaporated. The new Council strengthened the autonomy of the university, the rector's extended term of office generated stability, and the appointment of prorectors increased the rectorate's effectiveness. Moreover, in the constitution, the university had defined its special relationship with its numerous affiliated institutes and the board of trustees as an affiliated municipal body, thereby preserving its distinctive profile. Even the prospect of a *Gruppenuniversität* was no longer a source of consternation. Professors held a majority on all committees. The dreaded politicization did not materialize. In the anniversary year of 1988, Rector Peter Hanau looked to the future with optimism: "Cologne's path to becoming a *Gruppenuniversität* is being taken in close cooperation with all member groups with the goal of harmoniously merging past and present. This is how a reform-oriented university with patina will emerge."[28]

← At a press conference on 27 February 1989, Rector Peter Hanau (r.) and Chancellor Johannes Neyses inform the public about the university's new form of joint administration.

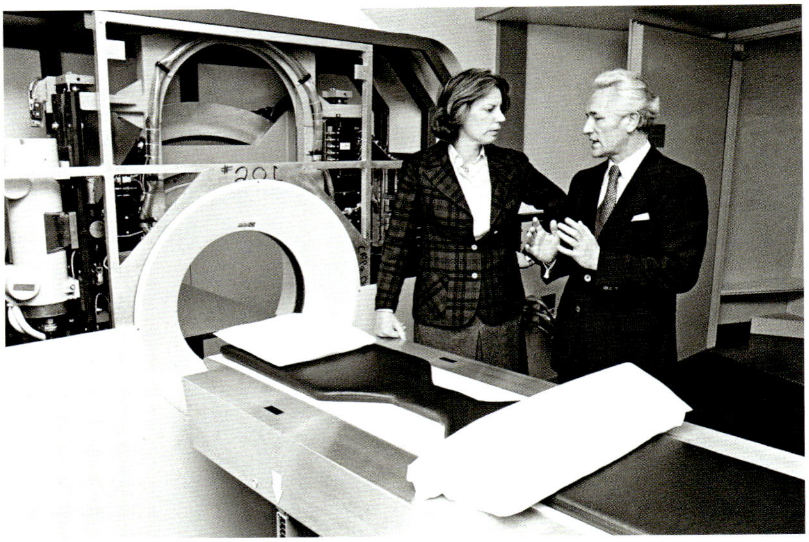

Full-Body CT Scanner

1976
Institute of Radiology

On 7 December 1976, Mildred Scheel, founder of German Cancer Aid, presented the first full-body CT scanner in North Rhine-Westphalia to Professor Gerd Friedmann, Director of the Institute of Diagnostic and Interventional Radiology of the University of Cologne. Gerd Friedmann and his colleague Ulrich Mödder praised the potential of full-body computer tomography, noting: "The introduction of computer tomography in 1972 is the most revolutionary technical development in diagnostic radiology since the discovery of X-rays." At a time when methods for the treatment of cancer were limited, the scanner, developed by the British electrical engineer and later Nobel Laureate for Medicine, Godfrey Hounsfield, significantly improved diagnostic possibilities. Computer tomography is a non-invasive method. An intravenous contrast agent is injected, allowing enhanced differentiation between normal and pathological tissue structures in various organs, especially the brain. The exposure to radiation in a CT scan is no higher than with conventional X-rays. Specialists such as Friedmann and Mödder expected that computer tomography would increasingly be used to examine organs. Their assumption was correct. By June 1978, there were already nearly 50 full-body CT scanners in Germany.[29]

Unimog with Excavator

1980
Institute of Prehistory and Early History

In September 1980, researchers from the Institute of Prehistory and Early History, the Institute of Geology and the Institute of Ethnology, together with colleagues from the Technical University of Berlin and Museum Koenig in Bonn, embarked on the University of Cologne's first Sahara expedition. Their destinations: the Gilf Kebir plateau in Egypt and Wadi Howar in Sudan. Their project: to study the connections between climate and changes in landscape in the eastern Sahara, as well as settlement and cultural development in the region.

The Unimog with excavator pictured above was of special significance for the project. Since the scientists could not hire any excavation workers locally, they needed a technical solution in order to examine the strata in silted lakes, for example. An excavator mounted onto the Unimog was the answer. Moreover, the vehicle itself offered lots of storage space. "For ten men to be able to live and work for months more than thirty-one kilometers from the nearest settlement in the largest dry desert on Earth, we had to carry large quantities of food, water, equipment and diesel fuel, so Daimler-Benz provided us with a truck," recalled Rudolph Kuper, who led the expedition and was head of the African Research Unit at the Institute of Prehistory and Early History for many years.[30]

Two New Faculties

In the mid-1970s, teacher training at Cologne was provided by three university faculties and two departments at the Rhineland College of Teacher Education. These had emerged from the Pädagogische Akademie in Cologne founded in 1946, which initially trained teachers for primary schools and later for primary and secondary schools. From 1949, the academy also offered curative education courses for teachers already working in special education. From the 1950s on, the academy developed its own academic standards and combined teaching with research. This included specializing in the study of curative education, for which an institute was set up in 1955. The introduction of a course of studies lasting six semesters instead of four, its research-based curricula and its own state examination authorities fostered the academic orientation of the Pädagogische Akademie. The academy moved to a new building on Frangenheimstraße near the university in 1957.

In 1962, the academy became a college of education. Its curative education program was recognized as a full-fledged degree program in 1963, and the college expanded its Institute of Curative Education into a teaching and research center. In 1965, both branches of the college were legally recognized as academic facilities and became departments of the new Rhineland College of Teacher Education. This advanced the position of curative education as a discipline in its own right, but at the same time, educational sciences lost their autonomy. In 1968, teacher training colleges in North Rhine-Westphalia were given the right to grant habilitations, and in 1970 the right to award doctorates. When the concept of training teachers for different levels of school was introduced in Germany in the mid-1970s, the colleges of education took over the training of teachers for primary and lower secondary schools. Students who wished to teach at upper secondary schools attended university.[31]

Academic orientation and the training of teachers for different levels of schooling dissolved the boundaries between colleges of education and universities. The government of North Rhine-Westphalia pushed to merge the two, putting an end to plans for the creation of independent universities of education. The draft of the Merger Act presented in 1978 defined this development. Education researchers and specialists in the didactics of specific subjects from the Rhineland College of Teacher Education in Cologne were to be integrated into the corresponding departments at the University of Cologne according to their teaching qualifications. The state government believed this association with each department would make systematic instruction more efficient and foster a "reflection on problems in school education" that was often "missing" at universities.[32]

The state's plans met with vehement opposition, especially the plans for integrating the specialists for didactics into corresponding departments at the university. A fundamental discord between the Rhineland College of Teacher Education and the University of Cologne was revealed here. The college believed its specialist systematic instruction was in jeopardy, while the university questioned the academic orientation of the college's teacher training programs. The college feared that its courses would become more geared toward the needs of the Gymnasium, whereas the university was concerned that its level of academic education would be threatened. The University Senate saw the Merger Act as an encroachment on the university's autonomy and decided in January 1979 to file a constitutional complaint. However, the complaint was never filed because a judicial review of the administrative decision, instigated by the political opposition, forced the state to revise the law. The new version of the law, adopted in January 1980, gave institutions of higher education more flexibility, and the University of Cologne then decided to set up two new faculties.[33]

Thus, both departments of the Rhineland College of Teacher Education located in Cologne were incorporated into the University of Cologne on 1 April 1980, becoming the Faculty of Educational Sciences and the Faculty of Curative Education without any changes to their organizational structure. This meant that the institutional separation of teacher training programs for different types of schools was in fact upheld. The Faculty of Philosophy and the Faculty of Mathematics and Natural Sciences continued to train teachers for comprehensive schools and Gymnasiums. The two new faculties were responsible for training teachers for primary and secondary schools, as well as curative teachers for special education schools. As before, the Faculty of Economics and Social Sciences offered a teaching training program for vocational colleges.[34]

Although the merger had not been voluntary, the preparatory work of the joint commission had shown that the two sides had much in common. Now it was a matter of breathing life into the new institutions. In the 1980s, the focus in educational sciences was on advancing teacher training and methods for "lifelong learning" outside the schools. Dean Heinrich Kronen explained in 1986 that pedagogy no longer dealt exclusively with the education of children and young people but included "research, teaching and studies in the entire field of education and training, in particular the conditions and forms of learning and teaching." The Faculty of Curative Education offered degree programs in social education, a diploma degree in education with a focus on special needs education and teaching foreign students, as well as teacher training courses in art therapy and new information technology. Within the university, this faculty was a driving force for inclusion in education.[35]

↑ The two departments of the Rhineland College of Teacher Education located in Cologne were incorporated into the University of Cologne in 1980. The two new faculties were housed in the building on Frangenheimstraße.

Günter Kohlmann 1933–2005

Professor in the Faculty of Law

Günter Kohlmann was a criminal defense lawyer and an expert in criminal tax law whose reputation reached well beyond Cologne's city limits. After his family fled from Upper Silesia, Poland, following World War II, he completed his Abitur in Jülich and began studying law in Cologne in 1954. He was a member of the Grotenburg Catholic student association, was actively involved in the AStA and represented his faculty in the Student Parliament. In 1960, Kohlmann was granted his doctorate in Cologne, and in 1963 he joined the university's Institute of Criminology as Ulrich Klug's research associate. He was awarded his habilitation in 1968 with a thesis titled *Der Begriff des Staatsgeheimnisses* (The concept of the state secret).

A year later, Kohlmann was appointed to the chair for criminal law, criminal procedural law and philosophy of law at Goethe University in Frankfurt am Main. In 1971, he assumed the professorship for criminal law, criminal procedural law and philosophy of law at Cologne and headed the Institute of Criminology until he retired in 1999. He served as dean from 1983 to 1985 and as first prorector of the university in 1993/1994. Kohlmann brought together theory and practice, particularly as a lawyer in economic crime cases. Spectacular court proceedings and high-profile clients such as the former CDU treasurer Walther Leisler Kiep often put the law professor in the public eye.[36]

Heinrich Lenzen 1921–2013

Professor in the Faculty of Curative Education

In 1965, Heinrich Lenzen, an expert in social education, became one of the first instructors of the Department for Curative Education at the newly established Rhineland College of Teacher Education in Cologne and the first director of the Department for General Curative Education and Social Pedagogy. In 1968, he was appointed first full professor in this area of studies. That same year, he founded the Support Desk for Trisomy Patients within his department. By the time Lenzen retired in 1986, it had provided support to more than 250 families. The Support Desk also developed new forms of care and designed practical courses to convey them to students and professionals. The main goal was to enable people with disabilities to experience their environment in new ways. For Lenzen, the combination of theory and practice was a matter of principle, and it led him to create the first self-help association for families caring for people with Down syndrome.

In 1980, Lenzen was involved in integrating the Department of Curative Education of the Rhineland College of Teacher Education into the University of Cologne as its seventh faculty. He was instrumental in setting up a *Diplom* degree program in education and in establishing the Audiovisual Media Center in 1977.[37]

Renate Mayntz
born 1929

Professor in the
Faculty of Economics and Social Sciences

Renate Mayntz is one of Germany's most distinguished sociologists. Born in Berlin in 1929, she completed her Abitur and then studied biochemistry at Wellesley College in the USA. In 1951, she began studying sociology at the Free University of Berlin, where she submitted her doctoral dissertation, *Die soziale Organisation des Industriebetriebes* (Social organization in industrial enterprises), in 1953. Mayntz obtained her habilitation in Berlin in 1957 with a study on the social stratification and social change in an industrial city in the Rhineland. She then spent two more years in the USA, which further strengthened the influence of empirically oriented American sociology on her work.

Mayntz returned to Berlin in 1960 and assumed a chair for sociology at the Free University in 1965. In 1971, she began working at the German University of Administrative Sciences in Speyer, and she was appointed to the chair for sociology at the University of Cologne in 1973. In 1985, she became a founding director of the Max Planck Institute for the Study of Societies in Cologne. She maintained close ties to the university as an honorary professor until retiring in 1997. Mayntz published many research papers, especially on organizational sociology and processes of political regulation. Numerous awards attest to the influence of her work in the public sphere. She has remained active in research, and at the age of 80, she founded an international working group to explore the regulation of financial markets.[38]

Peter Mittelstaedt
1929–2014

Professor in the
Faculty of Mathematics and Natural Sciences

As a child, Peter Mittelstaedt met the physicist Werner Heisenberg at his parent's home in Leipzig. His subsequent physics studies took him from Jena and Bonn to Göttingen, where he obtained his doctorate in 1956 under Heisenberg's supervision. He then worked at prestigious research centers such as the European Organization for Nuclear Research (CERN), the Max Planck Institute for Physics and Astrophysics, and Massachusetts Institute of Technology (MIT). In 1961, he completed his habilitation at the Ludwig-Maximilians-Universität in Munich.

The University of Cologne appointed Mittelstaedt full professor of theoretical physics in 1965. He was also active in the university's academic self-government until retiring in 1995. He served as dean in 1968/1969. A year later, in 1970/1971, he was the first rector not to have been professionally socialized during the Nazi era; he was appointed prorector from 1971 to 1973 and again from 1991 to 1994.

Mittelstaedt linked basic research in physics with philosophical reflection. His main fields of work ranged from relativity and quantum theory to the philosophy of science, theory of science and ethics of science. His books include *Philosophical Problems of Modern Physics* (1963), *The Concept of Time in Physics* (1976) and *Quantum Logic* (1978). Mittelstaedt continued his work on a temporal logic for the foundation of quantum theory to an advanced age.[39]

Collaborative Research

From the 1970s, research conducted by individual scholars was increasingly complemented by cooperative, interdisciplinary and internationally networked projects. "Collaborative research" was the magic phrase, a model recommended by the Wissenschaftsrat (German Council of Science and Humanities) in its first report in 1960. This approach was largely rejected by the University of Cologne and other universities, since the recommendations called for a departure from the traditional concept of a professorial university in favor of specific areas of focus. In 1967, the council then proposed to set up *Sonderforschungsbereiche* or SFBs (Collaborative Research Centers). This idea met with much greater interest and was implemented a year later by the German Research Foundation (DFG). SFBs were meant to be efficient and innovative university research units that worked across disciplines and boasted excellent working conditions.[40]

The first two SFBs at Cologne were set up in 1970, followed by a third in 1974. Cologne physicists worked together with colleagues at RWTH Aachen University and the Jülich Nuclear Physics Institute in SFB 125 (Magnetic Moments and Chaos Phenomena in Metals)—a promising form of regional collaborative research at an international level. Other important partners from major research facilities outside the university in the 1980s included the German Aerospace Center and the Gesellschaft für Mathematik und Datenverarbeitung, a research center for applied mathematics and data processing. Two other Collaborative Research Centers highlighted Cologne's strength in physics. Set up in 1985, SFB 301 (Physics and Chemistry of Interstellar Molecular Clouds) used a radio telescope on a Swiss mountain to receive signals from the universe. SFB 341 (Physics of Mesoscopic and Low-dimensional Metallic Systems), launched in 1989, conducted research on extremely small phenomena.[41]

The Cologne Tumor Center, which opened in 1977, pursued a special form of research collaboration involving twenty-six facilities in the Faculty of Medicine. One of its funders was German Cancer Aid, which also sponsored visiting lectureships by internationally renowned scientists.[42]

The university's collaboration with Max Planck institutes (MPIs) was also pioneering. In 1978, a department of the Frankfurt Max Planck Institute for Brain Research located at Merheim Hospital in Cologne became the Cerebrovascular Research Unit. This was subsequently transformed into an independent MPI for Neurological Research in 1982. Its first directors, Konstantin-Alexander Hossmann and Wolf-Dieter Heiss, were also untenured professors at the University of Cologne. Heiss was awarded a professorship in 1985 and became head of the University Psychiatric Clinic. The institute, which moved to the campus of the University Hospital in 1990, later became the MPI for Metabolism Research and is closely linked to the university.[43]

There was also in-depth professional networking between the biosciences and the MPI for Breeding Research in Cologne-Vogelsang. Former biology professor and MPI director Joseph Straub was a co-founder of Cologne's Institute of Genetics. The director of that institute, Peter Starlinger, and the new MPI directors Jozef Schell and Heinz Saedler together turned the University of Cologne into an internationally renowned center for molecular plant genetics. Close cooperation in the molecular biosciences led to the founding in 1984 of a Research Training Group funded by the Fritz Thyssen Foundation—another new form of collaboration meant to foster early-career researchers in particular, by giving them the opportunity to work in research teams. This group at Cologne was the first of its kind in Germany and served as a model for later collaborative endeavors. For this interdisciplinary project, based in the

Faculty of Medicine, scientists from the university's institutes for biochemistry, genetics and physiological chemistry and the MPI for Breeding Research worked together. This successful cooperation made Cologne a "stronghold" in genetics, as experts from the German Research Foundation noted when they approved the establishment of two more Collaborative Research Centers in 1989: SFB 243 (Molecular Analysis of Cellular Systems) and SFB 274 (Modular Structure of Genetic Material). One of the four research centers for gene technology that opened in Germany in 1989 was at Cologne, which confirmed the university's outstanding status in genetic research.[44]

Collaborative research also enhanced Cologne's traditionally strong research in the social sciences. Renate Mayntz, founding director of the Max Planck Institute for the Study of Societies, which was set up in Cologne in 1985, had previously been a full professor of sociology at the university. The MPI carried out fundamental research, working on an empirically grounded theory of society. Mayntz, who boasted an international reputation, was an early advocate of research collaboration. She coordinated the Forschungsverbund Implementation politischer Programme (Research Alliance on the Implementation of Public Policy) until 1982. Cooperation was also the guiding principle for the Gesellschaft Sozialwissenschaftlicher Infrastruktureinrichtungen—GESIS (German Social Science Infrastructure Service) founded in 1986, of which the Zentralarchiv für Empirische Sozialforschung (Central Archive for Empirical Social Research) in Cologne was an original member. The Institute of Applied Social Research opened a Research Training Group for social sciences in 1989 and was itself supported by the MPI for the Study of Societies, the Central Archive and the Forschungsinstitut für Soziologie (Research Institute for Sociology). Funded by the Volkswagen Foundation, the new Research Training Group explored the "networking and dynamics of social structures"—a traditional area of work by sociologists in Cologne.[45]

↓ An independent Max Planck Institute for Neurological Research was established in 1982; this photograph was taken in the department headed by Professor Wolf-Dieter Heiss.

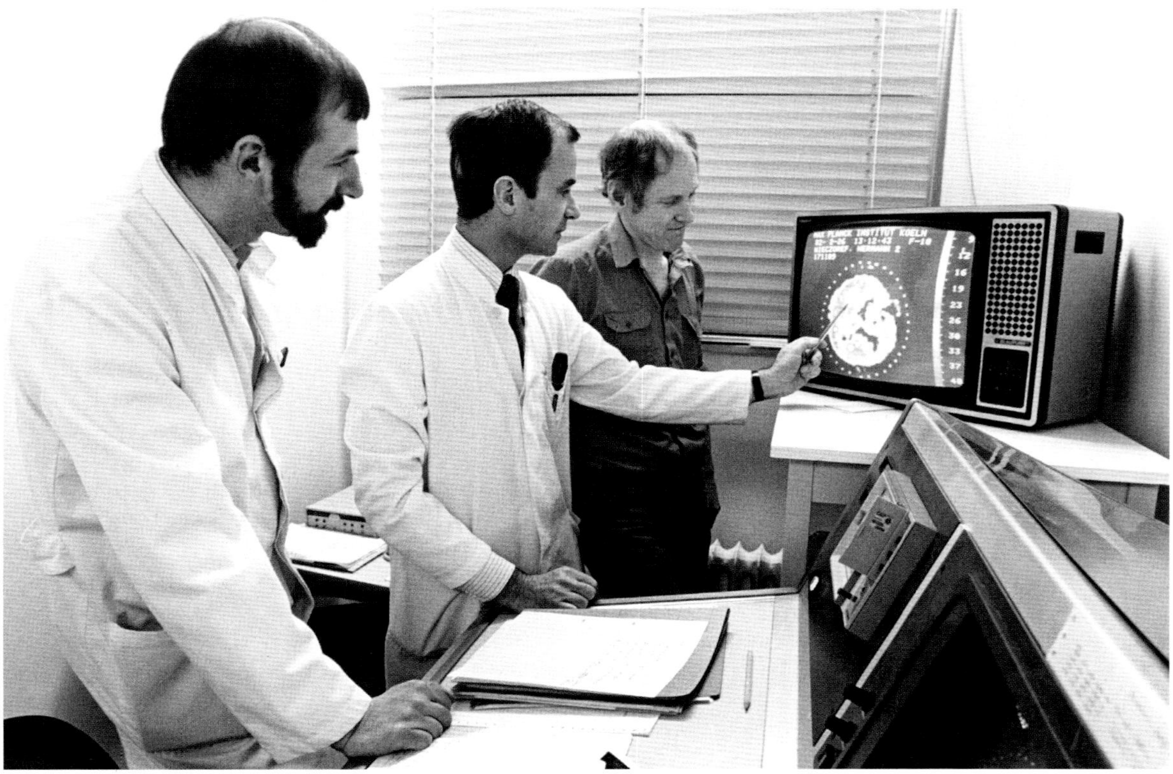

University Prize

1981
Press and Communications Department

The University of Cologne awarded "its" University Prize for the first time in 1981. Rector Herbert Wiedemann presented the first four certificates when he took office. The prizes went to Renate Bresgen-Bönner and Heinz-Günther Nesselrath, both members of the Faculty of Philosophy, to Bernhard Dick of the Faculty of Mathematics and Natural Sciences, and to Stephan von Zellewski of the Faculty of Economics and Social Sciences. With the University Prize, the Senate aimed to recognize the research achievements of the university's young academics. The recipients were selected by a prize committee composed of the rector of the university, the chairman of the Association of Friends and Sponsors, and the Senate commissioner for university honors and research. The prizes were endowed with 3,000 German marks each for dissertations and 2,000 German marks for diploma theses. The prize money was donated by local companies; in 1981, by Bayer AG Leverkusen, Kaufhof AG, Klöckner-Humboldt-Deutz AG and the Rudolf Siedersleben'sche Otto Wolff Foundation. Cologne's University Prize exists to this day. It is now also awarded for outstanding achievements and projects in the categories of research, studies and teaching, and administration, at a ceremony during the rector's annual reception. The prize is sponsored by Köln-Alumni e.V.—the Association of Friends and Sponsors of the University of Cologne.[46]

Three-Meter Radio Telescope

1982
First Physics Institute

The reflector of the radio telescope hovered above Cologne like a UFO while being hoisted by a mobile crane from a heavy-load truck onto the roof of the First Physics Institute of the University of Cologne on Zülpicher Straße. The work was carried out by Colonia, a special-purpose vehicle company, on 10 November 1982. On that rainy morning, the institute's astrophysicists stood fascinated, watching the spectacular installation of the three-meter radio telescope they had developed.

The scientists had collaborated with Krupp in Rheinhausen to have the four-ton telescope built. It was funded by the German Research Foundation as part of the grant for SFB 131, a radio astronomy research group. Construction took three years. Cologne became the first German university to acquire a radio telescope designed to work at short millimeter and submillimeter wave lengths. The instrument could be adjusted to one-thousandth of a degree, meaning that it could be accurately aimed at a person standing 100 kilometers away. According to the research group, the "scientific activities to be conducted once the telescope was operational" included the "observation of galactic regions where star formation is thought to take place."[47]

Changing Student Life

Students attending university in the 1970s and 1980s faced many challenges. Some had difficulty adjusting to the large, overcrowded university and its urban environment. Despite recommended standard durations of study, students took longer and longer to complete their degrees, and the number of dropouts rose. The University of Cologne tried to assist students by offering improved, centralized and subject-related academic counseling, but students often dropped out for private reasons. A university survey in 1976 revealed that many were dealing with unfavorable personal circumstances, family issues and a lack of money. Financial problems were often the reason for longer durations of study, with more and more students forced to earn money on the side. Although by the end of the 1970s, nearly one-third of the Cologne student body was receiving financial aid based on Germany's 1971 *Bundesausbildungsförderungsgesetz* or BAföG (Federal Training Assistance Act), for many their economic situation remained precarious. The university therefore set up a student grant fund in 1977 which supported students in need, especially regarding preventive healthcare. It was not without reason that in 1980 the West German Rectors'

Conference warned of the danger of a "social form of numerus clausus." After further restrictions, the number of BAföG recipients at Cologne fell below twenty percent in the mid-1980s. Such developments ran counter to the purported political will to open university education to young people from working-class and low-income families.[48]

By contrast, the rising share of female students was a success story; women made up thirty percent of the student body in 1975 and this figure increased from year to year. The addition of new faculties for educational sciences and curative education, in which two-thirds of the students were women, boosted this trend. The proportion of women at Cologne grew from just under thirty-seven percent in the winter semester of 1979/1980 to about forty-one percent in the summer of 1980. Cologne therefore ranked above the national average of approximately thirty-eight percent. The number of women studying in the Faculty of Philosophy was particularly high, overtaking the number of male students by the mid-1970s and reaching sixty percent by 1980. Women in the Faculty of Medicine constituted forty-two percent of students during the winter semester of 1986/1987. In the Faculty of Law, previously dominated by men, women made up some thirty-eight percent, and in the Faculty of Mathematics and Natural Sciences, they accounted for nearly thirty-six percent of the students. The figure for the Faculty of Economics and Social Sciences was the lowest at twenty-nine percent. The university responded to this trend and issued the first student ID cards with gender-neutral language for the winter semester of 1986/1987, a change initiated by the AStA's Autonomous Women's Department. The Commission for Women's Equality, set up in 1990, created the first platform for advancing equal rights throughout the university.[49]

Degree programs were also internationalized, changing the everyday life of students. The number of foreign students attending the University of Cologne grew steadily, and from the mid-1970s, more and more Cologne students went abroad. The ERASMUS program adopted in May 1986 by the education ministers of the European Community (EC) member states reinforced this trend. There were eighty ERASMUS scholarship holders at the University of Cologne in the fall of 1988; a year later, there were almost twice that number. The expansion of a European exchange network meant that, for the first time in the winter semester of 1989/1990, there were nearly forty students from seven European countries studying at Cologne.[50]

While studies abroad and support for foreign students by the Academic Foreign Office were well organized, people with disabilities at the University of Cologne struggled with numerous problems. A 1983 survey by the AStA revealed that only seventeen percent of the rooms were easily accessible to students with disabilities. The university was aware of the problem and in 1982, at the initiative of the Faculty of Curative Education, the Senate elected an authorized representative to address the issue—a first step on the long road to inclusion. In 1990, Cologne became the first German institution of higher education to assist students with disabilities in managing their everyday university lives—with the help of young men conscripted into community service. They provided assistance mostly in the library, on the way to and from events, and at mealtimes. A guide for students with disabilities was published in June 1990 as part of a package of measures designed to improve conditions for students with disabilities.[51]

During the 1980s, the university opened its doors to senior citizens interested in studying. About 110 students between the ages of sixty and eighty enrolled in 1984—some as full-fledged students, others auditing courses. Most of them were enrolled in the Faculty of Philosophy, especially in archeology and art history courses. Quite a few aimed to acquire a degree and several were even pursuing a doctorate. By 1988, there were already 650 senior citizens at the University of Cologne, and that summer, the University Senate decided to expand degree programs for older people and integrate them into the university's general research and teaching activities. At the same time, however, the Senate emphasized that academic education would take priority over the continuing education of older students. During the 1989 summer semester, the University of Cologne for the first time offered students over fifty the opportunity to attend orientation events and introductory courses on academic working methods. This made Cologne one of Germany's pioneers in university programs for seniors.[52]

← Housing for Cologne students was in short supply in the 1980s. At night, students looked at ads in the morning paper as soon as it was released for delivery.

Heinz Pichlmaier 1930–2019

Professor in the Faculty of Medicine

Heinz Pichlmaier is considered a pioneer of palliative medicine in Germany. He studied medicine and dentistry at Ludwig-Maximilians-Universität in Munich, where he obtained doctorates in both fields. From 1959 to 1966, he worked as a resident at the Surgical University Clinic in Munich and completed his habilitation there in 1965. He assumed his first untenured professorship in Munich in 1971.

In 1974, the University of Cologne appointed Pichlmaier to the chair of general surgery, as the successor to Georg Heberer, and made him director of the Surgical Clinic, which he headed until he retired in 1996. He served as dean and chairman of his faculty's ethics commission. He headed the Central Ethics Committee of the German Medical Association from 1995 to 2004 and significantly influenced the development of medical ethics.

His main areas of specialization included esophageal surgery, vascular surgery and kidney transplants. Pichlmaier broke new ground in 1983 when he set up Germany's first palliative care center in Cologne with the aim of improving tumor patients' quality of life; it became a model for further centers. In 1994, Pichlmaier founded the German Association for Palliative Medicine. He was awarded the Paracelsus Medal of the German Medical Association in 2005.[53]

Klaus Stern born 1932

Professor in the Faculty of Law

Klaus Stern shaped constitutional law and made an outstanding contribution to the interpretation and development of Germany's Basic Law as the author of five volumes on *Das Staatsrecht der Bundesrepublik Deutschland* (Constitutional law in the Federal Republic of Germany), published between 1977 and 2011. Stern studied law and economics in Erlangen and Munich, receiving his doctorate in Munich in 1956. In 1962, only a year after obtaining his habilitation, the Free University of Berlin appointed him to a full professorship. In 1966, he assumed the professorship of public law, administrative law and general jurisprudence at the University of Cologne and held this position until retiring in 1997. He was also appointed director of the Institute of Constitutional and Administrative Law. Stern was one of the founding directors of the Institute of Broadcasting Law in 1968. He served as rector from 1971 to 1973.

Stern was an internationally acclaimed expert in law who specialized in constitutional law, European law, administrative law, municipal and commercial law, and media and postal law. He was a member of the standing committee of the Deutscher Juristentag, an association of German jurists, and first chairman of the Vereinigung der Deutschen Staatsrechtler, the association of German scholars of constitutional law. Stern served on many state commissions and acted as an advisor during negotiations on German unification. He was also a member of the Constitutional Court of the State of North Rhine-Westphalia.[54]

Wilhelm Stoffel
born 1928

Professor in the
Faculty of Medicine

Wilhelm Stoffel is one of Germany's leading researchers in the field of molecular medicine and cell research. He studied medicine at Cologne and completed his doctorate in medicine at the university's Institute of Physiological Chemistry in 1952. He was then awarded a scholarship to study at the Institute of Biochemistry at the University of Uppsala, Sweden. In 1953, he began studying chemistry at the University of Bonn, where he completed his degree in 1957. He then worked as a research associate at the Rockefeller Institute in New York for two years. In 1959, Stoffel also completed a doctorate in chemistry at the University of Cologne and then went to the ETH Zurich for a year, before returning to Cologne in 1960 and working as a research associate at the University of Cologne's Institute of Biochemistry. He obtained his habilitation there in 1962 with a research paper titled *Biosynthese der Polyenfettsäuren* (Biosynthesis of polyene fatty acids).

Stoffel became a lecturer in Cologne in 1964 and was appointed to the chair for biochemistry at the University of Cologne in 1967, a position he held until retiring in 1995. He designed and set up Germany's first Research Training Group, which began work in 1984. The resulting cooperation between the Institute for Biochemistry, the Institute of Genetics and the Cologne Max Planck Institute for Breeding Research led in 1994 to the founding of the Center of Molecular Medicine in Cologne, the first of its kind in Germany, which Stoffel headed until 1996.[55]

Heinz Vater
1932–2015

Professor in the
Faculty of Philosophy

Heinz Vater, whose mother was Jewish, survived the Nazi era with his family by hiding in a basement. He studied German language and literature with a focus on linguistics at Humboldt University in Berlin in East Germany. He then worked at East Berlin's Academy of Sciences in a group focusing on structural grammar. In 1961, he submitted a dissertation titled *Artikelformen im gegenwärtigen Deutsch* (Article forms in contemporary German). Before completing his thesis defense, Vater fled to West Germany after having come into conflict with the socialist state due to critical remarks. He obtained his doctorate in 1963 at the University of Hamburg with the same doctoral thesis. After being awarded his habilitation in Hamburg in 1969, he was an associate professor at Indiana University in Bloomington, Indiana, for three years.

The University of Cologne appointed Vater to the chair of German linguistics in 1972. He established a department focusing on linguistics at the Institute of German Language and Literature, where he lectured and conducted research until retiring in 1997. An internationally acclaimed linguist who was also exceptionally gifted in languages and musically accomplished, Vater authored several introductory textbooks on linguistics in addition to publishing influential research monographs. As co-founder of the German Society of Linguistics and editor of numerous series of publications, he contributed significantly to the international position and profile of German linguistics.[56]

“Presenting Scholarship”—the University of Cologne Turns 600

By October 1980, the Senate had already decided to celebrate the University of Cologne’s anniversary in 1988 on a grand scale. It appointed two professors from the Faculty of Economics and Social Sciences to prepare the event, and it set up two senate commissions. From November 1986 on, an office with three full-time staff organized an ambitious and deeply symbolic program. More than three hundred events were held between the opening ceremony on 20 May 1988, which marked the date when the founding charter was issued on 21 May 1388, and 6 January 1989, six hundred years after the old university opened on Epiphany Day.[57]

All anniversary activities were held under the slogan of “Presenting Scholarship.” The university’s goal was to enter into a dialog with a variety of partners and present its achievements to a broader public. This assertive self-portrayal was unusual, but in times of tight budgets and low public interest in higher education, the University of Cologne aimed to enhance its profile and demonstrate its social relevance. The “faculty weeks” were the focal point of the program—an innovative idea which opened each faculty to interested parties for a week between May and July 1988. A summer festival on the campus attracted 15,000 visitors and showed another facet of the university. Here and at the four-day anniversary event in October, the university celebrated with Cologne’s citizens at Neumarkt square in the heart of the city. On countless occasions, speakers highlighted the university’s traditionally close connection to the city. The fact that the citizens of Cologne had founded their university twice, and their “willingness to make sacrifices” to fund it, were central elements of the anniversary narrative.[58]

These traditional and innovative forms of presentation showcased the university and its social relevance, local ties and historical continuity. Commemorative medals issued by Cologne’s savings bank were more traditional in style, while the anniversary logo had a rather modern look: a pictogram of the Three Wise Men above the words “600 Years Cologne University 1388–1988.” The official ceremony in the Cologne Philharmonic Hall, which marked the beginning of the week of celebrations on 4 November, was an old academic ritual at which prominent representatives of the groups that supported the university—the rector of the university, the mayor of the city, the premier of the state of North Rhine-Westphalia, and Germany’s president—gave speeches. A live program broadcast by the television station ARD was more contemporary, and music composed by Karlheinz Stockhausen, who had studied at Cologne, was decidedly avant-garde. Students were not an official part of the ceremony—a clear expression of the prevalent dislike of the *Gruppenuniversität*. Four days later, students were invited to the first *dies academicus* in twenty-one years, an event sponsored by the university leadership—the AStA, however, did not participate.[59]

The university underlined its progressive aspects at specialist events that were an important part of the anniversary celebrations. Three major interdisciplinary symposia featured experts from around the world who talked about the day’s big issues: the media, computer science and the environment. The symposia were designed to demonstrate Cologne’s academic achievements. More than eighty specialist conferences focused on research. Here, the university presented itself as part of an international network of innovative research facilities that worked toward finding solutions to important contemporary challenges.[60]

History was a recurrent theme in all of these activities. Four major anniversary talks on the past, present and future of the university linked the events together. A history of the university in three volumes was the first scholarly and comprehensive presen-

tation of the history of Cologne's higher education institutions, and it offered a nuanced historical account that did not leave out discontinuities. By contrast, at the ceremony commemorating the anniversary of the founding of the university on 20 May 1988, Rector Peter Hanau emphasized the continuities and commonalities that extended to the present day, including the close connection between university and city, the mediation between theory and practice at the new university, and the presence of an international community of scholars and students at the old university. These contrasting positions revealed the strong tensions between critical scholarship and affirmative self-representation. The representatives of the University of Cologne aimed to be traditional and innovative, critical and collaborative at the same time. This corresponded to a mixture of dynamic academic development and persistence in teaching and self-administration. The anniversary celebrations came and went, but a new concept for the university had not been proposed.[61]

The attempt to create an identity through tradition-building during the anniversary year met with criticism. This mostly applied to how the university dealt with the Nazi era, since the anniversary fell two years after the bitter dispute among historians in Germany that came to be called the Historikerstreit. For its six-hundredth anniversary, the University of Cologne had commissioned Frank Golczewski to compile a study on its Nazi past, and it had commemorated the "victims of National Socialist tyranny" on 9 November 1988. But the university's self-portrayal at public events and speeches during the celebrations did not address Golczewski's findings on the Nazi affiliation of many university instructors at Cologne. Students published the critical *Nachhilfe zur Erinnerung* (Lessons for remembrance). Even though the university protested against the criticism, it did not address the involvement of its members in the Nazi regime. Continuities before 1933 and after 1945, some of which concerned emeritus professors who were still alive, were never mentioned.[62]

↑ The 1988 anniversary logo combined a pictogram of the Three Wise Men and the anniversary slogan.

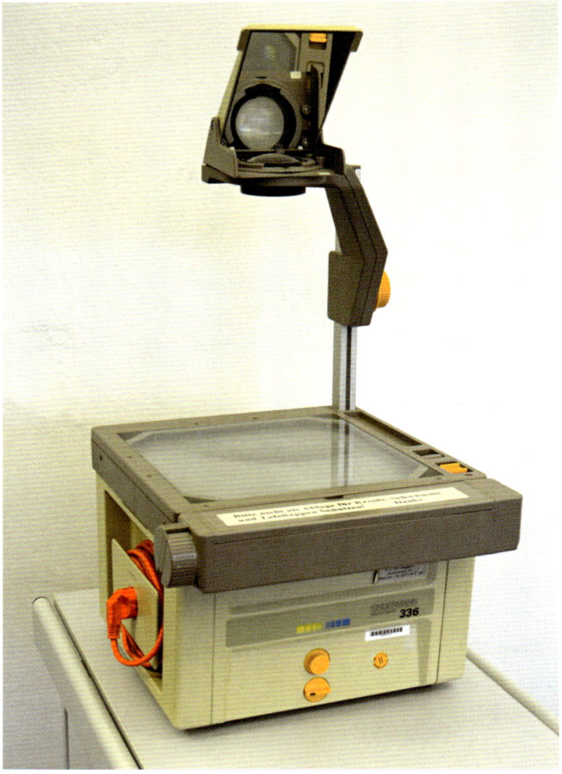

Overhead Projector

circa 1985
Faculty of Human Sciences

Nowadays, overhead projectors seem quite outmoded; they are considered relics of a pre-digital age. But according to the Infrastructural Facility Management Office of the University of Cologne, even in the university's 2019 anniversary year, nearly every seminar room and lecture hall is still equipped with one of these devices. The overhead projector accompanied generations of instructors and students. The machine pictured above dates from the mid-1980s and has long been relegated to a storage room at the Faculty of Human Sciences. The first overhead projector was launched by 3M in 1960. The model had its antecedents in Belsazar, a projection apparatus developed in 1931 based on an idea of Carl Zeiss'. Using an image projector, enlarged versions of texts, images, graphs, and reading lists on transparencies are projected onto a screen without having to darken the room completely. When the lecture hall building was completed in 1966, the university equipped the rooms with this state-of-the-art technology. Overhead projectors quickly became an indispensable aid for the teaching staff. The principle is the same as that of a slide projector. A lamp evenly illuminates the working surface through a lens; the light shines through the transparencies placed on the working surface and is projected onto a screen via the reflector.[63]

Stamp

1988
University of Cologne Archives

600 Years of Cologne University: The Deutsche Bundespost issued a 35 by 35 millimeter commemorative stamp on 5 May 1988, just in time for the anniversary celebrations on 20 May 1988. The eighty-pfennig stamp was issued in an edition of 31.5 million and was valid until 30 June 2002. Unlike the stamps of previous years, stamps issued in 1988 were only valid for a limited time due to the scheduled introduction of the euro as the single European currency on 1 January 2002. The artwork for the special edition stamp pictured above was based on a design by Otto Rohse, a well-known book designer and graphic artist from Hamburg who designed some sixty stamps for the Deutsche Bundespost. The top row of the stamp depicts the three church spires characteristic of Cologne's skyline: the basilica of St. Ursula, Cologne Cathedral and Great St. Martin (from left to right). The lecture hall building (left) and the Philosophikum (right)—two central buildings of the campus university, which was not completed until the early 1970s,—are grouped together in the second row. The bottom row shows an elongated view of the facade of the university's main building opened in the 1930s. The selection of stylized buildings was intended to express the traditional bonds between the city and the University of Cologne, which was founded and financed by the city and its citizens in 1388 and 1919.[64]

Reorientation

Chapter 7

1990–2007

1990–2007

1990

A New Constitution

The new constitution goes into effect. It bolsters self-administration, increases participation in decision-making processes and implements affirmative action measures for women for the first time.

1995

Online

The university's first website goes online in 1995, completely in black and white. A year later, students are able to set up a personal university email account. The University of Cologne enters the internet era.

1995

First SFB in the Faculty of Philosophy

The Faculty of Philosophy's first Collaborative Research Center (SFB) is established and dedicated to Cultural and Environmental Change in Arid Africa: Development Processes under Extreme Ecological Conditions.

1996

Germany's Largest University

Cologne boasts nearly 63,000 students, making it Germany's largest university for the first time. Overcrowding and underfunding remain a constant problem, not only at Cologne.

1997

"Lucky Strike"

In the largest nationwide protests since 1968, students demand better study conditions, reject a shorter duration of studies and oppose the introduction of tuition fees. Student blockades and occupations in Cologne result in violent clashes with the police.

2001

An Independent University Hospital

The University Hospital becomes an autonomous institution under public law. A cooperation agreement with the university maintains the connection between medical research and regional healthcare established by the Academy for Medicine in 1904.

2004

Between Failure and Success

The University of Cologne is not selected for funding in the first round of the Excellence Initiative. In the second round three years later, the university succeeds in receiving grants for a cluster of excellence and a graduate school.

2004

The Bologna Process

The University of Cologne begins implementing the Bologna Process. The first bachelor's and master's degree programs are offered in the winter semester of 2006/2007.

Although the university administration was strengthened by the new constitution of 1990, it continued to face familiar problems: after a brief period of stagnation, student enrollment again rose faster than the budget, and the state government continued to pursue its regulatory policy. It was not until 1995 that the introduction of a global budget gave the university greater autonomy. Cologne, which became Germany's largest university for the first time in 1996, distinguished itself in the academic arena as an internationally networked university with a focus on research and its applications. When the University Hospital became an autonomous legal entity in 2001, this marked the beginning of a decade of transformation. The launch of the Bologna Process and the Excellence Initiative in 2004, as well as plans to establish a new Faculty of Human Sciences in 2007, opened up new horizons for the University of Cologne.

Germany's Largest University

The fact that the entire university administration was now incorporated within the rectorate increased the effective autonomy of the university, which expanded and professionalized its control mechanisms during the 1990s. At the same time, the demands placed on the administration grew. Following a phase of stagnation, student numbers rose from around 53,000 in 1994 to almost 63,000 in 1996. Cologne was now the largest university in Germany and would hold this position for about a decade. Overcrowding and underfunding remained constant issues. There were 119 students for every full professor at Cologne in 1996, compared with a national average ratio of seventy to one.[1]

For years, the German public was barely aware of the chronic problems at its universities. This changed in the early 1990s, thanks in part to university rankings published by major magazines, which assessed the conditions of study, as well as the quality of teaching at German universities based on statistical data. Policymakers reacted by introducing new standards. The Quality of Teaching program launched by North Rhine-Westphalia's Ministry of Science and Research in 1991 tied additional funding to the implementation of concrete measures to improve studies. Two years later, the Eckdatenverordnung (Benchmarking Regulation) led to a sweeping restructuring of master's degree programs. This was part of an amendment to the state-level Higher Education Act, which also consolidated the administrative control powers of the rectorate and the deans. Whereas the state government felt the new law strengthened the autonomy of higher education institutions, for the University of Cologne it signaled further restrictions. A paper jointly drafted with other universities stated that the universities were prepared to undertake reforms, but that these had to respect tradition and "undo the serious damage done to the universities by the higher education policy of recent decades."[2]

↖ Into the 1990s, there were long registration lines at the beginning of each semester.

← Unauthorized parking of bicycles and cars in front of the main building was one of the many problems caused by overcrowding in the 1990s.

Global Budget and Research Funding

The University of Cologne's participation in a pilot project entitled Universities and Financial Autonomy in the mid-1990s opened up new horizons. From 1 January 1995, the University of Cologne was entrusted with a global budget, a turning point in education finance policy. Budgetary autonomy created new opportunities. Agreement on a Pact on Quality in 1999 and a reform of the Higher Education Act in 2000 further extended the universities' discretionary powers, but these changes were also tied to further demands for reform and massive cuts in public funding. Again, one aim was to improve the quality of teaching, but also to strengthen their competitive edge domestically and internationally by raising their profiles, cooperating with non-university research institutions and other universities, and expanding top-level research. By encouraging competition among universities, policymakers pressured them to become more entrepreneurial. Management approaches were introduced into university governance. The acquisition of additional funds and strategic investment in promising new fields of research built a foundation for future success, but this was at the expense of disciplines with less potential for economic exploitation. This increasing "economization" fundamentally changed the university.[3]

Although the University of Cologne continued to protest against what it saw as unnecessary interference in its governance, it also took advantage of the possibilities presented by deregulation and distinguished itself as a modern research university. The key to this success was a focus on areas where it had a reputation for excellence, on international collaboration and on applied research. The university increased its potential through local and regional cooperation with external research institutions and the neighboring universities of Bonn and Aachen.[4]

External funding continued to be a decisive factor in expanding research, and the importance of prize money for individual research achievements increased. The university also benefited from new forms of public funding from the European Union and the Federal Ministry of Education and Research (BMBF). From 1995 on, the ministry supported the interdisciplinary Center for Molecular Medicine at the University of Cologne (ZMMK), founded a year earlier as one of nine model institutions in Germany dedicated to conducting internationally competitive basic research. In 1996, the University of Cologne won the BMBF's BioRegio competition and set about establishing a research center for biosciences. The Center for Advanced European Studies and Research (CAESAR) in Bonn, which was founded by the Federal Republic of Germany and the state of North Rhine-Westphalia and began its work in 1998, was a special form of regional collaboration. The universities of Bonn and Cologne cooperated in this showcase project, which was exceptionally well funded.[5]

By the turn of the millennium, the volume of external funding to the University of Cologne had increased to roughly fifty-seven million euros. Almost four fifths of this was raised by the medical, mathematics and natural science faculties. Nine Collaborative Research Centers (SFBs)—including two of them for

↑ Ulrich Walter (left) studied physics at Cologne. The seal of his alma mater accompanied him on his flight to outer space; he is pictured here at a reception hosted by Rector Ulrich Matz in 1993.

the first time at the Faculty of Philosophy—along with seven graduate schools and one research group were focal points of top-level research at Cologne. By early 2001, roughly 3,000 projects in over 260 departments, institutes and clinics testified to the wide range of scholarship at the University of Cologne. More than 500 professors and some 1,500 members of the academic staff were involved in research and teaching.[6]

Repositioned

The year 2001 saw a fundamental change: the University Hospital became an autonomous institution under public law. The separation of research and teaching from healthcare severed a link created almost one hundred years earlier with the founding of the Academy for Medicine in 1904, which had advanced the development of Cologne as a site for higher education and research. A new cooperation agreement defined the future interplay between theory and practice.[7]

That same year, the expert council created by the state government to assess the performance of universities and other institutions of higher education certified that the University of Cologne was a "research-oriented, interdisciplinary and internationally active university." The university emphasized these strengths in its marketing endeavors, which began on an international level in 2001. In 2002, a marketing coordination office was established, which cooperated closely with the alumni network KölnAlumni e.V. founded that same year. The university, which increasingly operated along entrepreneurial lines, no longer relied solely on recognition from the academic community and contact with policymakers and civil servants, but instead worked systematically to boost its public image.[8]

The recommendations of the expert council were incorporated into the first Target Agreement, which the university and the Ministry of Science and Research concluded in the summer of 2002 to cover a period of two years. These agreements represented a new form of ministerial leadership adopted from corporate management. Besides strengthening research and teaching, the university would focus on expanding its international networks, including faculty-level contacts. With the Center for International Relations at the Faculty of Economics and Social Sciences, the University of Cologne had created a successful institution that was to become a model for others. In order to comply with the quality assurance requirements stipulated in the agreements, the university developed an evaluation mechanism for the first time and planned the establishment of international research advisory boards.[9]

The university also explored new ways of transferring research findings to other sectors. These included the Bioriver Science biotechnology network, which was founded in collaboration with the University of Düsseldorf. In 2002, the university additionally began working with the patent management agency PROvendis. Furthermore, the hochschulgründernetz cologne, which was set up in the winter semester of 2002/2003 as a collaborative project involving the University of Cologne, Cologne's University of Applied Sciences, and its Sports College, promoted business start-ups by Cologne-based scientists. Cologne thus positioned itself early on as a hub for academic start-ups and spinoffs. In late 2003, the university appointed its first rectorate commissioner for research transfer and business start-ups. This link between research and revenue transformed the university's self-understanding, and economic exploitability became more and more significant.[10]

In addition to applied research, the university increasingly promoted practice-oriented education. The Cologne Qualification Transfer Initiative (KIQ), which was launched in 1998, integrated professional training into academic studies and established contacts with business enterprises. From 2002, this became the Career Service. The growing role of ongoing academic education was reflected in the creation of the Center for Continuous Education (CCE) in 2001. The university expanded its scope to include internal and external services, representing a further fundamental change in how it interpreted its role. At the same time, it increased the fields of study and degrees offered. By 2004, there were about 140 undergraduate degree programs and, with almost 15,000 students, the University of Cologne was the largest teacher training college in Europe. Beginning with the winter semester 2003/2004, the Teacher Training Center (LBZ) coordinated and implemented the numerous reform measures initiated in the aftermath of the PISA (Programme for International Student Assessment) shock of 2001 (German students' scores in reading, mathematics and science were found to be lower than the OECD average).[11]

In Flux

The year 2004 began with the surprising news that the federal government was planning a competition to promote elite, high-performing universities. This Excellence Initiative met with great interest and approval in Cologne because it was seen as confirming the path already taken to create centers of top-level research. The disappointment was therefore great when the university emerged empty-handed from the first round of the competition in 2005/2006. In the second round in 2006/2007, Cologne was more successful and received funding for a cluster of excellence and a graduate school. Another project that was to change the university also began to take shape in 2004: the introduction of bachelor's and master's degree programs as part of the Bologna Process. Within three years, the university converted fifty-six *Magister* and twenty-three *Diplom* programs to the new system.[12]

In response to accelerated globalization, the university expanded its worldwide network. It assumed principal responsibility for the coordination of university relations between China and the state of North Rhine-Westphalia. In late 2004, the Senate established a fourth prorectorship for international affairs and public relations. A year later, the university for the first time adopted a set of guidelines for internationalization. At the end of 2006, the International Office registered around 7,000 foreign students from 154 countries. Sixteen official university partnerships in ten countries and 200 partnerships by faculties and departments in more than forty countries is a further testament to the breadth of the university's international network.[13]

The introduction of study vouchers and semester fees for "long-term students" in 2004 resulted in a short-term reduction in the official number of students, from 60,000 to 47,000, but these statistics no longer included guest auditors. However, demand remained so great that the university had to impose admission limits on almost all subjects. In 2006, when the state government decided to introduce tuition fees for all, protests erupted throughout the state. In Cologne, students occupied the rector's office for ten days and 1,500 of them held up a senate session. The rector called the police, who put an end to both protests.[14]

The civil service salary reform adopted in late 2004 was another landmark. It introduced age-independent basic salaries for professors with civil service status, to which variable bonuses could be added based on pre-contract negotiations or for special achievements in research, teaching or university self-administrative service. The rectorate responded to this reform with skepticism. The new "junior professorship," introduced on 1 January 2005, also met with little enthusiasm. There was great relief, however, that the traditional path to a professorship via habilitation was to be retained. The second Target Agreement from March 2005 continued to promote fields of research excellence and strengthened the internationalization of the university. In the same year, the Senate decided to merge the Faculty of Educational Sciences and the Faculty of Curative Education with the Department of Psychology and the Department of Pedagogy to form the Faculty of Human Sciences. This came into effect on 1 January 2007, kicking off a year of radical change.[15]

↗ Since the remodeling of the auditorium in the university's main building, professors and students have gathered there for the opening ceremonies at the beginning of each new semester.

→ A children's university was launched as part of the university's repositioning; young auditors at a chemistry lecture in 2003.

The Beginnings of Affirmative Action for Women

North Rhine-Westphalia was one of the first German states to pursue an active gender equality policy in the 1980s. The Affirmative Action for Women Act of 1990 was unique in stipulating that, given equal aptitude, qualifications and performance, women were to be given preferential consideration for appointment or promotion. At the time, there were almost as many female as male students in Cologne, but the proportion of female professors was in the low single digits. The new 1990 university constitution provided for the election of a Commission for Equality for Women and the appointment of a women's affairs officer. However, this reform was not implemented until 1991, making Cologne one of the last universities in North Rhine-Westphalia to act. Professor Ilse Müller became the acting women's affairs officer.[16]

The first election to the commission took place in January 1991. Over 29,000 women were eligible to vote, yet only slightly more than four percent of them did. While only a small portion of the female students took part in the election, fifty-eight percent of the female professors and thirty-five percent of the female research staff voted. Just eight percent of the female non-academic staff cast a vote. In contrast to the other university committees, the commission realized parity with two representatives from each of these groups. This in itself represented a step toward greater democratization of the university. From among its members, the commission elected the women's affairs officer, who was confirmed by the Senate. Candidates for this office were required to have an academic degree and be employed by the university. The women's affairs officer provided advice on issues such as scholarships for women, returning to work after parental leave, or dealing with sexual harassment. She was also authorized to cast a special vote in the committees that selected new professors.[17]

The first elected women's affairs officer was Dr. Karin Klees, a researcher at the Department of Pedagogy. She was followed in 1992 by Elisabeth Knust, professor at the Institute of Developmental Biology, and in 1993 by Christel Tomson, head of the Department of Budgetary Affairs, Student Affairs and (in some periods) Law. In 1992/1993, the university, with the help of the Women's Research Network, established dedicated professorships for women in African Studies and in historical research on reading. By the mid-1990s, eleven career re-entry fellowships and five Lise Meitner habilitation fellowships had been awarded to women as part of the University Special Program II. The women's affairs officer organized a public lecture series on women's issues, and, in 1993, the Commission for Equality for Women presented its first report on the situation of women at the University of Cologne. Since 1995, the Women's Affairs Office has published *FrauenInfo*, an information leaflet for women.[18]

Despite the many activities that had been introduced, the overall picture presented in the first annual progress report of the women's affairs officer in 1995 was sobering. Although about fifty-two percent of all students at Cologne were women, just twenty-nine percent of the academic staff was female, and the twenty-nine female professors represented less than six percent of all professorships. The university lacked the staff structure and affirmative action plan for women that was needed to fundamentally change this situation. There was neither an official university agreement to protect against sexual harassment nor a complaints office. The Women's Affairs Office was understaffed. Other areas where there was urgent need for action included the expansion of interdisciplinary women's and gender research, the use of gender-equitable language, and support for those dealing with family responsibilities while studying or pursuing a career. Christel Tomson noted that most offices and committees at all levels were still in

Chemie und Frauen

Kein Potential für Frauenthemen: Chemievorlesungen bleiben pure Naturwissenschaft

Feminin geprägtes Chemiestudium

Pech für die Frauenbeauftragte der Universität zu Köln. Auf der Suche nach Seminaren, die „einen Beitrag zu frauenspezifischen Fragen" leisten, konnte die mathematisch-naturwissenschaftliche Fakultät nicht mit einer einzigen Veranstaltung aufwarten.

Chemieprofessor Dieter Naumann, 52, versicherte indes, sein Institut sei „unerschütterlich" tolerant. Ohnehin sei der ganze Studienverlauf „feminin geprägt", schließlich müßten Studierende *die* Vorlesung hören, *die* Klausur schreiben und *die* Prüfung ablegen. „Ein paar geschlechtsneutrale Veranstaltungen, wie *das* Praktikum, *das* Seminar und *das* Kolloquium" hätten die Chemiker bloß, um „männliche Studenten nicht gänzlich abzuschrecken".

Focus 24.10.94

male hands. Despite the measures taken, she said, "it has not yet been possible to effectively break through the patriarchal structures at the university and remove the stumbling blocks to women's academic careers."[19]

The University of Cologne did not present a draft plan for affirmative action for women until March 1998. The delay was partly due to the rejection of gender-equal representation on selection committees and of quotas for academic appointments. The all-male university management considered these reforms to be inappropriate. It was not until 1999 that Ursula Hedwig Frost, a professor of pedagogy, became the first woman to assume the office of prorector. The 1999 Act on Equality of Women and Men obliged universities to draw up a three-year affirmative action plan for women, which was to define specific measures to promote equal opportunities, support those managing family life and careers, and increase the representation of women. In 2001, Cologne was one of the first universities in Germany to adopt an affirmative action plan for women and at the same time set up a fund to support four projects a year. These were to be selected by the rectorate together with the equal opportunities officer.[20]

For its commitment to the advancement of women, the university received the E-Quality Award for the first time in 2004. At that time, thirteen percent of professorships were held by women, and nearly twenty percent of Cologne academics completing their habilitation were female. These numbers represented a significant increase, but they were still far too low. That same year, a change in the university constitution promoted the advancement of women by setting up the Advisory Council for Equal Opportunities for Women to advise the Commission for Equality for Women. By 2006, the proportion of female students in Cologne had risen to fifty-eight percent and the share of female professors to around sixteen percent. There was still much to be done.[21]

↑ In 1994 the weekly news magazine *Focus* published a commentary on "feminine-style chemistry studies" at the University of Cologne.

Juergen B. Donges
born 1940

Professor in the Faculty of
Economics and Social Sciences

The international focus that distinguishes economist Juergen B. Donges was acquired early in his life. He was born in Seville, attended the German international school in Madrid and obtained both the Spanish *bachillerato* and the German Abitur there. Upon completing his training as an industrial administrator in Heidenheim, he studied economics at Saarland University and took a position there as a researcher at the Institute for European Economic Policy. He earned his doctorate in 1969 and then joined the Kiel Institute for the World Economy, where he was appointed director and professor in 1978. He served as the institute's vice-president in 1983. During his time in Kiel, Donges headed the Collaborative Research Center for Global Economy and International Trade Relations.

In 1989, the University of Cologne appointed Juergen B. Donges to the chair of political economics, which he held until he retired in 2007. At the same time, he was director of the Institute for Political Economy and the Otto Wolff Institute for Economic Studies. Donges was chairman of the German federal government's Deregulation Commission from 1989 to 1991. He was a member of the German Council of Economic Experts (also called the "Five Sages") from 1992 to 2002 and was its chairman from 2000 to 2002.[22]

Werner Eck
born 1939

Professor in the
Faculty of Philosophy

Werner Eck is considered a leading expert on Imperial Rome and Roman epigraphy. He studied history, Latin, Greek, German language and literature, and archeology at the University of Erlangen-Nuremberg, where he completed his doctorate in ancient history in 1968. He assumed a post as assistant professor at the University of Cologne in 1969, earning his habilitation in 1975 with a study titled *Die staatliche Organisation Italiens in der hohen Kaiserzeit* (The organization of the state in Italy during the High Imperial period). He was an academic advisor and professor, then full professor at Saarland University. The University of Cologne appointed him to a chair of ancient history in 1979, which he held until he retired in 2007.

Eck served as dean of the Faculty of Philosophy from 1985 to 1989 and was later a member of the university's Senate. He wrote over two dozen books and authored around a thousand articles, mostly on Roman administrative and social history and Roman epigraphy. He has been one of the editors of the journal *Zeitschrift für Papyrologie und Epigraphik* since 1979. Eck has been honored with numerous awards, including the Max Planck Research Prize for International Cooperation in 2000. His name is closely linked to *Geschichte der Stadt Köln*, a multi-volume history of the city of Cologne, as its editor and the author of the first volume on the city in Roman times.[23]

Peter Grünberg
1939–2018

Professor in the Faculty of Mathematics and Natural Sciences

Physicist Peter Grünberg discovered the GMR (giant magnetoresistance) effect—at the same time as Albert Fert, who was working independently—which revolutionized data storage on hard drives. Using the GMR effect, Grünberg and Fert developed sensors that employ the quantum mechanical properties of electron spin to read out data. The capacity of data storage devices could thus be greatly increased. Data-intensive applications such as cloud computing, big data, social media and the internet of things would not be possible without the GMR effect. Grünberg und Fert were awarded the 2007 Nobel Prize in Physics for their discoveries, which laid the foundation for the innovative field of spintronics.

Grünberg received his doctorate in 1969 from Technische Universität Darmstadt with a thesis titled *Spektroskopische Untersuchungen an einigen Selten-Erd-Granaten* (Spectroscopic investigations of selected rare earth garnets). After a three-year research appointment at Carleton University in Canada, he joined the Jülich Nuclear Physics Institute in 1972, where he worked as a research associate at the Institute for Solid State Research. Grünberg obtained his habilitation from the University of Cologne in 1984, where he was initially a *Privatdozent* and then an untenured professor from 1992 until retiring in 2004. In 2007, the Forschungszentrum Jülich (Jülich Research Center) awarded Grünberg the first Helmholtz professorship.[24]

Herbert Hax
1933–2005

Professor in the Faculty of Economics and Social Sciences

Although Herbert Hax was born in Cologne and his father, Karl Hax, had begun his academic career there as a student of Eugen Schmalenbach, Hax himself did not study in his native city. Only after obtaining his *Diplom* in business administration in Frankfurt am Main did he return to Cologne to work as Erich Gutenberg's associate. Hax assumed professorships in Saarbrücken and Vienna after completing his doctorate in 1960 and his habilitation in 1964. The University of Cologne appointed him to the chair of general business administration and business finance in 1976, which he held until retiring in 1998.

Hax's interests and areas of research were broad and ranged from decision theory to organizational theory and the theory of capital markets. His major works include *Die Koordination von Entscheidungen* (Coordinating decisions, 1965) and *Investitionstheorie* (Investment theory, 1970). His last book, *Unternehmen und Unternehmer in der Marktwirtschaft* (Enterprises and entrepreneurs in the market economy, 2005) was published posthumously. He spent many years as the editor of the *Zeitschrift für betriebswirtschaftliche Forschung*. Hax gained public recognition as a member of the German Council of Economic Experts from 1989 to 2000 and as its chairman from 1992 to 2000.[25]

Under Observation

An article in Germany's news magazine *Der Spiegel* in December 1989 opened up a new debate on higher education. Drawing on a survey of 6,000 students by the Berlin sociologist Friedhelm Neidhardt and the EMNID Institute, the magazine compiled a ranking of West German universities and technical colleges. The article was subsequently published in a large print-run as an extra edition. It was the first time that university rankings reached such a wide readership in Germany. Cologne came out in the top third of the overall ranking, as number seventeen in a field of fifty-one. However, in one of its leading disciplines, economics, Cologne was only thirty-ninth. The university reacted with displeasure. The Cologne-based sociologist Erwin K. Scheuch sharply criticized the methodology of the study. He accused *Der Spiegel* of having arbitrarily chosen and failed to explicitly weight the ranking criteria. He also claimed that the study drew on insufficient data and that the evaluation method distorted the results. He complained that the study, because of the public resonance it achieved, had caused considerable damage, as politicians were already using it as a basis for the allocation of funding. According to Scheuch, competition among universities was needed, but more rigorous ranking methods were required.[26]

Another ranking positioned Cologne among the top 100 European universities, which eased the pain of the *Der Spiegel* publication. Although that study, published by the French magazine *Libération*, was not very representative, being based solely on a survey of 600 European professors, the university was nonetheless pleased at its high placement in the subjects of history and political science. Numerous other university rankings that followed in the ensuing years heightened the influence of mass media in debates over higher education policy, even though the results varied significantly. For example, *Der Spiegel* ranked Cologne University thirty-sixth in Germany in 1993, while *Stern* magazine put it in ninth place and the business magazine *Forbes* ranked it number one. The differences between these ratings, which also affected other universities, led to a public debate about the validity of such rankings. The main focus of this debate was on the data, methodology and decontextualization of the results. For example, in most of the studies, the number of respondents was too small and their selection too arbitrary to yield far-reaching and generally valid results about teaching performance. The selection of criteria for comparing universities and subjects of different sizes and orientations was often considered problematic. The service-oriented publication of the rankings in journals, magazines and special issues also reduced complex facts to simple criteria for choosing a place of study.[27]

Despite their weaknesses, the popular rankings were important for universities, which were increasingly obliged to justify themselves to the public and policymakers. The large discrepancies in the results, however, led each university to select the evaluations that best suited them. In its 1997/1998 annual statement, the Cologne rectorate reported in detail on a recent survey by *Focus* magazine. The professors surveyed had placed Cologne in tenth place, while personnel managers ranked it third. The university was especially pleased with the praise from personnel departments. This was seen as proof that the university provided an education that was particularly well tailored to professional practice. On the other hand, the rectorate dismissed as incomprehensible the low score it received from students. The university at times felt obliged to respond publicly to poor ranking results. For example, in a 1998 *Der Spiegel* survey of universities across Europe, Cologne was among the lowest ranked. The university responded by organizing a panel discussion with the telling title "What is 'inadequate'—the University of Cologne or the *Der Spiegel* ranking?"[28]

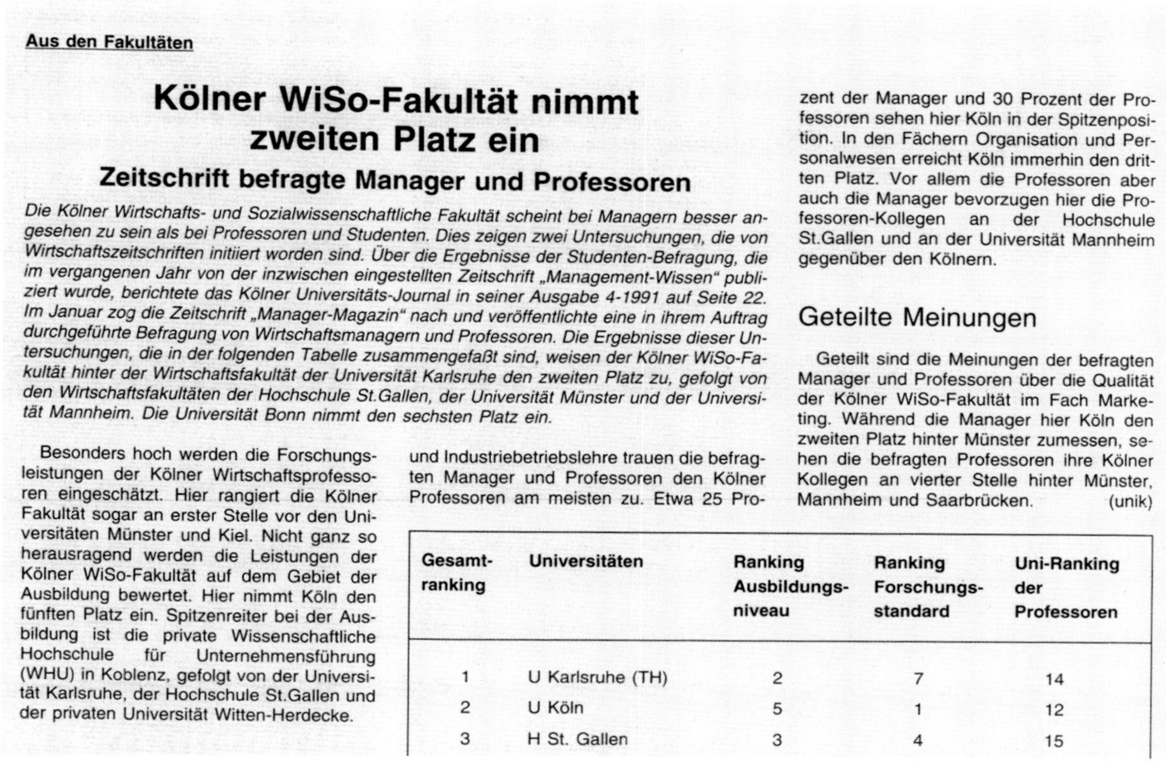

Aus den Fakultäten

Kölner WiSo-Fakultät nimmt zweiten Platz ein

Zeitschrift befragte Manager und Professoren

Die Kölner Wirtschafts- und Sozialwissenschaftliche Fakultät scheint bei Managern besser angesehen zu sein als bei Professoren und Studenten. Dies zeigen zwei Untersuchungen, die von Wirtschaftszeitschriften initiiert worden sind. Über die Ergebnisse der Studenten-Befragung, die im vergangenen Jahr von der inzwischen eingestellten Zeitschrift „Management-Wissen" publiziert wurde, berichtete das Kölner Universitäts-Journal in seiner Ausgabe 4-1991 auf Seite 22. Im Januar zog die Zeitschrift „Manager-Magazin" nach und veröffentlichte eine in ihrem Auftrag durchgeführte Befragung von Wirtschaftsmanagern und Professoren. Die Ergebnisse dieser Untersuchungen, die in der folgenden Tabelle zusammengefaßt sind, weisen der Kölner WiSo-Fakultät hinter der Wirtschaftsfakultät der Universität Karlsruhe den zweiten Platz zu, gefolgt von den Wirtschaftsfakultäten der Hochschule St.Gallen, der Universität Münster und der Universität Mannheim. Die Universität Bonn nimmt den sechsten Platz ein.

Besonders hoch werden die Forschungsleistungen der Kölner Wirtschaftsprofessoren eingeschätzt. Hier rangiert die Kölner Fakultät sogar an erster Stelle vor den Universitäten Münster und Kiel. Nicht ganz so herausragend werden die Leistungen der Kölner WiSo-Fakultät auf dem Gebiet der Ausbildung bewertet. Hier nimmt Köln den fünften Platz ein. Spitzenreiter bei der Ausbildung ist die private Wissenschaftliche Hochschule für Unternehmensführung (WHU) in Koblenz, gefolgt von der Universität Karlsruhe, der Hochschule St.Gallen und der privaten Universität Witten-Herdecke.

Und Industriebetriebslehre trauen die befragten Manager und Professoren den Kölner Professoren am meisten zu. Etwa 25 Prozent der Manager und 30 Prozent der Professoren sehen hier Köln in der Spitzenposition. In den Fächern Organisation und Personalwesen erreicht Köln immerhin den dritten Platz. Vor allem die Professoren aber auch die Manager bevorzugen hier die Professoren-Kollegen an der Hochschule St.Gallen und an der Universität Mannheim gegenüber den Kölnern.

Geteilte Meinungen

Geteilt sind die Meinungen der befragten Manager und Professoren über die Qualität der Kölner WiSo-Fakultät im Fach Marketing. Während die Manager hier Köln den zweiten Platz hinter Münster zumessen, sehen die befragten Professoren ihre Kölner Kollegen an vierter Stelle hinter Münster, Mannheim und Saarbrücken. (unik)

Gesamtranking	Universitäten	Ranking Ausbildungsniveau	Ranking Forschungsstandard	Uni-Ranking der Professoren
1	U Karlsruhe (TH)	2	7	14
2	U Köln	5	1	12
3	H St. Gallen	3	4	15

The first university rankings prepared by academic institutions appeared in the late 1990s. In 1997, the German Research Foundation (DFG) published a precursor to its *Förderatlas* (*Funding Atlas*), covering the years 1991 to 1995. This showed the distribution of external funding awarded by the DFG, which had become the most important instrument in the financing of high-level research at German institutions of higher education. Cologne was ranked twenty-first out of seventy, and for the period 2005 to 2007 it came eleventh. The ranking of the Alexander von Humboldt Foundation was also very important, as it showed the preferences of foreign researchers who received its funding. The University of Cologne was regularly listed among the top institutions in this ranking.[29]

The Center for Higher Education (CHE), a think tank established by the Bertelsmann Foundation and the German Rectors' Conference, first published its controversial ranking in 1998. The University of Cologne took tenth place in 2003. However, the evaluation did not include the strong research departments of physics, chemistry and biology, as they had not submitted their data to the CHE in time. The new Cologne rector Axel Freimuth lamented this "failure" in early 2005, but he also criticized the CHE, which, he pointed out, was responsible for ensuring the "soundness" of their survey. International rankings also gained importance. These included the Shanghai Ranking, published for the first time in 2003, in which the University of Cologne was initially ranked among the top 150 universities worldwide and later among the best 200. The narrow database, arbitrary criteria and lack of comparability were also criticized in these rankings. Despite their shortcomings, the rankings promoted competition among universities, an effect desired by policymakers. In Cologne, they led in particular to a professionalization of the way in which the university was presented to the public.[30]

↑ The Faculty of Economics and Social Sciences took second place in a field of sixty-five in the *Manager-Magazin* university rankings in January 1992.

Switchboards

1993

Museum for Communication, Frankfurt am Main

0221-470-0—Whoever calls this number reaches the University of Cologne's main telephone reception service, where operators forward all incoming calls. This hasn't changed from the time when operators worked at the switchboard pictured above in the basement of the main building. This photo was taken shortly before services were moved to the current telecommunications center in September 1993. Brigitte Schnitzler (second from left), who has worked at the telephone reception service since 1980, recalls: "Those were the old switchboards with lights that flashed when a call came in, and we would use a keypad to forward the call. In 1993, computer workstations with screens replaced the old system. It was dismantled and the new one installed at the same time. Then it was learning by doing. Thank God, we knew most of the professors' and the administration offices' numbers by heart. Our work has changed over the past thirty years. There used to be staff members who could only use their telephones to call numbers within the university. If they wanted to make external calls, they had to go through us." Today, the University of Cologne has some 8,500 extensions. Operators at the telecommunications center still forward calls, since many callers don't know the extension of the person they are calling. The old switchboards are now exhibits at the Museum for Communication in Frankfurt am Main.[31]

The Ecological Rhine Station

1997
Institute of Zoology

Moored on the left bank of Germany's longest river is a unique research laboratory: the Ecological Rhine Station of the University of Cologne. Hartmut Arndt, professor of ecology at Cologne, originated the idea for the laboratory. In 1997, when rowers from the Sports College, who had used the boat as their base, were moved to the regatta lake facilities on the Fühlinger See, Arndt convinced the university leadership to set up a research station for the Institute of Zoology on the Rhine to study animal habitats and the effect of climate change on the river. The floating structure, which measures sixty meters in length and eleven meters in width, is made up of two former Rhine ships. The *Baden 24*, built in 1885, was used for the front, and the *Desdemona*, built in 1912, for the rear. It is located at Rhine kilometer 684.5 adjacent to the fairway. As a floating facility, it must be staffed at all times and has an apartment for the boat keeper at the bow. Two flowing water labs are the centerpiece of the research center. "We bring up the Rhine and study its waters under the microscope," Hartmut Arndt explains. "Ten cubic meters of water are pumped through the lab every hour and end up in various basins and channels. This allows us to provide various cultures with a continuous supply of fresh water, and varying flow rates simulate different types of habitats."[32]

Quality of Teaching

Fundamental reforms of university study had been on the agenda of higher education policy since the 1960s. The issues addressed included limiting the duration of studies, structuring study programs, introducing compulsory student counseling, and new examination regulations. Most of the measures implemented were aimed at controlling rising student numbers in a period of ongoing austerity. The quality of teaching was not a key consideration, but that began to change around 1990. In 1988/1989, the student UNiMUT movement, which originated in West Berlin, demanded better study conditions and a different form of teaching with more participation by students and tutors. In 1990, the university rankings published by popular magazines brought the issue to the attention of the public. A year later, the state government of North Rhine-Westphalia launched the twelve-million-mark Quality of Teaching program. The goal was to realize a structural reform of undergraduate degree programs, strengthen teaching, improve orientation aids for students, involve them more in designing study programs, and provide incentives for reform activities and special achievements in teaching. The program promoted

new formats such as tutorials and student evaluations of lectures and seminars.[33]

The University of Cologne saw this program as a further intervention in the autonomy of higher education institutions. In particular, the rectorate rejected evaluations by students. In the eyes of the senators, any deficiencies in courses were due not to the quality of instruction but to a shortage of staff, money and equipment. The university was also opposed to the state's Benchmarking Regulation, which came into effect in 1993 as part of an amendment to the Higher Education Act. The new State Higher Education Act set out far-reaching requirements for the scope of studies, their maximum duration, the number of credits required and the processing time for final theses. The University of Cologne, together with other higher education institutions, faculty members and student representation bodies, lodged a constitutional complaint, which was rejected by the Federal Constitutional Court.[34]

These discussions about the quality of teaching took place against the background of a new debate on education. As had been the case thirty years earlier, there was again talk of a "crisis" and the "miserable state of German education policy." The persistent overcrowding and underfunding of universities and, in particular, the lack of a concept for integrating the universities of the former GDR into the national system of higher education institutions provoked criticism. At the Education Summit convened by Chancellor Helmut Kohl in November 1993, the federal government, the states, business representatives, trade unions and representatives from academia and schools discussed the future of German education policy. The result was sobering: "The Education Summit did not change anything and did not achieve anything," wrote *Die Zeit*. Students refused to tolerate this standstill. Some 3,000 students from the University of Cologne and the University of Applied Sciences in Cologne demonstrated in front of the main university building for the right to education. They called for increased investment, better teaching, the opening up of universities to all interested parties, funding support for the entire duration of study, the empowerment of women, and more participation in decision-making processes.[35]

"Lucky Strike" was the motto of the largest nationwide student protests since 1968, which took place in the winter semester of 1997/1998. In late November 1997, 40,000 students demonstrated in Bonn. The striking students, who for the first time used the internet to organize and network while acting locally, renewed the demands of 1993 and rejected the draft of a new framework law for higher education, which proposed shorter, more employment-oriented courses and the introduction of tuition fees. As the Cologne students blockaded streets and intersections, attempted to storm a hotel and occupied the main railway station, they also clashed violently with the police. The university administration, which supported some of the student demands, responded by investing 100,000 German marks in new teaching resources. The protests did not achieve much more than that. The state government worked through its agenda and followed up the Quality of Teaching program with the Study Reform 2000 Plus project in 2001. Additional funds were invested in counseling for new students, cooperation with schools, professional qualifications for students, and supporting female students. The evaluation of the quality of instruction was now required by law. In 2002, the university began to develop its own evaluation mechanisms.[36]

Beginning in 2004, a fundamental change in both study and teaching came with the implementation of the Bologna Process, which twenty-nine European nations had agreed upon in 1999. Its aim was to promote student mobility in Europe, the international recognition of European qualifications, and faster entry into professional life by introducing a two-tier system of bachelor's and master's degrees. The introduction of a modular design would more clearly structure students' selection of courses. Further innovations included examinations held during the course of studies, a European credit point system that reflected the time invested in courses, and the possibility for students to enter the job market as soon as they obtained a bachelor's degree. Again, improving the quality of teaching was not the main focus of this reform. Critics regarded the new system, which coincided with the further opening of universities and an increase in the number of secondary school graduates eligible to enter universities, as the end of the traditional university.[37]

← Some professors showed their solidarity with the student strike in December 1997 by holding their lectures or seminars in Cologne's city center.

Wolf-Dieter Heiss
born 1939

Professor in the
Faculty of Medicine

Austrian-born Wolf-Dieter Heiss studied medicine at the University of Vienna, where he obtained his medical degree in 1965. After conducting research at MIT in Cambridge, Massachusetts, the Institute of Physiology in Stockholm and the University of Buffalo, New York. Heiss earned his habilitation in neurology in 1970 at the University of Vienna, where he became an untenured professor in 1976.

Heiss was appointed director of the Neurological Clinic in Cologne-Merheim in 1978, where he also headed the newly established Cerebrovascular Research Unit of the Max Planck Institute for Brain Research in Frankfurt am Main. From 1979 on, Heiss taught as an untenured professor in the Faculty of Medicine. In 1982, he was named director of the Max Planck Institute for Neurological Research, which had emerged from the research unit. The University of Cologne appointed him full professor in 1985 and made him head of the Department of Neurology at the Lindenthal Clinic. He held both positions until retiring in 2005.

Heiss studied the effects of strokes on the brain, developed methods for the investigation of brain functions and was actively committed to the care of stroke patients, including as founder of the Cologne Against Stroke initiative. He served as president of the International Stroke Society and of the European Federation of Neurological Societies.[38]

Bettina Hurrelmann
1943–2015

Professor in the
Faculty of Educational Sciences

Bettina Hurrelmann brought together German studies and education to yield a fruitful synthesis. Her research on literature for children and young people set new standards. After completing a teaching degree, Hurrelmann initially worked as a teacher before pursuing a second degree in German language and literature, education and philosophy. She completed her doctorate at Münster in 1974 with a dissertation on the weekly publication *Der Kinderfreund*, which aimed to convey Enlightenment ideas to children. Hurrelmann earned her habilitation in 1983 at the Gesamthochschule Essen with a thesis on children's literature in a social context, a reception analysis of how literature was dealt with in the classroom.

Hurrelmann assumed her first professorship in 1984 at Tilburg University in the Netherlands. She was then appointed to a professorship for German literature and didactics in 1998 at Cologne, where she was the director of the Reading and Children's and Young Adult Literature Research Unit until retiring in 2008. Under her leadership, the unit was expanded to become the Children's and Young Adult Media Research Unit (ALEKI). From 1998 to 2006, she headed the DFG priority program Reading Socialization in the Media Society. Hurrelmann contributed significantly to her field of studies with her research and as an editor of numerous publications. She also supported contemporary literature for young people, for example as chair of the jury for the German Youth Literature Prize.[39]

Siglinde Kunert
1926–2010

Professor in the
Faculty of Curative Education

Joachim Lang
1940–2018

Professor in the
Faculty of Law

Siglinde Kunert was a pioneer in the field of education and in promoting the development of children with physical disabilities. As a young teacher in the early 1950s, she helped set up a hospital school in Cologne's university clinics. In 1954, this became the Municipal School for the Sick, with Kunert as its first principal. Five years later, she was involved in the founding of the Rhenish School for the Physically Disabled. In the early 1960s, together with Berta and Karel Bobath, two physiotherapists from London, she developed a therapy of remedial gymnastics for children with severe disabilities. In 1964, Kunert set up Das körperbehinderte Kind, a research group that addressed the specific psycho-physical needs of physically disabled children, methods for early care and development, and special education. This later evolved into the Center for Early Care and Development.

In addition to her work, Kunert studied psychology and pursued training in psychoanalysis. Her dissertation on behavioral disorders and psychagogic measures for physically disabled children was published in 1966. From 1971 on, Kunert taught as a professor of education for the disabled at the Rhineland College of Teacher Education in Cologne. When the college's branch in Cologne was incorporated into the University of Cologne in 1980, Kunert assumed Germany's first professorship in her field at the Faculty of Curative Education.[40]

Upon completing his Abitur, Joachim Lang first attended Max Reinhardt's theater school in Berlin, but in 1960, he decided to study law in Munich. After passing the state examination, Lang worked in the financial administration of North Rhine-Westphalia and later at the German Ministry of Finance. During this time, he completed his dissertation titled *Systematisierung der Steuervergünstigungen* (Systematization of tax concessions) under the supervision of Klaus Tipke, the founder of the Cologne school of tax law research. Lang obtained his doctorate in 1974.

Lang was awarded his habilitation by the University of Cologne in 1982 for a study titled *Die Bemessungsgrundlage der Einkommensteuer* (The assessment base for income tax), which influenced the 1982 landmark decision of the German Constitutional Court on tax splitting for married couples. He taught as a full professor at the Technische Universität Darmstadt, returning to Cologne in 1988 where he assumed the chair of tax law formerly held by his mentor Tipke. Lang held this post until retiring in 2006. He also continued his predecessor's work in preparing numerous revised editions of *Steuerrecht*, a standard reference book on tax law known simply as "Tipke/Lang." Lang pursued the systemization of tax law and presented several proposals for reforms. The internationally acclaimed expert was chairman of the German Tax Law Society and publisher of the journal *Steuer und Wirtschaft*.[41]

Recognized for Excellence

Academic prizes typically recognize achievements in research, but rarely in teaching. They bestow prestige on the institutions where the laureates work. Cologne professors have twice been recipients of the most renowned international award, the Nobel Prize, which was presented in 1950 to the chemist Kurt Alder and in 2007 to the physicist Peter Grünberg. They were free to decide whether to keep the prize money or invest it in further research. The situation was similar with awards bestowed in Germany. Prizes that were to be used specifically as funding instruments for further research, thus supplementing external funding at the individual level, were first awarded in the 1980s. Universities benefited from these awards in several ways: they enhanced their scientific reputation, raised their profile and financed new jobs and projects over a longer period of time, albeit only in the narrow sector of top-level research and not in the broad spectrum of their academic work.[42]

One of the first highly endowed and prestigious research funding prizes established in Germany was the Gottfried Wilhelm Leibniz Prize, launched in 1985 by the German Research Foundation (DFG). Since 1986, up to ten of these awards have been presented annually to outstanding and promising researchers in Germany or at German institutes abroad. The prize money initially amounted to the equivalent of up to 1.55 million euros per award, but in 2007 it was increased to 2.5 million euros. To ensure that the award-winners would be able to focus on their work, they were allowed to decide how the money would be spent without fulfilling bureaucratic requirements. Between 1992 and 2007, eight scholars from five faculties at the University of Cologne were awarded the coveted prize; three came from the Faculty of Mathematics and Natural Sciences, two from the Faculty of Philosophy and one each from the Faculty of Educational Sciences, the Faculty of Economics and Social Sciences, and the Faculty of Medicine. The awards demonstrated the extent of excellent research conducted in Cologne and confirmed the university's strategy of maintaining its profile as an institution offering the full range of academic subjects, as well as attractive conditions for research. The first winner of the Leibniz Prize in Cologne was the mathematician Peter Schneider, who was honored in 1992 for his work in arithmetic-algebraic geometry together with three colleagues from other North Rhine-Westphalian universities. This was exceptional, as the prize is usually awarded to individuals. The second Cologne prize-winner was also noteworthy: in 1995, Thomas Schweitzer became the first ethnologist to receive the DFG award. Schweitzer achieved international renown through the use of empirical research methods in data collection and evaluation.[43]

The Max Planck Research Award, which has been presented since 1990, honors German and foreign researchers who cooperate internationally on projects in new and promising fields of research. The number of awards was limited to twelve in 1995, and since 2004 only two awards have been presented annually. The prize money, which initially amounted to 250,000 German marks, was increased to 750,000 euros in 2004. From 1990 to 2007, five scholars from the University of Cologne received this prize. Two came from the Faculty of Medicine, two from the Faculty of Mathematics and Natural Sciences, and one from the Faculty of Philosophy. The two faculties which attracted the highest amount of external funding thus came out on top. The first two prize-winners were the physicians Thomas Krieg in 1991 and Wilhelm Stoffel in 1992. A few years later, Krieg and Stoffel established the Center for Molecular Medicine Cologne (ZMMK), which enhanced basic medical research through close cooperation with molecular biology.[44]

Several awards also helped to promote early-career scholars. The Gerhard Hess Award, which was presented by the DFG from 1988 to 2000 and was later

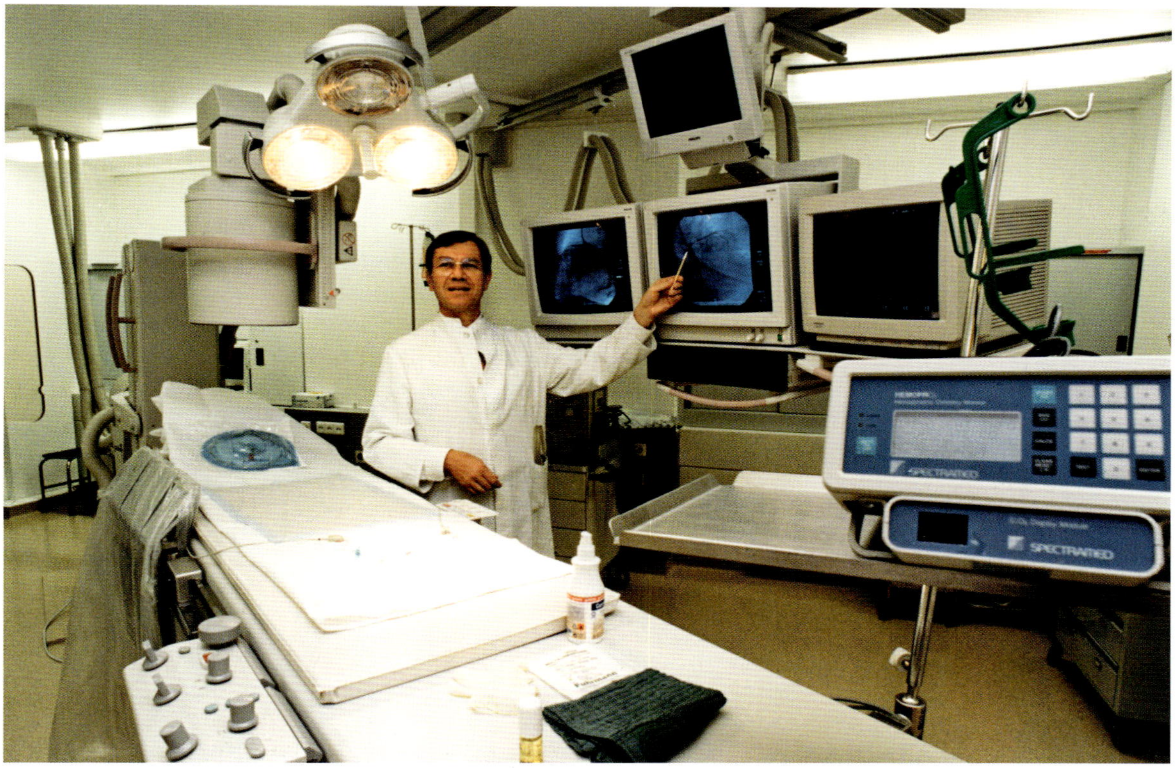

merged with the Emmy Noether Program established in 1997, was one of the first such measures. One of the most generously endowed prizes of this kind is the Alexander von Humboldt Foundation's Sofja Kovalevskaja Award, which was established in 2002 and recognizes excellent foreign post-doctorate researchers working in Germany or early-career German scholars working abroad. The prize money amounts to a maximum of 1.65 million euros. Award-winners select an institution in Germany at which to set up a working group to continue their research for five years. In the first year, Manuel Koch from Switzerland was awarded the prize and chose the Medical Faculty of the University of Cologne as the site for conducting his research on protein networks between cells. Also in 2002, German scholar Joachim Schultze, who had been working at Harvard Medical School's Dana Farber Cancer Institute in Boston, Massachusetts, was awarded the prize. He used the grant to help set up the Molecular Tumor Biology and Tumor Immunology research unit.[45]

These well-endowed and prestigious awards are supplemented by numerous less well-known ones from universities themselves, professional associations, foundations and sponsors. Since 1990, for example, the University of Cologne has awarded the Cologne Prize, which is sponsored by the Sparkasse savings bank, to young researchers working on Cologne-related issues. Sometimes awards are combined with other forms of sponsorship in order to strengthen existing research focal points. Thus, the first cluster of excellence in Cologne, Cellular Stress Responses in Aging-Associated Diseases (CECAD), was established in 2007 following the university's successful submission to the second round of the nationwide Excellence Initiative. The CECAD spokesperson was the molecular biologist Jens Brüning, who received the Leibniz Prize that same year.[46]

↑ In 1997, the intensive care unit of Clinic III for Internal Medicine was equipped with another cardiac catheterization unit for acute emergencies; Professor Erland Erdmann in the cardiac catheterization unit.

Mixing Console

2002

Kölncampus–Cologne University Radio

The University of Cologne has been on air since 30 April 2002. This was the day Kölncampus—Cologne University Radio was officially launched. The button was pushed by Rector Tassilo Küpper, Mayor Norbert Burger and project manager Georg Luppertz. The first broadcast was a live transmission during the party that took place on campus to celebrate the opening of the station. Kölncampus is a radio channel run by students for students. Its programming, music selection and presentation are completely in the hands of a young team of broadcasters who provide their listeners with the latest university news and entertain them twenty-four hours a day with a diverse mix of pop, jazz and chansons.

The beginnings of the station go back to 1995, when the first hour of community programming was broadcast on Radio Köln. Another milestone was the meeting in late November 1998 at which an association called Köln-campus e.V. was founded to support the project. Mayor Norbert Burger stressed that having a campus radio station at the largest university in North Rhine-Westphalia should be a matter of "political interest." In his view, this was an important part of media education, which would help support "opening up the university to the citizens of the city." Despite the voices of those who dismissed the university radio station as "fashionable nonsense," Köln-campus e.V. applied for a broadcasting license from the State Broadcasting Authority.[47]

Driverless Transportation System

2003

Cologne University Hospital

In 2003, after several years of preparation, the University Hospital of Cologne put its electronic driverless transportation system (DTS) into operation. It utilizes a 6.3-kilometer route to transport almost all the goods needed by people in the city's largest hospital: from medicines and sterile supplies to food for patients, and mail. The thirty-million-euro project, funded by the German federal government and the state of North Rhine-Westphalia, replaced the old circular overhead conveyor from 1972. The new ground-based transportation system was installed by the Austrian company TMS Automotion. Since January 2003, the computerized transportation vehicles have been running daily from 5 a.m. to 10 p.m. Initially there were fifty-three, but by 2016 their number had risen to eighty-six. Their construction is low so that they can drive under containers. When a container in the supply center is loaded with cargo, its personal identification number and freight destination code are entered into the system. A transponder transmits the number of the container, which is pushed onto the next free collection point. From then on, everything is automated. The activated vehicle picks up the container and heads toward the destination with the aid of sensors. All routes are stored in the computer system. The transporters can even use elevators autonomously, which take them up to the top floor of the hospital ward building.[48]

The Dawn of the Digital Age

In the beginning was the network—not the internet, but the University of Cologne Local Area Network (UKLAN), which linked all of the university's institutes. This turned the numerous personal computers that had been installed throughout the university since the mid-1980s from mere computing devices into portals to the digital world. The UKLAN had been set up by the Regional Computing Center of the University of Cologne (RRZK) using the latest technology of the time: fiber-optic cables. By 1990, most of the university's departments and institutes were online. The university's *Journal* explained the future to its readers in early 1991: "The university computer network is a prerequisite for any kind of telecooperation. It connects the individual workstations, provides access to the university's central computers, makes library services accessible, integrates lecture halls and laboratories into the university network, and provides connectivity to external networks." In "the medium term," the *Journal* went on to say, "text-oriented communication" would also be replaced by multimedia communication consisting of "voice, video and graphics." [49]

While this intranet simplified internal cooperation and data exchange, from the mid-1980s on, the internet opened up entirely new possibilities for information and communication. This applied not only to research and teaching. The University of Cologne press office celebrated its "leap into the age of electronic communication" in 1990. It was one of the first such offices at a German university to begin using email to share articles and essays. Ten years later, the press office switched to paperless communication. Instead of mailing 1,500 letters a week, it now relied exclusively on email to send out its press releases. Having an internet presence also became increasingly important for the university. The University of Cologne's first website went online in 1995, at a time when this was still uncharted territory for many universities. The first relaunch occurred just two years later. The website was made more user-friendly and colorful, with blue complementing the initial black-and-white design. The next step was to present the website in two languages. Meanwhile, some of the university's institutes had also set up their own websites.[50]

In 1990, the University and City Library (USB) introduced computer terminals, allowing users to search the library catalog, check the circulation status of books, place orders, and manage their accounts. Beginning in 1994, university students and staff had access to USB services such as literature and essay databases or book orders via the UKLAN. The opportunity to research on CD-ROMs was also available. The USB collaborated with the department and institute libraries to create a shared, publicly accessible online catalog known as OPAC. The administration also began using digital technology early on. The student secretariat, for example, employed LOVERNET, a local administrative network within the university, in conjunction with the new ZUL-UNIX admission system from 1995 on to process the significantly growing number of applications.[51]

Digital technology developed rapidly until the mid-1990s. The University of Cologne kept pace with this process from the outset by defining the framework for the work of the Regional Computing Center in its new constitution of 1990 and by instituting a Senate commission. In 1995, in view of the major changes in information technology and the considerable expansion of the RRZK's role in establishing and developing the technical infrastructure, the Senate recommended turning the RRZK into a Center for Practical Computer Science. Two years later, this central university institution known as the Center for Applied Computer Science (ZAIK), which included the Research and Teaching Department and the University-wide Services Department, went into operation.[52]

In 1996, the RRZK organized a university research day entitled Using the Internet for Research and Teaching. It was open to university staff and students, as well as interested citizens of Cologne. In the space of just a few years, the World Wide Web had made the internet accessible to a wide audience. Three thousand people came to watch the website of the Ministry of Science and Research of North Rhine-Westphalia being accessed online for the first time. They also received information about the development of the internet in Germany and plans to make it universally accessible. Experts introduced listeners to this new world in a series of talks. Rector Ulrich Matz proudly announced that all students would now have the opportunity to set up a university email account.[53]

A year later, the RRZK held an open house day to inform university members and the general public about "multimedia," a topic central to the future of research and teaching. German universities had a lot of catching up to do in comparison to their European counterparts. The 3,000 visitors learned about the use of multimedia systems in everyday university life, about databases, video conferencing and placing phone calls via the internet.[54]

The digital revolution was a constant challenge. The number of internet workstations was in short supply around the turn of the millennium, and wireless LAN was made available for the first time at thirty access points on campus in 2001. For security reasons, the ZAIK set up a virtual private network (VPN) in 2002 for external access to the UKLAN. The last two departmental libraries were connected to the USB electronic lending system in 2003. In 2004, the rectorate decided to introduce a new IT infrastructure to cope with the upcoming switch to the bachelor's and master's system.[55]

← The University and City Library introduced CD-ROM databases for research purposes in the early 1990s.

Gerd Lehmkuhl
born 1948

Professor in the
Faculty of Medicine

Gerd Lehmkuhl is a leading German child and adolescent psychiatrist and a pioneer in his field. After earning his medical doctorate in 1973, he obtained a *Diplom* in psychology from the Technical University of Aachen in 1979. Accredited as a psychoanalyst in 1985, he earned his habilitation in Heidelberg in 1986. The University of Cologne appointed him in 1988 to the newly created chair of child and adolescent psychiatry and psychotherapy, and named him head of the Department for Psychiatry and Psychotherapy for Children and Adolescents at the University Hospital.

Lehmkuhl developed the field of child and adolescent psychiatry at Cologne. The focus of his research was on craniocerebral trauma, ADHD and sleep disorders. As chairman of the Alfred Adler Institute Aachen/Cologne, he initiated the training and further education of psychotherapists for children and adolescents, among other things. Lehmkuhl was one of the founders of Villa Kunterbunt, opened in 1995, which provided therapy for children and adolescents with mental illnesses. He served as a dean from 2000 to 2004. Lehmkuhl also published the journals *Zeitschrift für Individualpsychologie* and *Zeitschrift für Kinder- und Jugendpsychiatrie und Psychotherapie*. After retiring in 2014, he became chairman of the board of Achtung! Kinderseele, a foundation dedicated to promoting the mental health of children throughout Germany.[56]

Jozef Schell
1935–2003

Honorary professor in the
Faculty of Mathematics and Natural Sciences

A Belgian national born in Ghent, Jozef Schell was one of the world's leading researchers in molecular plant biology and a pioneer in genetic engineering in plants. He was responsible for making Cologne an internationally recognized center of plant genetics. After studying zoology, he earned his doctorate in microbiology at the University of Ghent. He was appointed professor of molecular biology there in 1967 and founded a laboratory for general genetics.

The Max Planck Institute for Breeding Research in Cologne, which was renamed the MPI for Plant Breeding Research in 2009, offered the prominent Belgian researcher a position in 1978, where he headed the Department for Molecular Foundations of Plant Breeding until 1998. The University of Cologne appointed Schell as an honorary professor in 1980, and in 1994 he assumed a professorship at the Collège de France in Paris.

In 1983, Schell and his colleague Marc Van Montagu successfully transferred genes from another species into the genome of a plant. This was a historic achievement, since the researchers demonstrated for the first time that the stable transformation of plants and thus their genetic modification was possible. Numerous international accolades and memberships in academies, including the New York Academy of Sciences and the German Academy of Sciences Leopoldina, were bestowed upon Schell, honoring him for his scientific achievements.[57]

Hartmut Schiedermair
born 1936

Professor in the
Faculty of Law

Hartmut Schiedermair approached the study of law from a philosophical perspective. Son of Gerhard Schiedermair, an expert in civil law, Schiedermair began studying philosophy, history and art history at Frankfurt, but then switched to law. In 1968, he wrote his doctoral thesis on the relationship between power and law in the work of Gottfried Wilhelm Leibniz. From 1966 on, he held an academic position at the Max Planck Institute for Comparative Public Law and International Law in Heidelberg, and he earned his habilitation in 1974 at the university there. That same year, he joined the academic staff of the Federal Constitutional Court. Saarland University in Saarbrücken appointed him full professor of constitutional law, administrative law and international law in 1976.

Hartmut Schiedermair assumed the Cologne chair of public law, international law and philosophy of law in 1983, which he held until his retirement in 2001. In 1980, he was appointed as a constitutional expert to the Commission of the States to Determine the Financial Needs of Germany's Public Broadcasting Networks. In addition to his legal publications, Schiedermair wrote on university policy issues and served from 1980 to 2004 as president of the Deutscher Hochschulverband, a German association of university professors and lecturers, which named him an honorary president when he retired.[58]

Wilhelm Voßkamp
born 1936

Professor in the
Faculty of Philosophy

German studies scholar Wilhelm Voßkamp published fundamental research on early novel theory, the history of education, and utopian studies. He also furthered a cultural studies perspective within his field. Voßkamp had already begun exploring the topics of time and history in seventeenth-century literature in 1965 while writing his dissertation at Kiel. He obtained his habilitation in Cologne in 1972 and in the same year was appointed professor of literature at the reform-oriented University of Bielefeld, where he also served as director of the Center for Interdisciplinary Research from 1978 to 1982.

In 1987, the University of Cologne appointed Voßkamp to the chair of literature and modern German literature. He served as dean of the Faculty of Philosophy in 1994 and 1995. In 1999, he was one of the founders of the Research Unit for Media and Cultural Communication, and he served as its director until his retirement in 2004. His most important publications include *Romantheorie in Deutschland. Von Martin Opitz bis Friedrich von Blanckenburg* (Theory of the novel in Germany: From Martin Opitz to Friedrich von Blanckenburg, 1973) and the three-volume anthology he published in 1982, *Utopieforschung* (Utopian studies). In 2018, another major work was published, *Emblematik der Zukunft. Poetik und Geschichte literarischer Utopien von Thomas Morus bis Robert Musil* (Emblematics of the future: Poetics and history of literary utopias from Thomas Morus to Robert Musil).[59]

In the Heart of the City

As part of its major anniversary in 1988, the university had invoked, staged and harnessed its close connection to the city of Cologne in a variety of ways. Through its faculty weeks, open house day and various public events on campus and in the city center, the university introduced new formats for encounters between people from the university and the citizens of Cologne. However, the strongest traditional and institutional link to the city remained the board of trustees, which brought together municipal and academic dignitaries. The new constitution of 1990 retained this body. As in Adenauer's day, the chair was held by the mayor of Cologne. Among other things, the board of trustees made recommendations on appointments and proposed candidates for the posts of chancellor and director of the University and City Library. It acted as a link between the university and the city and advised the former on key issues.[60]

The university was present at important municipal events. In 1995, these included the commemoration of the fiftieth anniversary of the end of World War II, the visit of the Dalai Lama to the city, and the inauguration of the replacement statues for the tower of City Hall. The old statues had been almost completely destroyed in World War II. Members of the university donated a statue of Pope Urban VI, who had signed the founding charter of the old university in 1388. The other new sculptures included one of University of Cologne professor Benedikt Schmittmann, who was murdered by the Nazis in 1939.[61]

The rector and the mayor jointly welcomed the new students beginning their first semester in 1997. Both spoke of Cologne as a place for learning and living. Mayor Norbert Burger did so in a manner typical of the city: "Give your heart fully to your studies and to this city—or even to some special person from Cologne." The university continued to hold open house days for all interested citizens. Although the first University Day in 2000 was primarily aimed at students, it was also open to all residents of Cologne. In its second year, the motto was "City—Economy—University." That year also marked the one-hundredth anniversary of the founding of the Cologne Commercial College. Numerous Cologne-based companies sponsored the commemorative event. A student protest held during the ceremony targeted the poor conditions for students rather than the much-criticized "economization" of the university. In general, the university's increasingly intensive cooperation with local and regional businesses, which led to a cooperation agreement with the Cologne Chamber of Industry and Commerce in 1994, met with very little criticism.[62]

The university also demonstrated its close links to the city in its research. Scholarship that dealt with Cologne was presented in a special portion of the press conference on the annual research report. The spectrum of this work ranged from geographical studies about the Cologne region to historical studies of Jewish patronage and aspects of municipal economic development. The university also made its expertise directly available to the city. In 2003, it was involved in the city's applications for the title of European Capital of Culture and City of Science 2005. Since 2004, the university has been part of the Cologne Science Round Table (KWR), which also includes other local institutions of higher learning and research, the city administration, and the Chamber of Industry and Commerce. The KWR promotes Cologne as a research location, forges links between the research community and industry, and communicates academic knowledge to the general public.[63]

Ever since the foundation of the Commercial College, citizens of Cologne have enjoyed access to public lectures and events. From the 1990s, this option expanded and took on new forms. "Studies for seniors" became an established part of the university's offerings. From 1993, the university opened itself to the younger generation through cooperation with local

schools and information days for their pupils. Beginning in 2001, the University of Cologne pioneered a program entitled Pupils at the University in cooperation with a foundation funded by the Cologne Kreissparkasse, a savings bank. This allowed gifted teenagers to take part in introductory courses in mathematics, physics, chemistry, and computer science, and later also in the humanities. The project became a model for other universities. The Cologne Children's University, which was held for the first time in 2003, also attracted a great deal of attention. Furthermore, the university offered Cologne residents a broad cultural program of concerts, exhibitions, films and theater performances. These were held at the university lecture halls, the University and City Library, Schloss Wahn, the studiobühne and the film workshop.[64]

Another cultural event is typical of Cologne: its annual carnival. In 2001, for the first time since its anniversary in 1988, the university took part in the iconic Shrove Monday parade. Together with the head of the Cologne Trade Fair, the rector and prorector rode on a float depicting the university main building with the statue of Albertus Magnus. The motto of the float was "Germany's largest university," in keeping with the parade's theme in that year: "Köln kann sich mit allen Messen," a play on words referring to both the city's trade fair and its ability to compete on all levels. The float and the candy traditionally thrown into the crowds lining the route were funded by the Cologne Trade Fair, which had helped to found the Institute of Trade Fair Management within the Faculty of Economics and Social Sciences in 1999. The first carnival event to be held at the university itself took place in 2004 with the Musikcorps Kölner Husaren grün-gelb, which raised money for the university children's hospital. In the same year, students founded the Greater Cologne Academic Carnival Society, which was included in the university register, with membership restricted to students of the University of Cologne.[65]

↑ The university is located in the middle of the city; a view of the high-rise Unicenter building, next to it low-rise university buildings in Cologne's Greenbelt; photograph taken in 1999.

CECAD Logo

2007
CECAD Cluster of Excellence

The Cluster of Excellence on Cellular Stress Responses in Aging-Associated Diseases (CECAD) was established by the federal and state governments on 1 November 2007 as part of the Excellence Initiative. It conducts research on the molecular mechanisms of aging and age-related diseases. When it was officially launched on 7 February 2008, Rector Axel Freimuth expressed his conviction that this development would position the university among the country's top institutions of higher learning. He said that Cologne's focus on life sciences ensured the university would be competitive at the European level. Mayor Fritz Schramma pointed out that "boosted by the CECAD, Cologne would become the hub of a region known for its excellent healthcare and outstanding competence in scholarship and research." Both would prove to be correct. Today, the cluster of excellence, supported by the Faculty of Mathematics and Natural Sciences and the Faculty of Medicine, and financed by the German Research Foundation (DFG), is in its third funding period. The researchers involved in the cluster come to Cologne from all over the world. Their work is interdisciplinary and links both basic research in various disciplines with clinical practice, and participating university institutes with Max Planck institutes. The logo was designed by mediomix, a communications agency, and illustrates the role of the CECAD Cluster of Excellence as a versatile builder of bridges.[66]

The Cologne Compendium on Air Law

2007

Institute of Air and Space Law

Lost your suitcase at the airport? Annoying night-time noise from planes taking off and landing? The *Kölner Kompendium Luftrecht* (Cologne compendium on air law) helps with these and other issues, at least as far as the legal aspects are concerned. On 6 December 2007, its two publishers—Professor Stephan Hobe, director of Germany's oldest institute of aerospace law at the University of Cologne, and Nicolai von Ruckteschell, general counsel of Deutsche Lufthansa—presented the first volume of the comprehensive work at Lufthansa's headquarters in Deutz. The first volume deals with the basics of current German, European and international air traffic law and addresses topics such as institutional principles, the organization of air traffic, airspace, air sovereignty, air traffic agreements and the registration and operation of aircraft. "This new work on aviation law aims to offer the benefits of commentary blended with the advantages of a manual," Hobe explained at the book launch. "Every aviation lawyer should keep it on their desk as a standard reference book." Since then, the two other volumes of the 2,000-page work have also been published. The second volume came out in 2009 and focuses on air traffic regulation and safety, while the third volume, which appeared a year later, concentrates on aspects of commercial aviation law.[67]

A University of Excellence

Chapter 8

2007–2019

The year 2007 brought a number of fundamental changes. The creation of the new Faculty of Human Sciences led to the reorganization of entire departments and of the teacher training program. The Freedom of Universities Act gave the university the extensive autonomy it had long been seeking but also reinforced its entrepreneurial orientation. Meanwhile, the introduction of bachelor's and master's degrees revolutionized its programs of study. First successes in the framework of the Excellence Initiative were a major boost to the top-level research conducted at the university. In 2012, Cologne was officially designated a "University of Excellence," an achievement that accelerated change. A hundred years after its founding, the University of Cologne presented itself as one of Germany's leading universities.

New Horizons

The year 2007 began with the opening of a sixth faculty, the Faculty of Human Sciences. This brought together related disciplines that had previously been housed in the faculties of education, curative education and philosophy. The new faculty was divided into departments of pedagogy, psychology, curative education and rehabilitation, music and its didactic functions, art and art education, and textile science. The merger was intended to promote greater exchange between the pedagogical, psychological and rehabilitation disciplines and to raise their profile, with the aim of also improving the chances of attracting external funding.

The formation of the Faculty of Human Sciences was closely linked to the reorganization of Cologne's teacher education program. This was a key element in the development of the university, as about twenty-seven percent of all students—more than 10,000—were pursuing a teaching degree in 2007. Following the incorporation of the teacher training colleges in 1980, teacher study courses were spread across several faculties. The aim was now to link them to the respective disciplines in order to assure the academic quality of teacher education. This change also entailed a reorganization of the faculties of philosophy and mathematics and natural sciences to integrate teaching with subject-specific didactical methodology. Courses focusing on general aspects of education within the university's teacher training program were the responsibility of the Faculty of Human Sciences.[1]

The reorganization of teacher training was an important component of the third Target Agreement between the university and the state, signed by Rector Axel Freimuth and State Science and Research Minister Andreas Pinkwart on 11 January 2007. The agreement also aimed to raise the profile of outstanding research conducted at the university in key areas such as the life sciences, media research, and the relationship between markets and society. The agreement was a first step toward implementing the structural reforms initiated by the Freedom of Universities Act, which came into effect on 1 January 2007 and would fundamentally reform the universities in the state of North Rhine-Westphalia (NRW).[2]

With this law, the state government of NRW, which had been led by the CDU and FDP since 2005, transformed its public universities into statutory corporations, thereby handing them a large degree of autonomy. The University of Cologne welcomed the reform, as it met long-standing demands for greater independence. The universities thus became legally independent and were merely subject to the legal supervision of the state, which continued to be responsible for financing. The universities were granted financial autonomy, as well as full discretion regarding staff appointments. From that point onward, NRW universities acted as employers of both academic and non-academic staff, made appointments autonomously and exercised economic independence, including with respect to business start-ups and investments. However, the state government continued to influence the strategic direction of the universities via its Target Agreements, so it did not cede control entirely.[3]

Supervision of the universities was in the hands of university councils, half of whose members had to come from outside the respective university. These councils mapped out the strategic course of each

↖ The main building of the Faculty of Human Sciences, which was opened in January 2007, is located between Clarenbachstraße and Frangenheimstraße.

← Many interdisciplinary and groundbreaking fields of research are pursued at the University of Cologne; researchers of the DFG Priority Program 1833 Building a Habitable Earth.

university and advised its management. In Cologne, the new University Council replaced the board of trustees, which had been in place since 1919. The University of Cologne emphasized the role of external expertise and appointed seven non-university and three university members to its University Council. An important criterion in addition to the specific expertise of the members was their relationship to Cologne. The University Senate lost relevance, while the powers of the rector and faculty deans were strengthened. After assuming power in the state government in 2010, the SPD and Greens implemented the University Future Act of 2014, which sought to revoke some of the autonomy previously granted. However, its impact was minimal. Following a further change of government in 2017, the new CDU/FDP government announced that the partial roll-back of autonomy would be repealed.[4]

In Competition

The new freedom enjoyed by the universities in North Rhine-Westphalia was combined with a mandate to think and act entrepreneurially. This reform sought to increase administrative efficiency by applying the new public management model and translating academic knowledge into commercially useful applications. It also intensified and internationalized competition among universities for the best minds and the most lucrative external funding. The University of Cologne, which was well connected in Europe and globally, opened its first international office in Beijing in 2007, which is also the liaison office of the Cologne-led "china consortium" of North Rhine-Westphalian universities. Two further University of Cologne offices abroad followed—in New Delhi in 2009 and New York in 2010. Since then, representatives of the university have been on site in three of the most important international markets for educational opportunities, recruitment of young talent and top-level research.[5]

At the national level, the Excellence Initiative, which is financed by the German federal government and the states, considerably stepped up competition between Germany's universities. While this offered a significant opportunity for the development of areas of research that demonstrate superior achievement and the capacity to network with other scholars, quite a few were concerned about maintaining the university's inner balance, diversity and breadth of academic research and teaching. In 2007, the second application submitted to the Excellence Initiative by the University of Cologne was successful: the Graduate School of Physics and Astronomy, which operates in conjunction with the University of Bonn as the Bonn-Cologne Graduate School (BCGS), was included in the first line of funding. Jülich Research Center and the Max Planck Institute for Radio Astronomy in Bonn were also involved. The BCGS was intended to be a prototype for the future of graduate education at both universities. As in the Anglo-Saxon system, students would earn their doctorate within five years of graduating with a bachelor's degree. The broad spectrum of topics here ranged from particle and nuclear physics to astrophysics and photonics.[6]

The Cluster of Excellence for Cellular Stress Responses in Aging-Associated Diseases (CECAD) was selected in the second funding line. In the CECAD, biologists and physicians from the University Hospital Cologne and the newly founded Max Planck Institute for the Biology of Ageing are investigating the molecular causes of the ageing process and associated diseases such as Alzheimer's, Parkinson's, cancer, diabetes and stroke. CECAD is a pioneer in the study of ageing, and its aim is to develop new therapies. Both the Cluster of Excellence and the Max Planck Institute (MPI) moved into new buildings on the campus of the Cologne University Hospital and became part of a regional life science network in which the Cologne MPI for Neurological Research (now the MPI for Metabolism Research), the German Center for Neurodegenerative Diseases (part of the Helmholtz Association) and the CAESAR Research Center in Bonn also participated. The funding of this internationally networked project was extended by a further seven years in early 2019.[7]

CECAD is an example of a successful model of Cologne research: institutes from different faculties work with external research institutions at interdisciplinary and international levels in key areas and are integrated into regional and global networks. Their basic research generally deals with socially relevant phenomena, and the results are aimed at practical application.

↗ The university campus offers students many opportunities to study or relax together—such as on the lawn behind the main building.

→ The renovation of the main building, which began in 2009, also involved remodeling the hallways.

STADT

Research Priorities

The Center for Molecular Medicine Cologne—the University of Cologne's pioneering collaboration between biological and medical life sciences, founded in 1994—moved into a modern building on the campus of the University Hospital in 2009. The campus is the hub of the university's high-level medical research, which includes the Cologne-Bonn Center for Integrated Oncology (CIO), founded in 2005 and funded since 2007 by German Cancer Aid as one of the then top four oncological centers. Since 2008, the CIO, which today also comprises the cancer centers of the universities of Aachen and Düsseldorf, has collaborated with the University of Pittsburgh Cancer Institute, one of the most successful cancer research centers in the United States. In 2007, the new Heart Center building was opened on campus. Biologists and physicians work together in sequencing genomes in the Cologne Center for Genomics, which was established in 2004. The center is one of the most internationally renowned institutions of its kind in Germany. Since 2018, it has also led the West German Genome Center, one of four DFG-funded competence centers for high-throughput sequencing in Germany.[8]

A highlight of 2007 was the awarding of the Nobel Prize in Physics to Peter Grünberg, who together with Paris-based Albert Fert was honored for his research on the GMR effect, a groundbreaking discovery in the field of magnetism that has led to increased storage capacities in hard disks. Grünberg, who worked at Jülich Research Center and taught at the University of Cologne, benefited from a research network that is now part of the ForschungsAllianz Köln. It forms the institutional framework for the university's close cooperation with non-university research institutions in the Rhineland; these include research centers of the Helmholtz Association, such as that in Jülich, as well as several Max Planck institutes and the GESIS – Leibniz Institute for Social Sciences. This institutional collaboration is embedded in a network connecting the University of Cologne to the other Rhenish universities in Aachen, Bonn and Düsseldorf.[9]

← In 2017, the *Meteor*, a research boat, set off on an expedition to the Atlantic Ocean lasting several weeks.

As in previous years, the vast majority of external funding in 2007 went to the Faculty of Medicine and the Faculty of Mathematics and Natural Sciences. This was due not only to the high financial requirements and commercial potential of the funded projects, but also to the fact that much of the funding was designed to meet the needs of research in the natural sciences. Competition for funding thus reigned not only between universities or between university and non-university research institutions, but also between faculties. Unlike the Faculty of Philosophy or the newly formed Faculty of Human Sciences, the Faculty of Economics and Social Sciences and the Faculty of Law experienced less funding pressure. They financed and conducted their research largely through their numerous associated research institutes, which were supported by business and private foundations.

Although the Faculty of Philosophy attracted the third-largest share of external funding, it lagged far behind the faculties of medicine and the natural sciences. The increasingly important programs for external funding have tended to meet the needs of the humanities much less than those of the natural sciences. According to an analysis by the Wissenschaftsrat (German Council of Science and Humanities) in 2006, the humanities are particularly dependent on the comparatively low core funding provided by the university. In addition, the humanities have lost some of their standing since the 1990s as a result of the universities' greater output orientation. At particular risk have been what are referred to in German as "orchid subjects," disciplines in the humanities which often have just a single professorship and fewer than 100 students. The German Council of Science and Humanities suggested their future could be secured through collaboration with other disciplines. Several targeted measures have been undertaken to address the precarious situation of the humanities. For example, the University of Cologne established the Morphomata International Center for Advanced Studies—Genesis, Dynamics and Mediality of Cultural Figurations in 2009. Overall, discussions on the appropriate distribution of financial resources between research, teaching and the increasingly important administrative tasks of funding, project and academic management played a key role at the university in this period. They reflected fundamental changes in the internal structures of academic work and life.[10]

A Fundamental Reorganization

The introduction of the bachelor's and master's programs in the winter semester of 2006/2007 was a major undertaking that absorbed considerable time and energy. Underlying what was probably the greatest administrative change in the history of the University of Cologne was a revolution in third-level education in Germany and throughout Europe. The traditional state exams and diplomas, as well as the *Magister* degree introduced at the end of the 1950s, disappeared almost completed. They were replaced by bachelor's and master's degrees derived from the Anglo-Saxon educational model with modular study programs and credit point systems, which had to be reconciled with the requirements of university education and its curricular traditions in Germany. While proponents cited the goals of improved structure and transparency in degree programs, easier transfers for students throughout Europe and more effective career preparation, critics pointed to the risk of higher education becoming more similar to secondary school curricula, the enormous organizational effort involved, the numerous required examinations, and uncertainty about the market value of the bachelor's degree. Many regarded themselves as "second-class students."[11]

The unrest among the students was intensified by the introduction of universal tuition fees in 2007. Despite high revenues generated at the University of Cologne, which rose to as much as twenty-six million euros per year, funds were not sufficient to cover the steadily increasing financial requirements as student numbers continued to grow. The first Higher Education Pact 2020, enacted in 2007, in which the federal and state governments agreed to make additional funds available, was intended to deal with these problems and also compensate for the double school-leaving cohort in 2013 resulting from the reduction of the secondary school cycle from nine to eight years. However, this special funding, which was made available a further two times, was still not enough to plug all the budgetary holes.[12]

Universities and schools were in turmoil. In 2009, secondary school pupils and university students throughout Germany protested against school grades for behavior and work skills, regimented conditions at universities, and tuition fees. At the end of the year, students at the University of Cologne took part in a nationwide strike and occupied the main auditorium. Following their eviction by police, they moved for one week into the auditorium of the Faculty of Human Sciences, with the dean's permission. The students condemned the ongoing underfunding of the university, tuition fees, regimented curricula and the heavy examination load. On 15 December 2009, the University Senate discussed the strike and unanimously voted in favor of withdrawing the trespassing charges against those who had occupied the auditorium. The rector referred to extensive discussions with the students and to a specially created website which provided information on how tuition fees were spent. In 2008/2009, for example, the full sum of around twenty-five million euros was invested in the improvement of studies and teaching. In the committees which discussed how the fees should be spent, student representatives had half of the votes. Nevertheless, the situation did not calm down until the newly elected state government abolished tuition fees from the 2011/2012 winter semester onward.[13]

By then, the transition to a system of bachelor's and master's degrees had been completed. The process had also entailed a fundamental reform of teacher training. The faculties with teaching degree programs developed the Cologne Model, which integrates educational science and didactic elements relevant to the professional field of teaching into the bachelor's degree program, offers a wide range of subjects with extensive combination options, includes student teaching phases, and enhances research. The Center for Teacher Education, which opened in fall 2011, integrates teacher training across faculties and disciplines, works closely with schools and centers for practical school education and is responsible for promoting young talent through the new Cologne Graduate School of Teacher Education.[14]

The university also improved conditions for research and study by constructing new buildings. As part of the pilot project for autonomous construction management, it independently planned the redevel-

↗ Students don't mind waiting in line for a good cappuccino or espresso at the coffee stand on Albertus Magnus Platz.

→ Bright and modern workplaces are available to students in all campus buildings; pictured here is a working area at the Faculty of Economics and Social Sciences.

Cappuccino
Rifugio Dolomites
MessnerMountainMuseum
K PK 143

opment and expansion of the campus. In order to quickly solve the problem of overcrowding, the university rented about 6,000 square meters of space close to the campus in spring 2009. In fall 2010, a new seminar building with 900 seats, mainly financed by tuition fees, opened its doors. This extended the existing ensemble comprising the University and City Library, the lecture hall building and the Philosophikum, which had been built some forty years earlier. As a result, room capacities for lectures and seminars increased by thirty percent. In addition, modular buildings were constructed all across the campus to meet the high demand for additional teaching and work spaces at short notice. These included a building with modern workspaces and seminar rooms for economics and social sciences, which was located in front of the existing faculty high-rise and was also largely paid for by tuition fees. Similar buildings were erected on the campus of the faculties of human sci-ences and mathematics and natural sciences. In 2010, construction began on the Student Service Center (SSC), which was inaugurated three years later. Since then, its 12,000 square meters have housed all administrative services for students, which had previously been spread across various buildings on the campus: the Central Student Advisory Office, the Student Secretariat, the International Office and the Professional Center. The task of refurbishing the older buildings remains on the agenda. With its Master Plan 2025 and Master Plan 2030, the university developed two comprehensive programs for expanding the campus as part of a concept for the future and in close connection with the city's urban planning department.[15]

Excellence

In 2012, the University of Cologne, together with just ten other German universities, was successful in all three pillars of the second round of the Excellence Initiative: two graduate schools, two clusters of excellence and the institutional strategy were deemed worthy of funding by the German Research Foundation (DFG) and the Council of Science and Humanities. Funding for the Bonn-Cologne Graduate School and CECAD was extended. In addition, funding was granted to a.r.t.e.s. Graduate School for the Humanities Cologne and to the Cluster of Excellence on Plant Sciences (CEPLAS), a joint effort with the University of Düsseldorf, the MPI for Plant Breeding in Cologne and Jülich Research Center.[16]

The new a.r.t.e.s. (Anthropology-Reception-Transculturation-Episteme-Language) Graduate School, which emerged from one of the first NRW research schools, now supervises all doctoral degrees in the Faculty of Philosophy. A research master's degree and a research lab for the postdoctoral phase complement the range of services which enable the Faculty of Philosophy, as a graduate faculty, to compete with the best graduate schools in the world. CEPLAS, located at Plant Science Center Cologne-Düsseldorf, investigates how plants adapt to changing environmental conditions. In response to climate change, expanding human populations, and increasing resource scarcity, it aims to develop sustainable strategies for plant production by applying insights from microbiology. Innovative training programs for students, doctoral candidates and postdocs foster the next generation of scientists. The university's research profile was strengthened by the establishment of the Global South Studies Center, which has been dedicated since 2014 to the transdisciplinary study of far-reaching changes occurring in Africa, Asia and Latin America, and is networked internationally through numerous partnerships between the participating disciplines.[17]

The university's institutional strategy, entitled The Challenge of Change and Complexity, served to integrate the various initiatives taken in previous years to establish a research-oriented and internationally networked university. It formulated the goal of turning the University of Cologne into "a leading institution with excellent research and teaching." To this end, Cologne first defined four and later six "key profile areas" of research, which are based on existing focal points and infrastructure such as research clusters. The key profile areas are embedded in broader, interdisciplinary and cross-faculty areas of competence: Ageing and Demographic Change, Social and Economic Behavior, Quantitative Modeling of Complex Systems, Cultures and Societies in Transition, Food Security, and Language and Education.[18]

Shaping the Future

In promoting cutting-edge research, the aim is not to create islands of excellence but rather to foster work throughout the university and contribute to the further development of a highly differentiated culture of research. Internal exchange between faculties and disciplines is intended to strengthen the unity of the university while preserving its traditional diversity. The institutional strategy includes the research profile and a teaching profile, though the latter is considerably less elaborated. Within the framework of its numerous study programs, the university offers many opportunities for both research- and career-oriented education—two paths that often lead to tensions. Teacher training and educational research are particularly prominent in Cologne. International networking through research partnerships and the International Faculty Program is also a component of the institutional strategy. An internal funding system supports academic excellence in all its forms—from individual studies to large-scale research projects. New models of management and organization are aimed at strengthening the university's flexibility and responsiveness. Additional services meet the growing requirements of scholars, whose professional and self-image is undergoing a fundamental change in the twenty-first century.[19]

In particular, seven interrelated measures have supported the implementation of the institutional strategy since 2012: the development of key profile and competence areas, a funding program for cutting-edge research, a program for early-career scholars, the organizational development of the university, the expansion of the Cologne Research Alliance, increased internationalization, and the promotion of gender equality. Outside the university, Cologne has an impact through German U15, which it co-founded in 2012. This strategic group repre-

↑ The Abertus Magnus statue was returned to its original location in front of the main building in 2005.

senting the interests of fifteen German universities with strong research profiles, especially in medicine, develops ideas on higher education and research policy and presents them in public debates. All of the participating universities are internationally oriented. German U15 is a member of the Research Universities International Network, which was founded in 2013 and includes around 180 research universities worldwide. Its aim is to sustainably support basic research, to promote research-oriented teaching and to transfer knowledge to society, politics and business.[20]

The Excellence Initiative was continued under the name of Excellence Strategy after its evaluation by an international commission in 2016. The funding of graduate schools was discontinued, the financing period was extended to seven years and the application to be considered a university of excellence no longer required an institutional strategy. On 27 September 2018, the German Research Foundation (DFG) announced its decision on the clusters of excellence. All four applications submitted by the University of Cologne were successful. The funding of CECAD and CEPLAS was continued. A new addition was the ECONtribute: Markets & Public Policy cluster developed with the University of Bonn, which is part of the Reinhard Selten Institute founded by both universities in 2017. The cluster aims to take a new look at markets and use recent findings from economics, psychology, politics and law to analyze the phenomenon of market failure. The second new cluster of excellence, Matter and Light for Quantum Computing (ML4Q), involves the universities of Bonn and Aachen and Jülich Research Center. The aim of the cluster is to design new computer and network architectures based on quantum mechanics. Quantum computers, the next step in computer development, are expected to connect extremely fast processors and thus solve highly complex tasks.[21]

After a Hundred Years

One hundred years after its new founding, the University of Cologne is now one of the largest and most successful universities in Germany. It collaborates with a broad national and international network of institutions in research and teaching. As of 2018, around 50,000 women and men study here at six faculties, including over 5,000 foreign students. Today more than sixty percent of the students are women. Six hundred and fifty professors, including numerous junior professors, conduct research and teach at the University of Cologne, yielding an average ratio of seventy-five students per professor. Nearly 4,900 members of research staff play a major role in teaching and research, while more than 6,000 additional employees are responsible for administration and technical services. Women make up almost half of the research staff, though they account for only thirty percent of the professors. The university strives for gender equality at all levels and promotes diversity, equal opportunity and inclusion with its cross-sectional area of Gender & Diversity. The democratization of the university thus acquires a social dimension. The university has also systematically promoted the careers of young academics, for example through the many graduate schools in every faculty, and, since 2018, through the support and guidance provided to all doctoral students by the Albertus Magnus Center. Junior professorships and tenure-track processes create defined paths to professorships and thus clearer career perspectives.[22]

The position of the faculties has changed. Although they continue to form the basic structure of the university, cross-faculty projects and institutions such as the sixteen research centers play an increasingly important role. In addition to the clusters of excellence and the Center for Teacher Education, these include internal institutions such as the ProfessionalCenter, founded in 2008 to support students in launching their careers, and Gateway, which is to be expanded in the coming years with thirty million euros of state funding to form an excellence start-up center. The COPT.ZENTRUM for organic electronics, which was inaugurated in 2015, offers work opportunities to small and medium-sized enterprises in the fields of organic, flexible and printed electronics. This is a central component of the technology transfer strategy of the University of Cologne. All three institutions are part of the university's third mission, which has been added to its classical missions of research and teaching. The third mission involves the transfer of university knowledge to society, politics and business, ongoing professional and academic training, and social engagement. Also of increasing importance is the communication of research results to ensure active participation in our knowledge society. The university is thus developing entirely new fields of activity and working methods; their acceptance and integration into existing structures represents a major challenge that some view with skepticism. At the same time, the increasing interaction between the university and various sectors of society and their fundamental concerns is becoming more clearly defined.[23]

Today, the Faculty of Philosophy is by far the largest with about 14,000 students, followed by economics and social sciences, human sciences, and mathematics and natural sciences. The faculties of law and medicine have the lowest student enrollment. The ranking of the faculties is quite different when it comes to attracting external funding, which makes up more than a quarter of the university's total budget of over 800 million euros. In this respect, the Medical Faculty is well ahead of the rest with ninety-five million euros; mathematics and the natural sciences receive about half as much. The humanities and cultural sciences obtain nearly twenty-five million euros in external funding. However, neither student numbers nor success in attracting funding directly reflect research output, educational performance or social significance, since the faculties continue to demonstrate considerable and even increasing differences when it comes to structures and forms of work.[24]

The inherently heterogeneous structure of the University of Cologne in 2019 offers ample space for generating new research findings via diverse paths, and for exploring these findings in depth through research-oriented forms of learning. It draws on deep and broad networks at local, regional, national and global levels. As a member of the Cologne Science Round Table, the university is working to strengthen Cologne's reputation as a site for scholarship, to increase its economic potential, and to promote the development of the city society in the long term. Its multi-level cooperation with the other Rhenish universities in Bonn, Aachen and Düsseldorf, its research alliance with non-university research institutions in the region, and other forms of cooperation such as the Digital Hub Cologne or the Geoverbund, contribute significantly to the development of cutting-edge research in Cologne. The International Office looks after students and scholars who come to Cologne from abroad or go abroad from there. It supports the internationally networked clusters of excellence and centers, represents the university in its three offices abroad, and maintains contact with almost 200 institutional cooperation partners all over the world.[25]

Today's University of Cologne bears little resemblance to the university of 1919, so profound have been the changes. However, certain developmental threads can be traced back to its inception and to the era of the Cologne Commercial College. These include the marriage of theory with practice, and critical reflection on society and the conditions under which new knowledge emerges. Indeed, the university founded in 1919 already had little in common with the medieval university of 1388, beyond certain symbolic references to the initial foundation. These include the slogan "Good Ideas. Since 1388," with which the University of Cologne now presents itself. This slogan demonstrates an awareness of tradition, even if it was the courageous founding objectives of 1919 and their further development, especially since the 1960s, that were decisive in forming the present-day character of the University of Cologne. Continuity amid change and radical upheavals always raise the question of what constitutes a university today and in the future.

New, Modern, Refurbished: Innovative Development

Since 2010, several new structures have been erected throughout the university campus, while existing buildings have been refurbished and modernized. One of the flagship projects of this second major phase of expansion is the seminar building designed by the architect Paul Böhm and opened in 2010 after just one year of construction. Other showcase projects include the CECAD building and the Student Service Center (SSC). Also planned is the refurbishment of the Albertus Magnus Platz building complex and the Faculty of Economics and Social Sciences, as well as the construction of a student union service building and new buildings for the chemistry and physics institutes. The Master Plan drafted in 2012 also aims to close the gap in usable space between the current building stock and the estimated demands for 2025. At the heart of the plan is the creation of a new campus on Zülpicher Wall.

"We would like to build there because these sites are close to the main campus," explains Rector Axel Freimuth. "The concept also provides for the *Mensa* to be moved back toward Zülpicher Wall, thus creating a larger green space. The planned buildings along Zülpicher Wall are normal buildings that will match existing structures, meaning in particular that no high-rises will be built. This project is very important for the University of Cologne. We still have the smallest amount of space per student in Germany and far too many buildings in scattered locations, which severely hampers the quality of teaching and research. On the other hand, I understand very well that the people of Cologne are anxious to maintain their Greenbelt. Green spaces enhance quality of life—we at the university recognize this and we do not want our construction projects to have a negative impact on this."[26]

↗ The research building on Joseph Stelzmann Straße that opened in 2013 to house CECAD is clearly structured with open and closed spaces. The glass roof highlights the building's open design. The public areas include a large reading space and a cafeteria.

→ The Student Service Center (SSC), completed in 2014, was designed by Schuster Architekten Düsseldorf. On the ground floor there is a light-filled atrium. From there, the main stairway—a floating staircase with intersecting flights—leads to the building's upper floors.

↑ The six-story Student Service Centre (SSC) has a floor area of 12,000 square meters. The side of the building facing Universitätsstraße is smooth, while the upper stories of its other facades have protruding and receding sections. The complex houses, among other things, the Student Secretariat, the International Office and the ProfessionalCenter.

Editors' Afterword

Universities have been celebrating their anniversaries as far back as the sixteenth century. However, it was not until the heyday of this practice in the nineteenth century that these celebrations acquired the function, which they retain to this day, of lending to various kinds of organizations a cohesion that transcends daily routines. Anniversaries temporalize the present by institutionalizing the past in terms of tradition and imagining the future in terms of innovation, uniting all three phases in a common experience. Where this attempt succeeds, universities present continuity and radical change as complimentary resources for mobilizing their members and demonstrating their success stories to the outside world. Such celebrations are not only legitimate but indeed indispensable in the context of growing competition among universities.

However, university anniversaries are no longer occasion for unreflective jubilation. This was still the case until well into the twentieth century, when jubilees inspired a historiography of academic achievements that were perceived as heroic deeds and moments of glory. These publications portrayed the university as a special kind of corporately organized culture of knowledge. The various elements of institutional anniversaries that were established in the nineteenth century served to underscore this effect: speeches, the conferral of honorary doctorates for outstanding individuals, the reception of delegations from other universities—all conducted at least partially in Latin. In the 1960s, the first cracks began to appear in this gala facade: students, as well as a few professors, demanded a critical reappraisal of the past, especially the period of National Socialism. In Cologne, this debate over interpretation did not escalate until 1988, when the 600th anniversary of the city's original university was celebrated.

Such debates have heightened the awareness of subsequent generations of the need for a critical approach to the history of their university. Thus, the University of Cologne has used the one-hundredth anniversary of its second founding to shed new light on its history from a variety of perspectives. This volume is one outcome of that process. In addition, a research group conducted four studies on the academic culture at the University of Cologne from the 1920s to the 1970s. Each of these studies focuses on a particular period, examining the official image projected by the university, its appointment policy, the research networks linking university, state and business, and the university as a political space. Moreover, a new monograph examines, for the first time, the role of Konrad Adenauer and his family in the development of the university. An international conference situated the establishment of the University of Cologne in the context of other universities founded in the twentieth and twenty-first centuries. Finally, the university commissioned an expert study to examine how individual honorees, foundations and associated institutes were influenced by or involved with the Nazi regime.

This volume documents the first 100 years of the new University of Cologne. It offers a general overview of the university's history, adding accents by presenting certain recurring and changing themes, as well as biographies and selected objects from the university's material history. While this account incorporates earlier work and more recent findings, a comprehensive history of the new University of Cologne has not yet been written—one that examines not only the second half of university's history since the 1960s, but also aspects of its history during the Weimar Republic, National Socialism and the early Federal Republic. In this, the University of Cologne is not alone. Even this volume cannot compensate for the existing gaps in research, particularly regarding the university's role under various political orders, the degree of academic self-mobilization under the Nazi regime and how this legacy was dealt with after 1945, nor indeed the history of university life, especially the relationship between professors and students. Recently developed research methods such as network analysis, examination of the generation and circulation of academic knowledge, and postcolonial and other diversity-oriented approaches are likely to yield fresh perspectives and insights regarding periodization. Moreover, exploring the university's history from a cultural studies perspective to examine how meaning was generated, to historicize symbolic orders and to deconstruct the seemingly familiar would result in many new findings.

Only a selection of the many events and structures that have shaped the university's history can be presented here. Following an invitation to tender, the editors entrusted the preparation of this volume to an experienced Cologne-based history agency. The concept, which was agreed between the editors and the agency, treats the university first and foremost as an organization. It is shaped by the interaction between structures, resources and goals, on the one hand, and the actions of its members, on the other. In order to reveal the continuities, ruptures and transformations that formed the University of Cologne, it is necessary to focus on basic processes shaped by the dominant political orders and requirements; on questions of financing, teaching capacities and structural development; and on debates about the social structure of academic instructors and students, and how they see their roles.

This history of the University of Cologne begins with the founding of a new university on the site of a medieval university that was closed in 1798. Several other universities founded in the twentieth century share a similar history. Moreover, together with Frankfurt (1914) and Hamburg (1919), Cologne is one of three German universities founded in the shadow of World War I whose formative development occurred during the transition from an authoritarian monarchy to the nascent democracy of the Weimar Republic. According to the conventional division of German university history into three periods, the University of Cologne entered the arena of higher education at the end of the "classical" phase, which was represented by the reform universities of the eighteenth and nineteenth centuries. By the time the University of Cologne was founded in 1919, the model of the research university had already been established. This contrasts with the institutions founded in the early modern era, which were intended as places where all extant knowledge would be stored and taught.

The University of Cologne adopted elements of the research model from the outset, although it initially focused on academically grounded professional training. While this orientation grew in importance under the Nazi regime, which favored politically and ideologically "useful" research—to which many academics were willing converts—most of those who led the university after 1945 were committed to the ideal of a university of scholars, which exalted the *Ordinarius* or full professor and distanced itself from professional education. This orientation would gradually change with the transition to the "post-classical" phase from the 1960s onward. This was especially apparent in the sharp increase in student numbers due to the opening up of higher education and the associated challenges for teaching.

In a reversal of the bourgeois-elitist character of the early post-war years, the University of Cologne, not least because of its size, became an exemplar of the expansion of educational opportunities and the rapid increase in the importance of academic knowledge in the twentieth century. Given all of these changes, this volume repeatedly highlights the academic culture of the University of Cologne: the academic habitus and the daily routines of research and teaching, the significance and changes that came with a more autonomous administration and central management, and the discourses and practices through which the university defined itself.

Any structural overview of a university's history must consider the evolution of its range of subjects and faculties. It is neither possible nor intended to provide a detailed description of the relevant profiles, persons and achievements here. In particular, the biographies included in this volume were selected as examples. Similarly, each of the faculties is accorded the same level of attention, regardless of its size. The range of subjects and faculties expanded soon after the university's founding: only a theology faculty was not established. Today, Catholic and Protestant theology is studied within the Faculty of Philosophy. This volume is also necessarily limited to describing trends and milestones: the long-dominant role of economics and the social sciences, for example, or the university's integration of sections of the Rhineland College of Education (Pädagogische Hochschule Rheinland), which ultimately formed the basis for the Faculty of Human Sciences.

In hardly any other area of university life have the changes of the past one hundred years been so great as in externally funded research, the importance of which has increased hugely in recent decades. This has been accompanied by a shift of emphasis in favor of the natural sciences and medicine. Thanks to interdisciplinary collaborative research centers, as well as various centers and clusters of excellence, well-staffed units with considerable resources have emerged alongside the faculties. These have changed the structure of the university and led to an expansion of its central administration. Funding management, public relations and the need to strike a balance between controlling impulses and the right to autonomy have become more important and time-consuming tasks, but they also generate creative potential.

Although the interactions between the university and its environment cannot be dealt with in detail here, they are nonetheless frequently mentioned—especially the political, social and spatial relations with the city of Cologne. Their significance is obvious, as the city was the sole financial sponsor of the university from its founding until the 1950s and exerted considerable influence through the board of trustees. By the mid-twentieth century, however, the limits of this model had become apparent. The city was unable to continue funding the university. The state government assumed this responsibility, and the federal government now also plays a greater role in funding. Nevertheless, to borrow a memorable phrase from Mitchell Ash, a historian of knowledge, the city and the university have been "resources for one another" ever since the university was founded.

This also applies to the broader context. The history of the new University of Cologne must be understood within the wider arena of politics, society and scholarship in the twentieth century. The dating of some chapters makes this clear: 1919 was the founding year of the Weimar Republic, 1933 was the beginning of the Nazi dictatorship, and 1945 saw its end and the transition to Germany's second democracy. These were also turning points at the University of Cologne. The later phases of the university's history also include important social transformations: the education revolution of the 1960s and 1970s, the internationalization of universities, and the expansion of interdisciplinary research since the 1990s.

If we examine the university as an organization, it is almost inevitable that "grand narratives" such as modernization, professionalization and differentiation will play a far greater role than they otherwise do in present-day historiography. In addition, both the reason for publishing the present volume and its genre imply that it will follow the "model of the classical bildungsroman" (Marian Füssel): the phase of foundation and early character formation is followed by crises, whose mastery brings maturity and self-reliance, setting the course for a future that has yet to unfold. It would require a more detailed analysis to establish whether path dependencies going back to the founding model of 1919 can be identified in this development or have long been left behind in the course of systemic adaptation processes.

The present volume makes particularly clear how the history of the new University of Cologne unfolded as a fundamentally variable relationship between the three essential features of a modern university: education, professional training and basic research. The organizational history approach chosen here reveals a fundamental tension that applies to all universities, which itself warrants examination as a historical phenomenon: is the university an organization sui generis, as many believe, pointing to the academic freedom of professors? Or is it fundamentally no different from any other organization, particularly business enterprises?

Those who regard the university as a special kind of organization tend also to subscribe to an ideal attributed to Wilhelm von Humboldt: that of the unity of research and teaching, the community of professors and students, the empowerment of all students to conduct research, the offer of universal education, the idea of an interdisciplinary unity of scholarship, the task of personality development according to humanistic ideals, and the internal autonomy of the university—despite its funding by the state. However, Humboldtian ideal is itself scarcely older than the new University of Cologne. Significantly, it was first formulated on the occasion of the 100th anniversary of the founding of Berlin's Friedrich Wilhelm University in 1910. It served as a timely and critical alternative to the utilitarian large-scale research structures of Imperial Germany's state-associated universities.

When the University of Cologne was founded, Humboldt was merely one of several resources of legitimacy strategically and flexibly used by its founding fathers, Christian Eckert and Konrad Adenauer. Even immediately after 1945, reference was made in Cologne not so much to Humboldt as to the supposed tradition of the "Christian *Abendland*." In fact, Humboldt was only invoked with passion when, in the 1960s, the university defended its internal autonomy against interference by the state government. But neither were the Humboldtian concepts mentioned in their entirety in this context, nor did the university fully adhere to them at the time.

This shows that the unified university attributed to Humboldt had ceased to exist long before more recent critics began decrying the betrayal of the "idea of the university" in favor of market-oriented large-scale research and business-oriented management. Indeed, a process that began at the end of the nineteenth century and transformed the university into a complex, knowledge-based organization—one which reflected and shaped manifest changes in the social order—made it increasingly difficult to legitimize this institution on the basis of a guiding ideal. Instead, the modern university must be designed as a free space for knowledge, in which reflection and innovation are in close interaction. The rightly invoked principle of academic freedom proves its value precisely when academics meet their social responsibility in a self-critical and conscientious dialog with the public. The history of the new University of Cologne testifies to the importance of this idea.

Professor Dr. Habbo Knoch
Professor Dr. Ralph Jessen
Professor Dr. Hans-Peter Ullmann

Appendix

Notes

Chapter 1

1 Quoted from Adenauer 1919, 9; Eröffnungsfeier 1919.
2 Pabst 1988.
3 Heimbüchel 1988a, 113–130; van Eyll 1990, 26–30.
4 Mevissen 1879; Heimbüchel 1988a, 134–138; Henning 1990, 67–70.
5 Franz 1998, 28–42; Henning 1990, 76f.
6 Zander 2004, 53–56 and 109–111; van Eyll 1990, 32–37.
7 Zander 2004, 112–116; Heimbüchel 1988a, 140–142.
8 Heimbüchel 1988a, 147–149; Zander 2004, 117f.
9 Heimbüchel 1988a, 149–157; Ludwig 1991, 15–89.
10 Zander 2004, 117.
11 Asmuth 1985, 128–137.
12 Asmuth 1985, 59–63 and 112; Heimbüchel 1988a, 169–175 and 207–211; Bolten 1987, 53–59; Franken 1995, 25–28; Gabel/Suthaus 2001, 31–35.
13 Henning 1988a; Henning 1988b; Heimbüchel 1988a, 158–160 and 164; Ludwig 1991, 27f., 41–45 and 90f.; Potthoff/Sieben 1988.
14 Heimbüchel 1988a, 152, 165f. and 176; Gabel/Suthaus 2001, 36–38 and 54.
15 Franz 1998, 48 and 51; Heimbüchel 1988a, 155–161 and 173–176; Zander 2004, 119–122; Asmuth 1985, Appendix, table 1.
16 Frank 2008a; Frank 2008b; Heimbüchel 1988a, 183–199.
17 Bolten 1987; Heimbüchel 1988a, 200–215.
18 Heimbüchel 1988a, 227–250; Heimbüchel 1988b, 248–251; Bolten 1987, 10f.
19 Eckert 1913.
20 Heimbüchel 1988a, 255–270.
21 Heimbüchel 1988a, 273–304.
22 Heimbüchel 1988a; 304–316; Schwarz 1986, 235–247.
23 Neubau Handelshochschule Cöln 1907, 36.
24 Alte Universität.

Chapter 2

1 Franken 1995, 34f.; Universität Köln 1925, 79; Gabel/Suthaus 2001, 41; Universität Köln 1925, 24–33, 53f. and 79–81; Heimbüchel 1988a, 563–573; Heimbüchel 1988b.
2 Quote from Eckert 1919, 14f.; Heimbüchel 1988a, 579–586; Heimbüchel 1988b; Universität Köln 1925, 6; Thieß 1924b, 25 and 28.
3 Heimbüchel 1988a, 336–339 and 561; Universität Köln 1925, 15–18.
4 Heimbüchel 1988a, 547–563.
5 Peil 1988, 93–97 and 142–148; Heimbüchel 1988a, 404–443.
6 Peil 1988, 127f., 172–175 and 200–202; Heimbüchel 1988a, 443–519.
7 Meuthen 1988, 11–16 and 29–31; Heimbüchel 1988a, 359–363.
8 Henning/Lauf/Ludwig 1988, 317–328; Wehler 2003, 469f.
9 Henning/Lauf/Ludwig 1988, 293; Kops/Hansmeyer/Kranski 1988, 389; Asmuth 1985, Appendix, table 1; Wehler 2003, 463; Kuske 1929, 244.
10 Düwell 1976, 186–191; Heimbüchel 1988a, 522–529.
11 Heimbüchel 1988b.
12 Kuske 1929, 233f.; Keussen 1929; Eckert 1926; Meuthen 1988, 13, 17 and 33.
13 Eckert 1919a; Eckert 1919c, 24–26.
14 Quoted from Eckert 1919b, 6f.; Eckert 1919c, 22f.; Eckert 1919a; Adenauer 1919, 9f.; Stier-Somlo 1926, 3f.; Adenauer 1929, 31.
15 Thieß 1924a; Denkrede 1921; Golczewski 1984, 363f.; Heimbüchel 1988a, 588–592.
16 Heimbüchel 1988a, 530–586 and 289–302; Heimbüchel 1988b.
17 Heimbüchel 1988a, 534–540 and 547–563; Universität Köln 1925, 18; Universität Köln 1929, 76.
18 Eckert 1919b, 7; Planitz 1929, 35f.; Kuske 1929, 231–233.
19 Quoted from Liebermann 1988, 66; Frank/Moll 2006, 483–487; Liebermann 1988.
20 Wehefritz 1995; Pflüger 2017.
21 Wittka 1995a, 34–41; Franken 1995, 33–35; Rosenbaum 2003.
22 Freitäger 2004; Rektorenportrait Moritz.
23 Universität Köln 1929, 89–127; Peil 1988, 93–97; Henning/Lauf/Ludwig 1988, 334; Heimbüchel 1988a, 404–429; Ludwig 1991, 17–173, especially 127.
24 Universität Köln 1929, 149–195; Peil 1988, 142–148; Henning/Lauf/Ludwig 1988, 346; Heimbüchel 1988a, 429–443.
25 Universität Köln 1929, 129–148; Peil 1988, 127f.; Henning/Lauf/Ludwig 1988, 340; Heimbüchel 1988a, 443–468; Becker 1988, 12–21.
26 Universität Köln 1929, 197–218; Peil 1988, 172–175; Henning/Lauf/Ludwig 1988, 352; Heimbüchel 1988a, 468–512.
27 Universität Köln 1929, 197–204 and 218–230; Peil 1988, 200–202; Heimbüchel 1988a, 512–519; Eckert 1926, 28–30.
28 Quoted from Schumacher 1903, 40.
29 Universität Köln 1925, 21.
30 Quoted from Von akademischen Obrigkeiten; Groten 1988, 31; Konrad der Große 2017, 113; Krayer 1988, 79.
31 Peil 1988, 317; Universität Köln 1925, 33–37, 61–66, 80–83 and 115–161; Krayer 1988, 77.
32 Quoted from Köhler 1997, 132; Heimbüchel 1988a, 557–563; Köhler 1997, 131–133.
33 Peil 1988, 317; Heimbüchel 1988a, 557–563; Krayer 1988, 79–82.
34 Heimbüchel 1988a, 400–522; Frank/Moll 2006, 322–369.
35 Quoted from Plessner 2001, 337; Wiese 1957, 58f.; Mader 1980, 94–114.
36 von der Leyen 1960, 165; Kruk 1984, 50–52, 74–77 and 85–90; Lehmann 1976, 113–118.
37 Wiese 1957, 58f.; von der Leyen 1960, 162, 165, 169f. and 180f.; Kisch 1966, 112–114.
38 Engelhardt 1986; von der Leyen 1960, 180; Lehmann 1976, 118–120; Kruk 1984, 75f.; Nipperdey 1988, 130–132 and 134–136.
39 Hollstein 2007; Hollstein 2013; Rückert 1999; Meuthen 1988, 47 and 80–81.

40 Franken 1995, 128–132; Paletschek 2006, 176–180.

41 Fischer 2014; Henckmann 1998; Henckmann 2005.

42 Kruk 1984; Potthoff/Sieben 1988; Schneider 2007.

43 Kuske 1929, 246–264; Wenge 2005, 235–239; Heimbüchel 1988a, 364f.; Wehler 2003, 464f.; Titze 1987, 226.

44 Kuske 1929, 250f.; Henning/Lauf/Ludwig 1988, 293; Franken 1996, 42–45 and 49–51.

45 Wenge 2005, 240–251; Heimbüchel 1988a, 362f., 375 and 382f.; Jarausch 1984, 117–127.

46 Vorlesungsverzeichnis 1920/21, 14f.

47 Quoted from Vorlesungsverzeichnis 1920/21, 14; Graven 1929; Kuske 1929, 263–268; Jarausch 1984, 141–145.

48 Groten 1988, 139f.; Konrad der Große 2017, 113; Von akademischen Obrigkeiten.

49 Quoted from Riegel 1996, 158f.

50 Quoted from Universität Köln 1925, 22f.

51 UAK 95/Findbuch; UAK 689/110.

52 Potthoff/Sieben1988; Franz 1998, 82–101; Schneider 2007.

53 Frank 2008b, 92–94; Schaper/Schaper 1995.

54 Heimbüchel 1988a, 441 and 464f.; Wetzell 2000, 63; Frank/Moll 2006, 483–489.

55 Fischer 2014; Sieg 2013, 171–186.

56 Alemann 1976; Stölting 1986, 124–129, 167–173 and 280–315; Kaesler 1997; Moebius 2017, 6–14.

57 Weller 2013; Hollstein 2013.

58 Heimbüchel 1988a, 453–461; Dreier 1999.

59 Clemens 1983; Morsey 2010.

60 Otto 2013; Gienow 1990; Rektorenportrait Stier-Somlo.

61 Freitäger 2003; Gräbel 2015, 80 and 118; Golczewski 1988, 63f.; Haupts 2007, 353.

62 Alemann 1988; Kaesler 1997; van Dyk/Schauer 2014, 46–57; Borggräfe/Schnitzler 2014; Moebius 2017, 6–14.

63 Heimbüchel 1988a, 348–350 and 374f.; Golczewski 1988, 24–40; Wenge 2005, 242–265 and 273–279.

64 Quoted from Wenge 2005, 282 and Wortmann 1980, 113; Wenge 2005, 279–289; Wortmann 1980, 106–109 and 114; Freitäger 2010, 118.

65 Wenge 2005, 289f.; Wortmann 1980, 115.

66 Kuske 1932, 4; Wenge 2005, 289–292.

67 Kuske 1932, 4.

68 Kuske 1932, 4f.; Heimbüchel 1988a, 373–399; Golczewski 1988, 39–49; Wenge 2005, 292f.

69 Quoted from Festschrift Suevia 2004, 10 and 32; Festschrift Suevia 2004, 27.

70 Quoted from Kandinsky/Niessen 1931; Kandinskys "Bilder einer Ausstellung" 2008.

Chapter 3

1 Quoted from Golczewski 1988, 72f.; Titze 1989, 224f.

2 Golczewski 1988, 50–73.

3 Titze 1989, 228; Golczewski 1988, 248–297.

4 Golczewski 1988, 115f.

5 Quoted from Becker 1988, 23 and 26; Golczewski 1988, 115–123.

6 Golczewski 1988, 445–456; Grüttner/Kienas 2007, 139–148 and 177–179.

7 Grüttner/Kienas 2007, 133–139 and 149–151; Golczewski 1988, 104–247.

8 Henning/Lauf/Ludwig 1988, 293, 317, 320, 325, 328 and 331.

9 Kops/Hansmeyer/Kranski 1988, 391–405.

10 Golczewski 1988, 304–306 and 315–317; Titze 1989, 224–238; Wehler 2003, 825–829; Hachtmann 2010; Peil 1988, 93–204 and 254–266.

11 Henning/Lauf/Ludwig 1988, 293, 317, 320 and 325; Golczewski 1988, 287f.; Schallner 2012, 314f.; Jarausch 1984, 202f.

12 Schallner 2012, 319–322; Golczewski 1988, 289–297.

13 Lemberg 2000, 31–46; Golczewski 1988, 294–297; Schallner 2012, 322.

14 Quoted from Heimbüchel 1988a, 592; Golczewski 1988, 71f.; Titze 1989, 224f.

15 Quoted from Golczewski 1988, 59; Golczewski 1988, 50–52 and 57–59; Matzerath 2009, 63–77.

16 Golczewski 1988, 59f., 62, 73 and 256f.

17 Golczewski 1988, 54–56 and 60–64.

18 Quoted from Golczewski 1988, 65, 67 and 69; Golczewski 1988, 64–69.

19 Golczewski 1988, 70 and 286; Krayer 1988, 79–82.

20 Nees; Curriculum Vitae Alder; Alder Biographical.

21 Baerlecken/Tiedau 2003; Tiedau 2009; Haupts 2007, 219–221.

22 Cohn-Vossen; Golczewski 1988, 452.

23 Hoffrath 2012.

24 Quoted from Treß 2008, 160; Golczewski 2008, 549f.

25 Quoted from Golczewski 2008, 545; Treß 2008, 71.

26 Quoted from Golczewski 2008, 546f.

27 Quoted from Treß 2008, 161; Golczewski 2008, 546–548; Treß 2008, 160f.

28 Quoted from Treß 2008, 160f. and 165; Golczewski 2008, 548f.; Treß 2008, 164–166.

29 Quoted from Treß 2008, 162f.; Golczewski 2008, 551.

30 Quoted from Treß 2008, 164 and Golczewski 2008, 552; Treß 2008, 163f.; Golczewski 2008, 551f.

31 Quoted from Bieroth 1933, 6; Neue Universität Köln 1938, 41–44; Deutsche Kriegswirtschaft 1940.

32 BArch R 9361-VIII KARTEI / 2070531; Parteigenosse 2009; Peil 1988, 109.

33 Golczewski 1988, 144–147, 208–211 and 448f.; Henning/Lauf/Ludwig 1988, 317, 320, 325 and 328; Grüttner/Kienas 2007, 178f.

34 Golczewski 1988, 67–69, 154–164, 205–207, 306–314 and 445–447; Henning/Lauf/Ludwig 1988, 317, 320, 325 and 328; Grüttner/Kienas 2007, 177–179.

35 Golczewski 1988, 125–128, 132–149, 169–171 and 449–452; Henning/Lauf/Ludwig 1988, 317, 320, 325 and 328; Grüttner/Kienas 2007, 178f.

36 Golczewski 1988, 109, 129–131, 148–153, 198–205, 213–222, 419–427 and 452–456; Henning/Lauf/Ludwig 1988, 317, 320, 325 and 328; Grüttner/Kienas 2007, 177–179.

37 Golczewski 1988, 222–234; Grüttner/Kienas 2007, 177.

38 This list is based on three previous versions: an older one compiled by Golczewski 1988, 445–456; on a revised version of that list (with differing assessments in some cases); and

on an amended version by Grüttner/Kinas 2007, especially 177–179; special thanks are also due to Michael Grüttner (TU Berlin), who made available current findings and assessments from his present DFG project (Die Vertreibung von Wissenschaftlerinnen und Wissenschaftlern aus den deutschen Universitäten 1933–1945, January 2019).

39 Golczewski 1988, 144–147 and 448; Mayer-Maly 1969; Haymann.

40 Weinke 2013; Hausmann 2007, 68f. and 259–268; Rektorenportrait Jahrreiß.

41 Walter 1977; Schaper/Schaper 1995; Matzerath 2014; Kisch 1966.

42 Engels 2007; Henning 1988b; Rektorenportrait Kuske.

43 Szöllösi-Janze/Freitäger 2005, 8–13, 17–26 and 44–46; Happ 2004, 285–287.

44 Szöllösi-Janze/Freitäger 2005, 45f. and 89–91; Happ 2004, 289f.

45 Szöllösi-Janze/Freitäger 2005, 46f. and 105–110; Happ 2004, 290–292.

46 Quoted from Szöllösi-Janze/Freitäger 2005, 84; Szöllösi-Janze/Freitäger 2005, 46f., 49–59 and 84–88; Happ 2004, 293f.

47 Quoted from Szöllösi-Janze/Freitäger 2005, 68; Szöllösi-Janze/Freitäger 2005, 46f. and 49–64; Happ 2004, 291.

48 Szöllösi-Janze/Freitäger 2005, 7–13 and 122.

49 Quoted from UAK 317-III/712, 100.

50 Quoted from UAK 571/72.

51 Quoted from Neue Universität Köln 1938, 57–60; Vergleichsmikroskop 1936.

52 Quoted from Kriminaltechnik 1958, 251; Vergleichsmikroskop 1936.

53 Titze 1989, 227f. and 231; Golczewski 1988, 88–98.

54 Golczewski 1988, 98–103; Freitäger 2010, 120–123 and 125–131; Jarausch 1984, 165–175; Grüttner 1995, 304; Schallner 2007, 21.

55 Quoted from Freitäger 2010, 123/note 39 and Grüttner 1995, 273; Schallner 2007, 19–24; Freitäger 2010, 123–125; Grüttner 1995, 348 and 440.

56 Schallner 2012, 309f. and 314–323; Henning/Lauf/Ludwig 1988, 293; Golczewski 1988, 289–297; Grüttner 1995, 378; Jarausch 1984, 200–210.

57 Ahrend 2010; Hansmeyer/Mackscheidt 1988; Herrmann 1990.

58 Franken 2008; Franken/Schäfer 2011.

59 Durschang et al. 2005; Wittka 1995b, 83–90; Golczewski 1988, 347–349; Clemens 1983, 220f.

60 Golczewski 1988, 334–337; Schwab 2013; Schäfer 2013, 318–327.

61 Quoted from Haupts 2008, 81.

62 Quoted from Haupts 2008, 81; Engels 2007, 68–364; Haupts 2008, 79–98; Klingemann 2003, 412f.

63 Golczewski 1988, 344–346; Fahlbusch 1999, 375f. and 422; Haupts 2008, 75–78.

64 Quoted from Golczewski 1988, 367; Golczewski 1988, 363–367.

65 Wenge 2005, 548–550 and 557–560; Franken 2008; Franken/Schäfer 2011; Frank/Moll 2006, 490.

66 Dillmann 1988, 102; Depping 2002, 66 and 88; Weller 2013, 39–42; Hollstein 2007, 66–76; Janssen 2009, 208–215; Hacke 2018, 163–167 and 338f.

67 Golczewski 1988, 294f.; Haupts 2007, 356–358; Weinke 2013, 168f. and 181–185; Hausmann 2007, 68f. and 259–268.

68 Endres 2009, 202–209.

69 Endres 2009, 202; Schmidt 2004, 68.

70 Quoted from Hoffrath 2009, 103.

71 Hoffrath 2009.

72 Groten 1988, 141–148.

Chapter 4

1 Heimbüchel 1988a, 600; Golczewski 1988, 296; Haupts 2007, 17f.

2 Haupts 2007, 33–35; Schildt 1997, 225–227.

3 van Dijk 2010, 270–274; Krayer 1988, 77–82; Haupts 2007, 43f.

4 Haupts 1996.

5 Henning/Lauf/Ludwig 1988, 293f. and 325–332.

6 Meuthen 1988, 48; Kleinen 2005, 255–264 and 358–390; Kroll 1946a; Kroll 1946b; Kroll 1947a; Kroll 1947b; Haupts 2007, 39f.

7 Heimbüchel 1988a, 604–606; Haupts 2007, 61f. and 98–114; Beckhough 1983, 82; Golczewski 1988, 404–436 and 439; Golczewski 1997.

8 Henning/Lauf/Ludwig 1988, 294; Oehler/Bradatsch 1998, 412–416.

9 Henning/Lauf/Ludwig 1988, 294, 307 and 317–360; UAK 331/7, Senatsprotokoll 1 March 1958, 86.

10 Tiggemann 2008, 136; Binding/Müller 1988, 24; Katner 1969, 35f. and 41; Heinemann 1991, 301; Festschrift Lindenburg 2008, 148f.; Meuthen 1988, 54 and 56; Rüegg 2004, 21.

11 Binding/Müller, 21 and 31f.; Kellenbenz 1969, 17; Funck 2004, 209; Knoch 2018, 111f.

12 Heimbüchel 1988a, 600–603; Haupts 2007, 17–19 and 34f.; Lemberg 2000, 46–48; Wiese 1957, 90; Kries 1995, 247.

13 Kleinen 2005, 111–113; Haupts 2007, 20–23; Golczewski 1988, 378 and 380–382; Hollstein 2007, 77; van Dijk 2010, 274f.

14 Haupts 2007, 23; Kleinen 2005, 33; Kries 1995, 248; Diederich 1976, 513f.

15 Kleinen 2005, 33–58 and 67; Euros 2016, 250; Kries 1995, 244; Haupts 1996, 331; Kleinen 2005, 67.

16 Kries 1995, 251; Haupts 2007, 24 and 44.

17 Quoted from Kroll 1945, 10; Kries 1995, 250; Kleinen 2005, 1; Euros 2016, 256.

18 Weber 2003; Altenhein 2005; Garber 2000.

19 Interview with Baum; curriculum vitae Baum.

20 Rektorenportrait Bohne; Dillmann 1988, 103; Haupts 2007, 23, 34, 44 and 49; Lang-Hinrichsen 1958.

21 Strohmeier 1998.

22 Quoted from Heimbüchel 1988a, 606; Heimbüchel 1988a, 606f.; Bartz 2005, 105; Haupts 2007, 36–39.

23 Hollstein 2007, 79–82; Haupts 2007, 33–39 and 50; Kroll 1931a; Kroll 1931b; Kroll 1945; Golczewski 1988, 387–391; Kleinen 2005, 1–9.

24 Quoted from Kroll 1945, 6f. and 3f.; Kroll 1947a, 22; Kroll 1945; Kroll 1946a; Kroll 1946b; Kroll 1947a; Kroll 1947b; Kroll 1947c.

25 Quoted from: Alewyn 1951, 9 and Koch 1953, 21 and 24; Schildt 1999, 29–33; Weisbrod 2002, 19–30; Alewyn 1951; Koch 1953.

26 Quoted from: LA NRW R, NW 1048 no. 33398, Appendix I/a; BArch R 9361-IX KARTEI / 8521322; Rektorenportrait Fellerer; de Vries 1998.

27 Quoted from Curriculum Vitae Alder; UAK 266/1.

28 van Dijk 2010, 270 and 274; Kleinen 2005, 26.

29 Quoted from Golczewski 1988, 380f.; van Dijk 2010, 274.

30 van Dijk 2010, 274–279; Golczewski 1988, 380–386; Weisbrod 2002.

31 van Dijk 2010, 275f.; Golczewski 1988, 386 and 439; Henning/Lauf/Ludwig 1988, 317f., 320f., 325f. and 331f.

32 van Dijk 2010, 279–281; Golczewski 1988, 394–399; Haupts 2007, 28 and 68–73; Haupts 1996, 337 and 351; Kleinen 2005, 32.

33 Golczewski 1988, 401 and 403.

34 Platthaus 2006; Balkhausen 2008.

35 Schmaus 1979; Meuthen 2001; Haupts 2007, 150–167; Geschichte Thomas-Institut.

36 Moebius 2015.

37 Hasselbach 1991, 117–158; Ptak 2004, 82–89; Kowitz 1998, 15–134; Engels 2007, 334–336.

38 Kleinen 2005, 75f., 80f., 87, 89f., 95f., 110, 133, 154, 158 and 164; vom Hagen 2007, 72; Kries 1995, 252–254; Kücking 2007, 121 and 132; Henning/Lauf/Ludwig 1988, 293f.

39 Jarausch 1984, 214; Kleinen 2005, 164, 166 and 417; Kries 1995, 255; Velke 2010, 187 and 205.

40 Schneider, C. 2007, 85; Flümann 2007, 80 and 82; Velke 2010, 200; Kleinen 2005, 46–51; vom Hagen 2007, 73 and 75f.

41 Kries 1995, 243 and 261f.; Kleinen 2005, 388, 391, 402 and 419; Jarausch 1984, 218f.

42 Kleinen 2005, 75, 295f. and 326–330; Euros 2016, 258; Universitätsführer 1951, 147 and 150.

43 Quoted from Universitätsführer 1951, 3 and 167.

44 Husserl Archive; Vongehr 2007.

45 Haupts 2007, 116–119; Peil 1988, 117, 123f., 138 and 256.

46 Hollstein 2013; Moebius 2015; Karpen 2001; Katterle 1998.

47 Kowitz 1998; Ellinger 1988; Detjen 2014.

48 Nonn 2013, 123–177; Haupts 2007, 238–297; Meuthen 2001; Peil 1988, 177; Hausmann 1997; Altenhein 2005.

49 Wenkell 2013, 33–58; Eckart 1961, 210; Rektorenportrait Tönnis.

50 Karpen 2001; Rektorenportrait Peters.

51 Seibold 2004; Strauch 2007.

52 Hondros 2015, 134f. and 154–158; 100 Jahre, 649–662; Rektorenportrait Tönnis.

53 Ortmann 1976; Ortmann 1986, 6–17 and 22–32; Golczewski 1988, 132, 137, 139–142 and 452.

54 Kries 1995, 244–251; Haupts 2001, 341–351; Haupts 2007, 90 and 106–113; Allebrodt 2001, 41f. and 45–47.

55 Quoted from Haupts 2001, 353f.; Haupts 2007, 92f.; Haupts 2001, 344f. and 353–355; Meuthen 1988, 51.

56 Quoted from Haupts 2001, 356f.; Meuthen 1988, 53.

57 Quoted from Haupts 2001, 357f.

58 Haupts 2001, 358f.; Meuthen 1988, 46 and 60; Löwer 1997, 97, 134–136 and 150f.; Hüttenberger/Wadischat 1986,149f., 154 and 158.

59 Groten 1988, 166; Kolberg 1989, 321–325; Opitz 1997.

60 Quoted from Wolf-Pommrich 1960, 104f.; GESIS.

Chapter 5

1 Wehler 2008, 380–385; Oehler/Bradatsch 1998, 413–417 and 426; Jessen 2018; Henning/Lauf/Ludwig 1988, 293–295; Kellenbenz 1969, 17.

2 Henning/Lauf/Ludwig 1988, 334–360; Hansmeyer 1988, 27f.

3 Henning/Lauf/Ludwig 1988, 318–322 and 325–333; Oehler/Bradatsch 1998, 415.

4 Peil 1988, 25–224; Kops/Hansmeyer/Kranski 1988, 410–412, 425, 426f. and 433f.

5 Wagner 1969, 195f.; Binding/Müller 1988, 2 and 24.

6 Wagner 1969; Binding/Müller 1988, 33–38; Krings 2011; Knoch 2018, 113–116.

7 Binding/Müller 1988, 21 and 39–41; Knoch 2018, 112.

8 Binding/Müller 1988, 24 and 42–53; Tiggemann 2008, 138–145; Knoch 2018, 112.

9 Jarausch 1985, 226–241; Bartz 2000; Holl/Glunz 2008; Dohms 2008a; Leggewie 2018; Keim/Lewejohann 2018b.

10 Bartz 1998; Bartz 2000, 113–115 and 117–119; Holl/Glunz 2008, 73; Paul 2010; Dammer 2018.

11 Hübner 1988, 53–58; Schiedermair 1988, 418–420; Dohms 2008a; Keim 2018.

12 Quoted from Hübner 1988, 59 and 62; Hübner 1988; Schiedermair 1988; Fellerer 1968a; Hübner 1968; Hübner 1971; Mittelstaedt 1971; Jessen 2018, 98f.

13 Oehler/Bradatsch 1998, 433–437; Bartz 2006, 174–178; Mitteilungen 1/1971, 13–15.

14 Hüttenberger/Wadischat 1986, 157f.; Bartz 2006, 63–94; Henning/Lauf/Ludwig 1988, 294.

15 Henning/Lauf/Ludwig 1988, 294, 318–332 and 335–359; UAK 331/7, Senatsprotokoll, 25 January 1962, 179f.; Kellenbenz 1969, 18f.

16 Henning/Lauf/Ludwig 1988, 294, 318–332 and 335–359; Hansmeyer 1988, 27–29.

17 Quoted from UAK 331/8, Senatsprotokoll, 13 January 1964, 61 and UAK 331/8, Senatsprotokoll, 27 June 1963, 42; UAK 331/8, Senatsprotokoll, 25 May 1963, 33.

18 Quoted from Hausmitteilungen 1/1968, 2; Henning/Lauf/Ludwig 1988, 294f. and 318–332; UAK 331/9, Senatsprotokoll, 30 May 1969, 290–294 and Senatsprotokoll, 13 February 1970, 397.

19 UAK 631; Preisliste; Historisches; Peil 1988, 223.

20 Wenkel 2013, 35–38; Katner 1969, 93; Curriculum Vitae Delbrück.

21 Kaufmann 2007; Paracelsus-Medaille 1988; Festschrift Lindenburg 2008, 175.

22 Ellinger 1988; Mantel 2009, 64, 139, 281–283, 456f., 522f. and 704–708.

23 Jessen 2010, 262–267.

24 Sauter 1969; Peil 1988, 205–224.

25 Katner 1969, 19, 58 and 98; Peil 1988, 119, 178 and 206.

26 Quoted from Katner 1969, 55; Katner 1969, 55–81; Peil 1988, 172–179 and 182–199; Martin-Buber-Institut.

27 Kellenbenz 1969, 15–22; Peil 1988, 93–126; Binding/Müller 1988, 31f.

28 Peil 1988, 127–141; Geschichte Rechtswissenschaftliche Fakultät.

29 Katner 1969, 32–54; Peil 1988, 142–171; Binding/Müller 1988, 46f.; Vogt 2008a, 152f.; Tiggemann 2008, 138–144.

30 Quoted from UAK 28/538a; Groten 1988, 170; Hausmitteilungen 1/1970, 1–4.

31 Quoted from Holl/Glunz 2008, 134; Dammer 2018, 121.

32 Quoted from Mitteilungen 17/1974, 26; UAK 331/7, Senatsprotokoll, 28 November 1959, 130; Nyborg 2014, 4–9; Rüegg 2010, 39f.; Rektorenportrait Jahrreiß.

33 UAK 331/7, Senatsprotokoll, 30 April 1959, 112; Meuthen 1988, 58; Merkelbach 1970; Ladendorf 1969, 147; Gudian 1974.

34 Ladendorf 1969; Meuthen 1988, 60.

35 Kaltefleiter 1971; Meuthen 1988, 58; Freitäger 2005, 13.

36 Schramm 1969; Meuthen 1988, 57; Peil 1988, 265; Afrikanum 2013.

37 Meuthen 1988, 58; Hausmitteilungen 3/1969, 1–6; Ladendorf 1969, 147; Peil 1988, 119; UAK 331/8: Senatsprotokoll, 23 February 1963, 24 and Senatsprotokoll, 16 January 1965, 104; UAK 727/46.

38 Hahn.

39 Heberer; In Memoriam Heberer; Festschrift Lindenburg 2008, 174.

40 Thümmler 2012; Detjen 2014.

41 Marquardt 1986; Kaufmann.

42 Wehler 2008, 380–385; Henning/Lauf/Ludwig 1988, 294; UAK 331/8, Senatsprotokoll, 24 July 1965, 124c.

43 Bartz 2006, 100–106 and 109–112.

44 Quoted from Scheid 1967, 13; Schmölders 1966, 11; Fellerer 1968b, 13.

45 Hausmitteilungen 1/1968, 9–11.

46 Quoted from Hübner 1988, 61f.; UAK 331/9, 248f., 270ff., 283, 317ff., 351 and 352f.; UAK 331/10a, Bl. 5f., 21ff. and 33f.; Hochschulgesetz 1970, 256f.; all study regulations from: Mitteilungen 2–3/1972, 7–11/1972, 14/1972, 2–3/1973, 5–8/1973, 10–11/1973, 1/1974, 3–5/1974, 8–12/1974, 14–16/1974.

47 Quoted from UAK 261/348; Trier 2007, 514f.; Geschichte RRZK.

48 Ortmann 1986, 38–41; Anatomische Sammlung.

49 Koischwitz 2017, 311–325; Bartz 2006, 109–133.

50 Quoted from Schiedermair 2007, 422; Schieder 1968; Hübner 1969; Schiedermair 2007; Nonn 2013, 320–333; Rektorenportrait Schieder; Rektorenportrait Hübner.

51 Quoted from Schieder 1968, 15f. and 18; Nonn 2013, 326f.

52 Quoted from Hübner 1969, 22, 25f., 30 and Nonn 2013, 326; Schieder 1968, 20.

53 Benkö 1994; Bittlinger 1989, 19–30.

54 Hausmann 1997; Hausmann 2005.

55 Gall 2005; Haupts 2007, 258–283; Nonn 2013; Haar 2017.

56 Baltz-Otto 2010; Streeck.

57 Holl/Glunz 2008, 44f.; Dohms 2008a, 88f.; Bartz 2000, 108f.; Müller 2018.

58 Dohms 2008a, 93f.; Bartz 2000, 109f.

59 Dohms 2008a, 89.

60 Quoted from Verfassung 1963, §§ 26 (2) and 52 (2); Dohms 2008a, 89; Bartz 2000, 110; Meuthen 1988, 62–64.

61 Dohms 2008a, 94–96; Dohms 2008b, 228; Holl/Glunz 2008, 133f. and 143; Bartz 2000, 111; Leggewie 2018, 18 and 26f.; Hübner 1988, 53f.; Freitäger 2018a.

62 UAK 331/9, Senatsprotokoll, 23 November 1968, 246f. and 252; Meuthen 1988, 64; Dohms 2008a, 90f.; Bartz 2000, 111; Freitäger 2018b.

63 Holl/Glunz 2008, 100; Dohms 2008a, 96f.; Leggewie 2018, 60f.; Bartz 2000, 112; Schwanke 2018.

64 Dohms 2008b, 229; Bartz 2000, 112f.; Meuthen 1988, 66; Hübner 1988, 56.

65 Quoted from: Maier 1966; Rürup 2017, 167–174; Kotowski 2017, 645; Martin-Buber-Institut.

66 Quoted from 40 Jahre Studiobühne; Marx 2018; Studiobühneköln.

67 Binding/Müller 1988, 33–38; Knoch 2018.

Chapter 6

1 Quoted from Isselhard 1975b, 16; Kops/Hansmeyer/Kranski 1988, 421f.; Oehler/Bradatsch 1998, 418f.; Jessen 2010, 271f.; Tiggemann 2008, 144; Mitteilungen 4/1978, 27.

2 Kops/Hansmeyer/Kranski 1988, 426f. and 433; Henning/Lauf/Ludwig 1988, 295; Willeke 1978, 18; Mitteilungen 2/1982, 3; Mitteilungen 1/1984, 10.

3 Quoted from Isselhard 1975b, 16; Isselhard 1975a; Isselhard 1975b, 13–17.

4 Menze 1976, 11–14; Menze 1977, 12–16; Willeke 1978, 12–14.

5 Mitteilungen 1/1978, 27; Menze 1977, 21; Willeke 1979, 12–14; Wiedemann 1980, 11.

6 Wiedemann 1980, 12.

7 Meuthen 1988, 74; König 1989, 31; Binding 1982, 3; Hansmeyer 1988, 27f.; Gutmann 1984; UAK 261/5, Appendix Senatsprotokoll, 10 July 1986, *Bericht des Dekans über die Situation der Erziehungswissenschaftlichen Fakultät in Fragen der Stellenzuweisungen und Kürzungen*, 2f.; UAK 261/5, Senatsprotokoll (Gen.), 18 June 1986, 7f.; Journal 1/1990, 17f.

8 Kops/Hansmeyer/Kranski 1988, 421–434 and 441; Hansmeyer 1988, 28f.; Tiggemann 2008, 144f.

9 Mitteilungen 3/1984, 6; Journal 4/1988, 18; Peil 1988, 176 and 212; UAK 261/5, Senatsprotokoll (Gen.), 10 July 1986, 7f.; Studienführer 1980/81, 126–131; Studienführer 1989/90, 156–161.

10 Binding 1982, 4; Kops/Hansmeyer/Kranski 1988, 427 and 433f.

11 Kops/Hansmeyer/Kranski 1988, 425, 427 and 433f.; Sonderforschungsbereiche 1997, 81, 83, 87 and 91; Hanau 1986, 28; Gutmann 1984, 12.

12 Peil 1988, 272; Mitteilungen 3/1984, 34; Journal 4/1988, 34f.; Hanau 1986, 26; Hanau 1987.

13 Quoted from Hanau 1988, 32; UAK 261/493b, Senatsprotokoll (Gen.), 26 October 1988, 2; UAK 543/964b, Senatsprotokoll (Gen.), 25 October 1989, 6; König 1989, 32.

14 Journal 4/1988, 4f.; Journal 4/1987, 77; UAK 261/493b, Senatsprotokoll (Gen.), 13 July 1988, 2; UAK 261/493a, Senatsprotokoll (Gen.), 7 December 1988, 2; UAK 261/493a, Protokoll Kuratorium, 7 November 1988; UAK 261/964b, Senatsprotokoll (Gen.), 10 May 1989, 2; UAK 261/964b, Senatsprotokoll (Gen.), 7 June 1989, 2; UAK 261/964b, Senatsprotokoll (Gen.), 5 July 1989, 2; Journal 1/1990, 17f.; Hanau 1988; König 1989.

15 Wehler 2008, 381–383; Isselhard 1975b, 13; Journal 4/1990, 6; Meuthen 1988, 74; Jessen 2010, 268; Oehler/Bradatsch 1998, 417.

16 Isselhard 1975b, 14; Wagner 1975; UAK 331/12, Senatsprotokoll, 24 November 1976, 246f.; Jessen 2010, 269; Mitteilungen 3/1980, 33f.; Mitteilungen 4/1984, 2; Mitteilungen 3/1985, 5; Journal 4/1987, 14; Journal 4/1988, 8; Journal 3/1989, 18; Journal 3/1990, 13.

17 Quoted from Journal 2/1988, 3; Hansmeyer 1988, 27; Henning/Lauf/Ludwig 1988, 295, 319 and 322; Journal 4/1989, 2f.; Journal 3/1988, 8.

18 Quoted from Mitteilungen 2/1982, 3 and Journal 4/1988, 3 and 27; Mitteilungen 4/1978, 27; Mitteilungen 1/1984, 10; Journal 4/1988, 3.

19 Quoted from Journal 4/1989, 8 and Journal 2/1990, 63; Mitteilungen 4/1981, 36; Mitteilungen 3/1979, 16; UAK 543/964b, Senatsprotokoll (Gen.), 25 October 1989, 2; UAK 261/541b, Senatsprotokoll (Gen.), 5 December 1990, 3.

20 Berg.

21 Frese 1988.

22 Johansen 2007; Johansen.

23 Sudmann 2014; Albers 2014.

24 Mitteilungen 1/1976, 35.

25 Quoted from Mitteilungen 2/1978, 1; Mitteilungen 2–3/1977, 23; Mitteilungen 1/1978, 11; UAK 331/12, Senatsprotokoll, Sondersitzung 15 February 1978, 341f. and 344f.

26 Mitteilungen 4/1979, 25; UAK 261/5, Senatsprotokoll (Gen.), 8 February 1984, 2–7; UAK 261/5: Senatsprotokoll (Gen.), 4 July 1984, 3–12, Senatsprotokoll (Gen.), 6 February 1985, 4–11, Senatsprotokoll (Gen.), 15 January 1986, 3, Senatsprotokoll (Gen.), 15 January 1986, 3–21 and Senatsprotokoll (Gen.), 23 April 1986, 6–14; UAK 261/6, Senatsprotokoll (Gen.), 23 January 1987, 1–10; Journal 4/1990, 2f.; UAK 261/541a, Senatsprotokoll (Gen.), 16 January 1991, 2.

27 UAK 543/964b: Senatsprotokoll (Gen.), 7 June 1989, 2, Senatsprotokoll (Pers.), 21 June 1989, 2 and Senatsprotokoll (Pers.), 15 November 1989, 2f.; Müller-Böling 2010, 357; Journal 4/1990, 2f.; Journal 4/1988, 11f.; Journal 1/1989, 8; UAK 261/541b, Senatsprotokoll (Gen.), 27 June 1990, 4.

28 Quoted from: Hanau 1988, 32; König 1989, 31.

29 Quoted from Friedmann/Mödder 1978, 2891; Eschbach 2009, 132; Mitteilungen 3/1980, 9f.

30 Quoted from Universitätsmagazin 1/2015, 31; Mitteilungen 3/1980, 20.

31 Peil 1988, 225–253; Heinen 1990; Jussen et al. 1991; Mitteilungen 2/1980, 2–4.

32 Quoted from Mitteilungen 4/1977, 11; LehrerInnenbildung in Köln 2018, 23; Heinen 1990, 91f.

33 LehrerInnenbildung in Köln 2018, 26f.; Mitteilungen 4/1978, 22; Mitteilungen 1/1978, 1; UAK 331/13: Senatsprotokoll, 24 January 1979, 64, Senatsprotokoll, 7 February 1979, 70 and Senatsprotokoll, 7 November 1979, 95; Mitteilungen 1–2/1979, 7; Willeke 1979, 12f.; Mitteilungen 4/1979, 26.

34 Meuthen 1988, 74; UAK 331/13, Senatsprotokoll, 23 April 1980, 126; LehrerInnenbildung in Köln 2018, 23 and 31.

35 Quoted from UAK 261/5, Appendix Senatsprotokoll,10 July 2019, *Bericht des Dekans über die Situation der Erziehungswissenschaftlichen Fakultät in Fragen der Stellenzuweisungen und Kürzungen*, 4; Wiedemann 1980, 11; Journal 2/1988, 27; UAK 261/5, Senatsprotokoll (Gen.), 15 July 1987, 2; LehrerInnenbildung in Köln 2018, 29; Jussen 1991, 33f.; UAK 331/14, Senatsprotokoll, 21 July 1982, 305.

36 Kohlmann 2013.

37 Jussen et al. 1991, 44f., 70, 76–79 and 245–251; Emmerich/Buchkremer 2013.

38 Mayntz 1996; Lebenslauf Mayntz; Grenzgängerin 2010.

39 Busch 2015; Rektorenportrait Mittelstaedt.

40 Bartz 2007, 93; Streiter 2008, 6f.

41 JB 1970, 304f. and 466; JB 1975, 406; Hanau 1987; Sonderforschungsbereiche 1997, 50–59, 87 and 91.

42 Willeke 1978, 18.

43 Henning/Kazemi 2011, 533, 563, 615 and 824; Mitteilungen 3/1982, 20f.

44 Quoted from Journal 1/1989,15; Mitteilungen 4/1986, 45f.; Henning/Kazemi 2011, 564; Starlinger; Heim/Kaulen 2010, 348 and 356f.; Mitteilungen 2–3/1983, 12; Hänßler 2010, 6f.; Mitteilungen 2/1986, 18f.; JB 1988, 870; JB 1989, 675–694; Hanau 1986, 28; König 1989, 31.

45 UAK 261/5, Senatsprotokoll (Gen.), 6 June 1984, 3; Mitteilungen 2/1985, 2f.; Mitteilungen 1/1986, 7; Leendertz 2014, 303f.; Mitteilungen 1/1983, 10f.; Hanau 1987; Journal 1/1989, 37.

46 Mitteilungen 4/1980, 4; Universitätspreis 2018.

47 Quoted from Winnewisser et al. 1982, 157; Mitteilungen 4/1982, 22; JB 18 (1982), 383f.

48 Quoted from Mitteilungen 4/1980, 27f.; Mitteilungen 5/1974, 22f.; Mitteilungen 1/1975, 22; Mitteilungen 4/1976, 6; Mitteilungen 1/1980, 28; Mitteilungen 3/1980, 6 and 25; Mitteilungen 3/1985, 6; Journal 3/1986, 8; Journal 3/1987, 39; Journal 2/1990, 63f.; Wehler 2008, 381f.

49 Henning/Lauf/Ludwig1988, 295, 299f. and 301; Mitteilungen 2/1980, 5; Mitteilungen 1/1983, 45; Journal 3/1986, 9.

50 Mitteilungen 1/1983, 2; Mitteilungen 4/1977, 6; Mitteilungen 1/1980, 32; Mitteilungen 1/1983, 53; Mitteilungen 1/1984, 51; Rothblatt 2010, 244f.; Journal 2/1987, 8; Journal 2/1988, 13f.; Journal 3/1989, 18; Journal 1/1990, 28.

51 Mitteilungen 4/1983, 10; UAK 331/14, Senatsprotokoll, 21 July 1982, 305; Journal 4/1989, 23; Journal 1/1990, 32f.; Journal 2/1990, 13f.; UAK 261/541b, Senatsprotokoll (Gen.), 27 June 1990, 2b.

52 Mitteilungen 2/1984, 13; UAK 261/6, Senatsprotokoll (Gen.), 1 June 1988, 3; Journal 2/1988, 10; Journal 3/1989, 13.

53 Paracelsus-Medaille 2005; Pichlmaier 2005.

54 Website Stern; Rektorenportrait Stern.

55 Stoffel; Stoffel CV; Thyssen Stiftung 1985, 173; Mitteilungen 2/1986, 18f.; Vogt 2008a, 153f.

56 Neef 2010.

57 UAK 331/13, Senatsprotokoll, 29 October 1980, 159; Mitteilungen 4/1981, 9f.; Journal 4/1987, 31; Huintges 1989, 325-342; 600 Jahre 1988.

58 Hansmeyer1989, 12; Rudorf 1989; Journal 2/1988, 20–29 and 33; Huintges 1989, 339f.; Journal 4/1988, 32; Hanau 1989a; Hanau 1989b, 112.

59 Journal 2/1987, 4f.; Journal 1/1988, 27f.; Festakt 1989; Journal 2/1988, 36; Journal 4/1988, 38f.

60 Hanau 1988, 31; Huintges, 1989, 337f.

61 Kölner Universitätsgeschichte 1988; Hanau 1988a, 26f.

62 Nachhilfe 1988; Golczewski 1988; Gedenkstunde 1989; Journal 4/1988, 12–15; Huintges 1989, 374–380; Hansmeyer 1989, 12.

63 Gebäudemanagement; Zeiß 1931; Kroell/Eber 2011; Katner 1969, 178.

64 Briefmarken1988; Hack/Schwarz1992; Journal 1/1988, 27f.

Chapter 7

1 UAK 543/1173, Rechenschaftsbericht Rektorat 1996, 5.

2 Quoted from Autonomie der Universitäten 1995, 4f.; UAK 261/541b, Senatsprotokoll (Gen.), 5 December 1990, 2f.; UAK 261/551, Senatsprotokoll (Gen.), 15 July 1992, 1ff.; Löwer 2018, 419f.; Universitäts-Journal 2/1994, 10–15; Universitäts-Journal 3/1994, 3f.; UAK 543/1172, Rechenschaftsbericht Rektorat 1995, 7–18; Autonomie der Universitäten 1995; UAK 543/580, Rechenschaftsbericht Rektorat 1995, 5.

3 UAK 543/1172, Rechenschaftsbericht Rektorat 1995, 32–34; Plassmann/Süßmuth 2015, 100f.; UAK 543/1175, Rechenschaftsbericht Rektorat 1998/99, 6f. and 10–12; Münch 2011, 361–380.

4 UAK 543/1175, Rechenschaftsbericht Rektorat 1998/99, 1–4.

5 Vogt 2008a, 153f.; UAK 543/1175, Rechenschaftsbericht Rektorat 1998/99, 31f.; UAK 543/1174, Rechenschaftsbericht Rektorat 1997/98, 30.

6 UAK 543/1176, *Die Universität zu Köln im Frühjahr 2001. Abschlussbericht des Rektorates der Universität zu Köln*, 8f.; UAK 543/1177, Jahresbericht Rektorat 2001/02, 41f.; Zahlen – Daten – Fakten 2004, 18.

7 UAK 543/1177, Jahresbericht Rektorat 2001/02, 13.

8 Quoted from UAK 543/1177, Jahresbericht Rektorat 2001/02, 9; Löwer 2018, 424; UAK 543/1177, Jahresbericht Rektorat 2001/02, 83; UAK 543/1178, Jahresbericht Rektorat 2002/03, 60f.; UAK 543/1179, Jahresbericht Rektorat 2003/04, 65ff.

9 UAK 543/1177, Jahresbericht Rektorat 2001/02, 15f. and 25f.; UAK 543/1178, Jahresbericht Rektorat 2002/03, 10f. and 59; UAK 543/1179, Jahresbericht Rektorat 2003/04, 4 and 9f.

10 UAK 543/1178, Jahresbericht Rektorat 2002/03, 43; UAK 543/1179, Jahresbericht Rektorat 2003/04, 40f. and 43.

11 UAK 543/1175, Rechenschaftsbericht Rektorat 1998/99, 16f.; UAK 543/1177, Jahresbericht Rektorat 2001/02, 34ff.; UAK 543/1180, Jahresbericht Rektorat 2004/05, 15 and 159f.; UAK 543/1178, Jahresbericht Rektorat 2002/03, 19 and 23f.; UAK 543/1178, UAK 543/1179, Jahresbericht Rektorat 2003/04, 7f.; LehrerInnenbildung in Köln 2018, 33–35.

12 UAK 543/1180, Jahresbericht Rektorat 2004/05, 8f.; Presse-Information, 19 October 2007; Vogt 2008a, 154f.; UAK 543/1179, Jahresbericht Rektorat 2003/04, 6; Universitäts-Journal 1/2005, 10f.

13 UAK 543/1180, Jahresbericht Rektorat 2004/05, 1–10; Zahlen – Daten – Fakten 2006, 20.

14 UAK 543/1180, Jahresbericht Rektorat 2004/05, 35–37; Mersch 2006; Himmelrath/Mersch 2006.

15 UAK 543/1180, Jahresbericht Rektorat 2004/05, 1–7; LehrerInnenbildung in Köln 2018, 33–35.

16 Mättig 2018, 234; Lehnert et al. 1998, 2; Universitäts-Journal 1/1993, 30f.; Journal 4/1990, 2f.

17 Journal 1/1991, 8–10; Universitäts-Journal 1/1993, 30f.

18 UAK 261/551, Senatsprotokoll (Gen.), 15 July 1992, 7; Rothkopf/Tomson 1995, 131f.; Universitäts-Journal 1/1993, 30f.

19 Quoted from Bericht der Frauenbeauftragten 1995, 16; Wittka 1995c, 97; Bericht der Frauenbeauftragten 1995.

20 UAK 543/1174, Rechenschaftsbericht Rektorat 1997/98, 32f. and 55; UAK 543/1175, Rechenschaftsbericht Rektorat 1998/99, 63f.; Gesetz zur Gleichstellung von Frauen und Männern 1999; UAK 543/1176, *Die Universität zu Köln im Frühjahr 2001. Abschlussbericht des Rektorates der Universität zu Köln*, 8f.

21 UAK 543/1179, Jahresbericht Rektorat 2003/04, 9f. and 66–73; Senatsprotokoll, 28 July 2004; Zahlen – Daten – Fakten 2006, 2; Zahlen | Daten | Fakten 2011/12, 46.

22 Donges; Vita Donges.

23 Schneider 2008, 11 and 13f.; Lebenslauf Eck.

24 Grünberg; Grünberg Biographical; Gross/Marx 2018, 300; Fert 2018; Über Grünberg.

25 Hax; Nachruf Hax 2005; Franke/Laux 1998.

26 Die neuen Unis 1989; Scheuch 1990.

27 Journal 1/1990, 18; Jessen 2010, 277; Universitäts-Journal 2/1993, 5f.; Universitäts-Journal 2/1994, 70f.; Universitäts-Journal 1/2004, 4; Universitäts-Journal 2/2004, 8; Universitäts-Journal 1/1998, 17–20.

28 UAK 543/1174, Rechenschaftsbericht Rektorat 1997/98, 41f.; UAK 543/1175, Rechenschaftsbericht Rektorat 1998/99, 58f.; Universitäts-Journal 2/1999, 5f.

29 DFG Förder-Ranking 1997, 40; DFG Förder-Ranking 2009, 54 and 158; Universitäts-Journal 2/2005, 4.

30 Quoted from Universitäts-Journal 1/2005, 101; Universitäts-Journal 4/2003, 7; Shanghai Ranking 2003; Shanghai Ranking 2006; Müller-Böling 2010, 360 and 362.

31 Quoted from Universitätsmagazin 15/2018, 34.

32 Quoted from Kohl 2018, 48; Kohl 2018; Ökologische Rheinstation.

33 UAK 261/551, Senatsprotokoll (Gen.), 15 July 1992, 1ff.; UAK 261/541b, Senatsprotokoll (Gen.), 5 December 1990, 2f.

34 Journal 2/1991, 6–8; Universitäts-Journal 3/1993, 25; UAK 261/551, Senatsprotokoll (Gen.), 15 July 1992, 1ff.; Universitäts-Journal 3/1994, 3f.; Löwer 2018, 419–421.

35 Quoted from Wunder 1993, 669, Etzold 1993 and Universitäts-Journal 4/1993, 5; Pfeifen an den Unis 1993.

36 Mohr 1997; Universitäts-Journal 4/1997, 1; UAK 543/1174, Rechenschaftsbericht Rektorat 1997/98, 43–45; Universitäts-Journal 1/1998, 14; Löwer 2018, 421–423; Universitäts-Journal 2/2002, 11; UAK 543/1177, Jahresbericht Rektorat 2001/02, 15f., 25f. and 29; UAK 543/1179, Jahresbericht Rektorat 2003/04, 4.

37 Barblan 2010, 500–504.

38 Curriculum Vitae Heiss; Vogt 2008b; Henning/Kazemi 2011, 533, 563, 615 and 824.

39 Nachruf Hurrelmann; Wissenschaftspreis 2000.

40 Leyendecker 2011; JCW-Schule; Geschichte Zentrum; Peil 1988, 250 and 252.

41 Laudatio Lang 2010; Lebenslauf Lang.

42 Löwer 2018, 465f.

43 PreisträgerInnen; UAK 543/1175, Rechenschaftsbericht Rektorat 1998/99, 1ff.; Universitäts-Journal 2/1999, 4; Finetti 2005, 94 and 117.

44 Max-Planck-Forschungspreis; Preisträgerinnen.

45 Sofja Kovalevskaja-Preis; PreisträgerInnen; Sofja Kovalevskaja-Preis 2002.

46 Journal 1/1990, 34f.; Brüning.

47 Quoted from Universitäts-Journal 1/1999, 7; Lorentz 2007; Universitätszeitung 1/2009, 7; Sender Kölncampus.

48 Kornmüller 2006; Risse 2016; Universitätsmagazin 1/2015, 13.

49 Quoted from Journal 1/1991, 14; Journal 1/1991, 14–16; Trier 2007, 519–522.

50 Quoted from Journal 1/1990, 29; Journal 1/1990, 29f.; Trier 2007, 524; UAK 543/1177, Jahresbericht Rektorat 2001/02, 95f.; UAK 543/1172, Rechenschaftsbericht Rektorat 1995, 30; Universitäts-Journal 1/1997, 18.

51 Universitäts-Journal 3/1994, 28; Universitäts-Journal 4/1995, 15f.

52 Quoted from Trier 2007, 527; UAK 543/1173, Rechenschaftsbericht Rektorat 1996, 64ff.; Trier 2007, 526f.

53 Universitäts-Journal 3-4/1996, 12f.

54 UAK 543/1174, Rechenschaftsbericht Rektorat 1997/98, 23; Universitäts-Journal 4/1997, 22f.

55 Trier 2007, 523f.; Universitäts-Journal 3/2003, 22; UAK 543/1180, Jahresbericht Rektorat 2004/05, 10–14.

56 Katzmarzik 2014; Festschrift Lindenburg 2008, 158 and 183; Lehmkuhl.

57 Saedler 2004; Van Montagu 2003; Verstraete 2003; Heim/Kaulen 2010, 356f.

58 Schiedermair.

59 Voßkamp.

60 Quoted from UAK 543/1174, Rechenschaftsbericht Rektorat 1997/98, 5; Universitäts-Journal 2/1997, 3; Universitäts-Journal 2/1994, 3–5; Journal 1/1991, 4; UAK 543/1174, Rechenschaftsbericht Rektorat 1997/98, 5f.

61 UAK 543/965, Senatsprotokoll (Gen.), 30 May 1990, 2; Journal 4/1990, 3; UAK 543/580, Rechenschaftsbericht Rektorat 1995, 14.

62 Quoted from Universitäts-Journal 4/1997, 3; UAK 543/1174, Rechenschaftsbericht Rektorat 1997/98, 6ff.; Universitäts-Journal 4/1997, 22f.; Universitäts-Journal 2/2000, 1 and 3–5; Universitäts-Journal 2/2001, 28f.

63 Universitäts-Journal 2/1993, 4f.; Universitäts-Journal 4/1994, 3; Universitäts-Journal 1/1997, 7f.; Universitäts-Journal 4/1998, 3; Senatsprotokoll, 7 January 2004, 2f.; UAK 543/1178, Jahresbericht Rektorat 2002/03, 68; Universitäts-Journal 3/2002, 18.

64 UAK 543/1177, Jahresbericht Rektorat 2001/02, 31–33; UAK 543/1179, Jahresbericht Rektorat 2003/04, 20f. and 66f.; Universitäts-Journal 4/1993, 13; Universitäts-Journal 4/2003, 13f.; Universitäts-Journal 4/2005, 2f.; UAK 543/1174, Rechenschaftsbericht Rektorat 1997/98, 6ff.; UAK 543/1172, Rechenschaftsbericht Rektorat 1995, 66ff.

65 Universitäts-Journal 2/2001, 10; Presse-Information, 26 November 2003; Universitäts-Journal 1/2004, 15f.; Presse-Information, 9 February 2004.

66 Lörch 2010; Wanko 2008; Website mediomix.

67 Quoted from Klaetke 2008; Kölner Kompendium.

Chapter 8

1 Burckhart 2007; LehrerInnenbildung in Köln 2018, 33; Zahlen | Daten | Fakten 2011/12, 47; Senatsprotokoll, 10 January 2007, 2–3.

2 Universitätszeitung 1/2007, 4.

3 Löwer 2018, 435–438; Lynen 2017, 121; Hochschulfreiheitsgesetz, § 2 para. 1; Krausnick 2012, 387.

4 Löwer 2018, 435–438 and 446–449; Universitätszeitung 4/2007, 4; Senatsprotokoll, 29 May 2013, 2; Senatsprotokoll, 2 July 2014, 3.

5 Bildhauer 2007; Internationale Verbindungsbüros.

6 Exzellenzinitiative 2013, 52.

7 Exzellenzinitiative 2013, 97; Zahlen | Daten | Fakten 2011/12, 24; Website CECAD; Vogt 2008a, 154f.; Universitätszeitung 5/2007, 1f.

8 Website CMMC; Website CIO; Vogt 2008a, 154–156; Website CCG.

9 Grünberg Biographical; Zahlen | Daten | Fakten 2016, 21; Forschungsallianz Köln.

10 Zahlen – Daten – Fakten 2006, 7 and 18; Universitätszeitung 2/2007, 1f.; Universitätszeitung 3/2007, 1f.; Presse-Information, 25 November 2009.

11 Quoted from Senatsprotokoll, 5 December 2007, 2.

12 Zahlen | Daten | Fakten 2011/12, 67; Senatsprotokoll, 3 March 2010, 2; Hochschulpakt 2020.

13 Protest gegen Bildungssystem; Senatsprotokoll, 15 December 2009, 2f.; Presse-Information, 10 February 2010.

14 LehrerInnenbildung in Köln 2018, 37–41.

15 Presse-Information, 18 December 2008; Presse-Information, 3 May 2010; Presse-Information, 6 October 2010; Presse-Information, 29 October 2010; Presse-Information, 9 September 2013.

16 Exzellenzinitiative 2013, 51.

17 Über a.r.t.e.s.; Exzellenzinitiative 2013, 51f., 82 and 97; Website CEPLAS; Website GSSC.

18 Quoted from Die Herausforderung von Wandel und Komplexität, 26; Spitzenforschung für die Gesellschaft.

19 Die Herausforderung von Wandel und Komplexität, 27–29 and 39f.; Exzellenzinitiative 2013, 118.

20 Die Herausforderung von Wandel und Komplexität, 29–42; Website German U15.

21 Exzellenzcluster ECONtribute; ECONtribute; Exzellenzstrategie; Website ML4Q.

22 Zahlen | Daten | Fakten 2017, 13f., 46, 51, 67 and 69; Gender & Diversity; Promovierende; Tenure Track.

23 UzK Zentren; Presse-Information, 8 October 2015; Third Mission.

24 Zahlen | Daten | Fakten 2017, 46 and 72f.

25 Kölner Wissenschaftsrunde; Zahlen | Daten | Fakten 2017, 14f. and 21; International.

26 Quoted from Dohmen/Hümmeler/Riße 2018.

Bibliography

Abbreviations

BArch: Federal Archives

LA NRW R: State Archives North Rhine-Westphalia, Rhineland Department

UAK: University of Cologne Archives (Historical Archive of the Universität of Cologne)

Unpublished sources

Autonomie der Universitäten 1995: *Autonomie der Universitäten. Universitätsidee, bildungspolitische Legitimation und institutionelle Prinzipien*. In UAK 543/580, Rechenschaftsbericht des Rektorats 1995, Appendix B.

BArch R 9361-VIII KARTEI / 2070531: Paul Berkenkopf, NSDAP-Zentralkartei (membership card).

BArch R 9361-IX KARTEI / 8521322: Karl Gustav Fellerer, NSDAP-Gaukartei (membership card).

Kandinsky/Niessen 1931: Wassily Kandinsky to Carl Niessen, 26 October 1931. Theater Studies Collection, Cologne University.

LA NRW R, NW 1048 Nr. 33398, Anlage I/a: Karl Gustav Fellerer, Entnazifizierungsakte (denazification file).

Presse-Information: Universität zu Köln. Presse-Information 1999–2007 (press releases). Presse- und Informationsstelle der Universität zu Köln; Presse-Information 2007–2019, https://www.portal. uni-koeln.de/presseinformationen.html [12 April 2019].

Senatsprotokoll: Senatsprotokolle 2003/04–2018/19 (senate minutes), https://strategy.uni-koeln.de/gremien__und_sonstige_akademische_angelegenheiten/gremien/senat/tagesordnung_und_sitzungsprotokolle/index_ger.html [10 April 2019].

UAK 28/538a: Patenschaft Clermont-Ferrand, Vol. 1, 1959–1961.

UAK 95/Findbuch: Findbuch Verein der Freunde und Förderer der Universität zu Köln e.V., 1924-2004 (finding aids).

UAK 261/5–6: Senatsprotokolle 1983–1988 (senate minutes).

UAK 261/348: Acquisition of a dataprocessing system for the computer center, 1965–1969.

UAK 261/493a–493b: Senatsprotokolle 1988/89 (senate minutes).

UAK 261/541a–541b: Senatsprotokolle 1990/91 (senate minutes).

UAK 261/551: Senatsprotokolle 1992/93 (senate minutes).

UAK 266/1: Nobel Prize in Chemistry, 1950: Diploma of 10 December 1950. Estate of Prof. Dr. Kurt Alder.

UAK 317-III/712: Personalakte Prof. Dr. Hans Ludwig Hamburger (personnel file).

UAK 331: Senatsprotokolle 1954–1983 (senate minutes).

UAK 543/580: Rechenschaftsbericht des Rektorats (rectorate's report and accounts) 1994 and 1995.

UAK 543/964b–965: Senatsprotokolle 1989/90 (senate minutes).

UAK 543/1172–1180: Rechenschafts- und Jahresberichte des Rektorats (rectorate's accounts and annual reports) 1995–2004/05.

UAK 571/72: Personalnebenakte des Rektors, Hans Ludwig Hamburger (supplementary personnel file).

UAK 631: Nachlass Prof. Dr. Marianne Baudler (estate).

UAK 689/110: Membership card of the Association of Friends and Sponsors of the University of Cologne. Nachlass Prof. Dr. Hans Ludwig Hamburger (estate).

UAK 727/46: Report on the meeting of the Kabul Commission of the Faculty of Economics and Social Sciences of 21 January 1981.

Published sources and works

40 Jahre Studiobühne: *40 Jahre Studiobühne*. In *Kölner Stadt-Anzeiger*, 12 May 2014, https://www.ksta.de/ratgeber/verbraucher/-40-jahre-studiobuehne--wir-sind-ein-durchlauferhitzer--944970 [20 February 2019].

100 Jahre: *100 Jahre Kaiser-Wilhelm-/Max-Planck-Gesellschaft zur Förderung der Wissenschaften*. Part II/1: *Handbuch zur Institutsgeschichte der Kaiser-Wilhelm-/Max-Planck-Gesellschaft zur Förderung der Wissenschaften 1911–2011. Daten und Quellen*. Eds. Eckart Henning and Marion Kazemi. Vol. 1. Berlin, 2016.

600 Jahre 1988: *600 Jahre Kölner Universität 1388/1988. Veranstaltete Wissenschaft. Jubiläumsprogramm*, Eds. Universität zu Köln, Karl-Heinrich Hansmeyer and Friedrich-Wilhelm Henning. Cologne, 1988.

Adenauer 1919: [Konrad] Adenauer [Address held on the occasion of the opening ceremony of the University of Cologne on 12 June 1919.] In Eröffnungsfeier 1919, 9–12.

Adenauer 1929: [Konrad] Adenauer [Speech at the cornerstone laying ceremony for the new university building on 26 October 1929.] In *Politische Freiheitsrechte*. Cologne, 1930 (*Kölner Universitäts-Reden* 24), 29–32.

Afrikanum 2013: *Afrikanum in Köln ist 50 Jahre alt* [2013], http://www.afrikamissionare.de/de/Afrikanum%2050.html [24 July 2018].

Ahrend 2010: Julia C. Ahrend, *Fritz Karl Mann: Ein Pionier der Finanzsoziologie und der Theorie der Parafiski im Schnittfeld deutscher und amerikanischer Wissenschaftskultur*. Marburg, 2010.

Albers 2014: Brigitte Albers, *Anna Gisela Johnen 1925–2014. Eine Erinnerung*. Cologne, [2014].

Alder Biographical: *Kurt Alder – Biographical*, https://www.nobelprize.org/prizes/chemistry/1950/alder/biographical/ [4 July 2018].

Alemann 1976: Heine von Alemann, *Leopold von Wiese und das Forschungsinstitut für Sozialwissenschaften in Köln 1919 bis 1934*. In *Kölner Zeitschrift für Soziologie und Sozialpsychologie* 28 (1976), 649–743.

Alemann 1988: Heine von Alemann, *Leopold von Wiese (1876 bis 1969)*. In *Kölner Volkswirte und Sozialwissenschaftler. Über den Beitrag Kölner Volkswirte und Sozialwissenschaftler zur Entwicklung der Wirtschafts- und Sozialwissenschaften*. Ed. Friedrich-Wilhelm Henning. Cologne/Vienna, 1988, 97–138.

Alewyn 1951: R[ichard] Alewyn, *Vom Geist der Universität*. In *Universitätsführer der Universität zu Köln 1951*. Ed. Studentenschaft. [Cologne], 1951, 9–14.

Allebrodt 2001: Barbara Allebrodt, *Robert Görlinger – Oberbürgermeister von Köln*. In *Köln in den 50er Jahren. Zwischen Tradition und Modernisierung*. Ed. Jost Dülffer. Cologne, 2001, 39–48.

Alte Universität: *Alte Universität*, http://www.bilderbuch-koeln.de/Denkmale/2808 [23 April 2018].

Altenhein 2005: Hans Altenhein, *Richard Alewyns Kölner Jahre*. In *Das Projekt Empfindsamkeit und der Ursprung der Moderne. Richard Alewyns Sentimentalismusforschungen und ihr epochaler Kontext*. Eds. Klaus Garber and Ute Széll. Munich, 2005, 25–34.

Anatomische Sammlung: Anatomische Sammlung im Zentrum Anatomie, http://www.anatomie.uni-koeln.de/21558.html [17 February 2019].

Asmuth 1985: Margaret Asmuth, *Die Studentenschaft der Handelshochschule Köln 1901 bis 1919*. Cologne/Vienna, 1985.

Baerlecken/Tiedau 2003: Marta Baerlecken/Ulrich Tiedau, *Das Deutsch-Niederländische Forschungsinstitut an der Universität Köln 1931–1945 und der Aufbau des Faches Niederlandistik in der frühen Bundesrepublik*. In *Griff nach dem Westen: Die „Westforschung" der völkisch-nationalen Wissenschaften zum nordwesteuropäischen Raum*. Eds. Burkhard Dietz, Helmut Gabel and Ulrich Tiedau. Münster et al., 2003, 851–885.

Balkhausen 2008: Dieter Balkhausen, *Alfred Herrhausen (1930–1989)*. In *Deutsche Bankiers des 20. Jahrhunderts*. Ed. Hans Pohl for Wissenschaftlicher Beirat of the Institut für bankhistorische Forschung e.V. Stuttgart, 2008, 211–225.

Baltz-Otto 2010: Ursula Baltz-Otto, *Sölle, Dorothee*. In *Neue Deutsche Biographie* 24 (2010), 530–532, https://www.deutsche-biographie.de/pnd11861519X.html#ndbconten [29 July 2018].

Barblan 2010: Andris Barblan, *Epilog. Von der „Universität in Europa" zu den Universitäten Europas*. In *Geschichte der Universität in Europa*. Ed. Walter Rüegg. Vol. 4: *Vom Zweiten Weltkrieg bis zum Ende des 20. Jahrhunderts*. Munich, 2010, 485–506.

Bartz 2000: Olaf Bartz, *Mauerblümchen des Protests oder Hort pragmatischer Hochschulpolitik? Die Universität zu Köln und die Studentenbewegung von 1968*. In *Geschichte in Köln* 47 (2000), 107–119.

Bartz 2005: Olaf Bartz, *Bundesrepublikanische Universitätsleitbilder: Blüte und Zerfall des Humboldtianismus*. In *Die Hochschule* 2/2005, 99–113.

Bartz 2006: Olaf Bartz, *Wissenschaftsrat und Hochschulplanung. Leitbildwandel und Planungsprozesse in der Bundesrepublik Deutschland zwischen 1957 und 1975*. Cologne, 2006.

Becker 1988: Hans-Jürgen Becker, *600 Jahre Rechtswissenschaft in Köln. Aus der Geschichte der Rechtswissenschaftlichen Universität*. In *Festschrift der Rechtswissenschaftlichen Fakultät zur 600-Jahr-Feier der Universität zu Köln*. Cologne et al., 1988, 3–30.

Beckhough 1983: Harry Beckhough, *The Role of the British University Control Officer in Post War Germany*. In *German Universities after the Surrender: British Occupation Policy and the Control of Higher Education*. Ed. David Phillips. [Oxford], 1983, 76–89

Benkö 1994: Marietta Benkö, *Meyer, Alex*. In *Neue Deutsche Biographie* 17 (1994), 326f., https://www.deutsche-biographie.de/pnd118581740.html#ndbcontent [4 September 2018].

Berg: Prof. Dr. phil. Christa Berg, https://www.hf.uni-koeln.de/32120 [28 February 2019].

Bericht der Frauenbeauftragten 1995: Bericht der Frauenbeauftragten (report by the women's affairs officer). In UAK 543/1172, Rechenschafts- und Jahresberichte des Rektorats 1995, Appendix 14.4, XIII–XVI.

Bieroth 1933: Ella Bieroth, *Schau Westdeutscher Wirtschaft*. Cologne, 1933.

Bildhauer 2007: Stefan Bildhauer, *China ist überall*. In Universitätszeitung 1/2007, 3f.

Binding 1982: Günther Binding, Geleitwort. In JB 1982/II, 3–5.

Binding/Müller 1988: Günther Binding/Georg Müller, *Die Bauten der Universität zu Köln*. Cologne, 1988.

Bittlinger 1989: Horst Bittlinger, *History of the Institute of Air and Space Law of the University of Cologne*. [Cologne, 1989].

Bolten 1987: Jochen Bolten, *Hochschulstudium für kommunale und soziale Verwaltung in Köln 1912–1929. Eine Studie zur Wiedererrichtung der Universität zu Köln*. Cologne/Vienna, 1987.

Borggräfe/Schnitzler 2014: Henning Borggräfe/Sonja Schnitzler, *Die Deutsche Gesellschaft für Soziologie und der Nationalsozialismus. Verbandsinterne Transformationen nach 1933 und nach 1945*. In *Soziologie und Nationalsozialismus. Positionen, Debatten, Perspektiven*. Eds. Michaela Christ and Maja Suderland. Berlin, 2014, 445–479.

Briefmarken 1988: Briefmarken-Jahrgang (stamp issues) 1988 der Deutschen Bundespost, https://de.wikipedia.org/w/index.php?title= Briefmarken-Jahrgang_1988_der_Deutschen_Bundespost& oldid=185958950 [10 March 2019].

Brüning: Prof. Dr. Jens C. Brüning, https://www.cecad.uni-koeln.de/index.php?id=75&type=0 [18 January 2019].

Burckhart 2007: Holger Burckhart, *Der Mensch im Mittelpunkt. Die neue Humanwissenschaftliche Fakultät*. In Universitätszeitung 1/2007, 5.

Busch 2015: Paul Busch, *Nachruf auf Peter Mittelstaedt*. In *Physik Journal* 14 (2015), issue 2, 46.

Clemens 1983: Gabriele Clemens, *Martin Spahn und der Rechtskatholizismus in der Weimarer Republik*. Mainz, 1983.

Cohn-Vossen: Stefan Cohn-Vossen, http://www.mi.uni-koeln.de/cohn-vossen [15 April 2019].

Curriculum Vitae Alder: *Curriculum Vitae Prof. Dr. Kurt Alder*, https://www.leopoldina.org/fileadmin/redaktion/Mitglieder/CV_Alder_Kurt_D.pdf [4 July 2018].

Curriculum Vitae Delbrück: *Curriculum vitae Prof. Dr. Max L. H. Delbrück*, https://www.leopoldina.org/fileadmin/redaktion/Mitglieder/CV_Delbrueck_Max_D.pdf [28 August 2018].

Curriculum Vitae Heiss: *Curriculum vitae Professor Dr. Wolf-Dieter Heiss*, http://www.leopoldina.org/fileadmin/redaktion/Mitglieder/CV_Heiss_Wolf-Dieter_EN.pdf [26 September 2018].

Dammer 2018: Dario Dammer, *Zwischen Weltrevolution und dem Kampf für „das saubere Klo"*. In Keim/Lewejohann 2018a, 118–127.

de Vries 1998: Henning de Vries, *Sonderstab Musik. Organisierte Plünderungen in Westeuropa 1940–45*. Berlin, 1998.

Denkrede 1921: *Denkrede von Martin Spahn am 50. Gedenktage der Reichsgründung mit Ansprache des Vertreters der Studentenschaft und Schlusswort des Rektors der Universität*. Cologne, 1921.

Depping 2002: André Depping, *Das BGB als Durchgangspunkt. Privatrechtsmethode und Privatrechtsleitbilder bei Heinrich Lehmann (1876–1963)*. Tübingen, 2002.

Detjen 2014: Joachim Detjen, *Ferdinand A. Hermens (1906–1998)*. In *Deutsche Politikwissenschaftler – Werk und Wirkung. Von Abendroth bis Zellentin*. Eds. Eckhard Jesse and Sebastian Liebold. Baden-Baden, 2014, 347–360.

Deutsche Kriegswirtschaft 1940: *Deutsche Kriegswirtschaft*. [Special exhibition dedicated to important areas of the German war economy]. Cologne, 1940.

DFG Förder-Ranking 1997: Deutsche Forschungsgemeinschaft, *Bewilligungen nach Hochschulen. Bewilligungsvolumen 1991 bis 1995. Anzahl kooperativer Projekte im Jahr 1996*. [Bonn, 1997], http://83.143.2.157/download/pdf/dfg_im_profil/zahlen_fakten/ranking/archiv/dfg-foerderranking_1997.pdf [15 February 2019].

DFG Förder-Ranking 2009: Deutsche Forschungsgemeinschaft, *Förder-Ranking 2009. Institutionen – Regionen – Netzwerke. Fachliche Profile von Hochschulen und außeruniversitären Forschungseinrichtungen im Licht öffentlich geförderter Forschung.* Weinheim, 2009, http://83.143.2.157/download/pdf/dfg_im_profil/zahlen_fakten/ranking/ranking_2009/dfg-foerderranking_2009.pdf [15 February 2019].

Die Herausforderung von Wandel und Komplexität: *Die Herausforderung von Wandel und Komplexität – Strategien für zukünftige Exzellenz in Forschung und Lehre. Zukunftskonzept zum projektbezogenen Ausbau der universitären Spitzenforschung,* https://www.portal.uni-koeln.de/index.php?id=11616 [12 December 2018].

Die neuen Unis 1989: *Die neuen Unis sind die besten.* In *Der Spiegel* 50/1989, 70–87, http://www.spiegel.de/spiegel/print/d-13497184.html [11 January 2019].

Diederich 1976: Toni Diederich, *Adenauer als Kölner Oberbürgermeister von Mai bis Oktober 1945.* In *Konrad Adenauer. Oberbürgermeister von Köln. Festgabe der Stadt Köln zum 100. Geburtstag ihres Ehrenbürgers am 5. Januar 1976.* Ed. Hugo Stehkämper. Cologne, 1976, 499–530.

Dillmann 1988: Franz Dillmann, *Beschweigen ist unverfänglicher als Aufdeckung. Die juristische Fakultät im Nationalsozialismus.* In Nachhilfe 1988, 98–109.

Dohmen/Hümmeler/Riße 2018: Maria Dohmen/Christian Hümmeler/Dirk Riße, *Uni-Rektor Axel Freimuth „Die Klinik-Fusion ist eine Riesenchance für Köln".* In *Kölner Stadt-Anzeiger,* 12 November 2018, https://www.ksta.de/koeln/uni-rektor-axel-freimuth--die-klinik-fusion-ist-eine-riesenchance-fuer-koeln--31579882 [15 April 2019].

Dohms 2008a: Peter Dohms, *Die Studentenbewegung an den traditionellen Hochschulen Nordrhein-Westfalens.* In Peter Dohms and Johann Paul, *Die Studentenbewegung von 1968 in Nordrhein-Westfalen.* Siegburg, 2008, 63–121.

Dohms 2008b: Peter Dohms, *Die Studentenbewegung von 1968 an den nordrhein-westfälischen Hochschulen.* In *Geschichte in Köln 55* (2008), 205–243.

Donges: *Donges, Juergen B.* In *Munzinger Online/Personen – Internationales Biographisches Archiv,* http://www.munzinger.de/document/00000019290 [26 September 2018].

Dreier 1999: Horst Dreier, *The Essence of Democracy – Hans Kelsen and Carl Schmitt Juxtaposed.* In *Hans Kelsen and Carl Schmitt. A Juxtaposition.* Eds. Dan Diner and Michael Stolleis. Gerlingen, 1999, 71–79.

Durschang et al. 2005: Katja Durschang et al.: *Dr. phil. Lotte Schlesinger, geb. Brauer.* In Szöllösi-Janze/Freitäger 2005, 111–118.

Düwell 1976: Kurt Düwell, *Universität, Schulen und Museen. Adenauers wissenschafts- und bildungspolitische Bestrebungen für Köln und das Rheinland (1917–1932).* In *Konrad Adenauer. Oberbürgermeister von Köln. Festgabe der Stadt Köln zum 100. Geburtstag ihres Ehrenbürgers am 5. Januar 1976.* Ed. Hugo Stehkämper. Cologne, 1976, 167–206.

Eckert 1913: Christian Eckert, *Die Cölner Universitätsfrage* (UAK 10c/62, Bl. 11–19), reprinted by Akira Hayashima, *Der Weg zum Promotionsrecht. Zur Geschichte einer deutschen Handelshochschule.* In *Kwansei Gakuin University Annual Studies.* Vol. 31 (1982), 21–88, here 58–62.

Eckert 1919a: Christian Eckert, *Die Kölner Universität* [Speech held before University of Cologne professors and lecturers]. In *Rheinischer Merkur* 27/29 January 1919.

Eckert 1919b: Christian Eckert, *Universität Köln. Denkschrift.* Cologne, 1919.

Eckert 1919c: Christian Eckert, [Address held at the opening ceremony of the University of Cologne on 12 June 1919]. In Reden 1919, 21–27.

Eckert 1926: *Rede des Prof. Dr. Chr. Eckert aus Anlaß des 25jährigen Bestehens des Handels-Hochschulstudiums.* In *Reden zur Gründungsfeier der Universität Köln am 15. Mai 1926.* Cologne, 1926, 16–30.

Eckert 1961: Willehad Paul Eckert, *Kleine Geschichte der Universität Köln.* Cologne, 1961.

ECONtribute: *ECONtribute,* http://selten.institute/econtribute/ [28 March 2019].

Ellinger 1988: Theodor Ellinger, *Erich Gutenberg (1897 bis 1984).* In *Betriebswirte in Köln. Über den Beitrag Kölner Betriebswirte zur Entwicklung der Betriebswirtschaftslehre.* Ed. Friedrich-Wilhelm Henning. Cologne/Vienna, 1988, 115–147.

Emmerich/Buchkremer 2013: Michaela Emmerich/Hansjosef Buchkremer, *Heinrich Lenzen – „Nestor" der Kölner Allgemeinen Heilpädagogik ist verstorben.* In *Newsletter des Departments Heilpädagogik und Rehabilitation der Universität zu Köln* 7/2013, 2, https://www.hf.uni-koeln.de/data/main/File/Newsletter_DP_HP/DHR-News-2013-7.pdf [26 November 2018].

Endres 2009: Sonja Endres, *Zwangssterilisation in Köln 1934–1945.* Cologne, 2009.

Engelhardt 1986: Werner W. Engelhardt, *Baugenossenschaft Kölner Universität 1920–1936.* In *Zeitschrift für öffentliche und gemeinwirtschaftliche Unternehmen* 9 (1986), issue 3, 317–324.

Engels 2007: Marc Engels, *Die „Wirtschaftsgemeinschaft des Westlandes". Bruno Kuske und die wirtschaftswissenschaftliche Westforschung zwischen Kaiserreich und Bundesrepublik.* Aachen, 2007.

Eröffnungsfeier 1919: *Eröffnungsfeier der Universität Köln. Reden gehalten bei dem Festakt im großen Saal des Gürzenich am 12. Juni 1919 und bei der Akademischen Feier in der Aula der Universität am 20. Juni 1919.* Cologne, 1919.

Eschbach 2009: O. Eschbach, *Neuroradiologie in der Neurologischen Klinik.* In *50 Jahre Neurologie in Köln-Merheim.* Eds. Heiko Bewermeyer and Volker Limmroth. Cologne, 2009, 130–137.

Etzold 1993: Sabine Etzold, *Ratlos nach dem Start.* In *Die Zeit* 48/1993, 41.

Euros 2016: Glesni Euros, *The Post-War British 'Re-Education' Policy for Universities and its Application at the Universities of Göttingen und Cologne (1945–1947).* In *Research in Comparative & International Education* 11 (2016), 247–266.

Exzellenzcluster ECONtribute: *Exzellenzcluster ECONtribute: Märkte und Public Policy,* https://wiso.uni-koeln.de/de/forschung/uzk-zukunfstkonzept/exzellenzcluster-econtribute [28 March 2019].

Exzellenzinitiative 2013: *Exzellenzinitiative auf einen Blick. Der Wettbewerb des Bundes und der Länder zur Stärkung der universitären Spitzenforschung. Die zweite Förderphase 2012 bis 2017. Graduiertenschulen – Exzellenzcluster – Zukunftskonzepte.* 5th revised edition, Bonn, 2013, http://www.dfg.de/download/pdf/dfg_im_profil/geschaeftsstelle/publikationen/exin_broschuere_de.pdf [25 March 2019].

Exzellenzstrategie: *Exzellenzstrategie des Bundes und der Länder,* http://www.dfg.de/foerderung/exzellenzstrategie/index.html [12 December 2018].

Fahlbusch 1999: Michael Fahlbusch, *Wissenschaft im Dienst der nationalsozialistischen Politik? Die „Volksdeutschen Forschungsgemeinschaften" von 1931–1945.* Baden-Baden, 1999.

Fellerer 1968a: [Karl Gustav] Fellerer, *Rechenschaftsbericht des scheidenden Rektors.* In KUR [N.S.] 40.1968, 6–24.

Fellerer 1968b: K[arl] G[ustav] Fellerer, *Jahresbericht des Rektors.* In JB 1968, 12–14.

Fert 2018: Albert Fert, *Peter Grünberg, a great name in the field of magnetism and 2007 laureate of Nobel Prize in Physics passed away on April 7, 2018*. In *Journal of Magnetism and Magnetic Materials* 466 (2018), A1–A2.

Festakt 1989: *Festakt in der Kölner Philharmonie am 4. November 1988*. In Hansmeyer/Henning/Huintges 1989, 107–142.

Festschrift 1938: *Festschrift zur Erinnerung an die Gründung der alten Universität Köln im Jahr 1388*. Ed. Hubert Graven. Cologne, 1938.

Festschrift Lindenburg 2008: *Festschrift des Universitätsklinikums Köln.100 Jahre Klinik „auf der Lindenburg"*. Cologne, 2008.

Festschrift Suevia 2004: *Festschrift 100 Jahre KStV Suevia im KV zu Köln 1904–2004*. Cologne, 2004.

Finetti 2005: Marco Finetti, *Von märchenhafter Freiheit. 20 Jahre Spitzenforschung im Gottfried Wilhelm Leibniz-Programm*. Bonn, 2005.

Fischer 2014: Joachim Fischer, *Die „Kölner Konstellation". Scheler, Hartmann, Plessner und der Durchbruch zur modernen Philosophischen Anthropologie*. In *Plessner in Wiesbaden*. Eds. Tilman Allert and Joachim Fischer. Wiesbaden, 2014, 89–121.

Flümann 2007: Tobias Flümann, *Die Ernährungssituation an der Universität Köln 1943 bis 1948*. In *Zwischen „Endsieg" und Examen. Studieren an der Universität Köln 1943–1948. Brüche und Kontinuitäten*. Ed. Margit Szöllösi-Janze. Nümbrecht, 2007, 78–83.

Forschungsallianz Köln: *Forschungsallianz Köln*, https://www.portal.uni-koeln.de/12411.html [27 March 2019].

Frank 2008a: Monika Frank, *Medizinisches Lehren und Lernen in Köln. Von Missionaren, Bahnärzten und Gesundheitsökonomen*. In Festschrift Lindenburg 2008, 57–74.

Frank 2008b: Monika Frank, *Medizinische Forschung in Köln bis zum Zweiten Weltkrieg. Zwischen Krankenbett und Laboratorium*. In Festschrift Lindenburg 2008, 75–98.

Frank/Moll 2006: Monika Frank/Friedrich Moll, with contributions by Heiko Bewermeyer: *Nervensachen. Psychiatrie, Neurologie und Neurochirurgie*. In *Kölner Krankenhaus-Geschichten. Am Anfang war Napoleon...* Eds. Monika Frank and Friedrich Moll. Cologne, 2006, 480–497.

Franke/Laux 1998: Günter Franke/Helmut Laux, *Vorwort*. In *Unternehmensführung und Kapitalmarkt. Festschrift für Herbert Hax*. Eds. Günter Franke and Helmut Laux. Berlin/Heidelberg/New York, 1998, V–VII.

Franken 1995: Irene Franken, *„Ja, das Studium der Weiber ist schwer!" Studentinnen und Dozentinnen an der Kölner Universität bis 1933. Katalog zur Ausstellung in der Universitäts- und Stadtbibliothek Köln 28. April – 10. Juni 1995*. Cologne, 1995.

Franken 2008: Irene Franken, *„... dass ich kein rabiater Nationalsozialist bin". NS-Medizin an Kölner Universitätskliniken am Beispiel von Hans C. Naujoks (1892–1959), Direktor der Universitäts-Frauenklinik*. In Festschrift Lindenburg 2008, 99–134.

Franken/Schäfer 2011: Irene Franken/Daniel Schäfer, *Professionelles Handeln in der Diktatur. Hans Christian Naujoks und die deutsche Frauenheilkunde während des „Dritten Reiches"*. In *Medizingeschichte in Schlaglichtern: Beiträge des „Rheinischen Kreises der Medizinhistoriker"*. Ed. Dominik Groß. Kassel, 2011, 243–250.

Franz 1998: Heike Franz, *Zwischen Markt und Profession. Betriebswirte in Deutschland im Spannungsfeld von Bildungs- und Wirtschaftsbürgertum 1900–1945*. Göttingen, 1998.

Freitäger 2003: Andreas Freitäger, *Franz Thorbecke (1875–1945)*. In *Gelehrte – Diplomaten – Unternehmer. Kölner Sammler und ihre Bücherkollektionen in der Universitäts- und Stadtbibliothek Köln*. Eds. Gernot Gabel and Wolfgang Schmitz. Cologne, 2003, 151–159.

Freitäger 2004: Andreas Freitäger, *Prof. Dr. Friedrich Moritz (1861–1938). Arzt – Lehrer – Forscher. Begleitheft zur Ausstellung anläßlich der Gründung der Kölner Akademie für praktische Medizin vor 100 Jahren*. Cologne, 2004.

Freitäger 2005: Andreas Freitäger, *Ehrenbürger und Ehrensenatoren der Universität zu Köln 1925–2004 mit einem Verzeichnis der Träger der Universitätsmedaille*. Cologne, 2005.

Freitäger 2010: Andreas Freitäger, *Gleichschaltung durch das Disziplinarrecht: Universitätsrat und Disziplinargericht 1928–1936*. In *„1933" – Hochschularchive und die Erforschung des Nationalsozialismus. Beiträge des Kolloquiums aus Anlass des 40jährigen Bestehens des Universitätsarchivs Köln am 8. April 2008*. Ed. Andreas Freitäger. Cologne, 2010, 109–136.

Freitäger 2018a: Andreas Freitäger, *Barrikaden und Teerfarbe. Die Verbarrikadierung des Universitätshauptgebäudes am 30. Mai 1968*. In Keim/Lewejohann 2018a, 168–173.

Freitäger 2018b: Andreas Freitäger, *Kleine Schönheitsfehler und verkehrte Hammelsprünge. Die Rektoratsbesetzung am 23./25. November 1968*. In Keim/Lewejohann 2018a, 176–181.

Frese 1988: Erich Frese, *Erwin Grochla (1921 bis 1986)*. In *Betriebswirte in Köln. Über den Beitrag Kölner Betriebswirte zur Entwicklung der Betriebswirtschaftslehre*. Ed. Friedrich-Wilhelm Henning. Cologne/Vienna, 1988, 195–222.

Friedmann/Mödder 1978: Gerd Friedmann/Ulrich Mödder, *Leistungsfähigkeit der Ganzkörper-Computertomographie*. In *Deutsches Ärzteblatt* 75 (1978), 2891–2899.

Funck 2004: Britta Funck, *Wilhelm Riphahn. Architekt in Köln. Eine Bestandsaufnahme*. Cologne, 2004.

Gabel/Suthaus 2001: *Von der Handelshochschule zur Universität. 100 Jahre wirtschafts- und sozialwissenschaftliche Lehre und Forschung in Köln. Katalog zur Ausstellung in der Universitäts- und Stadtbibliothek Köln*. Eds. Gernot Gabel and Christiane Suthaus. Cologne, 2001.

Gall 2005: Lothar Gall, *Schieder, Theodor*. In *Neue Deutsche Biographie* 22 (2005), 732–734, https://www.deutsche-biographie.de/sfz111935.html#ndbcontent [12 April 2019].

Garber 2000: Klaus Garber, *Richard Alewyn (1902–1979)*. In *Wissenschaftsgeschichte der Germanistik in Porträts*. Eds. Christoph König, Hans-Harald Müller and Werner Röcke. Berlin/New York, 2000, 211–220.

Gebäudemanagement: Infrastrukturelles Gebäudemanagement, https://verwaltung.uni-koeln.de/abteilung54/content/sachgebiet_1/index_ger.html [10 March 2019].

Gebrochene Wissenschaftskulturen 2010: *Gebrochene Wissenschaftskulturen. Universität und Politik im 20. Jahrhundert*. Eds. Michael Grüttner, Rüdiger Hachtmann, Konrad H. Jarausch, Jürgen John and Matthias Middell. Göttingen, 2010.

Gedenkstunde 1989: *Gedenkstunde für die Opfer der nationalsozialistischen Gewaltherrschaft am 9. November 1988*. In Hansmeyer/Henning/Huintges 1989, 172–183.

Gender & Diversity: *Gender Equality & Diversity*, https://vielfalt.uni-koeln.de [28 March 2019].

Geschichte Rechtswissenschaftliche Fakultät: *Geschichte der Fakultät*, http://www.jura.uni-koeln.de/13760.html [11 October 2018].

Geschichte RRZK: *Die Geschichte des RRZK im Überblick*, https://rrzk.uni-koeln.de/geschichte.html?&L=0 [4 March 2019].

Geschichte Thomas-Institut: *Geschichte des Thomas-Instituts*, http://www.thomasinstitut.uni-koeln.de/11862.html [26 July 2018].

Geschichte Zentrum: Zentrum für Frühbehandlung und Frühförderung, Geschichte, https://www.fruehbehandlung.de/de/unsere-einrichtung/11.html [8 November 2018].

Gesetz zur Gleichstellung von Frauen und Männern 1999: *Gesetz zur Gleichstellung von Frauen und Männern für das Land Nordrhein-Westfalen und zur Änderung anderer Gesetze vom 9. November 1999*. In *Gesetz- und Verordnungsblatt* (GV. NRW) 1999, no. 45, 19 November 1999, 589f., https://recht.nrw.de/lmi/owa/br_vbl_detail_text?anw_nr=6&vd_id=2377&vd_back=N590&sg=&menu=1 [15 February 2019].

GESIS: *GESIS – Leibniz-Institut für Sozialwissenschaften*, https://www.gesis.org/institut [15 March 2019].

Gienow 1990: Ina Gienow, *Leben und Werk von Fritz Stier-Somlo*. Diss. Cologne, 1990.

Golczewski 1984: Frank Golczewski, *Jüdische Hochschullehrer an der neuen Universität Köln vor dem Zweiten Weltkrieg*. In *Köln und das rheinische Judentum. Festschrift Germania Judaica 1959–1984*. Eds. Jutta Bohnke-Kollwitz, Willehad Paul Eckert, Frank Golczewski and Hermann Greive. Cologne, 1984, 363–396.

Golczewski 1988: Frank Golczewski, *Kölner Universitätslehrer und der Nationalsozialismus*. Cologne/Vienna, 1988.

Golczewski 1997: Frank Golczewski, *Rückkehr aus dem Exil an die Universität – Überlegungen zu Lebens- und Organisationsentscheidungen*. In *Unter Vorbehalt. Rückkehr aus der Emigration nach 1945*. Publ. Verein EL-DE-Haus Köln, eds. Wolfgang Blaschke, Karola Fings and Cordula Lissner. Cologne, 1997, 33–43.

Golczewski 2008: Frank Golczewski, *Köln*. In *Orte der Bücherverbrennungen in Deutschland 1933*. Eds. Julius Schoeps and Werner Treß. Hildesheim et al., 2008, 544–555.

Gräbel 2015: Carsten Gräbel, *Die Erforschung der Kolonien. Expeditionen und koloniale Wissenskultur deutscher Geographen, 1884–1919*. Bielefeld, 2015.

Graven 1929: [Hubert] Graven, *Die Entwicklung der studentischen Wirtschaftsarbeit an der Universität Köln*. In Universität Köln 1929, 293–305.

Grenzgängerin 2010: *Grenzgängerin zwischen Sozialwissenschaft und politischer Praxis*. 12 November 2010, https://www.mpg.de/599149/innovationspreis_renate_mayntz [28 February 2019].

Gross/Marx 2018: Rudolf Gross/Achim Marx, *Festkörperphysik*. 3rd ed. Berlin/Boston, 2018.

Groten 1988: Manfred Groten, *Älteste Stadtuniversität Nordwesteuropas. 600 Jahre Kölner Universität. Ausstellung des Historischen Archivs der Stadt Köln 4. Oktober bis 14. Dezember 1988*. Cologne, [1988].

Grünberg: *Grünberg, Peter*. In *Munzinger Online/Personen – Internationales Biographisches Archiv*, http://www.munzinger.de/document/00000026327 [26 September 2018].

Grünberg Biographical: *Peter Grünberg. Biographical*, https://www.nobelprize.org/prizes/physics/2007/grunberg/autobiography/ [13 November 2018].

Grüttner 1995: Michael Grüttner, *Studenten im Dritten Reich*. Paderborn et al., 1995.

Grüttner/Kinas 2007: Michael Grüttner/Sven Kinas, *Die Vertreibung von Wissenschaftlern aus den deutschen Universitäten 1933–1945*. In *Vierteljahrshefte für Zeitgeschichte* 55 (2007), issue 1, 123–186.

Gudian 1974: Gunter Gudian, *Partnerschaft zu Clermont ausgeweitet. Fruchtbare Kontakte zwischen den Juristischen Fakultäten*. In Mitteilungen 7/74, 7.

Gutmann 1984: Gernot Gutmann, *Jahresbericht des Rektors*. In JB 1984, 11f.

Haar 2017: Ingo Haar, *Theodor Schieder*. In *Handbuch der völkischen Wissenschaften. Akteure, Netzwerke, Forschungsprogramme*. Eds. Michael Fahlbusch, Ingo Haar and Alexander Pinwinkler. Tome 1.2, completely expanded and revised edition. Berlin/Boston, 2017, 714–725.

Haarmann/Huder/Siebenhaar 1983: *„Das war ein Vorspiel nur ..." Bücherverbrennung Deutschland 1933: Voraussetzungen und Folgen, Ausstellung der Akademie der Künste vom 8. Mai bis 3. Juli 1983*. Eds. Hermann Haarmann, Walter Huder and Klaus Siebenhaar. Berlin/Vienna, 1983.

Hachtmann 2010: Rüdiger Hachtmann, *Die Wissenschaftslandschaft zwischen 1930 und 1949. Profilbildung und Ressourcenverschiebung*. In Gebrochene Wissenschaftskulturen 2010, 193–205.

Hack/Schwarz 1992: *Otto Rohse und seine Presse*. Eds. Bertold Hack and Herta Schwarz. Hamburg, 1992.

Hacke 2018: Jens Hacke, *Existenzkrise der Demokratie. Zur politischen Theorie des Liberalismus in der Zwischenkriegszeit*. Frankfurt a.M., 2018.

Hahn: *Hahn, Ulla*. In *Munzinger Online/Personen – Internationales Biographisches Archiv*, http://www.munzinger.de/document/00000017976 [25 June 2018].

Hanau 1986: Peter Hanau, *Jahresbericht des Rektors*. In JB 1986, 26, 28.

Hanau 1987: Peter Hanau, *Jahresbericht des Rektors*. In JB: 1987, 31.

Hanau 1988: Peter Hanau, *Jahresbericht des Rektors*. In JB 1988, 31f.

Hanau 1989a: Peter Hanau, *Begrüßung* [20 May 1988]. In Hansmeyer/Henning/Huintges 1989, 23–27.

Hanau 1989b: Peter Hanau, *Begrüßung* [4 November 1988]. In Hansmeyer/Henning/Huintges 1989, 111–113.

Hansmann/Perschke 2007: Lisa Hansmann/Birgit Perschke, *Frauen an der Universität Köln, 1943–1948: Studentinnen, Dozentinnen*. In *Zwischen „Endsieg" und Examen. Studieren an der Universität Köln 1943–1948. Brüche und Kontinuitäten*. Eds. Margit Szöllösi-Janze et al. Nümbrecht, 2007, 59–68.

Hansmeyer 1988: *600 Jahre Kölner Universität 1388/1988. Von der mittelalterlichen Alma mater zum zukunftsorientierten Zentrum der Wissenschaft. Historischer Überblick und aktuelle Bestandsaufnahme aus Anlaß der 600. Wiederkehr des Gründungsdatums*. Ed. Karl-Heinrich Hansmeyer with contributions by Erich Meuthen et al. Cologne, [1988].

Hansmeyer 1989: Karl-Heinrich Hansmeyer, *Vorwort*. In Hansmeyer/Henning/Huintges 1989, 12–15.

Hansmeyer/Henning/Huintges 1989: *600 Jahre Kölner Universität 1388–1988. Reden und Berichte zur Geschichte, Gegenwart und Zukunft der Universität*. Eds. Karl-Heinrich Hansmeyer and Friedrich-Wilhelm Henning with contributions by Robert Huintges. Cologne, 1989.

Hansmeyer/Mackscheidt 1988: Karl-Heinrich Hansmeyer/Klaus Mackscheidt, *Fritz Karl Mann (1883 bis 1979)*. In *Kölner Volkswirte und Sozialwissenschaftler. Über den Beitrag Kölner Volkswirte und Sozialwissenschaftler zur Entwicklung der Wirtschafts- und Sozialwissenschaften*. Ed. Friedrich-Wilhelm Henning. Cologne/Vienna, 1988, 15–38.

Hänßler 2010: Boris Hänßler, *Vom Modell zur Erfolgsgeschichte. Graduiertenkollegs: Promovierende erkannten schnell den Nutzen*. In *20 Jahre Graduiertenkollegs. Nährböden für neue Promotionskulturen: innovativ, interaktiv, international*. [Bonn, 2010], 6–9, https://www.dfg.de/download/pdf/dfg_im_profil/geschaeftsstelle/publikationen/20_jahre_graduiertenkollegs.pdf [16 November 2018].

Happ 2004: Sabine Happ, *Politisch und nicht politisch motivierte Aberkennung von akademischen Graden. Eine Auswertung der Rundschreiben deutscher Universitäten in der NS-Zeit*. In *Vielfalt der Geschichte. Lernen, Lehren und Erforschen vergangener Zeiten*. Eds. Sabine Happ and Ulrich Nonn. Berlin, 2004, 283–296.

Haselbach 1991: Dieter Haselbach, *Autoritärer Liberalismus und Soziale Marktwirtschaft. Gesellschaft und Politik im Ordoliberalismus*. Baden-Baden, 1991.

Haupts 1996: Leo Haupts, *Befreiung durch Restauration. Der Neubeginn an der Universität Köln im Herbst 1945*. In *Wir haben schwere Zeiten hinter uns. Die Kölner Region zwischen Krieg und Nachkriegszeit*. Ed. Jost Dülffer. Vierow bei Greifswald, 1996, 330-354.

Haupts 2001: *Leo Haupts, Die Stadt Köln, „ihre" Universität und die Parteien. Von der städtischen Universität zur Landesuniversität 1945–1955*. In *Köln in den 50er Jahren. Zwischen Tradition und Modernisierung*. Ed. Jost Dülffer. Cologne, 2001, 337–360.

Haupts 2007: Leo Haupts, *Die Universität zu Köln im Übergang vom Nationalsozialismus zur Bundesrepublik*. Cologne/Weimar/Vienna, 2007.

Haupts 2008: *Lebensraum im Westen. Der Beitrag der Universität zu Köln speziell in der „Hochschularbeitsgemeinschaft für Raumforschung"*. In *Wissenschaftsgeschichte im Rheinland unter besonderer Berücksichtigung von Raumkonzepten*. Eds. Gertrude Cepl-Kaufmann, Dominik Groß and Georg Mölich. Kassel, 2008, 75–106.

Hausmann 1997: Frank-Rutger Hausmann, *Fritz Schalk und die Romanistik in Köln von 1945 bis 1980*. In *Deutsche Literaturwissenschaft 1945–1965. Fallstudien zu Institutionen, Diskursen, Personen*. Eds. Petra Boden and Rainer Rosenberg. Berlin, 1997, 35–60.

Hausmann 2005: Frank-Rutger Hausmann, *Schalk, Fritz*. In *Neue Deutsche Biographie* 22 (2005), 551, https://www.deutsche-biographie.de/pnd118606379.html#ndbcontent [29 August 2018].

Hausmann 2007: Frank-Rutger Hausmann, *„Deutsche Geisteswissenschaft" im Zweiten Weltkrieg. Die „Aktion Ritterbusch" (1940–1945)*. 3rd expanded edition. Heidelberg, 2007.

Hausmitteilungen: *Hausmitteilungen der Universität zu Köln* 1968–1970.

Haymann: *Haymann, Franz*. In *Catalogus Professorium Rostochiensium*, http://purl.uni-rostock.de/cpr/00003397 [16 November 2017].

Hax: *Hax, Herbert*. In *Munzinger Online/Personen – Internationales Biographisches Archiv*, http://www.munzinger.de/document/00000020371 [26 September 2018].

Heberer: *Heberer, Georg. In Munzinger Online/Personen – Internationales Biographisches Archiv*, https://www.munzinger.de/search/document?id=00000013597&type=text%2fhtml&template=%2fpublikationen%2fpersonen%2fdocument.jsp&key=%24param%5b%27key%27%5d&- terminate=%24param%5b%27terminate%27%5d [1 August 2018].

Heim/Kaulen 2010: Susanne Heim/Hildegard Kaulen, *Müncheberg – Köln. Das Max-Planck-Institut für Pflanzenzüchtungsforschung*. In *Denkorte. Max-Planck-Gesellschaft und Kaiser-Wilhelm-Gesellschaft. Brüche und Kontinuitäten 1911–2011*. Eds. Peter Gruss and Reinhard Rürup with contributions by Susanne Kiewitz. Dresden, 2010, 348–358.

Heimbüchel 1988a: Bernd Heimbüchel, *Die neue Universität. Selbstverständnis – Idee und Verwirklichung*. In Kölner Universitätsgeschichte 1988. Vol. 2, 101–692.

Heimbüchel 1988b: Bernd Heimbüchel, *„Neuartige Universitas". Zur Geschichte der Kölner Hochschulidee im 19. und 20. Jahrhundert*. In *Geschichte in Köln* 23 (1988), 247–265.

Heinemann 1991: Helmut Heinemann, *Universitätsbauten*. In *Köln. Seine Bauten 1928–1988*. Ed. Heribert Hall. Cologne, 1991, 295–309.

Heinen 1990: Ernst Heinen, *Aspekte der Geschichte der Erziehungswissenschaftlichen Fakultät der Universität zu Köln*. In *Von den Generalstudien zur spezialisierten Universität. Vier Kolloquiumsvorträge zur deutschen Bildungs- und Wissenschaftsgeschichte*. Ed. Carl August Lückerath. Cologne, 1990, 73–94.

Henckmann 1998: Wolfhart Henckmann, *Max Scheler*. Munich, 1998.

Henckmann 2005: Wolfhart Henckmann, *Scheler, Max*. In *Neue Deutsche Biographie* 22 (2005), 644–646, https://www.deutsche-biographie.de/gnd118606964.html#ndbcontent [19 August 2018].

Henning 1988a: Friedrich-Wilhelm Henning, *Christian Eckert*. In *Kölner Volkswirte und Sozialwissenschaftler. Über den Beitrag Kölner Volkswirte und Sozialwissenschaftler zur Entwicklung der Wirtschafts- und Sozialwissenschaften*. Ed. Friedrich-Wilhelm Henning. Cologne/Vienna, 1988, 1–13.

Henning 1988b: Friedrich-Wilhelm Henning, *Bruno Kuske (1876 bis 1964)*. In *Kölner Volkswirte und Sozialwissenschaftler. Über den Beitrag Kölner Volkswirte und Sozialwissenschaftler zur Entwicklung der Wirtschafts- und Sozialwissenschaften*. Ed. Friedrich-Wilhelm Henning. Cologne/Vienna, 1988, 69–95.

Henning 1990: Friedrich-Wilhelm Henning, *Von der Handelsakademie zur Handelshochschule (18. bis 20. Jahrhundert)*. In *Handelsakademie – Handelshochschule – Wirtschafts- und Sozialwissenschaftliche Fakultät. Der Weg von der Handelsakademie und Handlungswissenschaft des 18. Jahrhunderts zur Wirtschafts- und Sozialwissenschaftlichen Fakultät und Betriebswirtschaftslehre des 20. Jahrhunderts*. Ed. Friedrich-Wilhelm Henning. Cologne/Vienna, 1990, 53–79.

Henning/Kazemi 2011: Eckart Henning/Marion Kazemi, *Chronik der Kaiser-Wilhelm-/Max-Planck-Gesellschaft zur Förderung der Wissenschaften 1911–2011. Daten und Quellen*. Berlin, 2011.

Henning/Lauf/Ludwig 1988: Friedrich-Wilhelm Henning/Peter Lauf/Hannelore Ludwig, *Statistik der Studierenden, der Lehrkörpers und der Promotionen*. In Kölner Universitätsgeschichte 1988. Vol. 3, 287–375.

Herrmann 1990: Walther Herrmann, *Mann, Fritz Karl*. In *Neue Deutsche Biographie* 16 (1990), 55–56, https://www.deutsche-biographie.de/pnd116732415.html#ndbcontent [14 August 2018].

Himmelrath/Mersch 2006: Armin Himmelrath/Britta Mersch, *Studentenproteste. Polizei räumt Kölner Rektorat*. In *Spiegel-Online*, 8 May 2006, https://www.spiegel.de/lebenundlernen/uni/studentenproteste-polizei-raeumt-koelner-rektorat-a-414965.html [10 December 2018].

Historisches: *Historisches*. University of Cologne website. Faculty of Mathematics and Natural Sciences. Department of Chemistry, http://www.chemie.uni-koeln.de/historisches4.html [8 August 2018].

Hochschulfreiheitsgesetz: *Hochschulfreiheitsgesetz (HFG) vom 31. Oktober 2006*, https://recht.nrw.de/lmi/owa/br_vbl_detail_text?anw_nr=6&vd_id=1460&vd_back=N474&sg=&menu=1 [4 December 2018].

Hochschulgesetz 1970: *Gesetz über die wissenschaftlichen Hochschulen des Landes Nordrhein-Westfalen (Hochschulgesetz – HSchG) vom 7. April 1970*. In *Gesetz- und Verordnungsblatt für das Land Nordrhein-Westfalen*. Edition A. 24 (1970), 254–262.

Hochschulpakt 2020: *Hochschulpakt 2020*, https://www.hrk.de/?id=628 [27 March 2019].

Hoffrath 2009: Christiane Hoffrath, *Bücherspuren. Das Schicksal von Elise und Helene Richter und ihrer Bibliothek im „Dritten Reich"*. Cologne/Weimar/Vienna, 2009.

Hoffrath 2012: Christiane Hoffrath, *Bibliotheksdirektor im Nationalsozialismus. Hermann Corsten und die Universitäts- und Stadtbibliothek Köln*. Cologne, 2012.

Holl/Glunz 2008: *1968 am Rhein. Satisfaction und ruhender Verkehr*. Eds. Kurt Holl and Claudia Glunz. New revised edition. Cologne, 2008.

Hollstein 2007: Thorsten Hollstein, *Die Verfassung als „Allgemeiner Teil". Privatrechtsmethode und Privatrechtskonzeption bei Hans Carl Nipperdey (1895–1968)*. Tübingen, 2007.

Hollstein 2013: Thorsten Hollstein, *Hans Carl Nipperdey (1895–1968). Kölner Rechtswissenschaftler, Präsident des BAG und juristisches Chamäleon?* In Kölner Juristen 2013, 197–209.

Hondros 2015: Michael Christian Hondros, *Die Geschichte der Neurologischen Klinik am Hansaplatz unter besonderer Berücksichtigung des Gesetzes zur Verhütung erbkranken Nachwuchses 1933/34*. Diss. Berlin, 2015.

Hübner 1968: Heinz Hübner, *Ansprache des Rektors*. In KUR [N.S.] 40.1968, 25–43.

Hübner 1969: Heinz Hübner, *Probleme von Forschung und Lehre heute*. In JB 1969, 18–30.

Hübner 1971: Heinz Hübner, *Ansprache des scheidenden Rektors Professor Dr. Heinz Hübner anläßlich der Rektoratsübergabe am 14. Oktober 1970*. In KUR [N.S.] 43.1971, 22–38.

Hübner 1988: Heinz Hübner, *Die Universität zu Köln in den Jahren 1968–1970*. In *Festschrift der Rechtswissenschaftlichen Fakultät zur 600-Jahr-Feier der Universität zu Köln*. Cologne, 1988, 53–63.

Huintges 1989: Robert Huintges, *Die Vorbereitung und Durchführung des Kölner Universitätsjubiläums 1988*. In Hansmeyer/Henning/Huintges 1989, 325–399.

Husserl-Archiv: *Husserl-Archiv der Universität zu Köln*, http://www.koelnerarchive.de/index.php?id=29 [23 February 2019].

Hüttenberger/Wadischat 1986: Peter Hüttenberger/Eberhard Frank Wadischat, *Hochschulpolitik*. In *Vierzig Jahre. Historische Entwicklungen und Perspektiven des Landes Nordrhein-Westfalen*. Ed. Peter Hüttenberger. 2nd edition, Düsseldorf, 1986, 149–170.

In memoriam Heberer: *In memoriam Prof. Dr. med. Dr. h.c. Georg Heberer*. Heidelberg, 2000.

International: Universität zu Köln, *International*, https://www.portal.uni-koeln.de/index.php?id=6766 [28 March 2019].

Internationale Verbindungsbüros: *Internationale Verbindungsbüros*, https://www.portal.uni-koeln.de/6808.html [27 March 2019].

Interview Baum: Interview mit Gerhart Baum, 27.11.2014. In *Quellen zur Geschichte der Menschenrechte*. Ed. Arbeitskreis Menschenrechte im 20. Jahrhundert, https://www.geschichte-menschenrechte.de/personen/gerhart-baum [9 August 2018].

Isselhard 1975a: [Wolf] Isselhard, *Vorwort*. In JB 1975, 5f.

Isselhard 1975b: W[olf] Isselhard, *Bericht des Rektors*. In JB 1975, 13–20.

Janssen 2009: Hauke Janssen, *Nationalökonomie und Nationalsozialismus. Die deutsche Volkswirtschaftslehre in den dreißiger Jahren des 20. Jahrhunderts*. 3rd revised edition. Marburg, 2009.

Jarausch 1984: Konrad H. Jarausch, *Deutsche Studenten 1800–1970*. Frankfurt a.M., 1984.

JB: *Jahrbuch der Universität zu Köln*. Ed. Rektor der Universität zu Köln. Cologne, 1966–1989.

JCW-Schule: JCW-Schule, *Mehr als 60 Jahre Schulgeschichte*, http://jcw-schule.de/index.php/ueber-die-jcw/schulgeschichte?showall=1&start=0 [8 November 2018].

Jessen 2010: Ralph Jessen, *Massenausbildung, Unterfinanzierung und Stagnation. Ost- und Westdeutsche Universitäten in den siebziger und achtziger Jahren*. In Gebrochene Wissenschaftskulturen 2010, 260–278.

Jessen 2018: Ralph Jessen, *Vom „Elfenbeinturm" zur „Massenuniversität". Hochschulreformen in den 1960er und 1970er Jahren*. In Keim/Lewejohann 2018a, 94–99.

Johansen: *Prof. Dr. Ulla C. Johansen*, http://ethnologie.phil-fak.uni-koeln.de/content.php?kid=193 [28 February 2019].

Johansen 2007: *Johansen, Ulla Christine*. In Bettina Beer, *Frauen in der deutschsprachigen Ethnologie. Ein Handbuch*. Cologne/Weimar/Vienna, 2007, 110–117.

Journal: Journal. *Berichte aus der Universität Köln* 3/1986–3/1992.

Jussen 1991: Heribert Jussen, *Zur Geschichte der Ausbildung von Sonderpädagogen in Köln – ein deskriptiver Rückblick*. In Jussen et al. 1991, 16–43.

Jussen et al. 1991: *Die Heilpädagogische Fakultät zu Köln. Geschichte, Gegenwartsprobleme, Perspektiven*. Ed. Heribert Jussen with contributions by Helga Fründt et al. Bonn, 1991.

Kaesler 1997: Dirk Kaesler, *Die Gründung des Forschungsinstituts für Soziologie der Universität zu Köln und die zwanziger Jahre*. In Dirk Kaesler: *Soziologie als Berufung. Bausteine einer selbstbewussten Soziologie*. Opladen, 1997, 235–247.

Kaltefleiter 1971: Werner Kaltefleiter, *10 Jahre Austauschprogramm zwischen der Pennsylvania State University und der Wirtschafts- und Sozialwissenschaftlichen Fakultät der Universität zu Köln*. In Mitteilungen 1/71, 9f.

Kandinskys „Bilder einer Ausstellung" 2008: *Kandinskys „Bilder einer Ausstellung": Skizzen zu Mussorgsky*. In *Neue Züricher Zeitung*, 3 November 2008, https://www.nrz.de/staedte/duesseldorf/kandinskys-bilder-einer-ausstellung-skizzen-zu-mussorgsky-id1121165.html [6 September 2018].

Karpen 2001: Ulrich Karpen, *Peters, Hans*. In *Neue Deutsche Biographie* 20 (2001), 240f., https://www.deutsche-biographie.de/pnd118740229.html#ndbcontent [25 July 2018].

Katner 1969: *Die Universität zu Köln 1919–1969*. Ed. Wilhelm Katner. Cologne, 1969.

Katterle 1998: Siegfried Katterle, *Gerhard Weissers Beitrag zur Theorie der Wirtschaftspolitik*. In *Gegen den gesellschaftspolitischen Imperialismus der reinen Ökonomie. Gedächtnisschrift für Gerhard Weisser*. Eds. Heinrich A. Henkel, Lothar F. Neumann and Hajo Romahn. Marburg, 1998, 63–85.

Katzmarzik 2014: Anja Katzmarzik, *Professor Dr. Gerd Lehmkuhl verlässt Köln. Nichts, was man fürchten müsste*. In *Kölner Stadt-Anzeiger*, 23 November 2014, https://www.ksta.de/koeln/professor-dr--gerd-lehmkuhl-verlaesst-koeln-nichts--was-man-fuerchten-muesste-578344 [8 November 2018].

Kaufmann: Hilde Kaufmann. In *Kieler Gelehrtenverzeichnis*, http://www.gelehrtenverzeichnis.de/bc1b3802-d3d9-1ade-a09e-4d4c60b5c3f0 [29 August 2018].

Kaufmann 2007: Werner Kaufmann, *Rudolf Gross 90 Jahre: Die Innere Medizin vorangebracht*. In *Deutsches Ärzteblatt* 104 (2007), A 2667, https://www.aerzteblatt.de/archiv/57053 [28 August 2018].

Keim 2018: Michaela Keim, *Zwischen Tradition und Reform. Die Universität zu Köln in den 1960er Jahren*. In Keim/Lewejohann 2018a, 86–91.

Keim/Lewejohann 2018a: *Köln 68! protest. pop. provokation*. Eds. Michaela Keim and Stefan Lewejohann. Mainz, 2018.

Keim/Lewejohann 2018b: Michaela Keim/Stefan Lewejohann, *Köln 68! Eine einordnende Darstellung*. In Keim/Lewejohann 2018a, 26–33.

Kellenbenz 1969: Hermann Kellenbenz, *Die Wirtschafts- und Sozialwissenschaftliche Fakultät*. In Katner 1969, 15–22.

Keussen 1929: Hermann Keussen, *Die alte Universität Köln 1388–1798*. In Universität Köln 1929, 11–52.

Kisch 1966: Bruno Kisch, *Wanderungen und Wandlungen. Die Geschichte eines Arztes im 20. Jahrhundert*. Cologne, 1966.

Klaetke 2008: Fabian Klaetke, *Kölner Kompendium des Luftfahrtrechts. Universität und Lufthansa stellen neues Standardwerk vor*. In Universitätszeitung 1/2008, 13.

Kleinen 2005: Karin Kleinen, *Ringen um Demokratie. Studieren in der Nachkriegszeit. Die akademische Jugend Köln (1945–1950)*. Cologne/Weimar/Vienna, 2005.

Klingemann 2003: Carsten Klingemann, *Soziologen in der „Westforschung" während des Nationalsozialismus*. In *Griff nach Westen. Die „Westforschung" der völkisch-nationalen Wissenschaften zum nordwesteuropäischen Raum (1919–1960)*. Tome 1. Eds. Burckhard Dietz, Helmut Gabel and Ulrich Tiedau. Münster et al., 2003, 407–445.

Knoch 2018: Habbo Knoch, *Unvollendete Utopie. Der Ausbau der Universität zu Köln in den 1960er und 1970er Jahren*. In Keim/Lewejohann 2018a, 110–117.

Koch 1953: Josef Koch, *Einige Gedanken über die Bedeutung der Universität in der Kulturkrise der Gegenwart*. In *Universitätsführer der Universität zu Köln 1953*. Ed. Studentenausschuss. Cologne, 1953, 21–24.

Kohl 2018: Peter Kohl, *Forschung mal anders: die Ökologische Rheinstation*. In *Universitätsmagazin* 16/2018, 46–48.

Köhler 1997: Henning Köhler, *Adenauer. Eine politische Biographie*. Vol. 1. Berlin, 1997.

Kohlmann 2013: Patrick Kohlmann, *Günter Kohlmann. Ein Juristen-Leben*. Cologne, 2013.

Koischwitz 2017: Svea Koischwitz, *Der Bund Freiheit der Wissenschaft in den Jahren 1970–1976. Ein Interessenverband zwischen Studentenbewegung und Hochschulreform*. Cologne/Weimar/Vienna, 2017.

Kolberg 1989: Gerhard Kolberg, *Die Außenskulpturen von Gerhard Marcks in Köln*. In *Gerhard Marcks. 1889–1981; Retrospektive*. Ed. Martina Rudloff. Munich, 1989, 318–336.

Kölner Juristen 2013: *Kölner Juristen im 20. Jahrhundert. Beiträge zur Ringvorlesung an der Universität zu Köln, Sommersemester 2010 und Wintersemester 2010/2011*. Eds. Steffen Augsberg and Andreas Funke. Tübingen, 2013.

Kölner Kompendium: Institut für Luftrecht, Weltraumrecht und Cyberrecht, *Kölner Kompendium des Luftrechts*. 3 vols., http://www.ilwr.jura.uni-koeln.de/13879.html [24 March 2019].

Kölner Universitätsgeschichte 1988: *Kölner Universitätsgeschichte*. Ed. Senatskommission für die Geschichte der Universität zu Köln. 3 vols. Cologne, 1988.

Kölner Wissenschaftsrunde: *Kölner Wissenschaftsrunde*, http://koelner-wissenschaftsrunde.de/koelner-wissenschaftsrunde/ [28 March 2018].

König 1989: Bernhard König, *Jahresbericht des Rektors*. In JB 1989, 31f.

Konrad der Große 2017: *Konrad der Große. Die Adenauerzeit in Köln 1917–1933*. Ed. Rita Wagner. Mainz, 2017.

Kops/Hansmeyer/Kranski 1988: Manfred Kops/Karl-Heinrich Hansmeyer/Bernd Kranski, *Die Finanzgeschichte der Universität zu Köln im Spiegel ihrer Haushaltspläne*. In Kölner Universitätsgeschichte 1988. Vol. 3, 377–467.

Kornmüller 2006: Arthur Kornmüller, *Bericht über den Einbau einer FTS im Klinikum zu Köln*. In www.awt-seminar.de. Event on 30 and 31 March 2006 in Cologne, 6–13, https://www.yumpu.com/de/document/read/24460905/download-handout-pdf-93kb-awt-seminar [20 March 2019].

Kotowski 2017: Elke-Vera Kotowski, *Martin-Buber-Institut für Judaistik*. In *Das Kulturerbe deutschsprachiger Juden. Eine Spurensuche in den Ursprungs-, Transit- und Emigrationsländern*. Ed. Elke-Vera Kotowski. Berlin, 2017.

Kowitz 1998: Rolf Kowitz, *Alfred Müller-Armack: Wirtschaftspolitik als Berufung – Zur Entstehungsgeschichte der Sozialen Marktwirtschaft und dem politischen Wirken des Hochschullehrers*. Cologne, 1998.

Krausnick 2012: Daniel Krausnick, *Staat und Hochschule im Gewährleistungsstaat*. Tübingen, 2012.

Krayer 1988: Susanne Krayer, *Rektoren und Dekane*. In Kölner Universitätsgeschichte 1988. Vol. 3, 75–84.

Kries 1995: Renate Kries, *Die Wiedereröffnung der Universität zu Köln*. In *Köln nach dem Krieg. Facetten der Stadtgeschichte*. Eds. Georg Mölich and Stefan Wunsch. Cologne, 1995, 241–264.

Kriminaltechnik 1958: *Grundfragen der Kriminaltechnik*. Wiesbaden, 1958.

Krings 2011: Ulrich Krings, *Rolf Gutbrods Bauten für die Universität zu Köln: Geschichte und aktueller Zustand*. In *Denkmalpflege im Rheinland* 28 (2011), issue 2, 72–83.

Kroell/Eber 2011: Clemens Kroell/Martin Eber, *Vom Overhead-Projektor zum iPad. Eine technische Übersicht*. In *Lehrbuch für Lernen und Lehren mit Technologien*. Eds. Martin Eber and Sandra Schön. Norderstedt, 2011, 23–30.

Kroll 1931a: [Josef Kroll], *Von der akademischen Freiheit. Aus einer Rede des Rektors der Universität Köln*. In KUZ, 18 April 1931, 3–5.

Kroll 1931b: [Josef] Kroll, *Hochschulprobleme. Rede des zurücktretenden Rektors Prof. Dr. Kroll bei der Rektoratsübergabe am 7. November 1931 im Gürzenich*. In KUZ, 21. November 1931, 9–11.

Kroll 1945: *Ansprache Seiner Magnifizenz des Rektors der Universität, Professor Dr. Kroll, anläßlich der festlichen Wiedereröffnung der Universität Köln verbunden mit der feierlichen Immatrikulation der Studenten am Montag, dem 10. Dezember 1945 vormittags 11 Uhr in der Aula der Universität*. In UAK 27/157.

Kroll 1946a: J[osef] Kroll, *Geleitwort*. In KUZ [N.S.] 1 (1946), 1f.

Kroll 1946b: [Josef Kroll], *Rede des Rektors*. In KUZ [N.S.] 1 (1946), 11f.

Kroll 1947a: Josef Kroll, *Die Universität in der Gegenwart*. Cologne, 1947.

Kroll 1947b: Josef Kroll, *Nach einem Jahre*. In KUZ [N.S.] 2 (1947), 25f.

Kroll 1947c: [Josef] Kroll, *Ansprache Sr. Magnificenz des Rektors Prof. Dr. Kroll bei der Eröffnung des ersten Ferienkursus ausländischer Studenten an der Universität zu Köln*. In KUZ [N.S.] 2 (1947), 61–63.

Kruk 1984: Max Kruk, *Leben und Wirken Schmalenbachs*. In *Eugen Schmalenbach. Der Mann – Sein Werk – Die Wirkung*. Ed. Walter Cordes. Stuttgart, 1984, 1–278.

Kücking 2007: Verena Kücking, *Keine weiße Weste: Die Entnazifizierung der Studierenden*. In *Zwischen „Endsieg" und Examen. Studieren an der Universität Köln 1943–1948. Brüche und Kontinuitäten*. Ed. Margit Szöllösi-Janze. Nümbrecht, 2007, 121–137.

KUR: *Kölner Universitätsreden* 1.1919–48.1943.

KUR [N.S.]: *Kölner Universitätsreden*. Neue Serie 1.1946–86.2001.

Kuske 1929: [Bruno] Kuske, *Stellung und Eigenart der Kölner Universität*. In Universität Köln 1929, 231–305.

Kuske 1932: [Bruno] Kuske, *Politik an Hochschulen*. In KUZ, 19 February 1932, 3–5.

KUZ: *Kölner Universitäts-Zeitung* 1919–1933.

KUZ [N.S.]: *Kölner Universitäts-Zeitung*. Neue Serie 1946–1948.

Ladendorf 1969: H. Ladendorf, *Internationale Verbindungen. Auslandsbeziehungen, ausländische Studenten, Partnerschaften, Stipendien. Das Auslandsamt*. In Katner 1969, 147f.

Lang-Hinrichsen 1958: Dietrich Lang-Hinrichsen, *Zum Gedenken an Gotthold Bohne*. In *Juristenzeitung* 13 (1958), 377f.

Laudatio Lang: *Laudatio*. In Klaus Tipke et al., *Festschrift für Joachim Lang zum 70. Geburtstag. Gestaltung der Steuerrechtsordnung*. Cologne, 2010, 1–17.

Lebenslauf Eck: Lebenslauf Werner Eck, https://alte-geschichte.phil-fak.uni-koeln.de/fileadmin/home/Abteilungen/Alte_Geschichte/Mitarbeiter/Eck/Lebenslauf__Dezember-2018.pdf [13 November 2018].

Lebenslauf Lang: Lebenslauf Joachim Lang, http://www.steuerrecht.uni-koeln.de/14195.html [8 November 2018].

Lebenslauf Mayntz: Lebenslauf Renate Mayntz, http://www.mpifg.de/people/rm/lebenslauf_de.asp [28 February 2019].

Leendertz 2014: Ariane Leendertz, *Die Politik der Entpolitisierung: Die Max-Planck-Gesellschaft und die Sozialwissenschaften in Starnberg und Köln*. In *„Dem Anwenden muss das Erkennen vorausgehen". Auf dem Weg zu einer Geschichte der Kaiser-Wilhelm-/Max-Planck-Gesellschaft*. Eds. Dieter Hoffmann, Birgit Kolboske and Jürgen Renn. Berlin, 2014, 287–306.

Leggewie 2018: Claus Leggewie, *50 Jahre '68. Köln und seine Protestgeschichte*. Cologne, 2018.

Lehmann 1976: *Heinrich Lehmann. Ein großer Jurist des Rheinlands. Jugend und Beruf. Seine Lebenserinnerungen*. Ed. Gerhard Kegel. Cologne, 1976.

Lehmkuhl: *Gerd Lehmkuhl*, https://de.wikipedia.org/w/index.php?title=Gerd_Lehmkuhl&oldid=179691707 [13 November 2018].

Lehnert et al. 1998: Nicole Lehnert et al., *Männer, Frauen und Frauenförderung. Eine Studie zur Situation von Frauen und Männern an der Universität Münster*. Münster et al., 1998.

LehrerInnenbildung in Köln 2018: *Kleine Geschichte der LehrerInnenbildung in Köln*. Ed. Zentrum für LehrerInnenbildung (ZfL), University of Cologne. Cologne, 2018.

Lemberg 2000: Margret Lemberg, *Schließung oder Verlegung – Die Kölner Universität im Wintersemester 1944/45*. In *Geschichte im Westen* 15 (2000), 31–48.

Leyendecker 2011: Christoph Leyendecker, *Zum Tod von Univ.-Prof. Dr. Siglinde Kunert*. In *Frühförderung interdisziplinär* 30 (2011), https://www.reinhardt-journals.de/index.php/fi/article/view/1362 [8 November 2018].

Liebermann 1988: Peter Liebermann, *Psychiatrie und Kriminologie. Zur Kontinuität wissenschaftlicher Kategorien und Diskurse*. In Nachhilfe 1988, 62–68.

Lörch 2010: Ulrike Lörch, *Schnelles Bauen für die Alterns- und Genomforschung. Medfacilities errichtet Forschungskomplex für Alternsforschung*. In Universitätszeitung 1/2010, 4.

Lorentz 2007: Frank Lorentz, *Der spannendste Sender des Landes*. In *WELT*, 2 December 2007, https://www.welt.de/wams_print/article1421315/Der-spannendste-Sender-des-Landes.html [24 March 2019].

Löwer 1997: Reiner Löwer, *Gesetzloses Hochschulrecht – Die Geschichte des Hochschulrechts in Nordrhein-Westfalen bis zum Inkrafttreten des Hochschulrahmengesetzes*. Diss. Bonn, 1997.

Löwer 2018: Wolfgang Löwer, *Traditionell modern! (1991–2018)*. In *Forschung und Lehre im Westen Deutschlands 1918–2018. Geschichte der Universität Bonn*. Vol. 2. Ed. Dominik Geppert. Göttingen, 2018, 407–500.

Ludwig 1991: Hannelore Ludwig, *Die wirtschafts- und sozialwissenschaftliche Lehre in Köln von 1901 bis 1989/90*. Cologne/Weimar/Vienna, 1991.

Lynen 2017: Peter Michael Lynen, *Typisierung von Hochschulen: Pädagogische Hochschulen, Kunst- und Musikhochschulen, kirchliche Hochschulen, private Hochschulen*. In *Hochschulrecht. Ein Handbuch für die Praxis*. Eds. Michael Hartmer and Hubert Detmer. 3rd edition. Heidelberg, 2017, 83–138.

Mader 1980: Wilhelm Mader, *Max Scheler*. Reinbek, 1980.

Maier 1966: Johann Maier, *Judaistik. Ein neues Studienfach an der philosophischen Fakultät* (1966), http://judaistik.phil-fak.uni-koeln.de/38630.html [22 February 2019].

Mantel 2009: Peter Mantel, *Betriebswirtschaftslehre und Nationalsozialismus. Eine institutionen- und personengeschichtliche Studie*. Wiesbaden, 2009.

Marquardt 1986: Helmut Marquardt, *Hilde Kaufmann. Eine Skizze ihres Lebens und ihres wissenschaftlichen Werkes*. In *Gedächtnisschrift für Hilde Kaufmann*. Eds. Hans Joachim Hirsch, Günther Kaiser and Helmut Marquardt. Berlin, 1986, 1–17.

Martin-Buber-Institut: Martin-Buber-Institut für Judaistik, *Bibliothek*, http://judaistik.phil-fak.uni-koeln.de/38644.html [22 February 2019].

Marx 2018: Peter W. Marx, *Spektakel, Provokation, Aufbruch und „kölsche Lösung". Köln als Theater- und Protestszene*. In Keim/Lewejohann 2018a, 311–317.

Mättig 2018: Ursula Mättig, *Frauenstudium und -politik, Frauenforschung und -förderung: 1968/1970 bis 2015*. In *Doch plötzlich jetzt emanzipiert will Wissenschaft sie treiben: Frauen an der Universität Bonn*. Eds. Andrea Stieldorf, Ursula Mättig and Ines Neffgen. Göttingen, 2018, 215–256.

Matzerath 2014: Horst Matzerath, *Professor Dr. Bruno Kisch (1890–1966). Ein jüdischer Arzt und Wissenschaftler im 20. Jahrhundert*. In *Für Köln. Leben für die Stadt*. Ed. Werner Eck. Cologne, 2014, 173–187.

Max-Planck-Forschungspreis: *Max-Planck-Forschungspreis*, https://de.wikipedia.org/wiki/Max-Planck-Forschungspreis [15 February 2019].

Mayer-Maly 1969: Theo Mayer-Maly, *Haymann, Franz*. In *Neue Deutsche Biographie* 8 (1969), 153f., https://www.deutsche-biographie.de/pnd119240998.html#ndbcontent [14 August 2018].

Mayntz 1996: Renate Mayntz, *Mein Weg zur Soziologie: Rekonstruktion eines kontingenten Karrierepfades*. In *Wege zur Soziologie nach 1945. Autobiographische Notizen*. Ed. Christian Fleck. Opladen, 1996, 225–235.

Menze 1976: Clemens Menze, *Jahresbericht des Rektors*. In JB 1976, 11–18.

Menze 1977: Clemens Menze, *Jahresbericht des Rektors*. In JB 1977, 12–22.

Merkelbach 1970: Reinhold Merkelbach, *Partnerschaft zwischen Universitäten Köln und Clermont-Ferrand*. In Hausmitteilungen 1/1970, 1–4.

Mersch 2006: Britta Mersch, *An der Uni Köln rumort es. Studentenproteste gegen Studiengebühren*. In *Deutschlandfunk*, 4 May 2006, https://www.deutschlandfunk.de/an-der-uni-koeln-rumort-es.680.de.html?dram:article_id=35512 [10 December 2018].

Meuthen 1988: Erich Meuthen, Chronik. In Kölner Universitätsgeschichte 1988. Vol. 3, 1–74.

Meuthen 1998: Erich Meuthen, *Kleine Kölner Universitätsgeschichte*. Köln 1998.

Meuthen 2001: Erich Meuthen, *Das Thomas-Institut. Vor- und Gründungsgeschichte*. In *Miscellanea Medieaevalis*. Publ. Thomas-Institut der Universität zu Köln. Vol. 29. Eds. Jan A. Aertsen and Martin Pickavé. Berlin/New York, 2001, 3–20.

Mevissen 1879: *Denkschrift des Herrn Geheimen Kommerzienrats Dr. Gustav von Mevissen in Köln, betreffend der Errichtung einer Handelsakademie in Köln, verfaßt bei Gelegenheit seiner ersten Schenkung zu diesem Zwecke im Jahre 1879*. Cologne [1900], http://www.ub.uni-koeln.de/cdm/ref/collection/koelnhs/id/9981 [6 November 2017].

Mitteilungen: *Mitteilungen der Universität zu Köln* 1971–2/1986.

Mittelstaedt 1971: Peter Mittelstaedt, *Ansprache des scheidenden Rektors Professor Dr. Peter Mittelstaedt anläßlich der Rektoratsübergabe am 15. Oktober 1971*. In KUR [N.S.] 45.1971, 27–42.

Moebius 2015: Stephan Moebius, *René König und die „Kölner Schule". Eine soziologiegeschichtliche Annäherung*. Wiesbaden, 2015.

Moebius 2017: Stephan Moebius, *Die Geschichte der Soziologie im Spiegel der „Kölner Zeitschrift für Soziologie und Sozialpsychologie* (KZfSS)". In *Soziologiegeschichte im Spiegel der „Kölner Zeitschrift für Soziologie und Sozialpsychologie"*. Eds. Hans Jürgen Andreß, Daniela Grunow and Thomas Schwinn. Wiesbaden, 2017 (*Kölner Zeitschrift für Soziologie und Sozialpsychologie*. Special edition 56/2017), 3–44.

Mohr 1997: [Joachim Mohr], *Der Zorn wächst ständig*. In *Der Spiegel* 49/1997, 32–35.

Morsey 2010: Rudolf Morsey, *Spahn, Martin*. In *Neue Deutsche Biographie* 24 (2010), 613–614, https://www.deutsche-biographie.de/gnd118615874.html#ndbcontent [10 July 2018].

Müller 2018: Rüdiger Müller, *Rowdies, Gammler, Müßiggänger! Die „KVB-Schlacht" im Oktober 1966*. In Keim/Lewejohann 2018a, 58–63.

Müller-Böling 2010: Detlef Müller-Böling, *Entfesselung von Wettbewerb. Von der Universität zum differenzierten Hochschulsystem*. In Gebrochene Wissenschaftskulturen 2010, 353–365.

Münch 2011: Richard Münch, *Akademischer Kapitalismus. Über die politische Ökonomie der Hochschulreform*. Berlin, 2011.

Nachhilfe 1988: *Nachhilfe zur Erinnerung. 600 Jahre Universität zu Köln*. Eds. Wolfgang Blaschke et al. Cologne, 1988.

Nachruf Hax 2005: *Nachruf Herbert Hax*. In *Der Spiegel* 50/2005, 206.

Nachruf Hurrelmann: *Trauer um Bettina Hurrelmann*, Obituary (Nachruf) published by Center for Reading Research and Children's and Youth Media at the University of Cologne. http://aleki.uni-koeln.de/sites/aleki/user_upload/Material/nachruf_bettina_hurrelmann.pdf [4 October 2018].

Neef 2010: Martin Neef, *Laudatio auf Heinz Vater anlässlich seiner Emeritierung im Juli 1997*. In *Linguistik und deutsche Grammatik im Fokus*. Eds. Heinz Vater and Andrzej Katny. Gdańsk, 2010, 7–12.

Nees: Kerstin Nees, *Kurt Alder*. In *Große Forscher und Forscherinnen von der Förde*, http://www.uni-kiel.de/grosse-forscher/index.php?nid=alder [4 July 2018].

Neubau Handelshochschule Cöln 1907: *Festschrift zur Eröffnung des Neubaues der Handelshochschule Cöln. 26 October 1907*. Cologne, 1907.

Neue Universität Köln 1938: *Die neue Universität Köln mit ihren Instituten und Seminaren*. Cologne, 1938.

Nipperdey 1988: *Thomas Nipperdey, Eine bürgerliche Jugend (1927–1945)*. In *Der Aquädukt 1763–1988. Ein Almanach aus dem Verlag C. H. Beck im 225. Jahr seines Bestehens*. Munich, 1988, 126–143.

Nonn 2013: Christoph Nonn, *Theodor Schieder. Ein bürgerlicher Historiker im 20. Jahrhundert*. Düsseldorf, 2013.

Nyborg 2014: Per Nyborg, *The roots of the European University Association*, EUA, April 2014, https://eua.eu/component/attachments/attachments.html?task=attachment&id=853 [21 September 2018].

Oehler/Bradatsch 1998: Christoph Oehler in collaboration with Christiane Bradatsch, *II. Hochschulen. Die Hochschulentwicklung nach 1945*. In *Handbuch der deutschen Bildungsgeschichte*. Vol. 4: *1945 bis zur Gegenwart*. Tome 1: *Bundesrepublik Deutschland*. Eds. Christoph Führ and Carl-Ludwig Furck. Munich, 1998, 412–443.

Ökologische Rheinstation: *Ökologische Rheinstation der Universität zu Köln*, https://rheinstation.uni-koeln.de/ [21 March 2019].

Opitz 1997: Silke Opitz, *Einzug eines Universalgeistes in Jena. Der bronzene „Albertus Magnus" von Gerhard Marcks im Hof des Philosophischen Instituts*. In *Weimar-Kultur-Journal. Zeitschrift für Weimar, Erfurt, Jena, Apolda*. Vol. 6, 4/1997, 21.

Ortmann 1976: R[olf] Ortmann, *Prof. Dr. Otto Veit. Ein Nachruf und ein Stück Geschichte der Kölner Anatomie*. In *Analecta anatomica* 94 (1976), 162–168.

Ortmann 1986: Rolf Ortmann, *Die jüngere Geschichte des Anatomischen Instituts der Universität zu Köln 1919–1984. 65 Jahre in bewegter Zeit*. Cologne, 1986.

Otto 2013: Martin Otto, *Stier-Somlo, Fritz*. In *Neue Deutsche Biographie* 25 (2013), 334–335; https://www.deutsche-biographie.de/gnd118982427.html#ndbcontent [21 September 2017].

Pabst 1988: Klaus Pabst, *Der Kölner Universitätsgedanke zwischen Französischer Revolution und Preußischer Reaktion (1794–1818)*. In Kölner Universitätsgeschichte 1988. Vol. 2, 1–99.

Paletschek 2006: Sylvia Paletschek, *Ermentrude und ihre Schwestern. Die ersten habilitierten Historikerinnen in Deutschland*. In *Politische Gesellschaftsgeschichte im 19. und 20. Jahrhundert. Festgabe für Barbara Vogel*. Eds. Henning Albrecht et al. Hamburg, 2006, 175–187.

Paracelsus-Medaille 1988: *Die Träger der Paracelsus-Medaille der Deutschen Ärzteschaft 1988*. In *Deutsches Ärzteblatt* 85 (1988), A 1475, https://www.aerzteblatt.de/archiv/111849/Die-Traeger-der-Paracelsus-Medaille-der-deutschen-Aerzteschaft-1988 [28 August 2018].

Paracelsus-Medaille 2005: *Die Träger der Paracelsus-Medaille der deutschen Ärzteschaft 2005*. In *Deutsches Ärzteblatt* 102 (2005), C 1009, https://www.aerzteblatt.de/archiv/46630/Die-Traeger-der-Paracelsus-Medaille-der-deutschen-Aerzteschaft-2005 [22 November 2018].

Parteigenosse 2009: *Wie wurde man Parteigenosse? Die NSDAP und ihre Mitglieder*. Ed. Wolfgang Benz. Frankfurt a.M., 2009.

Paul 2010: Johann Paul, *Reaktionen der Kölner Studentenschaft auf den Radikalenerlass von 1972*. In *Geschichte in Köln* 57 (2010), 163–187.

Peil 1988: Peter Peil with contributions by Ernst Heinen, Heribert Jussen and Wilhelm Koll, *Die akademischen Einrichtungen und ihre Leiter 1919–1987*. In Kölner Universitätsgeschichte 1988. Vol. 3, 85–275.

Pfeifen an den Unis 1993: *Pfeifen an den Unis*. In *Der Spiegel* 45/1993, 61–65.

Pflüger 2017: Hans-Joachim Pflüger, *Professor Ernst Bresslau, Founder of the Zoology Departments at the Universities of Cologne and Sao Paulo: Lessons to Learn from His Life history*. In *Zoology* 122, (2017), 1–6.

Pichlmaier 2005: EB, *Geburtstage: Heinz Pichlmaier*. In *Deutsches Ärzteblatt* 102 (2005), A 3136, https://www.aerzteblatt.de/archiv/49079/Geburtstage [22 November 2018].

Planitz 1929: [Hans] Planitz, [Speech at the cornerstone laying ceremony for the new university building on 26 October 1929.] In KUR 24.1930, 34–36.

Plassmann/Süssmuth 2015: Max Plassmann/Hans Süssmuth, *Heinrich-Heine Universität Düsseldorf. Von der Gründung bis zur Exzellenz*. Düsseldorf, 2015.

Platthaus 2006: Andreas Platthaus, *Alfred Herrhausen. Eine deutsche Karriere*. Berlin, 2006.

Plessner 2001: Helmuth Plessner, *Erinnerungen an Max Scheler*. In *Helmuth Plessner: Politik – Anthropologie – Philosophie. Aufsätze und Vorträge*. Eds. Salvatore Giammusso and Hans-Ulrich Lessing. Munich, 2001, 337–346.

Potthoff/Sieben 1988: Erich Potthoff/Günter Sieben, *Eugen Schmalenbach (1873 bis 1955)*. In *Betriebswirte in Köln. Über den Beitrag Kölner Betriebswirte zur Entwicklung der Betriebswirtschaftslehre*. Ed. Friedrich-Wilhelm Henning. Cologne/Vienna, 1988, 1–33.

Preisliste: List of awards (Preisliste) granted by the German Chemical Society, https://www.gdch.de/gdch/preise-und-auszeichnungen/gdch-preise.html [8 August 2018].

PreisträgerInnnen: *PreisträgerInnen*, https://portal.uni-koeln.de/universitaet/universitaet-auf-einen-blick/preistraegerinnen [12 November 2018].

Promovierende: Promovierende (doctoral candidates), https://www.portal.uni-koeln.de/9541.html [28 March 2019].

Protest gegen Bildungssystem: *Protest gegen Bildungssystem. „Bildungsstreik": Studenten bekommen prominente Unterstützung*. Koeln.de, 26 November 2009, https://www.koeln.de/koeln/bildungsstreik_studenten_bekommen_prominente_unterstuetzung_246542.html [12 December 2018].

Ptak 2004: Ralf Ptak, *Vom Ordoliberalismus zur Sozialen Marktwirtschaft. Stationen des Neoliberalismus in Deutschland*. Wiesbaden, 2004.

Rektorenportrait Bohne: Rector profile Gotthold Bohne, https://rektorenportraits.uni-koeln.de/rektoren/gotthold_bohne/ [27 February 2018].

Rektorenportrait Fellerer: Rector profile Karl Gustav Fellerer, https://rektorenportraits.uni-koeln.de/rektoren/karl_gustav_fellerer/ [23 February 2019].

Rektorenportrait Hübner: Rector profile Heinz Hübner, https://rektorenportraits.uni-koeln.de/rektoren/heinz_huebner [18 October 2018].

Rektorenportrait Jahrreiß: Rector profile Hermann Jahrreiß, https://rektorenportraits.uni-koeln.de/rektoren/hermann_jahrreiss/ [4 July 2018].

Rektorenportrait Kuske: Rector profile Bruno Kuske, https://rektorenportraits.uni-koeln.de/rektoren/bruno_kuske/ [13 June 2018].

Rektorenportrait Mittelstaedt: Rector profile Peter Mittelstaedt, https://rektorenportraits.uni-koeln.de/rektoren/peter_mittelstaedt/ [22 November 2018].

Rektorenportrait Moritz: Rector profile Friedrich Moritz, https://rektorenportraits.uni-koeln.de/rektoren/friedrich_moritz [10 February 2019].

Rektorenportrait Peters: Rector profile Hans Peters, https://rektorenportraits.uni-koeln.de/rektoren/hans_peters [25 July 2018].

Rektorenportrait Schieder: Rector profile Theodor Schieder, https://rektorenportraits.uni-koeln.de/rektoren/theodor_schieder [18 October 2018].

Rektorenportrait Stern: Rector profile Klaus Stern, https://rektorenportraits.uni-koeln.de/rektoren/klaus_stern/ [28 February 2019].

Rektorenportrait Stier-Somlo: Rector profile Fritz Stier-Somlo, https://rektorenportraits.uni-koeln.de/rektoren/fritz_stier_somlo [10 February 2019].

Rektorenportrait Tönnis: Rector profile Wilhelm Tönnis, https://rektorenportraits.uni-koeln.de/rektoren/wilhelm_toennis/ [27 February 2018].

Riegel 1996: Ernst Riegel, *Goldschmied zwischen Historismus und Werkbund*. Compiled by Carl Benno Heller and Wolfgang Glüber. Heidelberg, 1996.

Risse 2016: Dirk Risse, *Kölner Uniklinik: Computer steuern Container zehn Meter unter der Erde*. In *Kölner Stadt-Anzeiger*, 26 June 2016, https://www.ksta.de/koeln/koeln-archiv/koelner-uniklinik-computer-steuern-container-zehn-meter-unter-der-erde-24285576 [20 March 2019].

Rosenbaum 2003: Wilhelm Rosenbaum, *Jenny Gusyk. Jüdin, Türkin, Solingerin. Die Biografie der ersten Studentin an der Universität zu Köln*. Solingen, 2003.

Rothblatt 2010: Sheldon Rothblatt, *Das Studium*. In *Geschichte der Universität in Europa*. Ed. Walter Rüegg. Vol. 4: *Vom Zweiten Weltkrieg bis zum Ende des 20. Jahrhunderts*. Munich, 2010, 217–247.

Rothkopf/Tomson 1995: Gabriele Rothkopf/Christel Tomson, *Frauenförderung ist Hochschulreform*. In *Genia – Nur für Frauen. Lese- und Handbuch für Studentinnen*. Ed. Frauenbeauftragte der Universität zu Köln. Cologne, 1995, 127–132.

Rückert 1999: Joachim Rückert, *Nipperdey, Hans Carl*. In *Neue Deutsche Biographie* 19 (1999), 280–282. https://www.deutsche-biographie.de/gnd118735519.html#ndbcontent [22 September 2017].

Rudorf 1989: Friedhelm Rudorf, *Interviews mit den Dekanen der Kölner Fakultäten anlässlich der Fakultätswochen im Sommersemester 1988*. In Hansmeyer/Henning/Huintges 1989, 47–79.

Rüegg 2004: Walter Rüegg, *Themen, Probleme, Erkenntnisse:* In *Geschichte der Universität in Europa*. Ed. Walter Rüegg. Vol. 3: *Vom 19. Jahrhundert zum Zweiten Weltkrieg (1800–1945)*. Munich, 2004, 17–41.

Rüegg 2010: Walter Rüegg, *Themen, Probleme, Erkenntnisse:* In *Geschichte der Universität in Europa*. Ed. Walter Rüegg. Vol. 4: *Vom Zweiten Weltkrieg bis zum Ende des 20. Jahrhunderts*. Munich, 2010, 21–45.

Rürup 2017: Miriam Rürup, *Alltag und Gesellschaft*. Paderborn, 2017.

Saedler 2004: Heinz Saedler, *Nachruf Jozef Stefaan Schell*. In *Max-Planck-Gesellschaft. Jahrbuch 2004*. Ed. Max-Planck-Gesellschaft. Munich, 2004, 119f.

Sauter 1969: Fritz Sauter, *Die Mathematisch-Naturwissenschaftliche Fakultät*. In Katner 1969, 82–98.

Schäfer 2013: Martina Schäfer, *Die Geschichte des Instituts für Ur- und Frühgeschichte an der Universität zu Köln 1925–1945*. In *Archäologie und Bodendenkmalpflege in der Rheinprovinz 1920–1945*. Eds. Jürgen Kunow, Thomas Otten and Jan Bemmann. [Bonn], 2013, 315–330.

Schallner 2007: Berit Schallner, *Repressionen, Restriktionen, Vorschriften: Kölner Studierende im Visier des Regimes*. In *Zwischen „Endsieg" und Examen. Studieren an der Universität Köln 1943–1948. Brüche und Kontinuitäten*. Eds. Margit Szöllösi-Janze et al. Nümbrecht, 2007, 19–38.

Schallner 2012: Berit Schallner, *Kameradinnen im Dienste der Volksgemeinschaft? Studentinnen an der Kölner Universität in Kriegs- und Nachkriegszeit*. In *Jahrbuch des Kölnischen Geschichtsvereins* 81 (2012), 297–355.

Schaper/Schaper 1995: W. Schaper/J. Schaper, *Bruno Kisch, Leben und Werk. Ein Versuch*. In *Zeitschrift für Kardiologie* 84/Suppl. 4 (1995), 1–10. https://historischesarchiv.dgk.org/files/2015/03/Schaper-W.-Bruno-Kisch-Leben-und-Werk.pdf [18 February 2018].

Scheid 1967: [Werner Scheid,] *Jahresbericht des Rektors*. In JB 1967, 13–15.

Scheuch 1990: Erwin K. Scheuch, *Ein wertloser Bericht*. In *Journal* 1/1990, 49–52.

Schieder 1968: Theodor Schieder, *Forschung und Universitätsstruktur*. In JB 1968, 15–20.

Schiedermair: *Dr. iur. Hartmut Schiedermair em. o. Univ.-Professor für Öffentliches Recht, Völkerrecht und Rechtsphilosophie. Lebenslauf* (January 2005), https://www.hochschulverband.de/fileadmin/redaktion/download/pdf/rest/schiedermair-ll.pdf [8 November 2018].

Schildt 1997: Axel Schildt, *Im Kern gesund? Die deutschen Hochschulen 1945*. In *Vertuschte Vergangenheit. Der Fall Schwerte und die NS-Vergangenheit der deutschen Hochschulen*. Eds. Helmut König, Wolfgang Kuhlmann and Klaus Schwabe. Munich, 1997, 223–240.

Schildt 1999: Axel Schildt, *Zwischen Abendland und Amerika. Studien zur westdeutschen Ideenlandschaft der 50er Jahre*. Munich, 1999.

Schmaus 1979: Michael Schmaus, *Koch, Joseph*. In *Neue Deutsche Biographie* 12 (1979), 268f., https://www.deutsche-biographie.de/pnd116272651.html#ndbcontent [26 July 2018].

Schmidt 2004: Klaus Schmidt, *Das gefährdete Leben. Der Kölner Arzt und Gesundheitspolitiker Franz Vonessen (1892–1970)*. Cologne, 2004.

Schmölders 1966: [Günter Schmölders,] *Jahresbericht des Rektors*. In JB 1966, 11–14.

Schneider 2007: Dieter Schneider, *Schmalenbach, Eugen*. In *Neue Deutsche Biographie* 23 (2007), 118–119, https://www.deutsche-biographie.de/gnd118608452.html#ndbcontent [11 February 2018].

Schneider, C. 2007: Carsten Schneider, *Die „Kleidungsnot" der Kölner Studierenden*. In *Zwischen „Endsieg" und Examen. Studieren an der Universität Köln 1943–1948. Brüche und Kontinuitäten*. Ed. Margit Szöllösi-Janze. Nümbrecht, 2007, 84–86.

Schneider 2008: Helmuth Schneider, *Werner Eck und die Erforschung der römischen Wasserversorgung. Laudatio für Werner Eck*. In Werner Eck, *Roms Wassermanagement im Osten. Staatliche Steuerung des öffentlichen Lebens in den römischen Provinzen? Vortrag anlässlich der Ehrenpromotion am 17. Januar 2007*. Kassel, 2008, 9–20.

Schramm 1969: O. Schramm, *Das Staatliche Studienkolleg für ausländische Studierende*. In Katner 1969, 147.

Schumacher 1903: Hermann Schumacher, *Die städtische Handels-Hochschule in Cöln, die erste selbständige Handels-Hochschule in Deutschland*. Berlin/Heidelberg, 1903.

Schwab 2013: Michael Schwab, *Walter Stokar von Neuforn (1901–1958)*. In *Archäologie und Bodendenkmalpflege in der Rheinprovinz 1920–1945*. Eds. Jürgen Kunow, Thomas Otten and Jan Bemmann. [Bonn], 2013, 331–351.

Schwanke 2018: Enno Schwanke, *„Ein Beitrag zum Umsturz der staatlichen Ordnung"? Die Ausstellung „Ungesühnte Nazijustiz" in Köln*. In Keim/Lewejohann 2018a, 184–189.

Schwarz 1986: Hans-Peter Schwarz, *Adenauer. Der Aufstieg: 1876–1952*. Stuttgart, 1986.

Seibold 2004: Eugen Seibold, *Martin Schwarzbach; 7. Dezember 1907–24. Dezember 2003*. In *Geologische Rundschau* 93 (2004), 652–655.

Sender Kölncampus: *Der Sender Kölncampus*, https://www.koelncampus.com/sender/ [24 March 2019].

Shanghai-Ranking 2003: *Academic Ranking of World Universities 2003*, http://www.shanghairanking.com/arwu2003.html [26 February 2019].

Shanghai-Ranking 2006: *Academic Ranking of World Universities 2006*, http://www.shanghairanking.com/arwu2006.html [26 February 2019].

Sieg 2013: Ulrich Sieg, *Geist und Gewalt. Deutsche Philosophen zwischen Kaiserreich und Nationalsozialismus*. Munich, 2013.

Sofja Kovalevskaja-Preis: *Sofja Kovalevskaja Award*, https://www.humboldt-foundation.de/en/explore/newsroom/dossier-sofja-kovalevskaja-award [15 February 2019].

Sofja Kovalevskaja-Preis 2002: *Sofja Kovalevskaja Award 2002 – Award Winners*, https://www.humboldt-foundation.de/en/explore/newsroom/dossier-sofja-kovalevskaja-award/sofja-kovalevskaja-award-winners-2002 [15 February 2019].

Sonderforschungsbereiche 1997: *Sonderforschungsbereiche in Nordrhein-Westfalen*. Ed. Ministry of Science and Research of North Rhine-Westphalia. Cologne, 1997.

Spitzenforschung für die Gesellschaft: *Zukunftskonzept. Spitzenforschung für die Gesellschaft*, https://www.portal.uni-koeln.de/11498.html [28 March 2019].

Starlinger: *Peter Starlinger (18th March 1931 to 1st September 2017)*, https://www.mpipz.mpg.de/4506635/starlinger [15 November 2018].

Stier-Somlo 1926: Fritz Stier-Somlo, *Ansprache und Verwaltungsbericht*. In *Reden zur Gründungsfeier der Universität Köln am 15. Mai 1926*. In KUR 15.1926, 3–15.

Stoffel: *Professor Dr. rer. nat., Dr. med., Dr. h.c. Wilhelm Stoffel*, http://www.awk.nrw.de/akademie/klassen/naturmedizin/ordentliche-mitglieder/stoffel-wilhelm.html [21 November 2018].

Stoffel CV: *Prof. Dr. med. Dr. rer. nat. Dr. h.c. Wilhelm Stoffel – Curriculum Vitae*, https://www.cmmc-uni-koeln.de/research/cmmc-researchers/wilhelm-stoffel-curriculum-vitae [21 November 2018].

Stölting 1986: Erhard Stölting, *Akademische Soziologie in der Weimarer Republik*. Berlin, 1986.

Strauch 2007: Friedrich Strauch, *Martin Schwarzbach – ein Leben für die Paläoklimatologie*. In *Geohistorische Blätter* 9/10 (2007) 1–2, 161–168.

Streeck: Nina Streeck, *Dorothee Sölle*, http://www.rheinische-geschichte.lvr.de/Persoenlichkeiten/dorothee-soelle/DE-2086/lido/57c9529636ad16.61654631 [29 July 2018].

Streiter 2008: Axel Streiter, *Der Zauber der runden Zahl*. In *40 Jahre Sonderforschungsbereiche*. Ed. Deutsche Forschungsgemeinschaft. Berlin, 2008 (*duz Special*, September 2008; supplement to *duz – das unabhängige Hochschulmagazin*, 19 September 2008), 6f., http://www.dfg.de/download/pdf/foerderung/programme/sfb/spektrum_beiheft_sfb_0809.pdf [14 November 2018].

Strohmeier 1998: Renate Strohmeier, *Lexikon der Naturwissenschaftlerinnen und naturkundigen Frauen Europas. Von der Antike bis zum 20. Jahrhundert*. Thun/Frankfurt a.M., 1998, 129f.

Studienführer 1980/81: *Universität zu Köln. Studienführer* 1980/81. Ed. Rektor der Universität zu Köln Professor Dr. Herbert Wiedemann. Cologne, 1980.

Studienführer 1989/90: *Universität zu Köln. Studienführer* 1989/90. Ed. Rektor der Universität zu Köln Professor Dr. Peter Hanau. Cologne, 1989.

Studiobühneköln: studiobühneköln, *Über uns*, https://studiobuehnekoeln.de/ueber-uns/ [22 February 2019].

Sudmann 2014: Stefan R. Sudmann, *In memoriam. Prof. Dr. Anna Gisela Johnen (1925–2014)*. In *Charadrius* 50 (2014), issue 1, 105–106.

Szöllösi-Janze/Freitäger 2005: Margit Szöllösi-Janze/Andreas Freitäger, *„Doktorgrad entzogen!" Aberkennung akademischer Titel an der Universität Köln 1933 bis 1945*. Nümbrecht, 2005.

Tenure Track: *Tenure Track und Juniorprofessuren*, https://strategy.uni-koeln.de/hochschulentwicklung_und_evaluationen/tenure_track_und_juniorprofessuren/index_ger.html [28 March 2019]

Thieß 1924a: Karl Thieß, *Politik und Hochschulunterricht*. In Thieß, *Universität im Kampf. Zwei Rektoratsreden*. Cologne, 1924 (KUR 10), 8–18.

Thieß 1924b: Karl Thieß, *Der Geist des deutschen Studiums*. In Thieß, *Universität im Kampf. Zwei Rektoratsreden*. Cologne, 1924 (KUR 10), 24–34.

Third Mission: *Third Mission*, https://www.portal.uni-koeln.de/13928.html [28 March 2019].

Thümmler 2012: Ellen Thümmler, *Ferdinand A. Hermens und die Formel der Demokratie*. In *Intellektuelle Emigranten. Zur Aktualität eines historischen Phänomens. Festgabe für Prof. Dr. Alfons Söllner*. Eds. Frank Schale, Ellen Thümmler and Michael Vollmer. Wiesbaden, 2012, 155–184.

Thyssen Stiftung 1985: *Fritz Thyssen Stiftung. Jahresbericht* 1984/85. Cologne, 1985.

Tiedau 2009: Ulrich Tiedau, *In memoriam: Marta Baerlecken (1909–2007)*. In *Internationale Neerlandistiek* 47 (2009), issue 3, S. 96.

Tiggemann 2008: Anselm Tiggemann, *Der Zentralbau des Universitätsklinikums Köln. Ein Klinikum der Superlative*. In Festschrift Lindenburg 2008, 135–146.

Titze 1987: Hartmut Titze, *Das Hochschulstudium in Preußen und Deutschland 1820–1944*. Göttingen, 1987.

Titze 1989: Hartmut Titze, *II. Hochschulen*. In *Handbuch der deutschen Bildungsgeschichte*. Vol. V. *1918–1945. Die Weimarer Republik und die nationalsozialistische Diktatur*. Eds. Dieter Langewiesche and Heinz-Elmar Tenorth. Munich, 1989, 209–240.

Treß 2008: Werner Treß, *„Wider den undeutschen Geist". Bücherverbrennung 1933*. Berlin, 2008.

Trier 2007: Wolfgang Trier, *Entwicklung des Rechenzentrums der Universität zu Köln*. In *Engagierte Verwaltung für die Wissenschaft. Festschrift für Johannes Neyses, Kanzler der Universität zu Köln, zum 60. Geburtstag*. Eds. Peter Hanau et al. Cologne, 2007, 513–528.

Über a.r.t.e.s.: *Über a.r.t.e.s. Profil*, http://artes.phil-fak.uni-koeln.de/14072.html [25 March 2019].

Über Grünberg: *Über Peter Grünberg (1939–2018)*, http://www.fz-juelich.de/pgi/DE/UeberUns/AboutPeterGruenberg/_node.html;jsessionid=8000F0887CC1E04E5035989DE2D52E05 [13 November 2018].

Universität Köln 1925: *Die Universität Köln im ersten Jahrfünft nach ihrer Wiederaufrichtung 1919 bis 1924*. Cologne, 1925.

Universität Köln 1929: *Universität Köln 1919–1929*. [Cologne, 1929].

Universitätsführer 1951: *Universitätsführer der Universität zu Köln 1951*. Ed. Studentenausschuss. Cologne, 1951.

Universitäts-Journal: *Kölner Universitäts-Journal. Berichte aus der Universität zu Köln* 4/1992–2/2006.

Universitätsmagazin: *Kölner Universitätsmagazin* 2015–2018.

Universitätspreis 2018: *Ausschreibung des Universitätspreises 2018*, https://www.portal.uni-koeln.de/universitaetspreis.html [10 March 2019].

Universitätszeitung: *Kölner Universitätszeitung* 3/2007–2014.

UzK Zentren: *UzK Zentren*, https://www.portal.uni-koeln.de/12214.html [28 March 2019].

van Dijk 2010: Saskia van Dijk, *„Entnazifizierungsklüngel". Die Personalpolitik der Universität zu Köln in der Nachkriegszeit*. In *Schlagschatten auf das „braune Köln". Die NS-Zeit und danach*. Eds. Jost Dülffer and Margit Szöllösi-Janze. Cologne, 2010, 269–286.

van Dyk/Schauer 2014: Silke van Dyk/Alexandra Schauer, *„... daß die offizielle Soziologie versagt hat". Zur Soziologie im Nationalsozialismus, der Geschichte ihrer Aufarbeitung und der Rolle der DGS*. 2nd edition. Wiesbaden, 2014.

van Eyll 1990: Klara van Eyll: *Der Gedanke zur Gründung einer Universität oder einer Handelshochschule in Köln bei Gustav Mevissen*. In *Handelsakademie – Handelshochschule – Wirtschafts- und Sozialwissenschaftliche Fakultät. Der Weg von der Handelsakademie und Handlungswissenschaft des 18. Jahrhunderts zur Wirtschafts- und Sozialwissenschaftlichen Fakultät und Betriebswirtschaftslehre des 20. Jahrhunderts*. Ed. Friedrich-Wilhelm Henning. Cologne/Vienna, 1990, 21–38.

Van Montagu 2003: Marc Van Montagu, *Obituary: Jeff Schell (1935–2003)*. In *Nature*, Vol. 423 (2003), 934.

Velke 2010: Marcus Velke, *Zwischen Universität und Lagerleben. Zum Studium von Displaced Persons in Bonn und Köln*. In *Geschichte im Westen* 25 (2010), 177–207.

Verfassung 1963: *Verfassung der Universität zu Köln*. [Cologne, 1963].

Vergleichsmikroskop 1936: *Vergleichsmikroskop für kriminalistische Zwecke mit photographischer Einrichtung*. Ed. Ernst Leitz. Wetzlar, 1936.

Verstraete 2003: W. Verstraete, *Jeff Schell, obituary*. In *Environmental Microbiology* 5 (2003), 537f.

Vita Baum: Vita Gerhart Baum, https://gerhart-baum.de/vita/ [9 August 2018].

Vita Donges: *Vita Juergen B. Donges*. In *Weltwirtschaftlicher Strukturwandel, nationale Wirtschaftspolitik und politische Rationalität. Festschrift für Juergen B. Donges zum 65. Geburtstag*. Ed. Andreas Freytag. Cologne, 2005, 301–304.

Vogt 2008a: Sina Vogt, *Uniklinik Köln 2008. Medizin und Forschung in Schlaglichtern*. In Festschrift Lindenburg 2008, 151–161.

Vogt 2008b: Sina Vogt, *"Leadership in Stroke Medicine Award" geht an Prof. Dr. Wolf-Dieter Heiss aus Köln*, 26. September 2008, https://idw-online.de/de/news280082 [26 September 2018].

vom Hagen 2007: Doreen vom Hagen, *Die Wohnsituation der Studierenden*. In *Zwischen „Endsieg" und Examen. Studieren an der Universität Köln 1943–1948. Brüche und Kontinuitäten*. Ed. Margit Szöllösi-Janze. Nümbrecht, 2007, 71–77.

Von akademischen Obrigkeiten: *Von akademischen Obrigkeiten und ihren Zeichen*, https://uniarchiv.uni-koeln.de/ausstellungen-publikationen/ausstellungen-des-archivs/onlineausstellung-zeit-vergleiche-2013/von-akademischen-obrigkeiten [10 June 2018].

von der Leyen 1960: Friedrich von der Leyen, *Leben und Freiheit der Hochschule. Erinnerungen*. Cologne, 1960.

Vongehr 2007: Thomas Vongehr, *Kurze Geschichte des Husserl-Archivs in Leuven und der Husserl-Edition*. In *Geschichte des Husserl-Archivs Leuven*. Ed. Husserl Archives Leuven. Dordrecht, 2007, 71–98.

Vorlesungsverzeichnis 1920/21: *Vorlesungsverzeichnis der Universität Köln. Winter-Semester 1920/21*. Cologne, 1920.

Voßkamp: *Prof. (em.) Wilhelm Voßkamp. Biographisches*, http://idsl1.phil-fak.uni-koeln.de/10230.html [13 November 2018].

Wagner 1969: Wolfgang Wagner, *Bauplanung und Baufortschritt der Universität*. In Katner 1969, 195–197.

Wagner 1975: W[olfgang] Wagner, *Jahresbericht des Kanzlers*. In JB 1975, 34f.

Walter 1977: Heinz Walter, *Kisch, Bruno*. In *Neue Deutsche Biographie* 11 (1977), 680–682, https://www.deutsche-biographie.de/pnd11619328X.html [14 August 2018].

Wanko 2008: Christoph Wanko, *Auftakt für exzellente Alternsforschung. CECAD-Cologne geht an den Start*. In Universitätszeitung 2/2008, 7.

Weber 2003: Regina Weber, *Alewyn, Richard Wolfram*. In *Internationales Germanistenlexikon 1800–1950*. Ed. Christoph König. Vol. 1. Berlin/NewYork, 2003, 18–21.

Website CCG: Cologne Center for Genomics website, http://portal.ccg.uni-koeln.de/ccg/ [28 March 2019].

Website CECAD: CECAD website, http://www.cecad.uni-koeln.de/home/ [23 March 2019].

Website CEPLAS: CEPLAS website, https://www.ceplas.eu/en/home/ [25 March 2019].

Website CIO: CIO website, https://www.cio-koeln-bonn.de/ [24 March 2019].

Website CMMC: Center for Molecular Medicine Cologne website, https://www.cmmc-uni-koeln.de/home/ [24 March 2019].

Website German U15: German U15 website, https://www.german-u15.de/ [28 March 2019].

Website GSSC: GSSC | Global South Studies Center website, https://gssc.uni-koeln.de/ [28 March 2019].

Website mediomix: mediomix. Real Science Communication website, http://www.mediomix.de/ [24 March 2019].

Website ML4Q: ML4Q. Matter and Light for Quantum Computing website, https://ml4q.de/ [28 March 2019].

Website Stern: Prof. Dr. Dr. h.c. mult. Klaus Stern website, http://www.klaus-stern.net/ [28 February 2019].

Wehefritz 1995: Valentin Wehefritz, *Ein Herz leidet an Deutschland – Prof. Dr. Ernst Bresslau (1877–1935). Ein deutsches Gelehrtenschicksal im 20. Jahrhundert*. Dortmund, 1995.

Wehler 2003: Hans-Ulrich Wehler, *Deutsche Gesellschaftsgeschichte*. Vol. 4. *Vom Beginn des Ersten Weltkriegs bis zur Gründung der beiden deutschen Staaten 1914–1949*. 2nd revised edition. Munich, 2003.

Wehler 2008: Hans-Ulrich Wehler, *Deutsche Gesellschaftsgeschichte*. Vol. 5. *Bundesrepublik und DDR 1949–1990*. Munich, 2008.

Weinke 2013: Annette Weinke, *Hermann Jahrreiß (1894–1992). Vom Exponenten des völkerrechtlichen „Kriegseinsatzes" zum Verteidiger der deutschen Eliten in Nürnberg*. In Kölner Juristen 2013, 163–195.

Weisbrod 2002: Bernd Weisbrod, *Dem wandelbaren Geist. Akademisches Ideal und wissenschaftliche Transformation in der Nachkriegszeit*. In *Akademische Vergangenheitspolitik. Beiträge zur Wissenschaftskultur der Nachkriegszeit*. Ed. Bernd Weisbrod. Göttingen, 2002, 11–35.

Weller 2013: Marc-Philippe Weller, *Heinrich Lehmann (1876–1963). Ein Pionier des Privat- und Wirtschaftsrechts*. In Kölner Juristen 2013, 33–52.

Wenge 2005: Nicola Wenge, *Integration und Ausgrenzung in der städtischen Gesellschaft. Eine jüdisch-nichtjüdische Beziehungsgeschichte Kölns 1918–1933*. Mainz, 2005.

Wenkel 2013: Simone Wenkel, *Die Molekularbiologie in Deutschland von 1945 bis 1975 – Ein internationaler Vergleich*. Diss. Cologne, 2013.

Wetzell 2000: Richard F. Wetzell, *Inventing the Criminal. A History of German Criminology, 1880–1945*. Chapel Hill, 2000.

Wiedemann 1980: [Herbert Wiedemann,] *Jahresbericht 1980*. In JB 1980, 11f.

Wiese 1957: Leopold von Wiese, *Erinnerungen*. Cologne/Opladen, 1957.

Willeke 1978: Rainer Willeke, *Jahresbericht des Rektors*. In JB 1978, 12–19.

Willeke 1979: [Rainer Willeke,] *Jahresbericht des Rektors*. In JB 1979, 12–16.

Winnewisser et al. 1982: G. Winnewisser et al., *Das neue 3 m-Radioteleskop der Universität Köln*. In *Mitteilungen der Astronomischen Gesellschaft* 55 (1982), 157–159.

Wissenschaftspreis 2000: *Wissenschaftspreis für Deutschdidaktik zum zweiten Mal vergeben*. In *Der Deutschunterricht* 52 (2000), 110.

Wittka 1995a: Marina Wittka, *Die Anfänge des Frauenstudiums im Köln des Kaiserreichs*. In *Genia – Nur für Frauen. Lese- und Handbuch für Studentinnen*. Ed. Frauenbeauftragte der Universität zu Köln. Cologne, 1995, 23–41.

Wittka 1995b: Marina Wittka, *Geschichte des Frauenstudiums in Köln*. In *Genia – Nur für Frauen. Lese- und Handbuch für Studentinnen*. Ed. Frauenbeauftragte der Universität zu Köln. Cologne, 1995, 42–96.

Wittka 1995c: Marina Wittka, *Nach den Meilensteinen der Vergangenheit die Stolpersteine der Gegenwart. Studentinnen und Akademikerinnen am Ende des 20. Jahrhunderts*. In *Genia – Nur für Frauen. Lese- und Handbuch für Studentinnen*. Ed. Frauenbeauftragte der Universität zu Köln. Cologne, 1995, 97–100.

Wolf-Pommrich 1960: Hedda Wolf-Pommrich, *Handbuch für die Stenotypistin und Sekretärin im Bank- und Sparkassenwesen. Handbuch für Sekretariatstechnik in Banken und Sparkassen*. Wiesbaden, 1960.

Wortmann 1980: Michael Wortmann, *Der Nationalsozialistische Deutsche Studentenbund an der Universität Köln (1927–1933)*. In *Geschichte in Köln* 8 (1980), 101–118.

Wunder 1993: Dieter Wunder, *Die Misere deutscher Bildungspolitik und ihre strukturellen Ursachen – Wohin geht die Reise?* In *Gewerkschaftliche Monatshefte* 11 (1993), 669–683.

Zahlen – Daten – Fakten 2004: *Zahlen – Daten – Fakten 2004*. Ed. Tassilo Küpper, Rektor der Universität zu Köln. Cologne, 2005.

Zahlen – Daten – Fakten 2006: *Zahlen – Daten – Fakten 2006*. Ed. Axel Freimuth, Rektor der Universität zu Köln. Cologne, 2007.

Zahlen | Daten | Fakten 2011/12: *Zahlen | Daten | Fakten*. Ed. Stabsstelle 01 – Planung und Controlling der Universität zu Köln on behalf of the rector. Cologne, 2012.

Zahlen | Daten | Fakten 2016: *Zahlen | Daten | Fakten*. Ed. Rektor der Universität zu Köln. Cologne, 2017.

Zahlen | Daten | Fakten 2017: *Zahlen | Daten | Fakten*. Ed. Rektor der Universität zu Köln. Cologne, 2018.

Zander 2004: Gunther Herbert Zander, *Gründung der Handelshochschulen im deutschen Kaiserreich (1898–1919)*. Diss. Cologne, 2004.

Zeiß 1931: Carl Zeiß, *Schreib-Projektionsapparat „Belsazar"*. Jena, 1931.

Image Credits

Despite extensive efforts, it was unfortunately not possible to find suitable images of adequate quality for all biographies.

Foreword

P. 4/5: drawing by Simon Jefferson.

Chapter 1

P. 14: UAK 614/87, detail.

P. 16: UAK 10c/04.

P. 19 top: Rheinisches Bildarchiv Köln, Emil Hermann, rba_166742.

P. 19 bottom: Christian Eckert: *Die städtische Handels-Hochschule in Cöln. Bericht über das fünfte Studienjahr*. Cologne, 1906, plate following p. 128.

P. 20 top: postcard.

P. 20 bottom: ullstein bild, photo by A. & E. Frankl.

P. 23 top: ullstein bild, photo by A. & E. Frankl.

P. 23 bottom: UAK 624/36.

P. 24 top: Rheinisches Bildarchiv Köln, circa 1908/1912, rba_062611.

P. 24 bottom: Rheinisches Bildarchiv Köln, rba_062622.

P. 27: UAK 614/87.

P. 29 top: Rheinisches Bildarchiv Köln, circa 1938, rba_165547.

P. 29 bottom: *Festschrift zur Eröffnung des Neubaues der Handelshochschule Cöln. 26.10.1907*. Cologne, 1907, 41.

P. 30/31: Rheinisches Bildarchiv Köln, rba_062570.

Chapter 2

P. 32: UAK 20/299, detail.

P. 36: *Kölner Universitäts-Zeitung*, 20 September 1919, no. 1, front page.

P. 39 top: UAK 20/299.

P. 39 bottom: UAK 20/299.

P. 40: ullstein bild/ullstein bild, detail.

P. 43: *Warum studiere ich in Köln*. Cologne, 1928, cover.

P. 44 left: UAK 20/273, undated.

P. 44 right: Rheinisches Bildarchiv Köln, rba_112651, before 1935.

P. 45: Rheinisches Bildarchiv Köln, August Kreyenkamp, rba_078226, 1931.

P. 46: *Festschrift zur Eröffnung des Neubaues der Handelshochschule Cöln*. 26 October 1907. Cologne, 1907, 53.

P. 48: UAK 614/141.

P. 49: Kölnisches Stadtmuseum, photo by Judith Fröhlich.

P. 50: UAK 20/299.

P. 52 left: UAK 20/146, undated.

P. 52 right: Historisches Archiv der Stadt Köln. Ingrid Bohn, Corinne Grabosch, Waltraud Siebke, Verena Staack, Kristina Wolff, *Wissenschaftlerinnen an der Christiana Albertina. Zu den Lebens- und Arbeitszusammenhängen der ersten Kieler Hochschullehrerinnen – Fragestellungen und biographische Skizzen*. In *Demokratische Geschichte. Jahrbuch für Schleswig-Holstein* 14 (2001), 15–54. Photo p. 26, undated.

P. 53 left: ullstein bild/ullstein bild, 1928.

P. 53 right: ullstein bild/ullstein bild, 1930.

P. 55: UAK 614/175.

P. 56: Universität zu Köln, Abt. Presse und Kommunikation.

P. 57: UAK 689/110.

P. 58: UAK 20/299.

P. 60 left: ullstein bild/ullstein bild, 1933.

P. 60 right: Rheinisches Bildarchiv Köln, rba_112665, 1925/26.

P. 61 left: UAK 20/162, undated.

P. 61 right: UAK 20/56, undated.

P. 63: UAK 70/52.

P. 64: UAK 614/199.

P. 65: Theaterwissenschaftliche Sammlung, University of Cologne, Wassily Kandinsky, *Scene XVI–The Great Gate of Kiev*, Mussorgsky's *Pictures at an Exhibition*, Dessau 1928.

Chapter 3

P. 66: UAK 20/299, detail.

P. 70 top: UAK 20/319.

P. 70 bottom: UAK 20/299.

P. 73 top: UAK 624/26.

P. 73 bottom: UAK 20/299.

P. 74 top: UAK 20/300.

P. 74 bottom: NS-Dokumentationszentrum der Stadt Köln, Bp 3344.

P. 77: Rheinisches Bildarchiv Köln, rba_168534.

P. 78: UAK 20/246, undated.

P. 79 left: Bildarchiv des Mathematischen Forschungsinstituts Oberwolfach, undated.

P. 79 right: Bundesarchiv, R 9361-VIII KARTEI 5331360, 1935.

P. 80: *Westdeutscher Beobachter*, no. 113, 18 May 1933.

P. 82: Ella Bieroth, *Schau Westdeutscher Wirtschaft*. Cologne, 1933, 15.

P. 83: Bundesarchiv, R 9361-VIII KARTEI / 2070531, 1933.

P. 85: NS-Dokumentationszentrum der Stadt Köln.

P. 88 left: UAK 20/35, undated.

P. 88 right: UAK 20/155, 1938.

P. 89 left: UAK 20/279, undated.

P. 89 right: UAK 20/295, undated.

P. 91: UAK 386/318.

P. 92: UAK 317-III/712.

P. 93: *Die neue Universität Köln mit ihren Instituten und Seminaren*. Cologne, 1938, 58.

P. 94: UAK 20/304.

P. 96 left: UAK 20/54, undated.

P. 96 right: UAK 20/239, undated.

P. 97 left: *Genia – Nur für Frauen. Lese- und Handbuch für Studentinnen*. Ed. Frauenbeauftragte der Universität zu Köln. Cologne, 1995, 84, dated 1933.

P. 97 right: Michael Schwab, *Walter Stokar von Neuforn* (1901–58). In *Archäologie und Bodendenkmalpflege in der*

Rheinprovinz 1920–1945. Eds. Jürgen Kunow, Thomas Otten and Jan Bemmann. [Bonn], 2013, 331–351. Photo p. 333, circa 1934.

P. 99: Rheinisches Bildarchiv Köln, August Kreyenkamp, rba_078097.

P. 100: Sonja Endres, *Zwangssterilisation in Köln 1934–1945*. Cologne, 2009, 203.

P. 101: *Kölner Universitätszeitung* 1-2009, 9. Photo: Cologne University.

P. 103 top: Bildarchiv Foto Marburg, photographer unknown. Dated 1936.

P. 103 bottom: UAK 624/28.

P. 104/105: ullstein bild/ullstein bild.

Chapter 4

P. 106: UAK 670/186-5, detail.

P. 110: UAK 20/324.

P. 113 top: UAK 670/186-5.

P. 113 bottom: ullstein bild/Imagno, photo by Franz Hubmann.

P. 114: Walter Dick Archiv.

P. 117: UAK 23/38.

P. 118 left: Deutsches Literaturarchiv Marbach D20110921-52, 1935/1936.

P. 118 right: ullstein bild/ullstein bild, 1973.

P. 119 left: Rechtswissenschaftliche Fakultät der Universität zu Köln, undated.

P. 119 right: Universität zu Köln, Abt. Presse und Kommunikation, undated.

P. 121: akg-images.

P. 122: LA NRW R, NW 1048, no. 33398.

P. 123: UAK 266/1.

P. 124: Rheinisches Bildarchiv Köln, rba_L007633_09.

P. 126 left: ullstein bild/Poly-Press, 1989.

P. 126 right: Thomas-Institut, Universität zu Köln, undated.

P. 127 left: ullstein bild, photo by Brigitte Friedrich, 1974.

P. 127 right: ullstein bild/AKG, 1960.

P. 129: UAK 20/335.

P. 130: *Universitätsführer der Universität zu Köln 1951*. Ed. Studentenausschuss. Cologne, 1951, cover.

P. 131: Husserl-Archiv, Universität zu Köln.

P. 133: akg-images/picture-alliance/dpa.

P. 134: Rechtswissenschaftliche Fakultät der Universität zu Köln, undated.

P. 135 left: Archiv Medizinische Fakultät der Universität zu Köln, Photo: MedizinFotoKöln, undated.

P. 135 right: Archiv Medizinische Fakultät der Universität zu Köln, Photo: MedizinFotoKöln, undated.

P. 136: ullstein bild/dpa.

P. 138: Museum Ludwig, Cologne, donated by Galerie Aenne Abels in 1957, ML 76/SK 0157.

P. 139: GESIS – Leibniz-Institut für Sozialwissenschaften, Bibliothek, Abt. Wissenstransfer.

Chapter 5

P. 140: photo by Joachim Schmidt von Schwind, detail.

P. 144: photo by Hansherbert Wirtz.

P. 147: Universität zu Köln, Abt. Presse und Kommunikation.

P. 148: photo by Joachim Schmidt von Schwind.

P. 151: bpk/Walter Vogel.

P. 152 left: Universität zu Köln, Abt. Presse und Kommunikation, undated.

P. 152 right: akg/Science Photo Library, circa 1969.

P. 153 left: Archiv Medizinische Fakultät der Universität zu Köln. Photo: MedizinFotoKöln, undated.

P. 153 right: Raimund Berg, Gernot Uwe Gabel, *Von der Handelshochschule zur Universität. 100 Jahre wirtschafts- und sozialwissenschaftliche Lehre und Forschung in Köln*. Cologne, 2001, 72, undated.

P. 155: UAK 670/11.

P. 156: UAK 28/538a.

P. 157: UAK [uncredited].

P. 159: UAK 670/103, photo by Georg Munker.

P. 160 left: ullstein bild, photo by Brigitte Friedrich, 1981.

P. 160 right: Archiv Medizinische Fakultät der Universität zu Köln. Photo: MedizinFotoKöln, undated.

P. 161 left: Universität zu Köln, Abt. Presse und Kommunikation, undated.

P. 161 right: Rechtswissenschaftliche Fakultät der Universität zu Köln, undated.

P. 162: Universität zu Köln, Abt. Presse und Kommunikation.

P. 164: IBM System/360 Model 30 Operating Guide. New York.

P. 165: Rolf Ortmann, *Die jüngere Geschichte des Anatomischen Instituts der Universität zu Köln 1919–1984. 65 Jahre in bewegter Zeit*. Cologne, 1986, fig. 27.

P. 167: bpk / Walter Vogel.

P. 168 left: Horst Bittlinger, *History of the Institute of Air and Space Law of the University of Cologne*. [Cologne, 1989], 22, undated.

P. 168 right: ullstein bild, photo by Fritz Eschen, circa 1962.

P. 169 left: ullstein bild, photo by Fritz Eschen, undated.

P. 169 right: ullstein bild, photo by Brigitte Friedrich, 1974.

P. 170: photo by Hans Herbert Wirtz.

P. 172: Martin-Buber-Institut für Judaistik.

P. 173: photo by Simon Jefferson.

P. 175 top: Universität zu Köln, Abt. Presse und Kommunikation.

P. 175 bottom: Universität zu Köln, Abt. Presse und Kommunikation.

P. 176/177: Rheinisches Bildarchiv Köln, rba_143486.

Chapter 6

P. 178: photo by Christian Dalchow, detail.

P. 182 top: Universität zu Köln, Abt. Presse und Kommunikation.

P. 182 bottom: photo by Frank Krabbe.

P. 185: photo by Christian Dalchow.

P. 187 top: photo by Frank Krabbe.

P. 187 bottom: photo by Frank Krabbe.

P. 189: photo by Frank Krabbe.

P. 190 left: Universität zu Köln, Abt. Presse und Kommunikation, undated.

P. 190 right: *Zukunftsaspekte der anwendungsorientierten Betriebswirtschaftslehre. Erwin Grochla zum 65. Geburtstag gewidmet.* Eds. Eduard Gaugler, Hans Günther Meissner and Norbert Thom. Stuttgart, 1986, p. III, undated.

P. 191 left: Universität zu Köln, Abt. Presse und Kommunikation, undated.

P. 191 right: Stefan R. Sudmann, *In memoriam Prof. Dr. Anna Gisela Johnen (1925–2014).* In *Charadrius 50* (2014), issue 1, 105–106. Photo p. 105 by Barbara C. Meyer, 2012.

P. 192: photo by Klaus Flesch.

P. 194: Presse- und Informationsamt der Bundesregierung, B 145 Bild-00206689, photo by Ulrich Wienke.

P. 195: photo by Frank Krabbe.

P. 197: Rheinisches Bildarchiv Köln, rba_104539.

P. 198 left: Rechtswissenschaftliche Fakultät der Universität zu Köln, undated.

P. 198 right: Universität zu Köln, Abt. Presse und Kommunikation, undated.

P. 199 left: Archiv der Max-Planck-Gesellschaft, Berlin-Dahlem, 1985.

P. 199 right: photo by Csaba Peter Rakoczy.

P. 201: Archiv der Max-Planck-Gesellschaft, Berlin-Dahlem.

P. 202: Universität zu Köln, Abt. Presse und Kommunikation.

P. 203: Universität zu Köln, Abt. Presse und Kommunikation, photographer unknown.

P. 204: ullstein bild, photo by Klaus Rose.

P. 206 left: Archiv Medizinische Fakultät der Universität zu Köln. Photo: MedizinFotoKöln, undated.

P. 206 right: Rechtswissenschaftliche Fakultät der Universität zu Köln, undated.

P. 207 left: Archiv Medizinische Fakultät der Universität zu Köln. Photo: MedizinFotoKöln, undated.

P. 207 right: Universität zu Köln, Abt. Presse und Kommunikation, undated.

P. 209: *600 Jahre Kölner Universität. Von der mittelalterlichen Alma mater zum zukunftsorientierten Zentrum der Wissenschaft. Historischer Überblick und aktuelle Bestandsaufnahme aus Anlaß der 600. Wiederkehr des Gründungsdatums.* Cologne, 1988, cover.

P. 210: photo by Georg Wamhof.

P. 211: UAK 640.

Chapter 7

P. 212: photo by Roman Oranski, detail.

P. 216 top: photo by Csaba Peter Rakoczy.

P. 216 bottom: Universität zu Köln, Abt. Presse und Kommunikation.

P. 218: Universität zu Köln, Abt. Presse und Kommunikation.

P. 221 top: photo by Roman Oranski.

P. 221 bottom: ullstein bild/JOKER, photo by David Ausserhofer.

P. 223: *FOCUS Magazin*, no. 43 (1994), 138.

P. 224 left: ullstein bild, photo by Kucharz, 1992.

P. 224 right: Universität zu Köln, Historisches Institut–Abteilung für Alte Geschichte, undated.

P. 225 left: ullstein bild/BNF, 2007.

P. 225 right: ullstein bild/Bonn-Sequenz, 1995.

P. 227: *Kölner Universitäts-Journal* 1/1992, 26.

P. 228: Universität zu Köln, Abt. Presse und Kommunikation.

P. 229: Universität zu Köln, Abt. Presse und Kommunikation.

P. 230: Universität zu Köln, Abt. Presse und Kommunikation.

P. 232 left: Archiv der Max-Planck-Gesellschaft, Berlin-Dahlem, undated.

P. 232 right: Universität zu Köln, Abt. Presse und Kommunikation, undated.

P. 233 left: Humanwissenschaftliche Fakultät der Universität zu Köln, undated.

P. 233 right: ullstein bild/Boness/IPON, 2006.

P. 235: photo by Eberhard Aug.

P. 236: Kölncampus – Das Kölner Hochschulradio [Cologne University Radio].

P. 237: photo by Merle Hettesheimer.

P. 238: photo by Roman Oranski.

P. 240 left: Archiv Medizinische Fakultät der Universität zu Köln. Photo: MedizinFotoKöln, undated.

P. 240 right: Archiv der Max-Planck-Gesellschaft, Berlin-Dahlem, undated.

P. 241 left: ullstein bild/Bonn-Sequenz, 1994.

P. 241 right: ullstein bild, photo by Galuschka, 2004.

P. 243: akg-images/euroluftbild.de.

P. 244: CECAD Exzellenzcluster.

P. 245: Kölner Kompendium des Luftfahrtrechts. Vol. 1. Ed. Stephan Hobe. Cologne, 2008, cover.

Chapter 8

P. 246: photo by Thomas Josek, JOSEKDESIGN, detail.

P. 248 top: photo: Netzwerk Medien.

P. 248 bottom: photo by Fabian Stürtz.

P. 251 top: photo by Fabian Stürtz.

P. 251 bottom: photo: format2d.

P. 252: photo by Johannes Werner.

P. 255 top: photo by Uta Konopka.

P. 255 bottom: photo by Uta Konopka.

P. 257: photo by Thomas Josek, JOSEKDESIGN.

P. 261 top: photo: format2d.

P. 261 bottom: photo: format2d.

P. 262/263: photo by Thomas Josek, JOSEKDESIGN.

Index of Persons

Publishing Information

Edited on behalf of the Rectorate by

Habbo Knoch
Ralph Jessen
Hans-Peter Ullmann

Department of History, University of Cologne

Project coordinator

Georg Wamhof

Department of History, University of Cologne

Researched and written by

Thomas Prüfer
(research/text: essays, topics, biographies)

Thekla Keuck
(research/text: objects, buildings, images)

Anne Crumbach, Christiane Fritsche,
Verena Kücking, Carl-Josef Virnich
(research)

Geschichtsbüro Reder, Roeseling & Prüfer, Cologne

Translation

Alexis Conklin,
Stephen Roche

WordzWork, Bielefeld

Copyediting

Jessica Spengler

Lost in Translation, Brighton (UK)

Book design

Jefferson & Högerle
Visuelle Kommunikation, Cologne

Printing and binding

Finidr, Czech Republic
Printed on acid-free and chlorine-free bleached paper
Printed in the European Union.

Deutsche Nationalbibliothek
Cataloging-in-publication data: http://dnb.d-nb.de

Vandenhoeck & Ruprecht Verlage

www.vandenhoeck-ruprecht-verlage.com

ISBN 978-3-412-51555-3